菲迪克（FIDIC）文献译丛

设计、施工和运营合同条件

Conditions of Contract for Design, Build and Operate Projects

国际咨询工程师联合会 编

唐 萍 张瑞杰 等译

（正式使用发生争执时，以英文原版为准）

机械工业出版社

本书是国际咨询工程师联合会（FIDIC，菲迪克）编写并出版的《设计、施工和运营合同条件》（DBO）的中英文对照版本。2008年版《设计、施工和运营合同条件》，是对1999年版《生产设备和设计-施工合同条件》（黄皮书）进行了大量的修改后编写而成的。DBO合同对于工程项目，特别是大型工程项目，可以简化项目程序、保证质量，其最大的优势是优化项目的全寿命周期成本，并具有以下特色：

1）从时间角度看，DBO合同可减少不必要的延误，使施工的周期更加合理；
2）从质量角度看，DBO合同可保证项目质量长期的可靠性；
3）从资金角度看，DBO合同仅需承担简单的责任，同时拥有长期的承诺保障；
4）从风险角度看，承包实体对工程项目融资或最终商业成功概不负责，几乎没有融资和商业风险。

本书内容包括设计、施工和运营合同条件的通用条件和专用条件，附有争端裁决协议书一般条件、争端裁决委员会成员程序规则，各担保函格式以及投标函、合同协议书和争端裁决委员会成员协议书等格式。

本书推荐用于由承包商设计的工程项目。这种合同的通常情况是，由承包商对工程项目进行设计、施工和运营（如20年运营期）并对其负责维护保养，以优化创新、质量和性能的协调，其重心是在"运营"的环节，鼓励承包商设计、施工和运营一肩挑。

读者对象：工程咨询（设计）单位，从事投资、金融和工程项目管理的部门和组织，各类项目业主，建筑施工监理企业，工程承包企业，环保企业，会计/律师事务所，保险公司以及有关高等院校等单位和人员。

版权所有。未经出版者事先书面许可，对本出版物的任何部分不得以任何方式或途径复制或传播，包括但不限于复印、录制、录音，或通过任何数据库、信息或可检索的系统。

本书封面贴有机械工业出版社和国际咨询工程师联合会（FIDIC，菲迪克）双方的防伪标签，无标签或标签不全者不得使用和销售。

北京市版权局著作权合同登记 图字：01-2020-1316

图书在版编目（CIP）数据

设计、施工和运营合同条件/瑞士国际咨询工程师职合会编；唐萍等译. —北京：机械工业出版社，2021.3

（菲迪克（FIDIC）文献译丛）

书名原文：Conditions of Contract for Design, Build and Operate Projects

ISBN 978-7-111-67630-0

Ⅰ.①设… Ⅱ.①瑞… ②唐… Ⅲ.①建筑工程-承包合同-条件-国外 Ⅳ.①D913.604 ②TU723.1

中国版本图书馆CIP数据核字（2021）第036172号

机械工业出版社（北京市百万庄大街22号 邮政编码100037）
策划编辑：何文军　责任编辑：何文军　李宣敏
责任校对：张　薇　封面设计：张　静
责任印制：李　昂
北京铭成印刷有限公司印刷
2021年5月第1版第1次印刷
210mm×297mm · 20.25印张 · 948千字
标准书号：ISBN 978-7-111-67630-0
定价：249.00元

电话服务　　　　　　　网络服务
客服电话：010-88361066　机　工　官　网：www.cmpbook.com
　　　　　010-88379833　机　工　官　博：weibo.com/cmp1952
　　　　　010-68326294　金　书　网：www.golden-book.com
封底无防伪标均为盗版　机工教育服务网：www.cmpedu.com

译者的话

本书是由国际咨询工程师联合会（FIDIC，菲迪克）编写，于 2008 年出版的第 1 版《设计、施工和运营合同条件》（DBO）中英文对照版本。设计、施工和运营合同的模式是将设计、施工、运营（长期运营和维护，通常 20 年运营期）合同授予一个具有设计、施工、运营资质的专业及技能的承包实体（联营体或财团），以优化创新、质量和性能的协调，而不是单独授予设计、施工和运营合同。DBO 合同模式是国际通行和非常成熟的一种工程项目建设模式。DBO 合同最大的优势是优化项目的全寿命周期成本。因此，DBO 合同对于工程项目，特别是大型工程项目，可以简化项目程序、保证质量、优化全寿命成本，具有诸多优势和广阔的应用前景。本书是在 1999 年第 1 版菲迪克《生产设备和设计 - 施工合同条件》（黄皮书）的基础上进行了大量修改后编写而成的。虽然黄皮书涵盖了 DBO 合同的设计和施工方面，但菲迪克（FIDIC）没有一份将设计、施工义务与长期运营承诺结合起来的文件，尤其是有关长期运营相关的风险和责任的文件。所以，DBO 合同的重心是在"运营"的环节，鼓励承包实体设计、施工和运营一肩挑。

希望本书的出版，对我国广大从事工程咨询（设计）、投资、金融和项目管理的部门和组织，各类项目业主、建筑施工监理企业、工程承包企业、环保企业、会计 / 律师事务所、保险公司以及有关高等院校等人员在学习和运用菲迪克合同条件时，能够有效地解决在国际、国内工程咨询和工程承包活动中的合同管理问题，更好地开拓国内外工程咨询和工程承包市场，提高工程建设的投资效益和社会效益，建立和完善工程项目总承包制度，促进我国工程建设管理体制与国际惯例接轨，推动我国工程咨询事业与工程建设管理模式和体制的全面深化改革。

翻译过程中，我们虽然尽力想使译文准确通顺，完整地传达原文的内容，汉语表达规范易懂，但限于专业知识与语言水平，译文中可能出现不妥乃至错误之处，敬请读者指正。本书以中英文对照方式编排，以便用户核对中译文、从而更准确地理解金皮书。

本书由唐萍、张瑞杰、贾志成、史骏、邓冰茹、张辰旭、郭文涛、李莉萍、莫伟平、郑海燕、秦春燕、曾家平、张荣芹等翻译，唐萍、张瑞杰、贾志成校译，唐萍、张瑞杰、邓冰茹、张辰旭审校。

译者

FIDIC is the international federation of national Member Associations of consulting engineers.

FIDIC was founded in 1913 by three national associations of consulting engineers within Europe. The objectives of forming the Federation were to promote in common the professional interests of the Member Associations, and to disseminate information of interest to their members. Today, FIDIC membership covers more than 70 countries from all parts of the globe and encompassing most of the private practice consulting engineers.

FIDIC is charged with promoting and implementing the consulting engineering industry's strategic goals on behalf of Member Associations. Its strategic objectives are to: represent world-wide the majority of firms providing technology-based intellectual services for the built and natural environment; assist members with issues relating to business practice; define and actively promote conformance to a code of ethics; enhance the image of consulting engineers as leaders and wealth creators in society; promote the commitment to environmental sustainability.

FIDIC arranges seminars, conferences and other events in the furtherance of its goals: maintenance of high ethical and professional standards; exchange of views and information; discussion of problems of mutual concern among Member Associations and representatives of the international financial institutions; development of the consulting engineering industry in developing countries.

FIDIC members endorse FIDIC's statutes and policy statements and comply with FIDIC's Code of Ethics which calls for professional competence, impartial advice and open and fair competition.

FIDIC, in the furtherance of its goals, publishes international standard forms of contracts for works and for clients, consultants, sub-consultants, joint ventures and representatives, together with related materials such as standard pre-qualification forms.

FIDIC also publishes business practice documents such as policy statements, position papers, guides, guidelines, training manuals, and training resource kits in the areas of management systems (quality management, risk management, business integrity management, environment management sustainability) and business processes (consultant selection, quality based selection, tendering, procurement, insurance, liability, technology transfer, capacity building).

FIDIC organises an extensive programme of seminars, conferences, capacity building workshops, and training courses.

FIDIC publications and details about events are available from the Secretariat in Switzerland. Specific activities are detailed in an annual business plan and the FIDIC website, www.fidic.org, gives extensive background information.

菲迪克（FIDIC）是咨询工程师国家（地区）成员协会国际联合会。

菲迪克（FIDIC）是由欧洲三个国家的咨询工程师协会于 1913 年成立的。组建联合会的目的是共同促进成员协会的职业利益，以及向其会员传播有益信息。今天，菲迪克（FIDIC）已有来自于全球各地 70 多个国家（地区）的会员，包括大多数私人执业的咨询工程师。

菲迪克（FIDIC）代表成员协会负责促进和实施咨询工程师行业的战略目标。其战略目标是：代表全世界为建设和自然环境提供以技术为基础的智力服务的大多数公司；协助会员处理与业务实践相关的问题；制订并积极促进遵守职业道德规范；提升咨询工程师作为社会领导者和财富创造者的形象；促进对环境可持续性的承诺。

菲迪克（FIDIC）举办各类研讨会、会议及其他活动，以促进其目标：维护高水平的道德和职业标准；交流观点和信息；讨论成员协会和国际金融机构代表共同关心的问题，以及发展中国家工程咨询业的发展。

菲迪克（FIDIC）会员认可菲迪克（FIDIC）章程和政策声明，并遵守其职业道德要求的专业技能、公正的建议和公开公平的竞争。

菲迪克（FIDIC）为了实现其目标，为客户、咨询工程师、分包咨询工程师、联营体和代表发布了国际标准格式的工程合同，以及资格预审标准格式等相关资料。

菲迪克（FIDIC）还出版比如政策声明、行动报告、指南、指导方针、培训手册和管理体系领域的培训资料包（质量管理、风险管理、业务廉洁管理、环境可持续管理）以及业务流程［咨询工程师的选择、根据质量选择（咨询服务）、招标、采购、保险、责任、技术转让、实力建设］的业务实践文件。

菲迪克（FIDIC）组织研讨会、会议、实力建设研讨会和培训课程等各类活动。

菲迪克（FIDIC）出版物以及有关活动的详细信息，可以从设在瑞士日内瓦的秘书处得到。具体活动详见年度业务计划和菲迪克（FIDIC）网站，www.fidic.org，网站提供了大量的背景信息。

COPYRIGHT

© FIDIC 2021 All rights reserved.

The Copyright owner of this document is the International Federation of Consulting Engineers - FIDIC.

Translation from English to Chinese has been performed by China Machine Press with FIDIC's permission.

The lawful purchaser of this document has the right to make a single copy of the duly purchased document for his or her personal and private use. No part of this publication may be shared reproduced, distributed, translated, adapted, stored in a retrieval system, or communicated, in any form or by any means, mechanical, electronic, magnetic, photocopying, recording or otherwise, without prior written permission from FIDIC. To request such permission, please contact FIDIC, Case 311, CH-1215 Geneva 15, Switzerland; fax +41 22 799 49 01, e-mail: fidic@fidic.org. Electronic copies can be obtained from FIDIC at www.fidic.org/bookshop.

FIDIC considers the official and authentic text to be the version in the English language and assumes no liability whatsoever for the completeness, correctness, adequacy or otherwise of the translation into Chinese for any use to which this document may be put.

Disclaimer

While FIDIC aims to ensure that its publications represent the best in business practice, the Federation accepts or assumes no liability or responsibility for any events or the consequences thereof that derive from the use of its publications, including their translations. FIDIC publications are provided "as is" without warranty of any kind, either express or implied, including, without limitation, warranties of merchantability, fitness for a particular purpose and non-infringement. FIDIC publications are not exhaustive and are only intended to provide general guidance. They should not be relied upon in a specific situation or issue. Expert legal advice should be obtained whenever appropriate, and particularly before entering or terminating a contract.

版权

©FIDIC 2021 版权所有。

本文件的版权所有人为国际咨询工程师联合会——菲迪克（FIDIC）。

经菲迪克（FIDIC）许可，中国机械工业出版社完成了英文版的中文翻译。

本文件的合法购买者有权将正式购买的文件制作副本，供其个人和私人目的使用。未经菲迪克(FIDIC)事先书面许可，不得将本出版物的任何部分分享复制、分发、翻译、改编、存储在检索系统中，或以任何格式或通过任何方式以机械、电子、磁性、影印、记录或其他方式传送。如有意获得此类许可，请联系菲迪克（FIDIC），地址：Case 311, CH-1215 Geneva 15, Switzerland；传真：+41 22 799 49 01，电子邮件：fidic@fidic.org。电子版本可从菲迪克（FIDIC）获取，网址为www.fidic.org/bookshop。

菲迪克（FIDIC）认为正式的和权威性的文本为英语版本，并对本文件的任何用途的中文翻译文本的完整性、正确性、充分性或其他方面不承担任何责任。

免责声明

尽管菲迪克（FIDIC）的目标是确保其出版物代表最佳业务实践，但对于使用其出版物及其翻译文本而引起的任何事件或后果，联合会（菲迪克，FIDIC）不承担任何责任或义务。菲迪克（FIDIC）出版物按"原样"提供，没有任何明示或暗示的保证，包括对可销售性、特定用途的适用性和非侵权性的无限保证。菲迪克（FIDIC）出版物并非详尽无遗，仅提供一般性指导。在特定的情况或问题上不应依赖它们。除此之外，适当时，尤其在签订或终止合同前，应获得专家法律建议。

CONTENTS

INTRODUCTION

Acknowledgements XII
Foreword XIV
Notes XVI
Flow Charts XX

GENERAL CONDITIONS

General Conditions of Contract 14
Index of Clauses and Sub-Clauses 180
Index of Principal Terminology 190
General Conditions of Dispute Adjudication Agreement 196
Procedural Rules for Dispute Adjudication Board Members 206

PARTICULAR CONDITIONS

Preamble 214
Part A – Contract Data 216
Part B – Special Provisions 226

SAMPLE FORMS

Introduction 256
Forms of Tender, Contract Agreement & Dispute Adjudication Board Agreement ... 258
Forms of Security and Guarantee 274

目录

引言

致谢	XIII
前言	XV
说明	XVII
流程图	XXI

通用条件

合同通用条件	15
条目和条款索引	181
主要术语索引	191
争端裁决协议书一般条件	197
争端裁决委员会成员程序规则	207

专用条件

序言	215
A 部分——合同数据	217
B 部分——特别规定	227

样本格式

引言	257
投标函和协议书样本格式	259
担保和保函样本格式	275

设计、施工和运营合同条件

Conditions of Contract for
DESIGN, BUILD AND OPERATE PROJECTS

引言
Introduction

引言
INTRODUCTION

通用条件
GENERAL CONDITIONS

专用条件
PARTICULAR CONDITIONS

样本格式
SAMPLE FORMS

ACKNOWLEDGEMENTS

Fédération Internationale des Ingénieurs-Conseils (FIDIC) extends special thanks to the following members of its DBO Task Group: Michael Mortimer-Hawkins (Group Leader), Consulting Engineer, UK; Axel-Volkmar Jaeger, Consulting Engineer, Germany; Des Barry, JB Barry & Partners, Ireland; Anton (Toni) Bauer, Obermeyer Planen + Beraten GmbH, Germany; Christoph Theune, Pöyry Environment GmbH, Germany; Erica Lund, JB Barry & Partners, Ireland; and Nael Bunni, Chartered Engineer, Ireland.

The preparation was carried out under the general direction of the FIDIC Contracts Committee which comprised Axel-Volkmar Jaeger, Consulting Engineer, Germany (Chairman); Christopher Wade, Consulting Engineer, UK (Former Chairman); Philip Jenkinson, Atkins, UK; Nael Bunni, Chartered Engineer, Ireland; Legal Adviser Christopher Seppala, White and Case LLP, France; and Special Adviser Michael Mortimer-Hawkins, Consulting Engineer, UK and Sweden.

FIDIC would also like to thank the persons listed below who reviewed the draft document and the Pre-Press Seminar Edition and gave valuable comment. Their comments were of great help to the Design-Build-Operate (DBO) Task Group when finalising the wording of the various clauses and sub-clauses which make up this First Edition: Gordon Jaynes, Lawyer, UK; Rusli bin Idrus, Tenaga Nasional Berhad, Malaysia; Patrick Gallagher, CDM, USA; European International Contractors; Wolf-Rainer Kruska, KfW, Germany; Niel McCole, PB Power, UK; Dr Götz-Sebastian Hök, Dr Hök Stieglmeier & Kollegen, Germany; Edward Corbett, Corbett & Co, UK; Anthony Harkness, Aon, Ireland; J.C.M. Stolwijk, Aon Risico Management, The Netherlands; Brian Bond, Consulting Engineer, Ireland; Sean Maher, Allianz Insurance, Ireland; Patrick Lane, Lawyer, UK; Mushtaq Ahmad Smore, Mushtaq Contracts, Pakistan; Robin Schonfeld, SMEC International, UAE; Brian Totterdill, Consulting Engineer, UK; the International Bar Association; and all other persons who sent in comments and feedback.

FIDIC wishes to record its appreciation of the time and effort devoted by all the above.

FIDIC also wishes to thank Geoff French, Executive Committee member responsible for the FIDIC Contracts Committee; Enrico Vink, Managing Director, FIDIC, and Peter Boswell, General Manager, FIDIC, for their support and help in producing this document.

The ultimate decision regarding the wording of the clauses and format of the document rests with FIDIC, and acknowledgement of the reviewers does not mean that they concur with or approve the wording of all clauses.

致谢

国际咨询工程师联合会（FIDIC，菲迪克）向其设计、施工和运营工作组的以下成员特致谢意：英国咨询工程师 Michael Mortimer-Hawkins（组长）；德国咨询工程师 Axel-Volkmar Jaeger；爱尔兰 JB Barry &Partners 公司的 Des Barry；德国 Obermeyer—Planen + Beraten GmbH 公司的 Anton（Toni）Bauer；德国 Pöyry Environment GmbH 公司的 Christoph Theune；爱尔兰 JB Barry &Partners 公司的 Erica Lund 以及爱尔兰特许工程师 NaelBunni。

本书是在菲迪克（FIDIC）合同委员会全面指导下进行编写的，该委员会成员包括：德国咨询工程师 Axel-Volkmar Jaeger（主席）；英国咨询工程师 Christopher Wade（前主席）；英国 Atkins 公司的 Philip Jenkinson；爱尔兰特许工程师 Nael Bunni；法国 White and Case LLP 公司的法律顾问 Christopher Seppala 以及英国和瑞典咨询工程师、特别顾问 Michael Mortimer-Hawkins。

菲迪克（FIDIC）也要感谢以下人员，他们审阅了书稿文件和出版前研讨会版本，并提出了宝贵意见。他们的意见对设计—施工—运营（DBO）工作组在最终确定构成第 1 版的各种条款和子条款的措辞时，给予了很大的帮助。这些人员是：英国的律师 Gordon Jaynes；马来西亚 Tenaga Nasional Berhad 公司的 Rusli bin Idrus；美国 CDM 公司的 Patrick Gallagher；欧洲国际承包商组织；德国 KfW 的 Wolf-Rainer Kruska；英国 PB Power 公司的 Niel McCole；德国 Dr Hök Stieglmeier & Kollegen 公司的 Dr Götz-Sebastian Hök；英国 Corbett & Co 公司的 Edward Corbett；爱尔兰 Aon 公司的 Anthony Harkness；荷兰 Aon Risico Management 公司的 J.C.M. Stolwijk；爱尔兰咨询工程师 Brian Bond；爱尔兰 Allianz Insurance 公司的 Sean Maher；英国律师 Patrick Lane；巴基斯坦 Mushtaq Contracts 公司的 Mushtaq Ahmad Smore；阿拉伯联合酋长国 SMEC International 公司的 Robin Schonfeld；英国咨询工程师 Brian Totterdill；国际律师协会以及所有其他发送和反馈意见的人员。

菲迪克（FIDIC）希望记录下其对上述所有人员付出的时间和精力的感激之情。

菲迪克（FIDIC）还要感谢负责 FIDIC 合同委员会的执行委员会成员 Geoff French；菲迪克（FIDIC）秘书长 Enrico Vink，以及菲迪克（FIDIC）总经理 Peter Boswell，感谢他们对本文件出版的支持和帮助。

有关条款的措辞和本文件格式的最终确定由菲迪克（FIDIC）负责，对审稿人的致谢并不表示他们同意或对所有条款措辞的赞同。

FOREWORD

In 1999, the Fédération Internationale des Ingénieurs-Conseils (FIDIC) published a new series of Conditions of Contract: (a) for Construction; (b) for Plant and Design-Build; and (c) for EPC/Turnkey Projects. This was followed by the *Short Form of Contract* for lower value or less complex projects, and the *Form of Contract for Dredging* and *Reclamation Works*. Following their publication, it became clear that there was a growing need for a document which combined a design-build obligation with a long-term operation commitment.

Whilst it is recognised that there are alternative scenarios encompassing the Design, Build and Operate (DBO) concept – for example the "green field" scenario of Design-Build-Operate, and the "brown field" scenario of Operate-Design-Build – it was also recognised that different scenarios required different contract conditions. Moreover, the conditions applicable to short-term operation differed considerably to those applicable to long-term operation. A further consideration was whether it was best to approach a DBO project as a single long-term contract or as two separate or linked contracts.

FIDIC has chosen to adopt the green-field Design-Build-Operate scenario, with a 20- year operation period, and has opted for a single contract awarded to a single contracting entity (which will almost certainly be a consortium or joint venture) to optimise the coordination of innovation, quality and performance, rather than award separate contracts for design-build and for operation. The Contractor has no responsibility for either financing the project or for its ultimate commercial success. This is the basis upon which this document has been prepared.

The document, as written, is not suitable for contracts which are not based on the traditional Design-Build-Operate sequence, or where the Operation Period differs significantly from the 20 years adopted.

The document is recommended for general use where tenders are invited on an international basis.

前言

1999年，菲迪克（FIDIC）发布了一系列新的合同条件：(a) **施工**；(b) **生产设备和设计 - 施工**；(c) **设计采购施工（EPC）/ 交钥匙工程**。紧随其后（其次）是价值较低或较不复杂工程的*简明合同格式*，以及*疏浚和开垦（填海）工程合同格式*。在它们发布后，很明显，越来越需要一份将设计 - 施工义务与长期运营承诺结合起来的文件。

虽然人们认识到，存在着包括**设计、施工和运营（DBO）** 概念的备选方案，例如**设计-施工-运营**的"绿地（绿色地带）"方案和**运营-设计-施工**的"棕地（棕色地带）"方案，但也认识到，不同的方案需要不同的合同条件。此外，适用于短期运营的条件与适用于长期运营的条件有很大的不同。另一个考虑是，最好是将一个 DBO 工程作为一个单独的长期合同，还是作为两个单独的或相互联系的合同来处理。

菲迪克（FIDIC） 选择采用 20 年运营期的绿地设计 - 施工 - 运营方案，并选择将单一合同授予单个承包实体（几乎肯定是财团或联营体），以优化创新、质量和性能的协调，而不是单独授予设计 - 施工和运营合同。**承包商**对工程项目融资或最终商业成功概不负责。这是编制本文件的依据（基础）。

如书面所述，本文件不适用于不基于传统**设计 - 施工 - 运营**顺序的合同，或运营期与所采用的 20 年期有显著不同的合同。

建议在国际招标时使用本文件。

NOTES

When preparing these Conditions of Contract for Design, Build and Operate Projects, the drafting task group has attempted to include all conditions of a general nature, which are likely to apply to the majority of DBO contracts, into General Conditions. However, it was recognised that there are many essential provisions which are particular to each individual project. These are to be included as Contract Data and are to be found in the Particular Conditions Part A – Contract Data.

In addition, it was recognised that many Employers or governments, or even different jurisdictions, particularly if the General Conditions were to be used on domestic contracts, may require special conditions of contract, or indeed particular procedures, which differ from those included in the General Conditions. For this reason, the document also allows for Particular Conditions Part B – Special Provisions which includes advice to drafters of contract documents who may wish to add Special Provisions to replace or supplement the clauses to be found in the General Conditions.

Users who wish to adopt these conditions for use on a different scenario or with an operation period significantly different to the 20-year period assumed, are referred to the *FIDIC DBO Contract Guide* (planned for publication by FIDIC at a later date), which identifies the areas which will require amending and gives comprehensive guidelines and suggestions on how they should be addressed. However, the Guide will not claim to address all issues requiring attention, and users should seek expert advice from FIDIC before attempting to make any significant changes to the document via Particular Conditions Part B – Special Provisions.

Drafters of contract documents are reminded that the General Conditions of all FIDIC contracts are protected by copyright and trademark and may not be changed without specific written consent, usually in the form of a licence to amend, from FIDIC. If drafters wish to amend the provisions found in the General Conditions, the place for doing this is in the Particular Conditions Part B – Special Provisions, as mentioned above, and not by making changes in the General Conditions as such.

FIDIC also recognises that the successful performance of a long-term DBO contract requires that the Parties understand the overall time framework and the need for a long-term commitment by both the Employer and the Contractor. In trying to achieve this understanding and commitment, it has been necessary to introduce new procedures and new terminology which are not to be found in the other FIDIC forms of contract.

The document also includes a number of sample forms to help both Parties have a common understanding of what is required by third parties such as providers of securities and guarantees, and what is considered to be accepted good practice by FIDIC and the major international funding agencies. While copyrighted, these forms are expressly provided to users of the Conditions of Contract for completion by users. Users are warned that if these forms are changed in any significant way, there is a great risk that the balance of the contract and the specific wording of the Clauses may be compromised.

The document begins with a series of comprehensive flow charts which show, in visual form, the critical sequences of activities which are specific and unique to the DBO form of contract. These have been included by the drafting task group to facilitate an understanding of the new procedures and new terminology found in these *FIDIC Conditions of Contract for Design, Build* and *Operate Projects*.

说明

在为**设计**、**施工**和**运营工程**编制这些合同条件时,起草工作组试图将可能适用于大多数 **DBO** 合同的一般性质的所有条件纳入**通用条件**。然而,人们认识到,有许多基本规定是针对每个单独的工程项目的。这些数据将作为**合同数据**包含在**专用条件 A 部分——合同数据**中。

此外,人们认识到,许多**雇主**或政府,甚至不同的管辖区域,特别是在国内的合同中使用**通用条件**的情况下,可能需要与**通用条件**中所包括的不同的特别合同条件,或实际上的特定程序。为此,本文件还考虑了**专用条件 B 部分——特别规定**,其中包括对合同文件起草者的建议,这些起草者可能希望增加**特别规定**,以取代或补充**通用条件**中的条款。

如果用户希望将这些条件用于不同的场景或运营期与假设的 20 年期有很大不同,请参考**菲迪克(FIDIC)DBO 合同指南**(FIDIC 计划在以后出版),它确定了需要修改的领域,并就如何解决这些问题提出了全面的指导方针和建议。但是,该**指南**并不要求解决所有需要注意的问题,用户在试图通过**专用条件 B 部分——特别规定**对本文件进行任何重大修改之前,应向**菲迪克(FIDIC)**寻求专家建议。

合同文件起草者应注意,所有**菲迪克(FIDIC)**合同的**通用条件**受版权和商标保护,未经**菲迪克(FIDIC)**通常以修改许可证的形式授予特别的书面同意,不得修改。如果起草者希望修改**通用条件**中的规定,则应在**专用条件 B 部分——特别规定**如上所述中修改,而不是修改已发布的**通用条件**。

菲迪克(FIDIC)还认识到,成功地履行长期 **DBO** 合同需要双方理解整个时间框架,以及**雇主**和**承包商**长期承诺的必要性,为了实现这一理解和承诺,有必要引入新的程序和新的术语,这在其他**菲迪克(FIDIC)**合同格式中是找不到的。

本文件还包括一些样本格式,以帮助双方就第三方如担保和保函的提供方的要求,以及**菲迪克(FIDIC)**和主要国际融资机构认为可接受的良好做法达成共识。虽然有版权,但这些表格是明确提供给用户的**合同条件**,由用户完成。提醒用户,如果这些表格有任何重大的改变会有很大的风险,合同的平衡和**条款**的具体措辞可能会受到损害。

本文件以一系列综合流程图开始,这些流程图以视觉形式展示了 **DBO** 合同形式的特定和独特的关键活动顺序。起草工作组已将其包括在内,以便理解**菲迪克(FIDIC)合同条件**中关于**设计-施工和运营工程**的新程序和新术语。

These flow charts cover:

- The Overall Contract Period
- The Design-Build Period
- Commencement to Design-Build Commissioning
- The Operation Service Period
- Payment during the Design-Build Period
- Payment during the Operation Service Period
- Determinations by the Employer's Representative
- Contractor's Claims – Submission
- Contractor's Claims – Determination
- Settlement of Disputes

These charts are illustrative and must not be taken into consideration in the interpretation of the Conditions of Contract.

这些流程图包括：

- 合同总工期
- 设计-施工期
- 开始设计-施工调试
- 运营服务期
- 设计-施工期间付款
- 运营服务期间付款
- 由雇主代表确定
- 承包商索赔——提交
- 承包商索赔——确定
- 争端的解决

这些图只是说明性的，不应作为**合同条件**的解释。

FLOW CHARTS

The Overall Contract Period
The Design-Build Period
Commencement to Design-Build Commissioning
The Operation Service Period
Payment during the Design-Build Period
Payment during the Operation Service Period
Determinations by the Employer's Representative
Contractor's Claims – Submission
Contractor's Claims – Determination
Settlement of Disputes

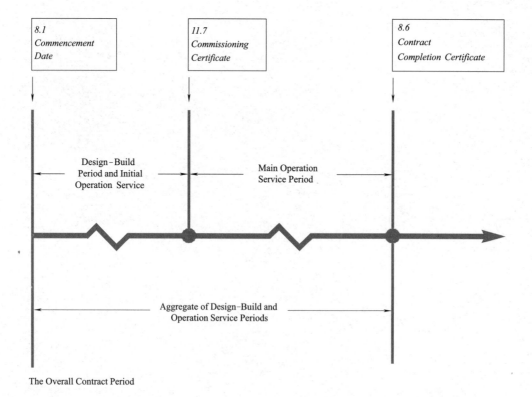

The Overall Contract Period

The Overall Contract Period

流程图

合同总工期
设计 - 施工期
开始设计 - 施工调试
运营服务期
设计 - 施工期间付款
运营服务期间付款
由雇主代表确定
承包商索赔——提交
承包商索赔——确定
争端的解决

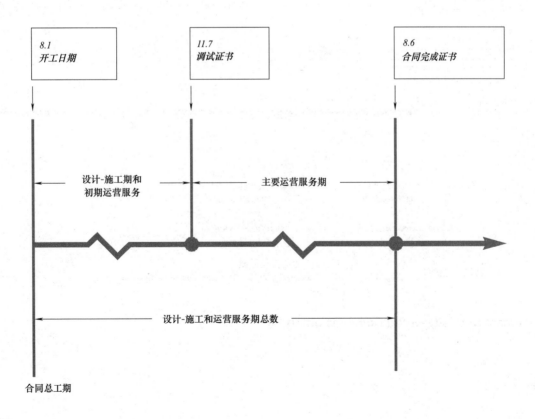

合同总工期

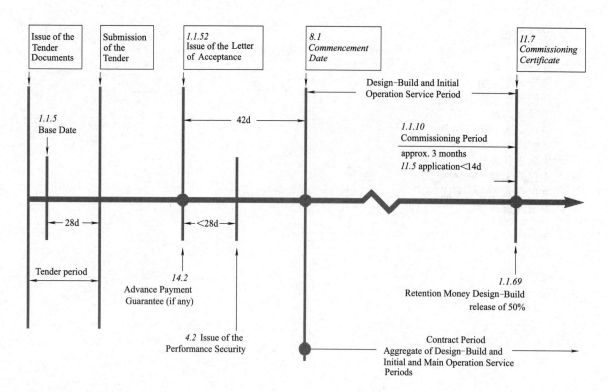

The Design-Build Period

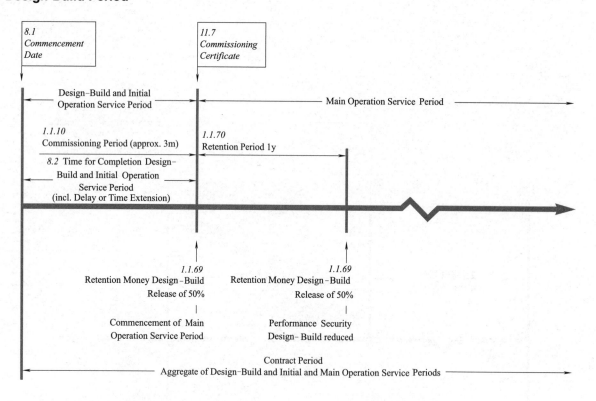

Commencement to Design-Build Commissioning

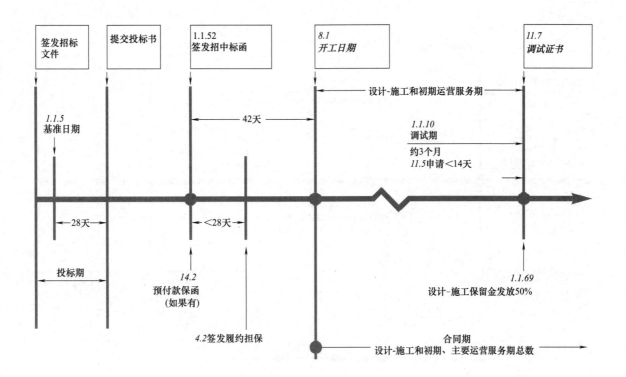

设计 - 施工期

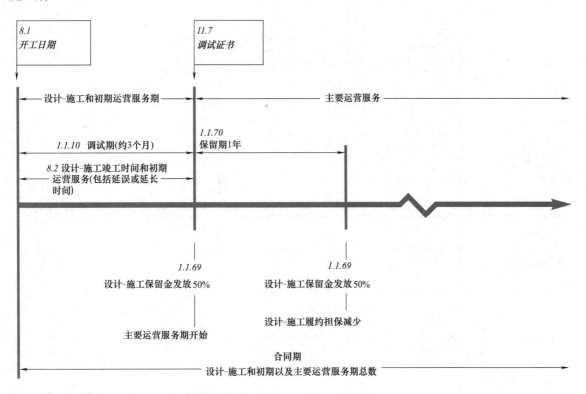

开始设计 - 施工调试

XXIII

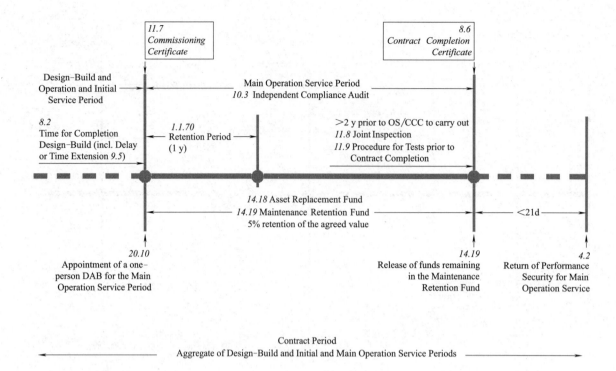

The Operation Service Period

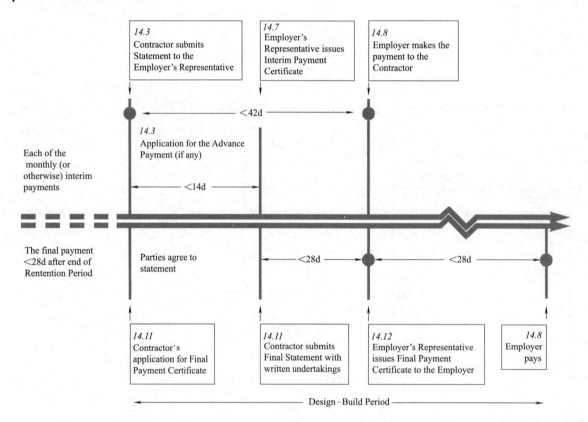

Payment during the Design-Build Period

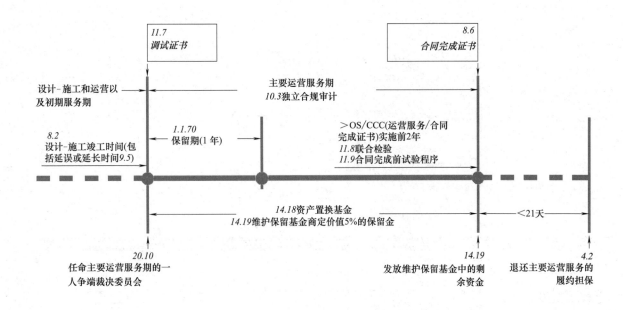

运营服务期

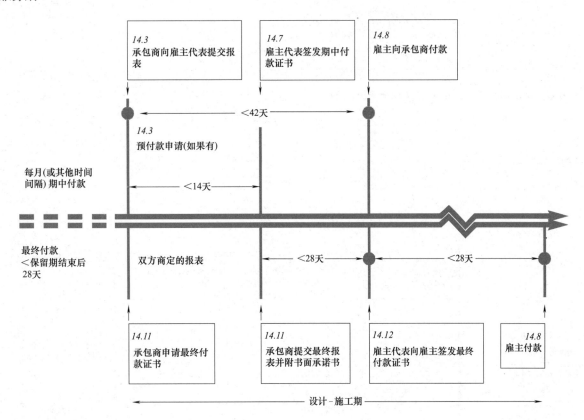

设计 - 施工期间付款

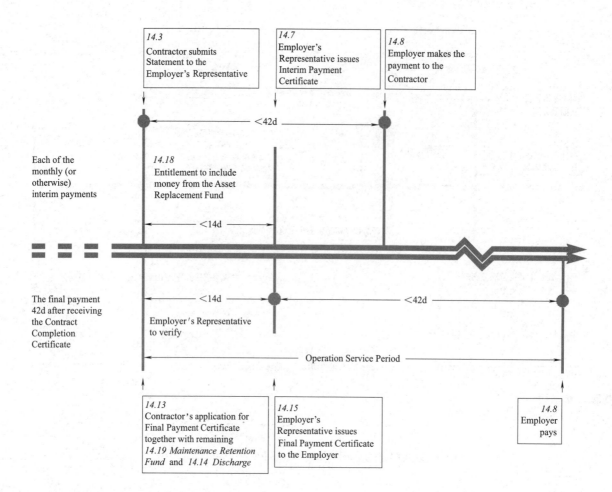

Payment during the Operation Service Period

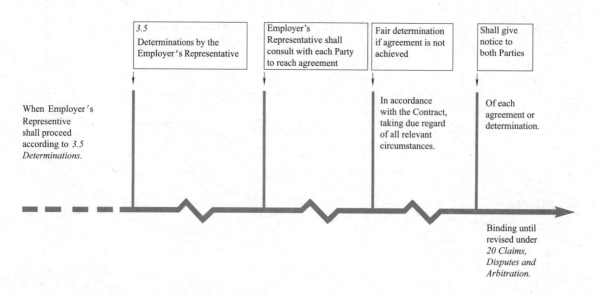

Determinations by the Employer's Representative

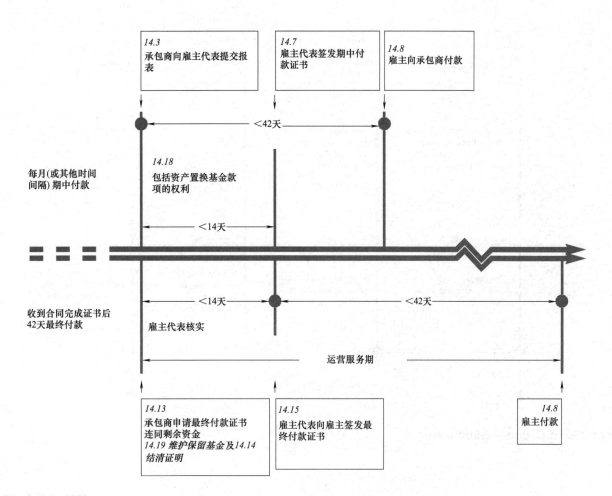

运营服务期间付款

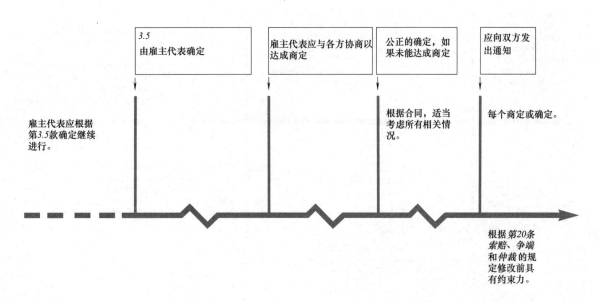

由雇主代表确定

XXVII

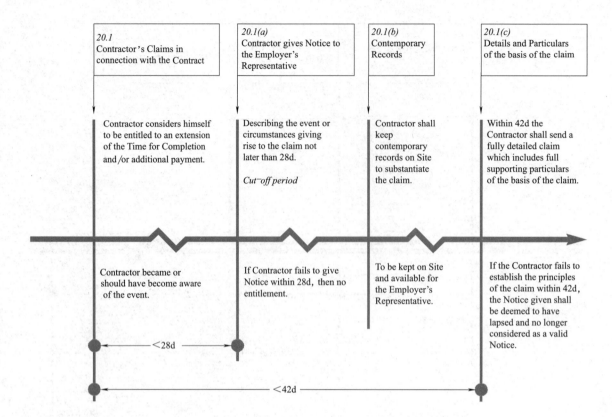

Contractor's Claims – Submission

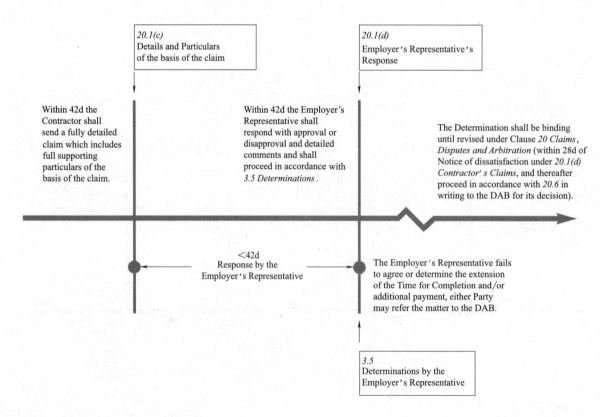

Contractor's Claims – Determination

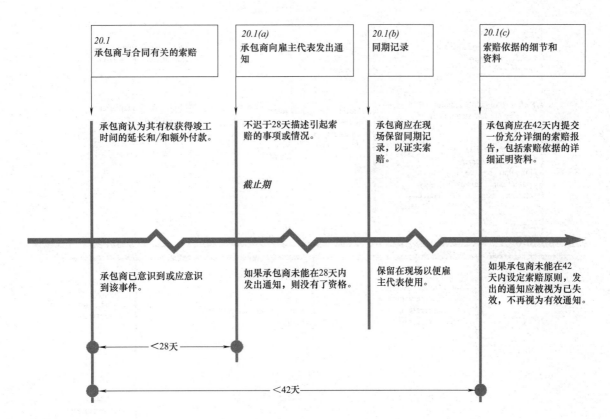

承包商索赔 - 提交

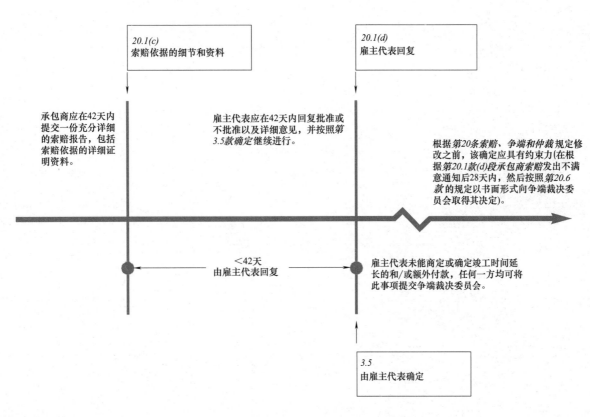

承包商索赔 - 确定

20.3 Appointment of the Dispute Adjudication Board	20.5 Avoidance of Disputes (If Parties so agree)	20.6 Obtaining Dispute Adjudication Board's Decision
Parties shall jointly appoint DAB by the date stated in the Contract Data. 20.4 Failure to Agree Dispute Adjudication Board: if the Parties fail to agree, then appointment made by the entity or official named in the Contract.	Parties may jointly refer to the DAB to provide assistance to resolve any disagreement. Parties are not bound by any advice given.	Either Party may refer a Dispute arising under 20.1 Contractor's Claims or 20.2 Employer's Claims within 28 d to the DAB in writing.

	Either Party may issue a Notice of dissatisfaction within 28d after receiving the DAB decision.	Both Parties shall attempt to settle the Dispute amicably before commencement of arbitration.	Arbitration may not be commenced until 56d after the Notice of No Dissatisfaction is issued.
	20.6 Obtaining Dispute Adjudication Board's Decision	20.7 Amicable Settlement (After Notice of dissatisfaction)	20.8 Arbitration (Final settlement by international arbitration)

Settlement of Disputes

争端的解决

20.3 争端裁决委员会的任命
双方应在合同数据中规定的日期共同任命争端裁决委员会。

20.4 对争端裁决委员会未能取得一致:
如果双方未能达成商定,则由合同中指名的实体或官方任命。

20.5 避免争端(如果双方同意)
双方可共同提请争端裁决委员会协助解决任何分歧。双方不受任何建议约束。

20.6 取得争端裁决委员会的决定
任何一方均可在28天内,以书面形式将第 *20.1 款承包商索赔* 或 *20.2 款雇主索赔* 规定发生的争端提交争端裁决委员会。

20.6 取得争端裁决委员会的决定
任何一方均可在收到争端裁决委员会的决定后28天内发出不满意通知。

20.7 友好解决(不满意通知后)
在开始仲裁之前,双方应努力友好地解决争端。

20.8 仲裁(由国际仲裁最终解决)
仲裁不得在发出不满意通知后56天内开始。

设计、施工和运营合同条件

Conditions of Contract for
DESIGN, BUILD AND OPERATE PROJECTS

通用条件
General Conditions

引言
INTRODUCTION

通用条件
GENERAL CONDITIONS

专用条件
PARTICULAR CONDITIONS

样本格式
SAMPLE FORMS

General Conditions of Contract

CONTENTS

CLAUSE INDEX 4

CLAUSES 1 - 20 14

INDEX OF CLAUSES AND SUB-CLAUSES 180

INDEX OF PRINCIPAL TERMINOLOGY 190

GENERAL CONDITIONS OF DISPUTE ADJUDICATION AGREEMENT 196

PROCEDURAL RULES FOR DISPUTE ADJUDICATION BOARD MEMBERS 206

合同通用条件

目　　录

条款索引 ··· 5

条款：1—20条 ·· 15

条目和条款索引 ·· 181

主要术语索引 ··· 191

争端裁决协议书一般条件 ··· 197

争端裁决委员会成员程序规则 ·· 207

General Conditions of Contract

CLAUSE INDEX

1	**General Provisions**	14

- 1.1 Definitions
- 1.2 Interpretation
- 1.3 Notices and Other Communications
- 1.4 Law and Language
- 1.5 Priority of Documents
- 1.6 Contract Agreement
- 1.7 Operating Licence
- 1.8 Assignment
- 1.9 Care and Supply of Documents
- 1.10 Errors in the Employer's Requirements
- 1.11 Employer's Use of Contractor's Documents
- 1.12 Contractor's Use of Employer's Documents
- 1.13 Confidential Details
- 1.14 Compliance with Laws
- 1.15 Joint and Several Liability

2	**The Employer**	34

- 2.1 Right of Access to the Site
- 2.2 Permits, Licences or Approvals
- 2.3 Employer's Personnel
- 2.4 Employer's Financial Arrangements

3	**The Employer's Representative**	36

- 3.1 Employer's Representative's Duties and Authority
- 3.2 Delegation by the Employer's Representative
- 3.3 Instructions of the Employer's Representative
- 3.4 Replacement of the Employer's Representative
- 3.5 Determinations

4	**The Contractor**	40

- 4.1 Contractor's General Obligations
- 4.2 Performance Security
- 4.3 Contractor's Representative
- 4.4 Subcontractors

合同通用条件

条款索引

1 一般规定 ·· 15

    1.1   定义
    1.2   解释
    1.3   通知和其他通信交流
    1.4   法律和语言
    1.5   文件优先次序
    1.6   合同协议书
    1.7   运营执照
    1.8   权益转让
    1.9   文件的照管和提供
    1.10   雇主要求中的错误
    1.11   雇主使用承包商文件
    1.12   承包商使用雇主文件
    1.13   保密事项
    1.14   遵守法律
    1.15   共同的和各自的责任

2 雇主 ·· 35

    2.1   现场进入权
    2.2   许可、执照或批准
    2.3   雇主人员
    2.4   雇主的资金安排

3 雇主代表 ·· 37

    3.1   雇主代表的任务和权利
    3.2   由雇主代表付托
    3.3   雇主代表的指示
    3.4   雇主代表的替代
    3.5   确定

4 承包商 ·· 41

    4.1   承包商的一般义务
    4.2   履约担保
    4.3   承包商代表
    4.4   分包商

4.5	Nominated Subcontractors
4.6	Co-operation
4.7	Setting Out
4.8	Safety Procedures
4.9	Quality Assurance
4.10	Site Data
4.11	Sufficiency of the Accepted Contract Amount
4.12	Unforeseeable Physical Conditions
4.13	Rights of Way and Facilities
4.14	Avoidance of Interference
4.15	Access Route
4.16	Transport of Goods
4.17	Contractor's Equipment
4.18	Protection of the Environment
4.19	Electricity, Water and Gas
4.20	Employer's Equipment and Free-Issue Material
4.21	Progress Reports
4.22	Security of the Site
4.23	Contractor's Operations on Site
4.24	Fossils
4.25	Changes in the Contractor's Financial situation

5 Design 60

5.1	General Design Obligations
5.2	Contractor's Documents
5.3	Contractor's Undertaking
5.4	Technical Standards and Regulations
5.5	As-Built Documents
5.6	Operation and Maintenance Manuals
5.7	Design Error

6 Staff and Labour 66

6.1	Engagement of Staff and Labour
6.2	Rates of Wages and Conditions of Employment
6.3	Persons in the Service of Employer
6.4	Labour Laws
6.5	Working Hours
6.6	Facilities for Staff and Labour
6.7	Health and Safety
6.8	Contractor's Superintendence
6.9	Contractor's Personnel
6.10	Records of Contractor's Personnel and Equipment
6.11	Disorderly Conduct

7 Plant, Materials, and Workmanship 70

7.1	Manner of Execution
7.2	Samples
7.3	Inspection
7.4	Testing
7.5	Rejection
7.6	Remedial Work

4.5	指定分包商	
4.6	合作	
4.7	放线	
4.8	安全程序	
4.9	质量保证	
4.10	现场数据	
4.11	中标合同金额的充分性	
4.12	不可预见的物质条件	
4.13	道路通行权和设施	
4.14	避免干扰	
4.15	进场通路	
4.16	货物运输	
4.17	承包商设备	
4.18	环境保护	
4.19	电、水和燃气	
4.20	雇主设备和免费提供的材料	
4.21	进度报告	
4.22	现场安保	
4.23	承包商的现场作业	
4.24	化石	
4.25	承包商资金（财务）状况的改变	

5　设计 ……………………………………………………………… 61

5.1	设计义务一般要求	
5.2	承包商文件	
5.3	承包商的承诺	
5.4	技术标准和法规	
5.5	竣工文件	
5.6	操作和维护手册	
5.7	设计错误	

6　员工 ……………………………………………………………… 67

6.1	员工的雇用	
6.2	工资标准和劳动条件	
6.3	为雇主服务的人员	
6.4	劳动法	
6.5	工作时间	
6.6	为员工提供设施	
6.7	健康和安全	
6.8	承包商的监督	
6.9	承包商人员	
6.10	承包商人员和设备的记录	
6.11	无序行为	

7　生产设备、材料和工艺 ……………………………………………………………… 71

7.1	实施方法	
7.2	样品	
7.3	检验	
7.4	试验	
7.5	拒收	
7.6	修补工作	

7.7	Ownership of Plant and Materials
7.8	Royalties

8 Commencement Date, Completion and Programme 76

8.1	Commencement Date
8.2	Time for Completion
8.3	Programme
8.4	Advance Warning
8.5	Delay Damages
8.6	Contract Completion Certificate
8.7	Handback Requirements
8.8	Unfulfilled Obligations

9 Design-Build 80

9.1	Commencement of Design-Build
9.2	Time for Completion of Design-Build
9.3	Extension of Time for Completion of Design-Build
9.4	Delays Caused by Authorities
9.5	Rate of Progress
9.6	Delay Damages relating to Design-Build
9.7	Suspension of Work
9.8	Consequences of Suspension
9.9	Payment for Plant and Materials in Event of Suspension
9.10	Prolonged Suspension
9.11	Resumption of Work
9.12	Completion of Design-Build
9.13	Failure to Complete

10 Operation Service 88

10.1	General Requirements
10.2	Commencement of Operation Service
10.3	Independent Compliance Audit
10.4	Delivery of Raw Materials
10.5	Training
10.6	Delays and Interruptions during the Operation Service
10.7	Failure to Reach Production Outputs
10.8	Completion of Operation Service
10.9	Ownership of Output and Revenue

11 Testing 96

11.1	Testing of the Works
11.2	Delayed Tests on Completion of Design-Build
11.3	Retesting of the Works
11.4	Failure to Pass Tests on Completion of Design-Build
11.5	Completion of the Works and Sections
11.6	Commissioning of Parts of the Works
11.7	Commissioning Certificate
11.8	Joint Inspection Prior to Contract Completion
11.9	Procedure for Tests Prior to Contract Completion
11.10	Delayed Tests Prior to Contract Completion

7.7 生产设备和材料的所有权
7.8 土地（矿区）使用费

8 开工日期、竣工和进度计划 ································· 77

8.1 开工日期
8.2 竣工时间
8.3 进度计划
8.4 预先警示
8.5 误期损害赔偿费
8.6 合同完成证书
8.7 移交要求
8.8 未履行的义务

9 设计 - 施工 ·· 81

9.1 设计 - 施工的开始
9.2 设计 - 施工竣工时间
9.3 设计 - 施工竣工时间的延长
9.4 部门造成的延误
9.5 工程进度
9.6 设计 - 施工的误期损害赔偿费
9.7 暂时停工
9.8 暂停的后果
9.9 暂停时对生产设备和材料的付款
9.10 拖长的暂停
9.11 复工
9.12 设计 - 施工的竣工
9.13 未能竣工

10 运营服务 ·· 89

10.1 一般要求
10.2 运营服务的开始
10.3 独立合规审计
10.4 原材料的交付
10.5 培训
10.6 运营服务期间的延误和中断
10.7 未能达到产量
10.8 运营服务的完成
10.9 产出和收入所有权

11 试验 ··· 97

11.1 工程试验
11.2 设计 - 施工竣工试验的延误
11.3 工程重新试验
11.4 未能通过设计 - 施工竣工试验
11.5 工程和分项工程的竣工
11.6 部分工程的调试
11.7 调试证书
11.8 合同完成前的联合检验
11.9 合同完成前试验程序
11.10 合同完成前试验的延误

11.11 Failure to Pass Tests Prior to Contract Completion
11.12 Retesting Prior to Contract Completion

12 Defects 106

12.1 Completion of Outstanding Work and Remedying Defects
12.2 Cost of Remedying Defects
12.3 Failure to Remedy Defects
12.4 Further Tests
12.5 Removal of Defective Work
12.6 Contractor to Search

13 Variations and Adjustments 110

13.1 Right to Vary
13.2 Value Engineering
13.3 Variation Procedure
13.4 Payment in Applicable Currencies
13.5 Provisional Sums
13.6 Adjustments for Changes in Legislation
13.7 Adjustments for Changes in Technology
13.8 Adjustments for Changes in Cost

14 Contract Price and Payment 116

14.1 The Contract Price
14.2 Advance Payment
14.3 Application for Advance and Interim Payment Certificates
14.4 Schedule of Payments
14.5 Asset Replacement Schedule
14.6 Payment for Plant and Materials intended for the Works
14.7 Issue of Advance and Interim Payment Certificates
14.8 Payment
14.9 Delayed Payment
14.10 Payment of Retention Money
14.11 Application for Final Payment Certificate Design-Build
14.12 Issue of Final Payment Certificate Design-Build
14.13 Application for Final Payment Certificate Operation Service
14.14 Discharge
14.15 Issue of Final Payment Certificate Operation Service
14.16 Cessation of Employer's Liability
14.17 Currencies of Payment
14.18 Asset Replacement Fund
14.19 Maintenance Retention Fund

15 Termination by Employer 136

15.1 Notice to Correct
15.2 Termination for Contractor's Default
15.3 Valuation at Date of Termination for Contractor's Default
15.4 Payment after Termination for Contractor's Default
15.5 Termination for Employer's Convenience
15.6 Valuation at Date of Termination for Employer's Convenience
15.7 Payment after Termination for Employer's Convenience

11.11	未能通过合同完成前试验	
11.12	合同完成前的重新试验	
12	**缺陷**	**107**
12.1	完成扫尾工作和修补缺陷	
12.2	修补缺陷的费用	
12.3	未能修补缺陷	
12.4	进一步试验	
12.5	移出有缺陷的工程	
12.6	承包商调查	
13	**变更和调整**	**111**
13.1	变更权	
13.2	价值工程	
13.3	变更程序	
13.4	以适用货币支付	
13.5	暂列金额	
13.6	因法律改变的调整	
13.7	因技术改变的调整	
13.8	因成本改变的调整	
14	**合同价格和付款**	**117**
14.1	合同价格	
14.2	预付款	
14.3	预付款和期中付款证书的申请	
14.4	付款计划表	
14.5	资产置换计划表	
14.6	拟用于工程的生产设备和材料的付款	
14.7	预付款和期中付款证书的签发	
14.8	付款	
14.9	延误的付款	
14.10	保留金的支付	
14.11	设计-施工最终付款证书的申请	
14.12	设计-施工最终付款证书的签发	
14.13	运营服务最终付款证书的申请	
14.14	结清证明	
14.15	运营服务最终付款证书的签发	
14.16	雇主责任的中止	
14.17	支付的货币	
14.18	资产置换基金	
14.19	维护保留金	
15	**由雇主终止**	**137**
15.1	通知改正	
15.2	由承包商违约的终止	
15.3	由承包商违约终止日期时的估价	
15.4	由承包商违约终止后的付款	
15.5	为雇主便利的终止	
15.6	为雇主便利终止日的估价	
15.7	为雇主便利终止后的付款	

| 16 | Suspension and Termination by Contractor | 140 |

16.1 Contractor's Entitlement to Suspend Work
16.2 Termination by Contractor
16.3 Cessation of Work and Removal of Contractor's Equipment
16.4 Payment on Termination

| 17 | Risk Allocation | 144 |

17.1 The Employer's Risks during the Design-Build Period
17.2 The Contractor's Risks during the Design-Build Period
17.3 The Employer's Risks during the Operation Service Period
17.4 The Contractor's Risks during the Operation Service Period
17.5 Responsibility for Care of the Works
17.6 Consequences of the Employer's Risks of Damage
17.7 Consequences of the Contractor's Risks resulting in Damage
17.8 Limitation of Liability
17.9 Indemnities by the Contractor
17.10 Indemnities by the Employer
17.11 Shared Indemnities
17.12 Risk of Infringement of Intellectual and Industrial Property Rights

| 18 | Exceptional Risks | 152 |

18.1 Exceptional Risks
18.2 Notice of an Exceptional Event
18.3 Duty to Minimise Delay
18.4 Consequences of an Exceptional Event
18.5 Optional Termination, Payment and Release
18.6 Release from Performance under the Law

| 19 | Insurance | 156 |

19.1 General Requirements
19.2 Insurances to be provided by the Contractor during the Design-Build Period
19.3 Insurances to be provided by the Contractor during the Operation Service Period

| 20 | Claims, Disputes and Arbitration | 164 |

20.1 Contractor's Claims
20.2 Employer's Claims
20.3 Appointment of the Dispute Adjudication Board
20.4 Failure to Agree Dispute Adjudication Board
20.5 Avoidance of Disputes
20.6 Obtaining Dispute Adjudication Board's Decision
20.7 Amicable Settlement
20.8 Arbitration
20.9 Failure to Comply with Dispute Adjudication Board's Decision
20.10 Disputes Arising during the Operation Service Period
20.11 Expiry of Dispute Adjudication Board's Appointment

16	**由承包商暂停和终止**	**141**
16.1	承包商暂停工作的权利	
16.2	由承包商终止	
16.3	停止工作和承包商设备的撤离	
16.4	终止时的付款	
17	**风险分配**	**145**
17.1	设计 - 施工期间雇主的风险	
17.2	设计 - 施工期间承包商的风险	
17.3	运营服务期间雇主的风险	
17.4	运营服务期间承包商的风险	
17.5	工程照管的职责	
17.6	雇主损害风险的后果	
17.7	承包商损害风险的后果	
17.8	责任限度	
17.9	由承包商保障	
17.10	由雇主保障	
17.11	保障分担	
17.12	知识产权和工业产权侵权风险	
18	**例外风险**	**153**
18.1	例外风险	
18.2	例外事件的通知	
18.3	将延误减至最小的义务	
18.4	例外事件的后果	
18.5	自主选择终止、付款和解除	
18.6	依法解除履约	
19	**保险**	**157**
19.1	一般要求	
19.2	承包商在设计 - 施工期间提供的保险	
19.3	承包商在运营服务期间提供的保险	
20	**索赔、争端和仲裁**	**165**
20.1	承包商索赔	
20.2	雇主索赔	
20.3	争端裁决委员会的任命	
20.4	对争端裁决委员会未能取得一致	
20.5	避免争端	
20.6	取得争端裁决委员会的决定	
20.7	友好解决	
20.8	仲裁	
20.9	未能遵守争端裁决委员会的决定	
20.10	运营服务期间发生的争端	
20.11	争端裁决委员会任命期满	

GENERAL CONDITIONS OF CONTRACT

1 General Provisions

1.1 Definitions

In the Conditions of Contract ("these Conditions"), which include Particular Conditions and these General Conditions, the following words and expressions shall have the meanings stated. Words indicating persons or parties include corporations and other legal entities, except where the context requires otherwise.

1.1.1 "**Accepted Contract Amount**" means the amount accepted in the Letter of Acceptance for the Design-Build of the Works and the provision of the Operation Service, including the amount of the Asset Replacement Fund.

1.1.2 "**Asset Replacement Fund**" means the fund provided for under Sub-Clause 14.18 [*Asset Replacement Fund*].

1.1.3 "**Asset Replacement Schedule**" means the schedule referred to in Sub-Clause 14.5 [*Asset Replacement Schedule*] prepared by the Contractor covering the identification and timing of asset replacements.

1.1.4 "**Auditing Body**" means the independent and impartial body appointed to conduct the Independent Compliance Audit in accordance with Sub-Clause 10.3 [*Independent Compliance Audit*].

1.1.5 "**Base Date**" means the date 28 days prior to the latest date for submission of the Tender.

1.1.6 "**Commencement Date**" means the date notified under Sub-Clause 8.1 [*Commencement Date*].

1.1.7 "**Commercial Risk**" means a risk which results in financial loss and/or time loss for either of the Parties, where insurance is not generally or commercially available.

1.1.8 "**Commissioning Certificate**" means the certificate issued by the Employer's Representative to the Contractor under Sub-Clause 11.7 [*Commissioning Certificate*] marking the end of the Design-Build Period under Sub-Clause 9.12 [*Completion of Design-Build*] and the commencement of the Operation Service Period.

1.1.9 "**Commissioning Period**" means that period of time when commissioning tests are being carried out.

1.1.10 "**Contract**" means the Contract Agreement, the Letter of Acceptance, the Letter of Tender, these Conditions, the Employer's Requirements, the Schedules, the Contractor's Proposal, the Operating Licence, and the further documents (if any) which are listed in the Contract Agreement or in the Letter of Acceptance.

1.1.11 "**Contract Agreement**" means the Contract Agreement (if any) referred to in Sub-Clause 1.6 [*Contract Agreement*].

合同通用条件

1 一般规定

1.1 定义

在**合同条件**("**本条件**"),包括**专用条件**和本**通用条件**中,以下词语和措辞应具有以下所述的含义。除上下文另有要求外,人员或当事各方等词语包括公司和其他合法实体。

1.1.1 "**中标合同金额**"系指在**中标函**中所认可的**工程**设计-施工和提供**运营服务**所需的费用,包括**资产置换基金**的金额。

1.1.2 "**资产置换基金**"系指根据第 14.18 款[*资产置换基金*]所规定的资金。

1.1.3 "**资产置换计划表**"系指**承包商**根据第 14.5 款[*资产置换计划表*]中提及的计划所编制的,包括资产置换的确认和时间安排。

1.1.4 "**审计机构**"系指根据第 10.3 款[*独立合规审计*]的规定,被任命进行**独立合规审计**的独立公正机构。

1.1.5 "**基准日期**"系指递交**投标书**截止日期前 28 天的日期。

1.1.6 "**开工日期**"系指根据第 8.1 款[*开工日期*]的规定通知的日期。

1.1.7 "**商业风险**"系指对任何一方造成经济损失和/或时间损失的风险,在一般情况下或在商业上没有获得保险。

1.1.8 "**调试证书**"系指**雇主代表**根据第 11.7 款[*调试证书*]的规定,向**承包商**签发的证书,该证书标志着第 9.12 款[*设计-施工的竣工*]规定的**设计-施工期**结束以及**运营服务期**的开始。

1.1.9 "**调试期**"系指进行调试试验的时间段。

1.1.10 "**合同**"系指**合同协议书**、**中标函**、**投标函**、**本条件**、**雇主要求**、**资料表**、**承包商建议书**、**运营执照**以及**合同协议书**或**中标函**中列出的进一步文件(如果有)。

1.1.11 "**合同协议书**"系指根据第 1.6 款[*合同协议书*]中所述的合同协议书(如果有)。

1.1.12 "**Contract Completion Certificate**" means the certificate issued by the Employer's Representative under Sub-Clause 8.6 [*Contract Completion Certificate*].

1.1.13 "**Contract Completion Date**" means the date contained in the Contract Completion Certificate as being the date on which the Operation Service has been completed.

1.1.14 "**Contract Data**" means the pages completed by the Employer entitled Contract Data which constitute Part A of the Particular Conditions.

1.1.15 "**Contract Period**" means the Design-Build Period plus the Operation Service Period.

1.1.16 "**Contract Price**" means the price defined in Sub-Clause 14.1 [*The Contract Price*], and includes adjustments in accordance with the Contract.

1.1.17 "**Contractor**" means the person named as Contractor in the Letter of Tender accepted by the Employer and the legal successors in title to this person.

1.1.18 "**Contractor's Equipment**" means all apparatus, machinery, vehicles and other things required for the execution and completion of the Works and the remedying of any defects. However, Contractor's Equipment excludes Temporary Works, Employer's Equipment (if any), Plant, Materials and any other things intended to form or forming part of the Works.

1.1.19 "**Contractor's Documents**" means the calculations, computer programs and other software, drawings, manuals, models and other documents of a technical nature supplied by the Contractor under the Contract; as described in Sub-Clause 5.2 [*Contractor's Documents*].

1.1.20 "**Contractor's Proposal**" means the document entitled proposal, which the Contractor submitted with the Letter of Tender, as included in the Contract.

1.1.21 "**Contractor's Personnel**" means the Contractor's Representative and all personnel whom the Contractor utilises on Site, including the staff, labour and other employees of the Contractor and of each Subcontractor, and any other personnel assisting the Contractor in the execution of the Works and provision of the Operation Service.

1.1.22 "**Contractor's Representative**" means the person named as such by the Contractor in the Contract or appointed from time to time by the Contractor under Sub-Clause 4.3 [*Contractor's Representative*] who acts on behalf of the Contractor.

1.1.23 "**Cost**" means all expenditure reasonably incurred (or to be incurred) by the Contractor, whether on or off the Site, including overhead and similar charges, but does not include profit.

1.1.24 "**Cost Plus Profit**" means Cost plus the applicable percentage agreed and stated in the Contract Data. Such percentage shall only be added where the Sub-Clause states that the Contractor is entitled to Cost Plus Profit.

1.1.25 "**Country**" means the country in which the Site (or most of it) is located, where the Permanent Works are to be executed.

1.1.12 "合同完成证书"系指雇主代表根据第 8.6 款［*合同完成证书*］的规定签发的证书。

1.1.13 "合同完成日期"系指合同完成证书中包含的**运营服务**完成日期。

1.1.14 "合同数据"系指由雇主填写完成的合同数据，构成专用条件 A 部分名为**合同数据**的文本。

1.1.15 "合同期"系指**设计 - 施工期**加上**运营服务期**。

1.1.16 "合同价格"系指第 14.1 款［*合同价格*］规定的价格，并包括根据合同进行的调整。

1.1.17 "承包商"系指在雇主接受的**投标函**中称为**承包商**的当事人，及其财产所有权的合法继承人。

1.1.18 "承包商设备"系指为实施和完成**工程**以及修补任何缺陷所需的所有仪器、机械、车辆和其他物品。但**承包商设备**不包括**临时工程**、**雇主设备**（如果有），以及拟构成或正构成**工程**一部分的**生产设备**、**材料**任何其他物品。

1.1.19 "承包商文件"系指第 5.2 款［*承包商文件*］中所述的，由**承包商**根据合同提交的所有计算、计算机程序和其他软件、图纸、手册、模型和其他技术性文件。

1.1.20 "承包商建议书"系指包括在合同中由**承包商**随**投标函**提交的名为建议书文件。

1.1.21 "承包商人员"系指**承包商代表**和**承包商**在**现场**聘用的所有人员，包括**承包商**和每个**分包商**的职员、工人和其他雇员，以及所有其他帮助**承包商**实施**工程**和提供**运营服务**的人员。

1.1.22 "承包商代表"系指由**承包商**在合同中指名的人员，或有时根据第 4.3 款［*承包商代表*］的规定，由**承包商**任命为其代表的人员。

1.1.23 "成本（费用）"系指**承包商**在**现场**内外发生（或将要发生）的所有合理开支，包括管理费和类似支出，但不包括利润。

1.1.24 "成本加利润"系指**合同数据**中同意和规定的**成本**加上适当的百分比。只有在本款规定**承包商**有权获得**成本加利润**时，该百分比才能加到**成本**中。

1.1.25 "工程所在国"系指实施**永久工程**的**现场**（或其大部分）所在的国家。

1.1.26 **"Cut-Off Date"** means the date, at the end of a specified period stated in the Contract Data, after the Time for Completion of the Design-Build or any extension thereto granted under Sub-Clause 9.3 [*Extension of Time for Completion of Design-Build*].

1.1.27 **"DAB"** means the person or three persons so named in the Contract, or other person (s) appointed under Sub-Clause 20.3 [*Appointment of the Dispute Adjudication Board*] or Sub-Clause 20.4 [*Failure to Agree Dispute Adjudication Board*], or Sub-Clause 20.10 [*Disputes Arising During the Operation Service Period*].

1.1.28 **"day"** means a calendar day.

1.1.29 **"Design-Build"** means all work to be performed by the Contractor under the Contract to design, build, test and complete the Works and obtain the Commissioning Certificate issued in accordance with Sub-Clause 9.12 [*Completion of Design-Build*].

1.1.30 **"Design-Build Period"** means the period from the Commencement Date to the date stated in the Commissioning Certificate.

1.1.31 **"Dispute"** means any situation where (a) one Party makes a claim against the other Party; (b) the other Party rejects the claim in whole or in part; and (c) the first Party does not acquiesce, provided however that a failure by the other Party to oppose or respond to the claim, in whole or in part, may constitute a rejection if, in the circumstances, the DAB or the arbitrator (s), as the case may be, deem it reasonable for it to do so.

1.1.32 **"Employer"** means the person named as Employer in the Contract Data and the legal successors in title to this person.

1.1.33 **"Employer's Equipment"** means the apparatus, machinery and vehicles (if any) made available by the Employer for the use of the Contractor in the execution of the Works and/or the Operation Service, as stated in the Employer's Requirements, but does not include Plant which has not been taken over by the Employer.

1.1.34 **"Employer's Personnel"** means the Employer's Representative, the assistants referred to in Sub-Clause 3.2 [*Delegation by the Employer's Representative*] and all other staff, labour and other employees of the Employer's Representative and of the Employer; and any other personnel notified to the Contractor, by the Employer or the Employer's Representative, as Employer's Personnel.

1.1.35 **"Employer's Representative"** means the person appointed by the Employer to act as Employer's Representative for the purposes of the Contract and named as such in the Contract Data, or other person appointed from time to time by the Employer and notified as such to the Contractor under Sub-Clause 3.4 [*Replacement of the Employer's Representative*].

1.1.36 **"Employer's Requirements"** means the document entitled Employer's Requirements, as included in the Contract, and any additions and modifications made thereto in accordance with the Contract. Such document specifies the purpose, scope, and/or design and/or other technical criteria for the execution of the Works and provision of the Operation Service.

1.1.37 **"Exceptional Event"** means an event or circumstance which is (a) beyond a Party's control; (b) which the Party could not reasonably have provided against before entering into the Contract; (c) which having arisen, such Party could not reasonably have avoided or overcome; and (d) which is not substantially attributable to the other Party.

1.1.26 "截止日期"系指在**合同数据**中规定的期限结束时，在**设计 - 施工竣工时间**或根据**第 9.3 款**［*设计 - 施工竣工时间的延长*］的规定，授予的任何延期之后的日期。

1.1.27 "DAB（争端裁决委员会）"系指合同中如此指名的一名或三名人员，或根据**第 20.3 款**［*争端裁决委员会的任命*］或**第 20.4 款**［*对争端裁决委员会未能取得一致*］或**第 20.10 款**［*运营服务期间发生的争端*］的规定任命的人员。

1.1.28 "日（天）"系指一个日历日。

1.1.29 "设计 - 施工"系指**承包商**根据合同为设计、施工、试验和完成**工程**所进行的所有工作，并获得根据**第 9.12 款**［*设计 - 施工的竣工*］签发的**调试运行证书**。

1.1.30 "设计 - 施工期"系指从**开工日期**到**调试证书**规定日期的期间。

1.1.31 "争端"系指下列情况：（a）一方向另一方提出索赔；（b）另一方拒绝全部或部分索赔；以及（c）第一方不认可，但另一方未能全部或部分反对或回复索赔，在这种情况下，如果 DAB 或仲裁员视情况认为拒绝是合理的，则可以构成拒绝。

1.1.32 "雇主"系指在**合同数据**中称为雇主的当事人，及其财产所有权的合法继承人。

1.1.33 "雇主设备"系指**雇主要求**中列明由**雇主**向**承包商**提供，在实施**工程**和 / 或**运营服务**中使用的仪器、机械和车辆（如果有），但不包括尚未经雇主接收的**生产设备**。

1.1.34 "雇主人员"系指**雇主代表**，**第 3.2 款**［*由雇主代表付托*］的规定中所称的助手，以及**雇主代表**和**雇主**的所有其他职员、工人和其他雇员；以及由**雇主**或**雇主代表**通知**承包商**作为**雇主人员**的任何其他人员。

1.1.35 "雇主代表"系指雇主为履行合同而任命的雇主代表，并在**合同数据**中指定的人员，或由雇主根据**第 3.4 款**［*雇主代表的替代*］的规定，不时任命并通知**承包商**的其他人员。

1.1.36 "雇主要求"系指合同中包含的名为**雇主要求**的文件，以及根据合同对该文件的任何补充和修改。此类文件规定了实施**工程**和提供**运营服务**的目的、范围和 / 或设计和 / 或其他技术标准。

1.1.37 "例外事件"系指以下事件或情况：（a）一方无法控制的；（b）该方在签订**合同**前，不能进行合理预防的；（c）发生后，该方不能合理避免或克服的；以及（d）不能主要归责于另一方的。

1.1.38 **"FIDIC"** means the Fédération Internationale des Ingénieurs-Conseils, the International Federation of Consulting Engineers.

1.1.39 **"Final Payment Certificate Design-Build"** means the payment certificate issued for the Design-Build under Sub-Clause 14.12 [*Issue of Final Payment Certificate Design-Build*].

1.1.40 **"Final Payment Certificate Operation Service"** means the payment certificate issued for the Operation Service under Sub-Clause 14.15 [*Issue of Final Payment Certificate Operation Service*].

1.1.41 **"Final Statement Design-Build"** means the Statement defined in Sub-Clause 14.11 [*Application for Final Payment Certificate Design-Build*].

1.1.42 **"Final Statement Operation Service"** means the Statement defined in Sub-Clause 14.13 [*Application for Final Payment Certificate Operation Service*].

1.1.43 **"Financial Memorandum"** means the document which details the Employer's financial arrangements and is attached to or forms part of the Employer's Requirements.

1.1.44 **"Foreign Currency"** means a currency in which part (or all) of the Contract Price is payable, but not the Local Currency.

1.1.45 **"Goods"** means Contractor's Equipment, Materials, Plant and Temporary Works, or any of them as appropriate.

1.1.46 **"Interim Payment Certificate"** means a payment certificate issued under Clause 14 [*Contract Price and Payment*], other than the Final Payment Certificates.

1.1.47 **"Laws"** means all national (or state) legislation, statutes, ordinances and other laws, and regulations and by-laws of any legally constituted public authority.

1.1.48 **"Letter of Acceptance"** means the letter of formal acceptance, signed by the Employer, of the Letter of Tender, including any annexed memoranda comprising agreements between and signed by both Parties. If there is no such Letter of Acceptance, the expression "Letter of Acceptance" means the Contract Agreement and the date of issuing or receiving the Letter of Acceptance means the date of signing the Contract Agreement.

1.1.49 **"Letter of Tender"** means the document entitled Letter of Tender, which was completed by the Contractor and includes the signed offer to the Employer for the execution of the Works and provision of the Operation Service.

1.1.50 **"Local Currency"** means the currency of the Country.

1.1.51 **"Maintenance Retention Fund"** and **"Maintenance Retention Guarantee"** mean the fund and guarantee respectively provided for under Sub-Clause 14.19 [*Maintenance Retention Fund*].

1.1.52 **"Materials"** means things of all kinds (other than Plant) whether on the Site or otherwise allocated to the Contract and intended to form or forming part of the Works, including the supply-only Materials (if any) to be supplied by the Contractor under the Contract.

1.1.38 "菲迪克"（FIDIC）系指国际咨询工程师联合会。

1.1.39 "设计 - 施工最终付款证书"系指根据第 14.12 款［*设计 - 施工最终付款证书的签发*］的规定，为设计 - 施工签发的付款证书。

1.1.40 "运营服务最终付款证书"系指根据第 14.15 款［*运营服务最终付款证书的签发*］的规定，为运营服务签发的付款证书。

1.1.41 "设计 - 施工最终报表"系指第 14.11 款［*设计 - 施工最终付款证书的申请*］中规定的报表。

1.1.42 "运营服务最终报表"系指第 14.13 款［*运营服务最终付款证书的申请*］中规定的报表。

1.1.43 "资金（财务）备忘录"系指详细说明雇主资金（财务）安排的文件，并作为雇主要求的附件或构成雇主要求的一部分。

1.1.44 "外币"系指可用于支付合同价格中部分（或全部）款项的当地货币以外的某种货币。

1.1.45 "货物"系指承包商设备、材料、生产设备和临时工程，或视情况指其中任何一种。

1.1.46 "期中付款证书"系指根据第 14 条［*合同价格和付款*］的规定签发的付款证书，最终付款证书除外。

1.1.47 "法律"系指所有全国性（或州）的法律、条例、法令和其他法律，以及任何合法成立的公共部门制定的规则和细则等。

1.1.48 "中标函"系指雇主签署的正式接受投标函的信函，包括其所附的由双方间签署的协议包含的任何附件备忘录。如无此类中标函，则"中标函"系指合同协议书，签发或收到中标函的日期系指签署合同协议书的日期。

1.1.49 "投标函"系指由承包商填写的名为投标函的文件，包括其已签字的向雇主提出的实施工程和提供运营服务的报价。

1.1.50 "当地货币"系指工程所在国的货币。

1.1.51 "维护保留基金"和"维护保留金保函"系指根据第 14.19 款［*维护保留金*］分别规定的基金和保函。

1.1.52 "材料"系指拟构成或正构成工程一部分的各类物品（生产设备除外），无论在现场或以其他方式按合同分配，包括根据合同要由承包商供应的只供材料（如果有）。

1.1.53 "**Notice**" means a written communication identified as a Notice and issued in accordance with the provisions of Sub-Clause 1.3 [*Notices and Other Communications*].

1.1.54 "**Operating Licence**" means the licence referred to in Sub-Clause 1.7 [*Operating Licence*] by which the Employer grants a royalty-free licence to the Contractor to operate and maintain the Works during the Operation Service.

1.1.55 "**Operation Management Requirements**" means the set of procedures and requirements, provided by the Employer, included in the Employer's Requirements for the proper implementation of the Operation Service.

1.1.56 "**Operation and Maintenance Plan**" means the plan for operating and maintaining the facility, submitted by the Contractor, and agreed and included in the Contract.

1.1.57 "**Operation Service**" means the operation and maintenance of the facility as set out in the Operation Management Requirements.

1.1.58 "**Operation Service Period**" means the period from the date stated in the Commissioning Certificate as provided for under Sub-Clause 10.2 [*Commencement of Operation Service*] to the date stated in the Contract Completion Certificate.

1.1.59 "**Party**" means the Employer or the Contractor, as the context requires.

1.1.60 "**Performance Security**" means the security under Sub-Clause 4.2 [*Performance Security*].

1.1.61 "**Permanent Works**" means the permanent works to be designed, executed and operated by the Contractor under the Contract.

1.1.62 "**Plant**" means the apparatus, machinery and vehicles intended to form or forming part of the Permanent Works.

1.1.63 "**Provisional Sum**" means a sum (if any) which is specified in the Contract by the Employer as a Provisional Sum, for the execution of any part of the Works or for the supply of Plant, Materials or services under Sub-Clause 13.5 [*Provisional Sums*].

1.1.64 "**Rates and Prices**" means the rates and prices inserted in the Schedules for the design, execution and completion of the Works and for the provision of the Operation Service as incorporated in the Contract.

1.1.65 "**Retention Money**" means the accumulated retention monies which the Employer retains under Sub-Clause 14.3 [*Application for Advance and Interim Payment Certificates*].

1.1.66 "**Retention Period**" means the period of 1 year after the date stated in the Commissioning Certificate for the completion of outstanding work.

1.1.67 "**Risk of Damage**" means a risk which results in physical loss or damage to the Works or other property belonging to either Party, other than a Commercial Risk.

1.1.68 "**Schedules**" means the document (s) entitled Schedules, completed by the Contractor and submitted with the Letter of Tender, as incorporated in the Contract. Such documents shall include the Asset Replacement Schedule, and may also include data, lists, Schedules of Payments and/or prices, and guarantees.

1.1.53 "**通知**"系指按照第 1.3 款［*通知和其他通信交流*］的规定发出的书面**通知**。

1.1.54 "**运营执照**"系指在第 1.7 款［*运营执照*］中提到的执照，**雇主**向**承包商**授予在**运营服务期**间运营和维护**工程**的免版税执照。

1.1.55 "**运营管理要求**"系指**雇主**提供的一套程序和要求，包括**雇主要求**中关于正确实施**运营服务**的规定。

1.1.56 "**运营和维护计划**"系指由**承包商**提交和同意并包含在**合同**中的设施运营和维护计划。

1.1.57 "**运营服务**"系指**运营管理要求**中规定的设施运营和维护。

1.1.58 "**运营服务期**"系指第 10.2 款［*运营服务的开始*］规定的，**调试证书**中规定的日期到**合同完成证书**中规定的日期的期间。

1.1.59 "**当事方（一方）**"系指**雇主**或**承包商**，根据上下文的需要。

1.1.60 "**履约担保**"系指根据第 4.2 款［*履约担保*］规定的担保。

1.1.61 "**永久工程**"系指**承包商**按照合同规定设计、实施和运营的永久性工程。

1.1.62 "**生产设备**"系指拟构成或正构成**永久工程**一部分的装备、机械和车辆。

1.1.63 "**暂列金额**"系指**雇主**在合同中规定为**暂列金额**的一笔款项（如果有），根据第 13.5 款［*暂列金额*］的规定，用于实施**工程**的任何部分，或用于提供**生产设备**、材料或服务。

1.1.64 "**费率和价格**"系指**资料表**中为**工程**设计、实施和竣工以及提供合同中包含的**运营服务**的费率和价格。

1.1.65 "**保留金**"系指**雇主**根据第 14.3 款［*预付款和期中付款证书的申请*］的规定扣留的累计保留金。

1.1.66 "**保留期**"系指从**调试证书**中的日期起 1 年内完成扫尾工作的期限。

1.1.67 "**损害风险**"系指对**工程**或属于任何一方的其他财产造成有形损失或损害的风险，商业风险除外。

1.1.68 "**资料表**"系指合同中名为各种资料表的文件，由**承包商**填写并随**投标函**一起提交。此类文件可包括**资产置换计划表**，也可包括数据、表册、**付款计划表**和／或价格表以及保函。

1.1.69 "**Schedule of Payments**" means those Schedules (if any) incorporated in the Contract showing the manner in which payments are to be made to the Contractor.

1.1.70 "**Section**" means a part of the Works specified in the Contract Data as a Section (if any).

1.1.71 "**Section Commissioning Certificate**" means a certificate issued by the Employer's Representative to the Contractor under Sub-Clause 11.7 [*Commissioning Certificate*].

1.1.72 "**Site**" means the places where the Permanent Works are to be executed and to which Plant and Materials are to be delivered, and where the Operation Service is to be provided, and any other places as may be specified in the Contract as forming part of the Site.

1.1.73 "**Statement**" means a financial Statement submitted by the Contractor as part of an application, under Clause 14 [*Contract Price and Payment*], for a payment certificate.

1.1.74 "**Subcontractor**" means any person named in the Contract as a subcontractor, or any person appointed as a subcontractor, for a part of the Works; and the legal successors in title to each of these persons.

1.1.75 "**Tender**" means the Letter of Tender and all other documents which the Contractor submitted with the Letter of Tender, as incorporated in the Contract.

1.1.76 "**Tests on Completion of Design-Build**" means the tests which are specified in the Contract or agreed by both Parties or instructed as a Variation, and which are to be carried out under Clause 11 [*Testing*] before the Works or a Section (as the case may be) are deemed to be fit for purpose as defined in the Employer's Requirements.

1.1.77 "**Tests Prior to Contract Completion**" means the tests (if any) which are specified in the Contract and any other such tests as may be agreed by the Employer's Representative and the Contractor or instructed as a Variation and which are to be carried out under Clause 11 [*Testing*] before the expiry of the Contract Period.

1.1.78 "**Time for Completion of Design-Build**" means the time for completing the Design-Build or a Section thereof (as the case may be) under Sub-Clause 9.2 [*Time for Completion of Design-Build*], as stated in the Contract Data (with any extension under Sub-Clause 9.3 [*Extension of Time for Completion of Design-Build*]), calculated from the Commencement Date.

1.1.79 "**Temporary Works**" means all temporary works of every kind (other than Contractor's Equipment) required on Site for the execution, completion and operation of the Works.

1.1.80 "**Unforeseeable**" means not reasonably foreseeable by an experienced contractor by the date for submission of the Tender.

1.1.81 "**Variation**" means any change to the Employer's Requirements or the Works, which is instructed or approved as a Variation under Clause 13 [*Variations and Adjustments*].

1.1.82 "**Works**" means the Permanent Works and Temporary Works or either of them as appropriate and the facility to be operated by the Contractor during the Operation Service Period.

1.1.83 "**Year**" means 365 days.

1.1.69 "付款计划表"系指合同中规定了向承包商付款方式的计划表（如果有）。

1.1.70 "分项工程"系指在合同数据中确定为分项工程（如果有）的工程组成部分。

1.1.71 "分项工程调试证书"系指雇主代表根据第11.7款[调试证书]的规定，向承包商签发的证书。

1.1.72 "现场"系指将实施永久工程和运送生产设备与材料到达的地点，将提供运营服务的地点以及合同中指定为现场组成部分的任何其他场所。

1.1.73 "报表"系指承包商根据第14条[合同价格和付款]的规定，提交的作为付款证书申请组成部分的资金报表。

1.1.74 "分包商"系指在合同中为分包商的任何人，或为部分工程任命为分包商的任何人员，以及这些人员各自财产所有权的合法继承人。

1.1.75 "投标书"系指投标函和合同中包括的由承包商随投标函一起提交的所有其他文件。

1.1.76 "设计－施工竣工试验"系指在合同中规定的，或双方商定的，或按指示作为一项变更的，在工程或某分项工程（视情况而定）被认为适合雇主要求中规定的目的之前，按照第11条[试验]的要求进行的试验。

1.1.77 "合同完成前试验"系指在合同中规定的试验（如果有），以及雇主代表和承包商商定的，或按指示作为一项变更的任何此类试验，并在合同期期满前按照第11条[试验]的要求进行的试验。

1.1.78 "设计－施工竣工时间"系指合同数据中规定的，自开工日期算起至设计－施工或某分项工程（视情况而定），根据第9.2款[设计－施工竣工时间]规定的要求竣工（连同根据第9.3款[设计－施工竣工时间的延长]的规定提出的任何延长期）的全部时间。

1.1.79 "临时工程"系指为实施、完成和运营工程，在现场所需的所有各类临时工程（承包商设备除外）。

1.1.80 "不可预见的"系指一个有经验的承包商在提交投标书前不能合理预见。

1.1.81 "变更"系指根据第13条[变更和调整]的规定，经指示或批准作为变更的，对雇主要求或工程所做的任何更改。

1.1.82 "工程"系指永久工程和临时工程，或视情况指其中任何一项，以及承包商在运营服务期内运营的设施。

1.1.83 "年"系指365天。

1.2 Interpretation

In the Contract, except where the context requires otherwise:

(a) words indicating one gender include all genders;
(b) words indicating the singular also include the plural and words indicating the plural also include the singular;
(c) provisions including the word "agree", "agreed" or "agreement" require the agreement to be recorded in writing;
(d) "written" or "in writing" means hand-written, type-written, printed or electronically made, and resulting in a permanent record;
(e) "shall" means that the Party or person referred to has an obligation under the Contract to perform the duty referred to; and

(f) "may" means that the Party or person referred to has the choice of whether to act or not in the matter referred to.

The marginal words and other headings shall not be taken into consideration in the interpretation of these Conditions.

1.3 Notices and Other Communications

Wherever these Conditions provide for the giving or issuing of a Notice or other communication including approvals, certificates, consents, determinations, instructions and requests, such Notice or communication shall be:

(a) where it is a Notice, identified as a Notice and include reference to the Clause under which it is issued;
(b) where it is another form of communication, identified as such, and include reference to the Clause under which it is issued where appropriate;
(c) in writing and delivered by hand (against receipt), sent by mail or courier, or transmitted by using any of the agreed systems of electronic transmission as stated in the Contract Data; and
(d) delivered, sent or transmitted to the address for the recipient's communications as stated in the Contract Data. However:

　(i) if the recipient gives Notice of another address, communications and Notices shall thereafter be delivered accordingly; and
　(ii) if the recipient has not stated otherwise when requesting an approval or consent, it may be sent to the address from which the request was issued.

Notices and other communications shall not be unreasonably withheld or delayed. When a certificate is issued to a Party, the certifier shall send a copy to the other Party. When a Notice is issued to a Party, by the other Party or the Employer's Representative, a copy shall be sent to the Employer's Representative or the other party, as the case may be.

1.4 Law and Language

The Contract shall be governed by the law of the country (or other jurisdiction) stated in the Contract Data.

If there are versions of any part of the Contract which are written in more than one language, the version which is in the ruling language stated in the Contract Data shall prevail.

The language for communications shall be that stated in the Contract Data. If no language is stated there, the language for communications shall be the ruling language of the Contract.

1.2 解释

在**合同**中，除上下文中另有要求外：

（a）表示一性别的词，包括所有性别；

（b）单数形式的词，也包括复数含义，复数形式的词亦包括单数含义；

（c）包括"同意（商定）""达成（取得）一致"或"协议"等词的各项规定都要求用书面记载；

（d）"书面"或"以书面形式"系指手写、打字、印刷或电子制作，并形成永久性记录；

（e）"应当"系指一方（当事人）或个人根据**合同**规定有义务履行规定的职责；（以及）

（f）"可以"系指一方（当事人）或个人有权选择是否就所述事项采取行动。

旁注和其他标题在**本条件**的解释中不应考虑。

1.3 通知和其他通信交流

本**条件**不论在何种场合规定发出或签发**通知**或其他通信交流包括批准、证明、同意、确定、指示和请求，此类**通知**或通信交流应：

（a）如果是**通知**，则应注明为**通知**，并包括签发的参考**条款**；

（b）如果是另一种通信方式，则应同样注明，并在适当情况下包括签发的参考**条款**；

（c）采用书面形式，由人面交（取得对方收据），邮寄或信差传送，或用**合同数据**中提出的任何商定的电子传输系统发送；（以及）

（d）交付、传送或传输至**合同数据**中规定的接收人的地址。但：

　　（i）如接收人**通知**了另外地址，随后通信交流和**通知**均应按新地址发送；（以及）

　　（ii）如接收人在请求批准或同意时，没有另外说明，可按请求发出的地址发送。

通知和其他通信交流，不得无故被扣压或拖延。当向一方签发证书时，证明人应抄送另一方。当另一方或**雇主代表**向一方发出**通知**时，应视情况抄送**雇主代表**或另一方。

1.4 法律和语言

合同应受**合同数据**中所述国家（或其他司法管辖区）的法律管辖。

如果**合同**任何部分的文本采用一种以上语言编写，则应以**合同数据**规定的主导语言文本为准。

通信交流应使用**合同数据**中规定的语言。如未规定，应使用**合同**的主导语言。

1.5 Priority of Documents

The documents forming the Contract are to be taken as mutually explanatory of one another. For the purposes of interpretation, the priority of the documents shall be in accordance with the following sequence:

(a) the Contract Agreement (if any),
(b) the Letter of Acceptance,
(c) the Letter of Tender,
(d) the Particular Conditions Part A – Contract Data,
(e) the Particular Conditions Part B – Special Provisions,
(f) these General Conditions,
(g) the Employer's Requirements,
(h) the Schedules, and
(i) the Contractor's Proposal and any other documents forming part of the Contract.

If an ambiguity or discrepancy is found in the documents, the Employer's Representative shall issue any necessary clarification or instruction.

1.6 Contract Agreement

The Parties shall enter into a Contract Agreement within 28 days after the Contractor receives the Letter of Acceptance, unless they agree otherwise. The Contract Agreement shall be based upon the sample form included in the tender documents. The costs of stamp duties and similar charges (if any) imposed by law in connection with entry into the Contract Agreement shall be borne by the Employer.

1.7 Operating Licence

Together with the Letter of Acceptance, the Employer shall issue to the Contractor the Operating Licence or equivalent legal authorisation to enable the Contractor to operate and maintain the Works during the Operation Service Period.

The Operating Licence shall automatically come into full force and effect upon the issue of the Commissioning Certificate upon completion of the Design-Build under Sub-Clause 9.12 [*Completion of Design-Build*] and shall remain in force until the issue of the Contract Completion Certificate under Sub-Clause 8.6 [*Contract Completion Certificate*].

The Operating Licence shall only extend to those parts of the Site which it is required to occupy for the purposes of carrying out the Works and Operation Service as set out in the Contract. The Operating Licence granted pursuant to this Sub-Clause shall not operate nor be deemed to operate as a tenement or a demise of the Site or any part thereof. The Contractor shall not have or be entitled to any estate right, title, or interest in the Site. The licence will immediately terminate upon the termination of this Contract for whatever reason.

1.8 Assignment

Neither Party shall assign the whole or any part of the Contract or any benefit or interest in or under the Contract. However, either Party:

(a) may assign the whole or any part with the prior agreement of the other Party, at the sole discretion of such other Party; and
(b) may, as security in favour of a bank or financial institution, assign its right to any monies due, or to become due, under the Contract.

1.5 文件优先次序

构成合同的文件应能够相互说明。为了便于解释，文件的优先次序如下：

(a) **合同协议书**（如果有）；
(b) **中标函**；
(c) **投标函**；
(d) 专用条件 A 部分——**合同数据**；
(e) 专用条件 B 部分——特别规定；
(f) 本通用条件；
(g) **雇主要求**；
(h) **资料表**；（以及）
(i) **承包商建议书**和构成合同组成部分的任何其他文件。

如发现文件中有歧义或不一致之处，**雇主代表**应发出任何必要的澄清或指示。

1.6 合同协议书

除非另有协议，双方应在**承包商**收到**中标函**后 28 天内签订**合同协议书**。**合同协议书**应以招标文件中的样本格式为依据。与签订**合同协议书**有关的，依法征收的印花税和类似费用（如果有）应由**雇主**承担。

1.7 运营执照

雇主应连同**中标函**一起，向**承包商**签发**运营执照**或同等法律授权书，使**承包商**能够在**运营服务期**内运营和维护**工程**。

运营执照应根据第 9.12 款 [设计 - 施工的竣工] 的规定，在**设计 - 施工**竣工后，在签发**调试证书**后自动完全生效，并在根据**第 8.6 款** [**合同完成证书**] 的规定签发**合同完成证书**之前保持有效。

运营执照仅适用于为履行**合同**规定的**工程**和**运营服务**所需要占用的**现场**部分。根据本款授予的**运营执照**不得运营，也不得视为运营**现场**或其他任何部分的公寓或出租。**承包商**不应拥有或有权享有**现场**的任何财产权、所有权或权益。本**合同**因任何原因终止后，执照应立即终止。

1.8 权益转让

任一方都不应将**合同**的全部或任何部分，或**合同**中或**合同**规定的任何利益或权益转让他人。但任一方：

(a) 在另一方完全自主决定的情况下，事先征得其同意后，可以将**合同**的全部或部分转让；（以及）
(b) 可作为以银行或金融机构为受款人的担保，转让其根据**合同**规定的任何到期或将到期应得款项的权利。

1.9 Care and Supply of Documents

Each of the Contractor's Documents shall be in the custody and care of the Contractor, unless and until taken over by the Employer. Unless otherwise stated in the Contract, the Contractor shall supply to the Employer's Representative six copies of each of the Contractor's Documents.

The Contractor shall keep, on the Site, a copy of the Contract, publications named in the Employer's Requirements, the Contractor's Documents, and Variations and other communications given under the Contract. The Employer's Personnel shall have the right of access to all these documents at all reasonable times.

If a Party becomes aware of an error or defect of a technical nature in a document which was prepared for use in executing the Works, the Party shall promptly give Notice to the other Party of such error or defect.

1.10 Errors in the Employer's Requirements

Notwithstanding the Contractor's obligations to scrutinise the Employer's Requirements under Sub-Clause 5.1 [*General Design Obligations*], if the Contractor finds an error in the Employer's Requirements, he shall immediately give a written Notice to the Employer's Representative advising him of the nature and details of the error and requesting instruction regarding its rectification.

After receiving this Notice, the Employer's Representative shall, without prejudice to other rights and obligations of the Parties, promptly confirm to the Contractor:

(a) whether or not there is an error in the Employer's Requirements as stated in the Contractor's Notice;
(b) whether or not an experienced contractor should have discovered the error when scrutinising the Employer's Requirements under Sub-Clause 5.1 [*General Design Obligations*]; and
(c) the measures which the Employer's Representative requires the Contractor to take to rectify the error.

If the Contractor suffers delay and/or incurs cost as a result of an error in the Employer's Requirements, and an experienced contractor exercising due care would not have discovered the error when scrutinising the Employer's Requirements under Sub-Clause 5.1 [*General Design Obligations*], the Contractor shall be entitled, subject to Sub-Clause 20.1 [*Contractor's Claims*], to:

(i) an extension of time for any such delay, if completion is or will be delayed under Sub-Clause 9.3 [*Extension of Time for Completion of Design-Build*]; and
(ii) payment of any such Cost Plus Profit, which shall be included in the Contract Price.

1.11 Employer's Use of Contractor's Documents

As between the Parties, the Contractor shall retain the copyright and other intellectual property rights in the Contractor's Documents and other design documents made by (or on behalf of) the Contractor.

The Contractor shall be deemed (by signing the Contract) to give to the Employer a non-terminable transferable non-exclusive royalty-free licence to copy, use and communicate the Contractor's Documents, including making and using modifications of them. This licence shall:

(a) apply throughout the actual or intended working life (whichever is longer) of the relevant part of the Works;

| 1.9 文件的照管和提供 | 每份**承包商文件**都应由**承包商**保存和照管，除非并直到被**雇主**接收为止，除非**合同**另有规定，**承包商**应向**雇主代表**提供**承包商文件**一式六份。

承包商应在**现场**保存一份**合同**、**雇主要求**中指名的文件、**承包商文件**、**变更**以及根据合同发出的其他通信交流。**雇主**人员有权在所有合理的时间使用所有这些文件。

如果一方发现在为实施**工程**编制的文件中有技术性错误或缺陷，应立即将该错误或缺陷**通知**另一方。 |

| 1.10 雇主要求中的错误 | 尽管**承包商**有义务根据第 5.1 款［*设计义务一般要求*］的规定，仔细审核**雇主要求**，如果**承包商**发现**雇主要求**中存在错误，**承包商**应立即向**雇主代表**发出书面**通知**，告知其错误的性质和细节，并要求其纠正错误。

在收到此通知后，**雇主代表**应在不损害双方其他权利和义务的情况下，立即向**承包商**确认：

（a）　**承包商通知**中所述的**雇主要求**中是否存在错误；

（b）　在根据第 5.1 款［*设计义务一般要求*］的规定，仔细审核**雇主要求**时，经验丰富的承包商是否会发现错误；（以及）

（c）　**雇主代表**要求**承包商**采取纠正错误的措施。

如因**雇主要求**中的错误而使**承包商**遭受延误和／或招致增加费用，且此错误是一个有经验的承包商在根据第 5.1 款［*设计义务一般要求*］的规定，对**雇主要求**进行认真详查也难以发现的，**承包商**应有权根据第 20.1 款［*承包商索赔*］的规定，获得：

（i）　根据第 9.3 款［*设计-施工竣工时间的延长*］的规定，如果竣工已经或将受到延误，对任何此类延误给予延长期；

（ii）　任何此类**成本加利润**，应计入**合同价格**，给予支付。 |

| 1.11 雇主使用承包商文件 | 就双方而言，由**承包商**（或其代表）编制的**承包商文件**以及其他设计文件，其版权和其他知识产权应归**承包商**所有。

承包商（通过签署**合同**）应被认为已给予**雇主**无限期的、可转让的、不排他的、免版税的，复制、使用和传送**承包商文件**的许可，包括对其做出的修改和使用。这项许可应：

（a）　适用于**工程**相关部分的实际或预期工作寿命期（取较长的）； |

(b) entitle any person in proper possession of the relevant part of the Works to copy, use and communicate the Contractor's Documents for the purposes of completing, operating, maintaining, altering, adjusting, repairing and demolishing the Works;

(c) in the case of Contractor's Documents which are in the form of computer programs and other software, permit their use on any computer on the Site and other places as envisaged by the Contract, including replacements of any computers supplied by the Contractor; and

(d) enable the Employer to relet the Contract as provided for under Sub-Clause 15.2 [*Termination for Contractor's Default*].

The Contractor's Documents and other design documents made by (or on behalf of) the Contractor shall not, without the Contractor's consent, be used, copied or communicated to a third party by (or on behalf of) the Employer for purposes other than those permitted under this Sub-Clause.

1.12 Contractor's Use of Employer's Documents

As between the Parties, the Employer shall retain the copyright and other intellectual property rights in the Employer's Requirements and other documents made by (or on behalf of) the Employer. The Contractor may, at his cost, copy, use, and obtain communication of these documents for the purposes of the Contract. They shall not, without the Employer's consent, be copied, used, or communicated to a third party by the Contractor, except as necessary for the purposes of the Contract.

1.13 Confidential Details

The Contractor shall disclose all such confidential and other information as the Employer's Representative may reasonably require in order to verify the Contractor's compliance with the Contract.

The Contractor shall treat the details of the Contract as private and confidential, except to the extent necessary to carry out his obligations under the Contract. The Contractor shall not publish, permit to be published, or disclose any particulars of the Contract in any trade or technical paper or elsewhere without the previous consent in writing of the Employer. The said consent shall not be unreasonably withheld.

The Employer shall treat all information designated by the Contractor as confidential, and shall not disclose it to third parties, except as maybe necessary when exercising his rights under Sub-Clause15.2 [*Termination for Contractor's Default*].

1.14 Compliance with Laws

The Contractor shall, in performing the Contract, comply with applicable Laws. Unless otherwise stated in the Employer's Requirements:

(a) the Employer shall have obtained (or shall obtain) the planning, zoning, building permit, or similar permission for the Permanent Works and for the Operation Service, and any other permissions described in the Employer's Requirements as having been (or being) obtained by the Employer; and the Employer shall indemnify and hold the Contractor harmless against and from the consequences of any failure to do so;

(b) the Contractor shall give all notices, pay all taxes, duties and fees, and obtain all further permits, licences and approvals, as required by the Laws, in relation to the design, execution and completion of the Works and Operation Service and the remedying of any defects; and the Contractor shall indemnify and hold the Employer harmless against and from the consequences of any failure to do so; and

(b) 允许具有**工程**相关部分正当占有权的任何人，为了完成、运行、维护、更改、调整、修复和拆除**工程**的目的，复制、使用和传送**承包商文件**；

(c) 如果**承包商文件**是计算机程序和其他软件形式，允许它们在**现场**和**合同**规定的其他场所的任何计算机上使用，包括更换**承包商**提供的任何计算机；（以及）

(d) 使**雇主**根据第 15.2 款［*由承包商违约的终止*］的规定，重新签订合同。

未经**承包商**同意，**雇主**（或其代表）不得在本款允许以外，为其他目的使用、复制**承包商文件**和由**承包商**（或其代表）编制的此类其他设计文件，或将其传送给第三方。

1.12 承包商使用雇主文件

就双方而言，由**雇主**（或其代表）编制的**雇主要求**和其他文件，其版权和其他知识产权应归**雇主**所有。**承包商**因合同的目的，可自费复制、使用和获得传送这些文件。除**合同**需要外，未经雇主同意，**承包商**不得复制、使用这些文件，或将其传送给第三方。

1.13 保密事项

对**雇主代表**为了证实**承包商**遵守**合同**的情况，合理需要的所有秘密和其他信息，**承包商**应当透露。

承包商应将**合同**的细节视为隐私和机密，但履行其在**合同**规定的义务所必需的情况除外。未经**雇主**事先书面同意，**承包商**不应在任何行业或技术文件或其他地方发布、允许发布或透漏合同的任何细节。上述同意不得无理拒绝。

雇主应将**承包商**指定的所有信息视为保密资料。不应向第三方透漏，除根据第 15.2 款［*由承包商违约的终止*］的规定，在履行其必要的权利时。

1.14 遵守法律

承包商在履行合同期间，应遵守所有适用**法律**。除非**雇主要求**中另有规定：

(a) **雇主**应已（或将）为**永久工程**和**运营服务**取得规划、区域划定、施工许可证或类似的许可证以及**雇主要求**中所述的**雇主**已（或将）取得的任何其他许可；**雇主**应保障和保持**承包商**免受未能完成上述工作带来的损害；

(b) **承包商**应发出所有通知，缴纳各项税费关税和费用，按照**法律**关于**工程**设计、实施和竣工、**运营服务**以及修补任何缺陷等方面的要求，办理并领取所需要的所有许可、执照和批准；以及**承包商**应保障和保持**雇主**免受因未能完成上述工作带来的损害；（以及）

(c) the Contractor shall at all times and in all respects comply with, give all notices under, and pay all fees required by any licence obtained by the Employer in respect of the Site or the Works or Operation Service, whether relating to the Works or Operation Service on or off the Site.

1.15 Joint and Several Liability

If the Contractor constitutes (under applicable Laws) a joint venture, consortium or other unincorporated grouping of two or more persons:

(a) these persons shall be deemed to be jointly and severally liable to the Employer for the performance of the Contract;
(b) these persons shall notify the Employer of their leader who shall have authority to bind the Contractor and each of these persons; and
(c) the Contractor shall not alter his composition or legal status without the prior consent of the Employer.

The 2 Employer

2.1 Right of Access to the Site

The Employer shall give the Contractor right of access to, and possession of, all or part of the Site within the time (or times) stated in the Contract Data. The right and possession may not be exclusive to the Contractor. If, under the Contract, the Employer is required to give the Contractor possession of any foundation, structure, plant or means of access, the Employer shall do so in the time and manner stated in the Employer's Requirements. However, the Employer may withhold any such right or possession until the Performance Security has been received.

If no such time is stated in the Contract Data, the Employer shall give the Contractor right of access to, and possession of, the Site within such times as may be required to enable the Contractor to proceed in accordance with the programme submitted under Sub-Clause 8.3 [*Programme*].

If the Contractor suffers delay and/or incurs cost as a result of a failure by the Employer to give any such right or possession within such time, the Contractor shall give Notice to the Employer's Representative and shall be entitled subject to Sub-Clause 20.1 [*Contractor's Claims*] to:

(a) an extension of time for any such delay, if completion is or will be delayed, under Sub-Clause 9.3 [*Extension of Time for Completion of Design-Build*]; and
(b) payment of any such Cost Plus Profit, which shall be included in the Contract Price.

After receiving this Notice, the Employer's Representative shall proceed in accordance with Sub-Clause 3.5 [*Determinations*] to agree or determine these matters.

However, if and to the extent that the Employer's failure was caused by any error or delay by the Contractor, including an error in, or delay in the submission of, any of the Contractor's Documents, the Contractor shall not be entitled to such extension of time or cost.

2.2 Permits, Licences or Approvals

The Employer shall provide, at the request of the Contractor, such reasonable assistance as to allow the Contractor to obtain:

（c）承包商应在任何时候和各方面遵守雇主关于现场或工程或运营服务获得的任何执照所要求的所有费用，如与现场内外的工程或运营服务有关，则承包商应根据雇主获得的任何执照发出所有通知，并支付所有费用。

1.15 共同的和各自的责任

如果承包商是由两个或两个以上当事人（根据适用法律）组成的联营体、财团或其他非法人团体：

（a）这些当事人应被认为对雇主履行合同负有共同的和各自的责任；

（b）这些当事人应通知雇主其负责人，该负责人有权约束承包商及其每个当事人；（以及）

（c）未经雇主事先同意，承包商不得改变其组成或法律地位。

2 雇主

2.1 现场进入权

雇主应在合同数据中规定的时间（或几个时间）内，给予承包商进入和占用现场全部或部分的权利。此项进入和占用权可不为承包商独享。如果根据合同，要求雇主向承包商提供任何基础、结构、生产设备的占用权或进场方法，雇主应按雇主要求规定的时间和方式提供。但是，雇主在收到履约担保前，可保留上述任何进入或占用权。

如果合同数据中没有规定上述时间，雇主应在要求的时间内，给予承包商进入和占用现场的权利，使承包商能够按照第8.3款［进度计划］规定提交的进度计划进行施工。

如果雇主未能及时给予承包商上述进入或占用的权利，使承包商遭受延误和/或招致增加费用，承包商应向雇主代表发出通知，并有权根据第20.1款［承包商索赔］的规定，获得：

（a）根据第9.3款［设计-施工竣工时间的延长］的规定，如果竣工已或将受到延误，对任何此类延误，给予延长期；（以及）

（b）任何此类成本加利润的支付，应计入合同价格。

在收到此通知后，雇主代表应按照第3.5款［确定］的规定，就这些事项进行商定或确定。

但是，如果雇主的违约是由于承包商的任何错误或延误，包括在任何承包商文件中的错误或提交延误造成的情况，承包商应无权获得此类延长期或费用。

2.2 许可、执照或批准

雇主应根据承包商的请求，应对其提供合理的协助，以便承包商可获得：

(a) copies of the Laws of the Country which are relevant to the Contract but are not readily available; and
(b) any permits, licences or approvals required by the Laws of the Country, including details of the information required to be submitted by the Contractor in order to obtain such permits, licences or approvals:

   (i) which the Contractor is required to obtain under Sub-Clause 1.14 [*Compliance with Laws*];
   (ii) for the delivery of Goods, including clearance through customs; and
   (iii) for the export of Contractor's Equipment when it is removed from the Site.

2.3 Employer's Personnel

The Employer shall be responsible for ensuring that the Employer's Personnel and the Employer's other contractors on the Site:

(a) co-operate with the Contractor's efforts under Sub-Clause 4.6 [*Co-operation*]; and
(b) take actions similar to those which the Contractor is required to take under subparagraphs (a), (b) and (c) of Sub-Clause 4.8 [*Safety Procedures*] and under Sub-Clause 4.18 [*Protection of the Environment*].

2.4 Employer's Financial Arrangements

The Employer's arrangements for financing the design, execution and operation of the Works, including the provision of the Asset Replacement Fund, shall be detailed in the Financial Memorandum.

If the Employer intends to make any material changes to the financial arrangements or has to do so because of changes in his financial or economic situation, the Employer shall give Notice to the Contractor, with detailed particulars. Within 28 days after receiving any request of the Contractor the Employer shall give reasonable evidence that financial arrangements have been made and are being maintained which will enable the Employer to pay the Contract Price.

3 The Employer's Representative

3.1 Employer's Representative's Duties and Authority

The Employer shall appoint the Employer's Representative prior to the signing of the Contract, who shall be suitably qualified and experienced and who shall carry out the duties assigned to him in the Contract. The Employer's Representative's staff shall include suitably qualified engineers and other professionals who are competent to carry out these duties.

The Employer's Representative shall have no authority to amend the Contract.

The Employer's Representative may exercise the authority attributable to the Employer's Representative as specified in or necessarily to be implied from the Contract.

The Employer undertakes not to impose further constraints on the Employer's Representative's authority, except as agreed with the Contractor.

However, whenever the Employer's Representative exercises a specified authority for which the Employer's approval is required, then (for the purposes of the Contract) the Employer shall be deemed to have given approval.

(a) 与**合同**有关，但不易得到的**工程所在国**的**法律**文本；（以及）

(b) **工程所在国法律**要求的任何许可、执照或批准，包括为取得此类许可、执照或批准，**承包商**需要提交的信息：

（i）根据第 1.14 款［*遵守法律*］的规定，**承包商**需要得到的；

（ii）为运送**货物**，包括清关需要的；（以及）

（iii）**承包商**设备运离**现场**时出口需要的。

2.3 雇主人员

雇主应负责保证**现场**的**雇主**人员和其他**承包商**做到：

（a）根据第 4.6 款［*合作*］的规定，与**承包商**努力合作；（以及）

（b）采取与根据第 4.8 款［*安全程序*］(a)、(b) 和 (c) 段和第 4.18 款［*环境保护*］的规定要求**承包商**采取的类似措施。

2.4 雇主的资金安排

雇主为**工程**设计、施工和运营所提供的资金安排，包括**资产置换基金**的规定，应在**资金（财务）备忘录**中详细说明。

如果**雇主**拟对资金安排做任何实质性变更，或由于**雇主**的资金或经济状况发生变化而必须这样做，**雇主**应向**承包商**发出**通知**，并提供详细资料。在收到**承包商**的任何要求后 28 天内，**雇主**应提供合理的证据，证明其已做并正在维持的资金安排，使**雇主**能够支付**合同价格**。

3 雇主代表

3.1 雇主代表的任务和权利

雇主应在签订**合同**前任命**雇主代表**，该代表应具有适当的资格和经验以执行**合同**中分配给其的任务。**雇主代表**的员工应包括合格的工程师和其他有能力执行任务的专业人员。

雇主代表无权修改**合同**。

雇主代表可行使**合同**中规定或必然隐含的应属于**雇主代表**的权利。

雇主承诺不进一步限制**雇主代表**的权利，除非与**承包商**达成商定。

但是，每当**雇主代表**行使需由**雇主**批准的规定权利时，则（就**合同**而言）应视为**雇主**已予批准。

Except as otherwise stated in these Conditions:

(a) whenever carrying out duties or exercising authority, specified in or implied by the Contract, the Employer's Representative shall be deemed to act for the Employer;
(b) the Employer's Representative has no authority to relieve either Party of any duties, obligations or responsibilities under the Contract; and
(c) any approval, check, certificate, consent, examination, inspection, instruction, Notice, proposal, request, test or similar act by the Employer's Representative (including absence of disapproval) shall not relieve the Contractor from any responsibility he has under the Contract, including responsibility for errors, omissions, discrepancies and non-compliances.

3.2 Delegation by the Employer's Representative

The Employer's Representative may from time to time assign duties and delegate authority to assistants, and may also revoke such assignment or delegation. These assistants may include independent inspectors (other than the Auditing Body) appointed to inspect and/or test items of Plant and/or Materials and/or workmanship or monitor the provision of the Operation Service. The assignment, delegation or revocation shall be in writing and shall not take effect until copies have been received by both Parties. However, unless otherwise agreed by both Parties, the Employer's Representative shall not delegate the authority to determine any matter in accordance with Sub-Clause 3.5 [*Determinations*].

Assistants shall be suitably qualified persons, who are competent to carry out these duties and exercise this authority, and who are fluent in the language for communications defined in Sub-Clause 1.4 [*Law and Language*].

Each assistant, to whom duties have been assigned or authority has been delegated, shall only be authorised to issue instructions to the Contractor to the extent defined by the delegation. Any approval, check, certificate, consent, examination, inspection, instruction, Notice, proposal, request, test or similar act by an assistant, in accordance with the delegation, shall have the same effect as though the act had been an act of the Employer's Representative. However:

(a) any failure to disapprove any work, Plant, Materials or any part of the Operation Service shall not constitute approval, and shall therefore not prejudice the right of the Employer's Representative to reject the work, Plant, Materials or any part of the Operation Service; and
(b) if the Contractor questions any determination or instruction of an assistant, the Contractor may refer the matter to the Employer's Representative, who shall promptly confirm, reverse or vary the determination or instruction.

3.3 Instructions of the Employer's Representative

The Employer's Representative may issue to the Contractor (at any time) instructions which may be necessary for the execution of the Works and the remedying of any defects, all in accordance with the Contract. The Contractor shall only take instructions from the Employer's Representative, or from an assistant to whom the appropriate authority has been delegated under this Clause. If an instruction constitutes a Variation, Clause 13 [*Variations and Adjustments*] shall apply.

The Contractor shall comply with the instructions given by the Employer's Representative or delegated assistant on any matter related to the Contract. These instructions shall be given in writing.

除非本条件中另有规定：

（a） 在执行任务或行使合同中规定或隐含的权利时，**雇主代表**应被认为代表**雇主**行事；

（b） **雇主代表**无权解除任何一方在**合同**中规定的任何任务、义务或职责；（以及）

（c） **雇主代表**的任何批准、校核、证书、同意、检查、检验、指示、**通知**、建议、要求、试验或类似行动（包括没有不批准），不得免除**承包商**根据**合同**规定应承担的任何责任，包括对错误、遗漏、不一致和不合规的责任。

3.2 由雇主代表付托

雇主代表有时可向其助手指派任务和付托权利，也可撤销这种指派或付托。这些助手可包括任命为检验和 / 或试验各项**生产设备**和 / 或**材料**和 / 或工艺，或监督**运营服务**提供的独立检验人员（**审计机构**除外）。以上指派、付托或撤销应用书面形式，在双方收到副本后才生效。但是，除非双方另有商定，**雇主代表**不应将按照**第 3.5 款**［**确定**］的规定确定任何事项的权利付托他人。

助手应为具有适当资质的人员，能履行这些任务，行使此项权利，并能流利地使用**第 1.4 款**［**法律和语言**］规定的交流语言。

应只授权被指派任务或付托权利的每位助手，在付托规定的范围内对**承包商**发出指示。由助手按照付托做出的任何批准、校核、证书、同意、检查、检验、指示、**通知**、建议、要求、试验或类似行动，应与**雇主代表**做出的行动具有同等效力。但是：

（a） 未对任何工作、**生产设备**、**材料**或**运营服务**的任何部分提出否定意见不应构成批准，因此不应影响**雇主代表**拒收该工作、**生产设备**、**材料**或**运营服务**任何部分的权利；（以及）

（b） 如果**承包商**对助手的确定或指示提出质疑，**承包商**可将此事项提交**雇主代表**，**雇主代表**应迅速对该确定或指示进行确认、取消或更改。

3.3 雇主代表的指示

雇主代表可（在任何时候）按照**合同**规定向**承包商**发出实施工程和修补缺陷可能需要的指示。**承包商**仅应接受**雇主代表**或根据本条被付托适当权利的助手的指示。如果指示构成一项变更，**第 13 条**［**变更和调整**］应适用。

承包商应遵守**雇主代表**或付托助手对**合同**有关的任何事项发出指示。这些指示应采用书面形式。

If the Contractor considers that any instruction of the Employer's Representative does not comply with applicable Laws or is technically impossible, he shall immediately notify the Employer's Representative in writing. The Employer's Representative shall then either confirm or amend such instruction.

3.4
Replacement of the Employer's Representative

If the Employer intends to replace the Employer's Representative, the Employer shall, not less than 42 days before the intended date of replacement, give Notice to the Contractor of the name, address and relevant experience of the intended replacement Employer's Representative.

The Employer shall not replace the Employer's Representative with a person against whom the Contractor raises reasonable objection by Notice to the Employer, with supporting particulars.

3.5
Determinations

Whenever these Conditions provide that the Employer's Representative shall proceed in accordance with this Sub-Clause to agree or determine any matter, the Employer's Representative shall consult with each Party in an endeavour to reach agreement. If agreement is not achieved, the Employer's Representative shall make a fair determination in accordance with the Contract, taking due regard of all relevant circumstances.

The Employer's Representative shall give Notice to both Parties of each agreement or determination, with supporting particulars. Each Party shall give effect to each agreement or determination unless and until revised under Clause 20 [*Claims, Disputes and Arbitration*].

4 The Contractor

4.1
Contractor's General Obligations

The Contractor shall design, execute and complete the Works and provide the Operation Service in accordance with the Contract and shall remedy any defects in the Works. When completed, the Works shall be fit for the purposes for which the Works are intended as defined in the Contract, and the Contractor shall be responsible for ensuring that the Works remain fit for such purposes during the Operation Service Period.

The Contractor shall provide the Plant and Contractor's Documents specified in the Contract, and all Contractor's Personnel, Goods, consumables and other things and services, whether of a temporary or permanent nature, required to meet the Contractor's obligations under the Contract.

The Works shall include any work which is necessary to satisfy the Employer's Requirements, Contractor's Proposal and Schedules, or is implied by the Contract, and all works which (although not mentioned in the Contract) are necessary for stability or for the completion, or safe and proper operation, of the Works.

The Contractor shall be responsible for the adequacy, stability and safety of all Site operations, of all methods of construction and of all the Works during both the Design-Build Period and the Operation Service Period.

The Contractor shall, whenever required by the Employer's Representative, submit details of the arrangements and methods which the Contractor proposes to adopt for the execution of the Works. No significant alteration to these arrangements and methods shall be made without this having previously been notified to the Employer's Representative.

如果**承包商**认为**雇主代表**的任何指示不符合适用**法律**或在技术上不可能，其应立即书面通知**雇主代表**。**雇主代表**应确认或修改此类指示。

3.4
雇主代表的替代

如果**雇主**拟替代**雇主代表**，**雇主**应在拟替代日期 42 天前**通知承包商**，告知拟替代**雇主代表**的姓名、地址和相关经验。

雇主不得用**承包商**根据本款对其发出的**通知**，提出合理反对并附有证明资料的人替代**雇主代表**。

3.5
确定

每当本**条件**规定**雇主代表**应按照本款的规定商定或确定任何事项时，**雇主代表**应与每一方协商，努力（尽量）达成商定。如果未能达成商定，**雇主代表**应对所有有关情况给予适当的考虑，按照**合同**做出公正的确定。

雇主代表应将每项商定或确定，向双方发出**通知**，并附证明资料。除非并直到根据**第 20 条**［*索赔、争端和仲裁*］的规定做出修改，每方均应履行每项商定或确定。

4 承包商

4.1
承包商的一般义务

承包商应按照**合同**设计、实施和完成**工程**以及提供**运营服务**，并修补**工程**中的任何缺陷。竣工后，**工程**应能满足合同规定的**工程**预期目的，以及**承包商**应确保**工程**在**运营服务**期内保持适合此目的。

承包商应提供**合同**中规定的**生产设备**和**承包商文件**，以及履行**合同**规定的**承包商**义务所需的临时性或永久性的所有**承包商人员**、**货物**、消耗品及其他物品和服务。

工程应包括满足**雇主要求**、**承包商建议书**和**资料表**所需的任何工作，或**合同**规定的，以及（尽管**合同**中未提及）**工程**的稳定或竣工或安全、正常运行所需的所有工作。

承包商应对所有**现场**作业、**设计 - 施工期**和**运营服务期**内的所有施工方法和所有**工程**的完备性、稳定性和安全性承担责任。

当**雇主代表**提出要求时，**承包商**应提交其拟采用的详细**工程**施工安排和方法。事先未通知**雇主代表**，不得对这些安排和方法进行重要改变。

The Contractor shall attend all meetings as reasonably required by the Employer or the Employer's Representative.

4.2 Performance Security

The Contractor shall obtain at his cost the Performance Security for proper performance of the Contract, in the amounts and currencies set out in the Contract Data. If no amount is stated in the Contract Data, this Sub-Clause shall not apply.

At the end of the Retention Period, the Contractor is entitled to a reduction of the amount of the Performance Security, as stated in the Contract Data.

The Contractor shall deliver the Performance Security to the Employer within 28 days after receiving the Letter of Acceptance, and shall send a copy to the Employer's Representative. The Performance Security shall be issued by an entity and from within a country (or other jurisdiction) approved by the Employer, and shall be based on the sample form included in the tender documents, or in another form approved by the Employer.

The Contractor shall ensure that the Performance Security is valid and enforceable until the issue of the Contract Completion Certificate. If the terms of the Performance Security specify its expiry date, and the Contractor has not become entitled to receive the Contract Completion Certificate by the date 28 days prior to the expiry date, the Contractor shall extend the validity of the Performance Security until the Works and the Operation Service have been completed (or alternatively, until the Contractor has been entitled to receive the Contract Completion Certificate). Failure by the Contractor to maintain the validity of the Performance Security shall be grounds for termination in accordance with Sub-Clause 15.2 [*Termination for Contractor's Default*].

The Employer shall not make a claim under the Performance Security except for amounts to which the Employer is entitled under the Contract in the event of:

(a) failure by the Contractor to extend the validity of the Performance Security as described in the preceding paragraph, in which event the Employer may claim the full or, in case of an earlier reduction, the reduced amount of the Performance Security;
(b) failure by the Contractor to pay the Employer an amount due, as either agreed by the Contractor or determined under Sub-Clause 3.5 [*Determinations*] or Clause 20 [*Claims, Disputes and Arbitration*], within 42 days after this agreement or determination;
(c) failure by the Contractor to remedy a default within 42 days after receiving the Employer's Notice requiring the default to be remedied; or
(d) circumstances which entitle the Employer to terminate under Sub-Clause 15.2 [*Termination for Contractor's Default*], irrespective of whether Notice of termination has been given.

The Employer shall indemnify and hold the Contractor harmless against and from all damages, losses and expenses (including legal fees and expenses) resulting from a claim under the Performance Security which the Employer was not entitled to make.

The Employer shall return the Performance Security to the Contractor within 21 days after receiving a copy of the Contract Completion Certificate.

4.3 Contractor's Representative

The Contractor shall appoint the Contractor's Representative and shall give him all authority necessary to act on the Contractor's behalf under the Contract.

承包商应当参加雇主或雇主代表合理要求的所有会议。

4.2 履约担保

承包商应自费取得履约担保以其恰当履行合同，保证金额和币种应符合合同数据中的规定。如合同数据中未明确保证金额，本款应不适用。

在保留期结束时，承包商有权按照合同数据的规定减少履约保证金的金额。

承包商应在收到中标函后 28 天内向雇主提交履约担保，并向雇主代表送一份副本。履约担保应由雇主批准的国家（或其他司法管辖区）内的实体签发，并采用招标文件中的样本格式或雇主批准的其他格式为依据（基础）。

承包商应在其合同完成证书签发前，确保履约担保保持有效和可执行。如果在履约担保的条款中规定了其期满日期，而承包商在该期满日期前 28 天尚无权拿到合同完成证书，承包商应将履约担保的有效期延长至工程和运营服务完成（或直到承包商有权收到合同完成证书）时为止。承包商未能保持履约担保的有效性应成为根据第 15.2 款［*由承包商违约的终止*］规定的终止。

除以下雇主根据合同规定有权获得的金额情况外，雇主不应根据履约担保提出索赔：

（a）承包商未能按前一段所述的要求延长履约担保的有效期，这时雇主可以索赔履约担保的全部金额，或在先前减少的情况下，减少履约担保金额；

（b）承包商未能在商定或确定后 42 天内，将承包商同意的，或按照第 3.5 款［*确定*］或第 20 条［*索赔、争端和仲裁*］的规定，确定的承包商应付金额向雇主支付；

（c）承包商未能在收到雇主要求纠正违约的通知后 42 天内进行纠正违约；（或）

（d）雇主有权根据第 15.2 款［*由承包商违约的终止*］的规定，终止合同的情况，无论是否已发出终止通知。

雇主应保障和保持使承包商免受因雇主无权提出履约担保规定的索赔，而产生的所有损害赔偿费、损失和开支（包括法律费用和开支）的损害。

雇主在收到合同完成证书副本后 21 天内，将履约担保退还承包商。

4.3 承包商代表

承包商应任命承包商代表，并授予其代表承包商根据合同采取行动所需的全部权利。

Unless the Contractor's Representative is named in the Contract, the Contractor shall, prior to the Commencement Date, submit to the Employer's Representative for consent the name and particulars of the person the Contractor proposes to appoint as Contractor's Representative. If consent is withheld or subsequently revoked, or if the appointed person fails to act as Contractor's Representative, the Contractor shall similarly submit the name and particulars of another suitable person for such appointment.

The Contractor shall not, without the prior consent of the Employer's Representative, revoke the appointment of the Contractor's Representative or appoint a replacement.

The whole time of the Contractor's Representative shall be given to directing the Contractor's performance of the Contract. If the Contractor's Representative is to be temporarily absent from the Site during the execution of the Works or provision of the Operation Service, a suitable replacement person shall be appointed, subject to the Employer's Representative's prior consent, and the Employer's Representative shall be notified accordingly.

The Contractor's Representative shall, on behalf of the Contractor, receive instructions under Sub-Clause 3.3 [*Instructions of the Employer's Representative*].

The Contractor's Representative may delegate any powers, functions and authority to any competent person, and may at any time revoke the delegation. Any delegation or revocation shall not take effect until the Employer's Representative has received prior Notice signed by the Contractor's Representative, naming the person and specifying the powers, functions and authority being delegated or revoked.

The Contractor's Representative and all these persons shall be fluent in the language for communications defined in Sub-Clause 1.4 [*Law and Language*].

4.4 Subcontractors

The Contractor shall not subcontract the whole of the Works. Unless otherwise agreed, the Contractor shall not subcontract the provision of the Operation Service.

The Contractor shall be responsible for the acts or defaults of any Subcontractor, his agents or employees, as if they were the acts or defaults of the Contractor. Unless otherwise stated in the Particular Conditions:

(a) the Contractor shall not be required to obtain consent to suppliers of Materials, or to a subcontract for which the Subcontractor is named in the Contract;
(b) the prior consent of the Employer's Representative shall be obtained to other proposed Subcontractors; and
(c) the Contractor shall give Notice to the Employer's Representative not less than 28 days' prior to the intended date of the commencement of each Subcontractor's work, and of the commencement of such work on the Site.

If any Subcontractor is entitled under any contract or agreement relating to the Works to relief from any risk on terms additional to or broader than those specified in the Contract, such additional or broader events or circumstances shall not excuse the Contractor's non-performance or entitle him to relief under the Contract.

除非**合同**中已写明了**承包商代表**的姓名，**承包商**应在**开工日期**前，将其拟任命为**承包商代表**的人员姓名和详细资料提交**雇主代表**取得同意。如未获得同意，或随后撤销了同意，或任命的人员不能担任**承包商代表**，**承包商**应同样提交另外适合人选的姓名、详细资料，以取得该项任命。

未经**雇主代表**事先同意，**承包商**不应撤销**承包商代表**的任命，或任命替代人员。

承包商代表应将其全部时间用于指导**承包商**履行**合同**。如果**承包商代表**在工程施工或提供**运营服务**期间临时离开**现场**，应事先征得**雇主代表**的同意，临时指定一名合适替代人员，并相应通知**雇主代表**。

承包商代表应代表**承包商**，接受根据第3.3款［*雇主代表的指示*］规定的指示。

承包商代表可向任何胜任的人员付托任何职权、任务和权利，并可随时撤销付托。任何付托或撤销应在**雇主代表**收到**承包商代表**签发的指明人员姓名，并说明付托或撤销的职权、职能和权利的事先**通知**后生效。

承包商代表和所有这些人员应能流利地使用第1.4款［*法律和语言*］规定的交流语言。

4.4	
分包商	**承包商**不得将整个**工程**分包出去。除非另有约定，**承包商**不得将**运营服务**的提供分包出去。

承包商应对任何**分包商**、其代理人或雇员的行为或违约，如同**承包商**自己的行为或违约一样负责。除非**专用条件**中另有规定：

（a） **承包商**在选择**材料**供应商或向**合同**中已指明的分包商进行分包时，无须取得同意；

（b） 对其他建议的**分包商**，应取得**雇主代表**的事先同意；（以及）

（c） **承包商**应在每个**分包商**工作拟定开工日期前不少于28天，向**雇主代表**发出**通知**并在**现场**开始此类工作。

如果任何**分包商**根据与**工程**有关的任何合同或协议，有权根据合同规定的附加或更广泛的条款免除任何风险，则此类附加或更广泛的条款或情况不应成为**承包商**不履行**合同**的理由，也不应使其有权根据合同获得救济。

4.5 Nominated Subcontractors

In this Sub-Clause, "nominated Subcontractor" means a Subcontractor named as such in the Employer's Requirements or whom the Employer's Representative, under Clause 13 [*Variations and Adjustments*], instructs the Contractor to employ as a Subcontractor. The Contractor shall not be under any obligation to employ a nominated Subcontractor against whom the Contractor raises reasonable objection by Notice to the Employer's Representative as soon as practicable, with supporting particulars.

4.6 Co-operation

The Contractor shall, as specified in the Contract or as instructed by the Employer's Representative, allow appropriate opportunities for carrying out work to:

(a) the Employer's Personnel;
(b) any other contractors employed by the Employer; and
(c) the personnel of any legally constituted public authorities;

who may be employed in the execution on or near the Site of any work not included in the Contract.

Any such instruction shall constitute a Variation if and to the extent that it causes the Contractor to incur Unforeseeable cost. Services for these personnel and other contractors may include the use of Contractor's Equipment, Temporary Works or access arrangements which are the responsibility of the Contractor.

The Contractor shall be responsible for his construction and operation activities on the Site, and shall co-ordinate his own activities with those of other contractors to the extent (if any) specified in the Employer's Requirements.

If, under the Contract, the Employer is required to give to the Contractor possession of any foundation, structure, plant or means of access in accordance with Contractor's Documents, the Contractor shall submit such documents to the Employer's Representative in the time and manner stated in the Employer's Requirements.

4.7 Setting Out

The Contractor shall set out the Works in relation to original points, lines and levels of reference specified in the Contract or notified by the Employer's Representative. The Contractor shall be responsible for the correct positioning of all parts of the Works, and shall rectify any error in the positions, levels, dimensions or alignment of the Works.

The Employer shall be responsible for any errors in these specified or notified items of reference, but the Contractor shall use reasonable efforts to verify their accuracy before they are used.

If the Contractor suffers delay and/or incurs cost from executing work which was necessitated by an error in these items of reference, and an experienced contractor could not reasonably have discovered such error and avoided this delay and/or cost, the Contractor shall give Notice to the Employer's Representative and shall be entitled subject to Sub-Clause 20.1 [*Contractor's Claims*] to:

(a) an extension of time for any such delay, if completion is or will be delayed, under Sub-Clause 9.3 [*Extension of Time for Completion of Design-Build*]; and

4.5 指定分包商

在本款中,"指定分包商"系指在**雇主要求**中指定的**分包商**,或**雇主代表**根据第 13 条[*变更和调整*]的规定指示**承包商**雇用的**分包商**。**承包商**不应有任何义务雇用指定**分包商**,**承包商**应尽快向**雇主代表**发出附有详细证明资料的**通知**,提出合理的反对意见。

4.6 合作

承包商应按照**合同**规定或**雇主代表**的指示,提供下列人员适当的工作机会:

(a) **雇主人员**;
(b) **雇主**雇用的任何其他**承包商**;(以及)
(c) 任何合法成立的公共部门的人员;

他们可能被雇用在**现场**或**现场**附近从事本**合同**中未计划进行的任何工作。

如果任何此类指示达到导致**承包商**增加**不可预见**费用时,该指示应构成一项**变更**。对这些人员和承包商的服务,可包括使用**承包商设备**,以及由**承包商**负责的**临时工程**或进入的安排。

承包商应负责其在**现场**的施工和运营活动,并应在本**雇主要求**中的规定范围内(如果有),协调其自己与其他承包商的这些活动。

如果根据**合同**,要求**雇主**按照**承包商文件**向**承包商**提供任何基础、结构、生产设备或进入手段(方式)的占用权,**承包商**应按**雇主要求**中提出的时间和方式,向**雇主代表**提交此类文件。

4.7 放线

承包商应根据**合同**中规定的或**雇主代表**通知的原始基准点、基准线和基准标高对**工程**放线。**承包商**应负责对**工程**的所有部分正确定位,并应纠正**工程**的位置、标高、尺寸或定线中的任何错误。

雇主应对规定或通知的这几项基准的任何错误负责,但**承包商**应在使用前,做出合理的努力,对其准确性进行核实。

如果**承包商**在执行必要的工作中由于这几项基准中的某项错误而遭受延误和/或招致增加费用,而有经验的承包商不能合理发现此类错误,并避免此延误和/或增加费用,**承包商**应**通知雇主代表**,有权根据第 **20.1 款**[*承包商索赔*]的规定,获得:

(a) 根据第 9.3 款[*设计-施工竣工时间的延长*]的规定,如果竣工已或将受到延误,对任何此类延误给予延长期;(以及)

(b) payment of any such Cost Plus Profit, which shall be included in the Contract Price.

After receiving this Notice, the Employer's Representative shall proceed in accordance with Sub-Clause 3.5 [*Determinations*] to agree or determine (i) whether and (if so) to what extent the error could not reasonably have been discovered, and (ii) the matters described in sub-paragraphs (a) and (b) above related to this extent.

4.8 Safety Procedures

The Contractor shall:

(a) comply with all applicable safety regulations;
(b) take care for the safety of all persons entitled to be on the Site;
(c) use reasonable efforts to keep the Site and Works clear of unnecessary obstruction so as to avoid danger to these persons;
(d) provide fencing, lighting, guarding and watching of the Works until the issue of the Contract Completion Certificate; and
(e) provide any Temporary Works (including roadways, footways, guards and fences) which may be necessary, because of the execution of the Works, for the use and protection of the public and of owners and occupiers of adjacent land.

4.9 Quality Assurance

The Contractor shall institute a quality assurance system to demonstrate compliance with the requirements of the Contract. The system shall be in accordance with the details stated in the Contract. The Employer's Representative shall be entitled to audit any aspect of the system.

Details of all procedures and compliance documents shall be submitted to the Employer's Representative for information before each design, execution and operation stage is commenced. When any document of a technical nature is issued to the Employer's Representative, evidence of the prior approval by the Contractor himself shall be apparent on the document itself.

Compliance with the quality assurance system shall not relieve the Contractor of any of his duties, obligations or responsibilities under the Contract.

4.10 Site Data

The Employer shall have made available to the Contractor for his information, prior to the Base Date, all relevant data in the Employer's possession on sub-surface, hydrological and climatic conditions at the Site, including environmental aspects. The Employer shall similarly make available to the Contractor all such data which come into the Employer's possession after the Base Date. The Contractor shall be responsible for interpreting all such data.

To the extent which was practicable (taking account of cost and time), the Contractor shall be deemed to have obtained all necessary information as to risks, contingencies and other circumstances which may influence or affect the Tender or Works or the provision of the Operation Service. To the same extent, the Contractor shall be deemed to have inspected and examined the Site, its surroundings, the above data and other available information, and to have been satisfied before submitting the Tender as to all relevant matters, including (without limitation):

(a) the form and nature of the Site, including sub-surface conditions;
(b) the hydrological and climatic conditions;

(b) 任何此类**成本加利润**的费用，应计入**合同价格**，给予支付。

雇主代表收到此类**通知**后，应按照**第3.5款**[**确定**]的规定，商定或确定：(i)错误是否不能合理发现，(如果是)不能合理发现的程度，以及(ii)与该程度相关的上述(a)和(b)段所述事项。

4.8 安全程序

承包商应：

(a) 遵守所有适用安全的规则；
(b) 照顾有权在**现场**所有人员的安全；
(c) 尽合理的努力保持**现场**、**工程**清除不需要的障碍物，以避免对这些人员造成危险；
(d) 在签发**合同完成证书**之前，提供**工程**的围栏、照明、保卫和看守；(以及)
(e) 因实施**工程**，为公众和邻近土地和财产的所有人、占用人使用和对其保护，提供可能需要的任何**临时工程**(包括道路、人行道、防护物和围栏等)。

4.9 质量保证

承包商应建立质量管理体系，以证明其符合**合同**要求。该体系应符合**合同**的详细规定。**雇主代表**应有权对体系的任何方面进行审查。

承包商应在每一设计、实施和运营阶段开始前，向**雇主代表**提交所有程序的细节和合规文件，供其参考。向**雇主代表**发出任何技术性文件时，**承包商**自己事先批准的证据应在文件上明显可见。

遵守质量保证体系，不应免除**合同**规定的**承包商**任何任务、义务和责任。

4.10 现场数据

雇主应在**基准日期**前，将其取得的**现场**地下、水文和气候条件和环境方面所有有关数据，提供给**承包商**。同样，**雇主**在**基准日期**后得到的所有此类资料，也应提供给**承包商**。**承包商**应负责解释所有此类资料。

在实际可行(考虑费用和时间)的范围内，**承包商**应被认为已取得可能对**投标书**或**工程**或提供**运营服务**的产生影响或作用的有关风险、偶发事件和其他情况的所有必要资料。同样，**承包商**应被认为在提交**投标书**前，已检验和检查了**现场**、周围环境、上述数据和其他得到的资料，并对所有相关事项感到满足要求，包括(但不限于)：

(a) **现场**的状况和性质，包括地下条件；
(b) 水文和气候条件；

(c) the extent and nature of the work and Goods necessary for the execution and completion of the Works and the remedying of any defects
(d) the Laws, procedures of regulatory and other authorities and labour practices of the Country; and
(e) the Contractor's requirements for access, accommodation, facilities, personnel, power, transport, water and other services.

4.11 Sufficiency of the Accepted Contract Amount

The Contractor shall be deemed to:

(a) have satisfied himself as to the correctness and sufficiency of the Accepted Contract Amount; and
(b) have based the Accepted Contract Amount on the data, interpretations, necessary information, inspections, examinations and satisfaction as to all relevant matters referred to in Sub-Clause 4.10 [*Site Data*], and any further data relevant to the Contractor's design.

The Accepted Contract Amount covers all the Contractor's obligations under the Contract (including those under Provisional Sums, if any) and all things necessary for the proper design, execution and completion of the Works, the remedying of any defects and the provision of the Operation Service.

4.12 Unforeseeable Physical Conditions

In this Sub-Clause, "physical conditions" means natural physical conditions and man-made and other physical obstructions and pollutants, which the Contractor encounters at the Site when executing the Works, including sub-surface and hydrological conditions but excluding climatic conditions.

If the Contractor encounters adverse physical conditions which he considers to have been Unforeseeable, the Contractor shall give Notice to the Employer's Representative as soon as practicable.

This Notice shall describe the physical conditions, so that they can be inspected by the Employer's Representative, and shall set out the reasons why the Contractor considers them to be Unforeseeable. The Contractor shall continue executing the Works, using such proper and reasonable measures as are appropriate for the physical conditions, and shall comply with any instructions which the Employer's Representative may give. If an instruction constitutes a Variation, Clause 13 [*Variations and Adjustments*] shall apply.

If and to the extent that the Contractor encounters physical conditions which are Unforeseeable, gives such a Notice, and suffers delay and/or incurs cost due to these conditions, the Contractor shall be entitled subject to Sub-Clause 20.1 [*Contractor's Claims*] to:

(a) an extension of time for any such delay, if completion is or will be delayed, under Sub-Clause 9.3 [*Extension of Time for Completion of Design-Build*]; and
(b) payment of any such Cost, which shall be included in the Contract Price.

After receiving such Notice and inspecting and/or investigating these physical conditions, the Employer's Representative shall proceed in accordance with Sub-Clause 3.5 [*Determinations*] to agree or determine (i) whether and (if so) to what extent these physical conditions were Unforeseeable, and (ii) the matters described in sub-paragraphs (a) and (b) above.

(c) 实施、完成**工程**和修补任何缺陷所需的工作和**货物**的范围和性质；
(d) **工程**所在国的**法律**、监管部门和其他部门的程序和劳务惯例；（以及）
(e) **承包商**对进入、食宿、设施、人员、电力、运输、水和其他服务的要求。

4.11 中标合同金额的充分性

承包商应被认为：

(a) 已确信**中标合同金额**的正确性和充分性；（以及）

(b) 已将**中标合同金额**建立在根据**第 4.10 款**[**现场数据**]中提到的所有相关事项的数据、解释、必要的资料、检验、检查和满意，以及与**承包商**设计相关的任何进一步数据的基础上。

中标合同金额包括**承包商**根据合同规定应承担的全部义务（包括根据**暂列金额**应承担的义务，如果有），以及为正确的设计、**工程**的实施和竣工、修补任何缺陷和提供**运营服务**的所需的全部有关事项的费用。

4.12 不可预见的物质条件

本款中的"物质条件"系指**承包商**在**现场工程**施工期间遇到的自然物质条件、人为的及其他物质障碍和污染物，包括地下和水文条件，但不包括气候条件。

如果**承包商**遇到其认为**不可预见**的有不利物质条件，应尽快**通知****雇主代表**。

此**通知**应说明该物质条件以便**雇主代表**进行检验，并应提出**承包商**为何认为**不可预见**的理由。**承包商**应采取适应物质条件的适当和合理措施继续**工程**施工，并应遵照**雇主代表**可能给出的任何指示。如某项指示构成**变更**，则**第 13 条**[**变更和调整**]应适用。

如果**承包商**遇到不可预见的物质条件，并发出**通知**，因这些条件达到遭受延误和/或增加费用的程度，**承包商**应有权根据**第 20.1 款**[**承包商索赔**]的规定，获得：

(a) 根据**第 9.3 款**[**设计-施工竣工时间的延长**]的规定，如果竣工已或将受到延误，对任何此类延误给予延长期；（以及）

(b) 任何此类**费用**应计入**合同价格**，给予支付。

雇主代表收到此类**通知**并对该物质条件进行检验和/或研究后，应按照**第 3.5 款**[**确定**]的规定，进行商定或确定：(i) 此类物质条件是否**不可预见**，(如果是) 此类物质条件不可预见的程度，(ii) 与此程度有关的上述 (a) 和 (b) 段所述事项。

However, before additional Cost is finally agreed or determined under (ii), the Employer's Representative may also review whether other physical conditions in similar parts of the Works (if any) were more favourable than could reasonably have been foreseen when the Contractor submitted the Tender. If and to the extent that these more favourable conditions were encountered, the Employer's Representative may proceed in accordance with Sub-Clause 3.5 [*Determinations*] to agree or determine the reductions in Cost which were due to these conditions, which may be included (as deductions) in the Contract Price and payment certificates. However, the net effect of all adjustments under sub-paragraph (b) and all these reductions, for all the physical conditions encountered in similar parts of the Works, shall not result in a net reduction in the Contract Price.

The Employer's Representative may take account of any evidence of the physical conditions foreseen by the Contractor when submitting the Tender, which may be made available by the Contractor, but shall not be bound by any such evidence.

4.13 Rights of Way and Facilities

The Contractor shall bear all costs and charges for special and/or temporary rights-of-way which he may require, including those for access to the Site. The Contractor shall also obtain, at his risk and cost, any additional facilities outside the Site which he may require for the purposes of the Works.

4.14 Avoidance of Interference

The Contractor shall not interfere unnecessarily or improperly with:

(a) the convenience of the public; or
(b) the access to and use and occupation of all roads and footpaths, irrespective of whether they are public or in the possession of the Employer or of others.

The Contractor shall indemnify and hold the Employer harmless against and from all damages, losses and expenses (including legal fees and expenses) resulting from any such unnecessary or improper interference.

4.15 Access Route

The Contractor shall be deemed to have been satisfied as to the suitability and availability of access routes to the Site. The Contractor shall use reasonable efforts to prevent any road or bridge from being damaged by the Contractor's traffic or by the Contractor's Personnel. These efforts shall include the proper use of appropriate vehicles and routes.

Except as otherwise stated in these Conditions:

(a) the Contractor shall (as between the Parties) be responsible for any maintenance which may be required as a result of his use of access routes;
(b) the Contractor shall provide all necessary signs or directions along access routes, and shall obtain any permission which may be required from the relevant authorities for his use of routes, signs and directions;
(c) the Employer shall not be responsible for any claims which may arise from the use or otherwise of any access route;
(d) the Employer does not guarantee the suitability or availability of particular access routes; and
(e) Costs due to non-suitability or non-availability, for the use required by the Contractor, of access routes shall be borne by the Contractor.

但是，根据上述（ii）最终商定或确定给予增加**费用**前，**雇主代表**还可审核工程类似部分（如果有），其他物质条件是否比**承包商**提交**投标书**时能合理预见的更为有利。如果并在一定程度上**达**到遇到这些更为有利的条件，**雇主代表**可按照**第3.5款**［**确定**］的规定，商定或确定因这些条件引起的**费用**减少额，并（作为扣减额）计入**合同价格**和付款证书。但对**工程**类似部分遇到的所有物质条件根据（b）段所做的调整和这些减少额的净作用，不应造成**合同价格**净减少的结果。

雇主代表可以考虑**承包商**提交**投标书**时可能提供的可预见的物质条件的任何证据，但不应受任何此类证据的约束。

4.13 道路通行权和设施

承包商应为其所需的专用和/或临时道路通行权，包括进入**现场**道路的通行权，承担全部费用和开支。**承包商**还应自担风险和费用，取得为**工程**目的可能需要的**现场**以外的任何附加设施。

4.14 避免干扰

承包商应避免对以下事项产生不必要或不当的干扰：

（a） 公众的便利；（或）
（b） 所有道路和人行道的进入、使用和占用，不论它们是公共的，或是**雇主**或其他人所有的。

承包商应保障和保持使**雇主**免受因任何此类不必要或不当的干扰造成的所有损害赔偿费、损失和开支（包括法律费用和开支）。

4.15 进场通路

承包商应被认为已对进入现场通路的适宜性和可用性感到满意。**承包商**应尽合理的努力，防止任何道路或桥梁因**承包商**的通行或**承包商**人员受到损坏。这些努力应包括正确使用适宜的车辆和通路。

除本**条件**另有规定外：

（a） **承包商**应（就双方而言）负责对其使用进场通路所需的任何维护；

（b） **承包商**应提供进场通路所有必需的标识或方向指示，还应为其使用这些通路、标识和方向指示，取得必要的有关部门的任何许可；

（c） **雇主**不应对因任何进场通路的使用或其他原因引起的任何索赔负责；

（d） **雇主**不保证特定进场通路的适宜性或可用性；（以及）

（e） 因**承包商**需要使用进场通路而产生的不适宜性和不可用性的**费用**均应由**承包商**承担。

4.16 Transport of Goods

Unless otherwise stated in the Particular Conditions:

(a) the Contractor shall give Notice to the Employer's Representative not less than 21 days prior to the date on which any Plant or a major item of other Goods will be delivered to the Site; and

(b) the Contractor shall be responsible for packing, loading, transporting, receiving, unloading, storing and protecting all Goods and other things required for the Works or provision of Operation Service; and

(c) the Contractor shall indemnify and hold the Employer harmless against and from all damages, losses and expenses (including legal fees and expenses) resulting from the transport of Goods, and shall negotiate and pay all claims arising from their transport.

4.17 Contractor's Equipment

The Contractor shall be responsible for all Contractor's Equipment. When brought on to the Site, Contractor's Equipment shall be deemed to be exclusively intended for the execution of the Works and provision of the Operation Service. The Contractor shall not remove from the Site any major items of Contractor's Equipment without the consent of the Employer's Representative. However, consent shall not be required for vehicles transporting Goods or Contractor's Personnel off Site.

4.18 Protection of the Environment

The Contractor shall take all reasonable steps to protect the environment (both on and off the Site) and to limit damage and nuisance to people and property resulting from pollution, noise and other results of his operations.

The Contractor shall ensure that emissions, surface discharges and effluent from the Contractor's activities shall not exceed the values indicated in the Employer's Requirements, and shall not exceed the values prescribed by applicable Laws.

4.19 Electricity, Water and Gas

Except as stated below, the Contractor shall be responsible for the provision of all electricity, water and other services he may require.

The Contractor shall be entitled to use for the purposes of the Works and provision of the Operation Service such supplies of electricity, water, gas and other services as may be available on the Site and of which details are given in the Employer's Requirements.

In such a case the Contractor shall take over in his own name and shall be responsible for payment of the electricity, water, gas and other services to the utility provider. The Contractor will be allowed to take over the existing service entry and provision points and shall be responsible for taking and recording such information as is necessary for the utility providers to correctly charge the Contractor from the Commencement Date.

4.20 Employer's Equipment and Free-Issue Materials

The Employer shall make the Employer's Equipment (if any) available for the use of the Contractor in the execution of the Works in accordance with the details, arrangements and prices stated in the Employer's Requirements. Unless otherwise stated in the Employer's Requirements:

(a) the Employer shall be responsible for the Employer's Equipment, except that

(b) the Contractor shall be responsible for each item of Employer's Equipment whilst any of the Contractor's Personnel is operating it, driving it, directing it or in possession or control of it.

4.16 货物运输	除非**专用条件**中另有规定：
	（a） **承包商**应在不少于 21 天前，将任何**生产设备**或每项其他主要**货物**将运到**现场**的日期，**通知雇主代表**；（以及）
	（b） **承包商**应负责**工程**需要的所有**货物**和其他物品的包装、装货、运输、接收、卸货、存储和保护，或提供**运营服务**；（以及）
	（c） **承包商**应保障并保持**雇主**免受因运输**货物**引起的所有损害赔偿费、损失和开支（包括法律费用和开支），并应协商和支付由于**货物**运输而引起的所有索赔。
4.17 承包商设备	**承包商**应负责所有**承包商设备**。**承包商设备**运到**现场**后，应被视作准备为**工程**施工和提供**运营服务**专用。未经**雇主代表**同意，**承包商**不得从**现场**运走任何主要**承包商设备**。但运送**货物**或**承包商人员**离开**现场**的车辆，无须经过同意。
4.18 环境保护	**承包商**应采取一切必要措施保护（**现场**内外）环境，限制由其施工作业引起的污染、噪声和其他后果对公众和财产造成的损害和妨害。 **承包商**应确保因其活动产生的气体排放、地面排水、排污，不得超过**雇主要求**规定的数值，也不得超过适用**法律**规定的数值。
4.19 电、水和燃气	除下述情况外，**承包商**应负责提供其所有电、水和需要的其他服务。 **承包商**应有权因**工程**和提供**运营服务**的需要使用**现场**可供的电、水、燃气和其他服务，其详细规定见**雇主要求**。 在这种情况下，**承包商**应以自己的名义接管，并负责向公用设施供应商支付电、水、燃气和其他服务。**承包商**将被允许接管现有的服务入口和供应点，并应负责获取和记录公用设施供应商，从**开工日期**起向**承包商**收费所需的准确信息。
4.20 雇主设备和免费提供的材料	**雇主**应准备**雇主设备**（如果有），供**承包商**按照**雇主要求**中规定的细节、安排和价格，在**工程**实施中使用。除非**雇主要求**中另有规定： （a） 除下列（b）项所列情况外，**雇主**应对**雇主设备**负责； （b） 当任何**承包商人员**操作、驾驶、指挥、占用或控制某项**雇主设备**时，**承包商**应对该项设备负责。

The appropriate quantities and the amounts due (at such stated prices) for the use of Employer's Equipment shall be agreed or determined by the Employer's Representative in accordance with Sub-Clause 20.2 [*Employer's Claims*] and Sub-Clause 3.5 [*Determinations*]. The Contractor shall pay these amounts to the Employer.

The Employer shall supply, free of charge, the "free-issue materials" (if any) in accordance with the details stated in the Employer's Requirements. The Employer shall, at his risk and cost, provide these materials at the time and place specified in the Contract. The Contractor shall then visually inspect them, and shall promptly give Notice to the Employer's Representative of any shortage, defect or default in these materials. Unless otherwise agreed by both Parties, the Employer shall immediately rectify the notified shortage, defect or default.

After this visual inspection, the free-issue materials shall come under the care, custody and control of the Contractor. The Contractor's obligations of inspection, care, custody and control shall not relieve the Employer of liability for any shortage, defect or default not apparent from a visual inspection.

4.21 Progress Reports

During the Design-Build Period, monthly progress reports, in a format agreed with the Employer's Representative shall be prepared by the Contractor and submitted to the Employer's Representative in one original and five copies, unless otherwise stated in the Employer's Requirements. The first report shall cover the period up to the end of the first calendar month following the Commencement Date. Reports shall be submitted monthly thereafter, each within 7 days after the last day of the period to which it relates.

Reporting on progress shall continue until the Contractor has received the Contract Completion Certificate. Details of the content of the progress reports for the Design-Build Period and the Operation Service Period shall be as specified in the Employer's Requirements.

Unless otherwise stated or agreed, each progress report shall include:

(a) charts and detailed descriptions of progress, including each stage of design, Contractor's Documents, procurement, manufacture, delivery to Site, construction or replacement, erection, testing, commissioning, trial operation and provision of Operation Service;

(b) photographs showing the status of manufacture or replacement and of progress on the Site;

(c) for the manufacture or replacement of each main item of Plant and Materials, the name of the manufacturer, manufacture location, percentage progress, and the actual or expected dates of:

  (i) commencement of manufacture,
  (ii) Contractor's inspections,
  (iii) tests, and
  (iv) shipment and arrival at the Site;

(d) the details described in Sub-Clause 6.10 [*Records of Contractor's Personnel and Equipment*];

(e) copies of quality assurance documents, test results and certificates of Materials;

(f) list of Variations, Notices given under Sub-Clause 20.1 [*Contractor's Claims*] and Notices given under Sub-Clause 20.2 [*Employer's Claims*];

使用**雇主设备**的适当数量和应付金额（按规定价格），应由**雇主代表**按照第 20.2 款［*雇主索赔*］和第 3.5 款［*确定*］的规定商定或确定。**承包商**应向**雇主**支付此金额。

雇主应按照**雇主要求**中规定的细节，免费提供"免费供应的材料"（如果有）。**雇主**应自担风险和费用，按照**合同**中规定的时间和地点供应这些材料。随后，**承包商**应对其进行目视（目测）检验，并将这些材料的短缺、缺陷或缺项迅速**通知****雇主代表**。除非双**方**另有商定，**雇主**应立即改正**通知**指出的短缺、缺陷或缺项。

目视检验后，这些免费供应的材料应由**承包商**照管、监护和控制。**承包商**的检验、照管、监护和控制的义务，不应免除**雇主**对目视检验时难发现的任何短缺、缺陷或缺项所负的责任。

4.21	
进度报告	除非**雇主要求**中另有规定，在**设计 - 施工期**，**承包商**应按照**雇主代表**同意的格式编制月度进度报告，一份原件、五份副本提交给**雇主代表**。第一次报告所包含的期间，应自**开工日**期起至当月底止。此后，应每月提交一次报告，在每次报告月最后一天后 7 日内报出。

进度报告应持续到**承包商**收到工程完成证书为止。**设计 - 施工期**和**运营服务期**进度报告的详细内容应符合**雇主要求**中的有规定。

除非另有规定或商定，每份进度报告应包括：

（a） 图表和详细进度说明，包括设计、**承包商文件**、采购、制造、送达**现场**、施工或更换、安装、试验、调试、试运行和提供**运营服务**的每个阶段；

（b） 反映制造或更换和**现场**内外进展情况的照片；

（c） 关于每项主要**生产设备**和**材料**的制造或更换、制造商的名称、制造地点、进度百分比，以及下列事项的实际或预计日期：

（i） 开始制造；
（ii） **承包商**检验；
（iii） 试验；（以及）
（iv） 发货和运抵**现场**；

（d） 第 6.10 款［*承包商人员和设备的记录*］中所述的细节；

（e） 材料的质量保证文件、试验结果和证书的副本；

（f） 变更清单，根据第 20.1 款［*承包商索赔*］的规定发出的**通知**，以及根据第 20.2 款［*雇主索赔*］的规定发出的**通知**；

(g) safety statistics, including details of any hazardous incidents and activities relating to environmental aspects and public relations; and

(h) comparisons of actual and planned progress, with details of any events or circumstances which may jeopardise the completion in accordance with the Contract, and the measures being (or to be) adopted to overcome delays.

The particular reporting requirements during the Operation Service Period shall be as specified in the Employer's Requirements.

4.22 Security of the Site

The Contractor shall be responsible for the security of the Site. Unless otherwise stated in the Particular Conditions:

(a) the Contractor shall be responsible for keeping unauthorised persons off the Site; and

(b) authorised persons shall be limited to the Contractor's Personnel and the Employer's Personnel, and to any other personnel notified to the Contractor, by the Employer or the Employer's Representative, as authorised personnel of the Employer's other contractors on the Site.

4.23 Contractor's Operations on Site

The Contractor shall confine his operations to the Site, and to any additional areas which may be obtained by the Contractor and agreed by the Employer's Representative as working areas. The Contractor shall take all necessary precautions to keep Contractor's Equipment and Contractor's Personnel within the Site and these additional areas, and to keep them off adjacent land.

At all times the Contractor shall keep the Site free from all unnecessary obstruction, and shall store or dispose of any Contractor's Equipment or surplus materials. The Contractor shall promptly clear away and remove from the Site any surplus material, wreckage, rubbish and Temporary Works which are no longer required.

Upon the issue of a Commissioning Certificate, the Contractor shall clear away and remove, from that part of the Site and Works to which the Commissioning Certificate refers, all Contractor's Equipment, surplus material, wreckage, rubbish and Temporary Works. The Contractor shall leave that part of the Site and the Works in a clean and safe condition.

The Contract Completion Certificate shall not be issued until the Contractor has removed any remaining Contractor's Equipment, surplus material, wreckage, rubbish and Temporary Works from the Site which are not required. The Contractor shall leave the Site and the Works in a clean and safe condition.

4.24 Fossils

All fossils, coins, articles of value or antiquity, and structures and other remains or items of geological or archaeological interest found on the Site shall be placed under the care and authority of the Employer. The Contractor shall take reasonable precautions to prevent Contractor's Personnel or other persons from removing or damaging any of these findings.

The Contractor shall, upon discovery of any such finding, promptly give Notice to the Employer's Representative, who shall issue instructions for dealing with it. If the Contractor suffers delay and/or incurs cost from complying with the instructions, the Contractor shall give a further Notice to the Employer's Representative and shall be entitled, subject to Sub-Clause 20.1 [*Contractor's Claims*], to:

(g) 安全统计，包括对有关环境方面和公共关系有危害的任何事件和活动的详细情况；（以及）

(h) 实际进度与计划进度的对比，包括可能影响按照**合同**规定竣工的任何不利事件或情况的详情，以及为消除延误正在（或准备）采取的措施。

运营服务期间的特别报告要求应符合**雇主要求**中的规定。

4.22 现场安保

承包商应负责**现场**的安全。除非**专用条件**中另有规定：

(a) **承包商**应负责阻止未经授权的人员进入**现场**；（以及）

(b) 由**雇主**或**雇主代表**向**承包商**发出通知，授权人员应仅限于**承包商人员**和**雇主人员**和被确定为授权人员的任何其他人员，作为**雇主**在**现场**的其他承包商。

4.23 承包商的现场作业

承包商应将其作业范围限制在**现场**，以及**承包商**可得到并经**雇主代表**同意作为工作场地的任何其他区域内。**承包商**应采取一切必要的预防措施，以保持**承包商设备**和**承包商人员**处在**现场**和此类其他区域内，避免其进入邻近区域。

在任何时间，**承包商**应保持**现场**没有一切不必要的障碍物，并应妥善存放或处置**承包商设备**或剩余的材料。**承包商**应立即从**现场**清除并运走任何剩余材料、残物、垃圾和不再需要的**临时工程**。

在签发一项**接收证书**后，**承包商**应从**调试证书**涉及的**现场**和**工程**部分，清除并运走所有**承包商设备**、剩余材料、残物、垃圾和**临时工程**。**承包商**应使该部分**现场**和**工程**处于清洁和安全的状态。

在**承包商**从**现场**清除并运走所有剩余的**承包商设备**、剩余材料、残物、垃圾和**现场**不需要的**临时工程**之前，不得签发合同完成证书。**承包商**应使**现场**和**工程**处于清洁和安全的状态。

4.24 化石

在**现场**发现的所有化石、硬币、有价值的物品或古物，以及具有地质或考古价值的结构物和其他遗迹或物品，应置于**雇主**的照管和权限下。**承包商**应采取一切合理的预防措施，防止**承包商人员**或其他人员移动或损坏任何此类发现物。

发现任何此类物品后，**承包商**应迅速**通知雇主代表**，**雇主代表**应就处理此类物品发出指示。如**承包商**因执行这些指示遭受延误和／或招致增加费用，**承包商**应向**雇主代表**发出进一步**通知**并有权根据**第 20.1 款**[**承包商索赔**]的规定，获得：

(a) an extension of time for any such delay, if completion is or will be delayed, under Sub-Clause 9.3 [*Extension of Time for Completion of Design-Build*]; and
(b) payment of any such Cost, which shall be included in the Contract Price.

After receiving this further Notice, the Employer's Representative shall proceed in accordance with Sub-Clause 3.5 [*Determinations*] to agree or determine these matters.

4.25 Changes in the Contractor's Financial Situation

If the Contractor becomes aware of any change in the Contractor's financial situation which will or could adversely affect his ability to complete and fulfil all his obligations under the Contract, he shall immediately give Notice to the Employer with detailed particulars. Within 28 days of receiving such Notice, the Employer shall advise the Contractor of what action he intends to take and/or what action the Employer requires the Contractor to take.

In any event, the Contractor shall provide the Employer annually with his audited financial statements and reports.

Design

5.1 General Design Obligations

The Contractor shall carry out, and be responsible for, the design of the Works. Design shall be prepared by qualified designers who are engineers or other professionals who comply with the criteria (if any) stated in the Employer's Requirements. Unless otherwise stated in the Contract, the Contractor shall submit to the Employer's Representative for consent the name and particulars of each proposed designer and design Subcontractor.

The Contractor warrants that he, his designers and design Subcontractors have the experience and capability necessary for the design. The Contractor undertakes that the designers shall be available to attend discussions with the Employer's Representative at all reasonable times.

Upon receiving Notice under Sub-Clause 8.1 [*Commencement Date*], the Contractor shall scrutinise the Employer's Requirements (including design criteria and calculations, if any) and the items of reference mentioned in Sub-Clause 4.7 [*Setting Out*]. Within the period stated in the Contract Data, calculated from the Commencement Date, the Contractor shall give Notice to the Employer's Representative of any error, fault or other defect found in the Employer's Requirements or these items of reference.

After receiving this Notice, the Employer's Representative shall determine whether Clause 13 [*Variations and Adjustments*] shall be applied, and shall give Notice to the Contractor accordingly. If and to the extent that (taking account of cost and time) an experienced contractor exercising due care would have discovered the error, fault or other defect when examining the Site and the Employer's Requirements before submitting the Tender, the Time for Completion shall not be extended and the Contract Price shall not be adjusted.

If the Contractor finds any error, fault or other defect in the Employer's Requirements after the period stated in the Contract Data, then Sub-Clause 1.10 [*Errors in the Employer's Requirements*] shall be applicable.

（a）根据第 9.3 款［*设计 - 施工竣工时间的延长*］的规定，如果竣工已或将受到延误，对任何此类延误给予延长期；（以及）

（b）任何此类**费用**应计入**合同价格**，给予支付。

雇主代表收到进一步**通知**后，应按照**第 3.5 款**［*确定*］的规定，商定或确定这些事项。

4.25 承包商资金（财务）状况的改变

如果**承包商**意识到其资金（财务）状况发生任何改变，将或可能对完成和履行合同规定的所有义务的能力产生不利影响，则应立即向**雇主**发出**通知**，并附详细资料。在收到此类**通知**后 28 天内，**雇主**应告知**承包商**其打算（拟）采取的措施和 / 或**雇主**要求**承包商**采取的措施。

在任何情况下，**承包商**应向**雇主**提供其经审计的资金（财务）报表和报告。

5 设计

5.1 设计义务一般要求

承包商应进行工程的设计并对其负责。应由符合**雇主要求**中规定标准（如果有）的**工程师**或其他专业人员等合格的设计人员进行设计。除非**合同**中另有规定，**承包商**应将拟雇用的每位设计人员和设计**分包商**的名称及详细情况，提交**雇主代表**，取得其同意。

承包商应保证其自身、其设计人员和设计**分包商**具备从事设计所必需的经验和能力。**承包商**承诺其设计人员在一切合理时间内，能参加与**雇主代表**的讨论。

在收到根据**第 8.1 款**［*开工日期*］的规定签发的**通知**后，**承包商**应仔细检查**雇主要求**（包括设计标准和计算书，如果有），以及**第 4.7 款**［*放线*］中提到的参考事项。在**合同数据**中规定的自开工日期算起的期间内，**承包商**应将**雇主要求**或这些参考事项中发现的任何错误、失误或其他缺陷**通知雇主代表**。

在收到此类通知后，**雇主代表**应确定**第 13 条**［*变更和调整*］的规定是否应适用，并相应地**通知承包商**。如果且在一定程度上（考虑费用和时间），一个经验丰富的承包商在提交**投标书**前，对**现场**和**雇主要求**进行细心的检查时，会发现的错误、失误或其他缺陷，则**竣工时间**应不予延长，**合同价格**应不予调整。

如果**承包商**在**合同数据**规定期限后发现**雇主要求**中的错误、失误或其他缺陷，**第 1.10 款**［*雇主要求中的错误*］将适用。

5.2 Contractor's Documents

The Contractor's Documents shall comprise the technical documents specified in the Employer's Requirements, documents required to satisfy all regulatory approvals, and the documents described in Sub-Clause 5.5 [*As-Built Documents*] and Sub-Clause 5.6 [*Operation and Maintenance Manuals*]. Unless otherwise stated in the Employer's Requirements, the Contractor's Documents shall be written in the language for communications defined in Sub-Clause 1.4 [*Law and Language*].

The Contractor shall prepare all Contractor's Documents, and shall also prepare any other documents necessary to instruct the Contractor's Personnel. The Employer's Personnel shall have the right to inspect the preparation of all these documents, wherever they are being prepared.

If the Employer's Requirements describe the Contractor's Documents which are to be submitted to the Employer's Representative for review leading to consent and/or for approval, they shall be submitted accordingly, together with a Notice as described below. The Employer's Representative gives his consent to a document when he is satisfied that the Contractor's Documents conform to the Employer's Requirements. In the following provisions of this Sub-Clause, (i) "review period" means the period required by the Employer's Representative for review leading to consent and (if so specified) for approval, and (ii) "Contractor's Documents" exclude any documents which are not specified as being required to be submitted for review leading to consent and/or for approval. The Contractor's Documents which require approval from the Employer's Representative shall be as listed in the Contract Data.

Unless otherwise stated in the Employer's Requirements or agreed with the Employer's Representative, each review period shall not exceed 21 days, calculated from the date on which the Employer's Representative receives a Contractor's Document and the Contractor's Notice. This Notice shall state that the Contractor's Document is considered ready for review leading to either approval (if so specified) or consent with regard to conformity with the Employer's Requirements, in accordance with this Sub-Clause and for use. The Notice shall also state that the Contractor's Document complies with the Contract, or the extent to which it does not comply.

The Employer's Representative may, within the review period, give Notice to the Contractor that a Contractor's Document fails (to the extent stated) to conform with the Contract. If a Contractor's Document so fails to conform, it shall be rectified, resubmitted and reviewed (and, if specified, approved) in accordance with this Sub-Clause, at the Contractor's cost. If such re-submission and review causes the Employer to incur additional costs, the Contractor shall, subject to Sub-Clause 20.2 [*Employer's Claims*], pay these costs to the Employer.

For each part of the Works, and except to the extent that the prior approval or consent of the Employer's Representative shall have been obtained:

(a) in the case of a Contractor's Document which has (as specified) been submitted for the Employer's Representative's approval or consent:

   (i) the Employer's Representative shall give Notice to the Contractor that the Employer's Representative gives his consent that the Contractor's Document conforms with the Employer's Requirements or is approved, or that it does not (to the extent stated) comply with the Contract;

   (ii) execution of such part of the Works shall not commence until the Employer's Representative has either approved or given his consent to the Contractor's Document; and

5.2	
承包商文件	**承包商文件**应包括**雇主要求**中规定的技术文件，为满足所有规章要求报批的文件，以及第5.5款[*竣工文件*]和第5.6款[*操作和维护手册*]中所述文件。除非**雇主要求**中另有说明，**承包商文件**应使用第1.4款[*法律和语言*]中规定的交流语言编写。

承包商应编制所有**承包商文件**，还应编制指导**承包商人员**所需要的任何其他文件。**雇主人员**应有权对所有此类文件的编制进行检验。

如果**雇主要求**中规定**承包商文件**要提交**雇主代表**以获得同意和/或批准，这些文件应按照要求，连同下述**通知**一并提交。当**雇主代表**确信**承包商文件**符合**雇主要求**，**雇主代表**同意该文件。在本款的以下规定中，(i) "审核期" 系指**雇主代表**审核以获得同意和批准（如有规定）需要的期限，以及 (ii) "**承包商文件**" 不包括未规定需要提交审核以获得同意和/或批准的任何文件。需要**雇主代表**批准的**承包商文件**应在**合同数据**中列出。

除非**雇主要求**中另有规定或与**雇主代表**商定，每项审核期，从**雇主代表**收到一份**承包商文件**和**承包商通知**的日期算起不应超过21天。该**通知**应说明，**承包商文件**已可供，按照本款规定可根据**雇主要求**的要求批准（如有规定）或同意其使用。**通知**还应说明本**承包商文件**符合合同规定的情况，或在哪些方面不符合规定。

雇主代表可在审核期内向**承包商**发出**通知**，指出**承包商文件**（在规定范围内）不符合**合同**的规定。如果**承包商文件**确实不符合要求，则应按照本**款**的规定对其进行修正、重新提交和审核（如有规定，应予以批准），费用由**承包商**承担。根据第20.2款[*雇主的索赔*]如果此类重新提交和审核引起**雇主**招致增加费用，则**承包商**应向**雇主**支付这些费用。

除应已取得**雇主代表**事先批准或同意的范围外，对**工程**的每一部分：

(a) 如果已经（根据规定）将**承包商文件**提交**雇主代表**批准或同意：

(i) **雇主代表**应**通知承包商**，说明**雇主代表**同意**承包商文件**符合**雇主要求**或获得批准，或（在规定范围内）不能符合**合同**规定；

(ii) 在**雇主代表**批准或同意**承包商文件**之前，**工程**的相应部分不应开工；（以及）

(iii) the Employer's Representative shall be deemed to have approved the Contractor's Documents or given his consent that the Contractor's Documents conform to the Employer's Requirements upon the expiry of the review periods for all the Contractor's Documents which are relevant to the design and execution of such part, unless the Employer's Representative has previously notified otherwise in accordance with sub-paragraph (i);

(b) execution of such part of the Works shall not commence prior to the expiry of the review periods for all the Contractor's Documents which are relevant to its design and execution;

(c) execution of such part of the Works shall be in accordance with those Contractor's Documents for which the Employer's Representative has given his consent as to the conformity with the Employer's Requirements, (and, if specified, approved); and

(d) if the Contractor wishes to modify any design or document which has previously been submitted for review (and, if specified, approval), the Contractor shall immediately give Notice to the Employer's Representative, accompanied by a written explanation of the need for such modification. Thereafter, the Contractor shall submit revised documents to the Employer's Representative in accordance with the above procedure.

Any such consent and/or approval (where specified) (under this Sub-Clause or otherwise) shall not relieve the Contractor from any obligation or responsibility.

5.3 Contractor's Undertaking

If the Employer's Representative reasonably instructs that further Contractor's Documents are required, the Contractor shall prepare them promptly at his own cost. The Contractor undertakes that the design, the Contractor's Documents, the execution and the completed Works will be in accordance with:

(a) the Laws of the Country; and
(b) the documents forming the Contract, as altered or modified by Variations.

5.4 Technical Standards and Regulations

Unless otherwise stated, the design, the Contractor's Documents, the execution and the completed Works shall comply with the Country's technical standards, building, construction and environmental Laws, Laws applicable to the product being produced from the Works, and other standards specified in the Employer's Requirements, applicable to the Works, or defined by the applicable Laws.

All these Laws shall, in respect of the Works and each Section, be those prevailing when the Commissioning Certificate is issued in accordance with Sub-Clause 11.7 [*Commissioning Certificate*]. References in the Contract to published standards shall be understood to be references to the edition applicable on the Base Date, unless stated otherwise.

If changed or new applicable standards come into force in the Country after the Base Date, the Contractor shall give Notice to the Employer's Representative and (if appropriate) submit proposals for compliance. In the event that:

(a) the Employer's Representative determines that compliance is required; and
(b) the proposals for compliance constitute a variation, then the Employer's Representative shall initiate a Variation in accordance with Clause 13 [*Variations and Adjustments*].

(iii) 除非**雇主代表**此前已按照（i）段发出通知，在与该部分**工程**的设计和施工相关的所有**承包商文件**的审核期期满时，**雇主代表**应被视为已批准**承包商文件**，或同意**承包商文件**符合**雇主要求**；

(b) 在有关该部分**工程**的设计和施工的所有**承包商文件**审核期尚未期满前，不得开工；

(c) 该部分**工程**的实施，应符合**雇主代表**已同意符合**雇主要求**的**承包商文件**（如有规定，应予以批准）；（以及）

(d) 如果**承包商**希望修改先前提交审核（如有规定，经批准）的任何设计或文件，**承包商**应立即**通知雇主代表**，并附上书面说明，说明是否需要修改。此后，**承包商**应按照上述程序，将修改后的文件提交**雇主代表**。

任何此类同意和／或批准（如有规定）（根据本**款**或其他规定），不得免除**承包商**的任何义务或责任。

5.3 承包商的承诺

如果**雇主代表**合理指示需要进一步的**承包商文件**，**承包商**应立即自费编制这些文件。**承包商**承诺其设计、**承包商文件**、实施和竣工的**工程**将符合：

（a）**工程所在国**的**法律**；（以及）
（b）经过**变更**做出更改或修正的，构成**合同**的各项文件。

5.4 技术标准和法规

除非另有规定，该设计、**承包商文件**、施工和竣工的**工程**，均应符合**工程所在国**的技术标准，建筑、施工和环境方面的**法律**，适用于**工程**将生产的产品的**法律**，以及**雇主要求**中规定的适用于**工程**，或适用**法律**规定的其他标准。

所有这些**工程**和各**分项工程**方面的**法律**，应是在根据第 11.7 款［*调试证书*］的规定签发**调试证书**时有效的。除非另有规定，否则**合同**中对已发布标准的引用应理解为对**基准日期**适用版本的引用。

基准日期后，如果在**工程所在国**有修订的或新的适用标准生效，**承包商**应向**雇主代表**发出**通知**，并（如适宜）提交合规建议书。如果：

（a）**雇主代表**确定需要遵守；（以及）
（b）合规建议书构成一项**变更**，**雇主代表**应按照第 13 条［*变更和调整*］的规定启动**变更**。

5.5
As-Built Documents

The Contractor shall prepare, and keep up-to-date, a complete set of "as-built" records of the execution of the Works, showing the exact as-built locations, sizes and details of the work as executed. These records shall be kept on the Site and shall be used exclusively for the purposes of this Sub-Clause. At least two copies shall be supplied to the Employer's Representative prior to the commencement of the Tests on Completion of Design-Build.

In addition, the Contractor shall supply to the Employer's Representative as-built drawings of the Works, showing all Works as executed, and submit them to the Employer's Representative for review under Sub-Clause 5.2 [*Contractor's Documents*]. The Contractor shall obtain the consent of the Employer's Representative as to their size, the referencing system, and other relevant details.

Prior to the issue of the Commissioning Certificate, the Contractor shall supply to the Employer's Representative the specified numbers and types of copies of the relevant as-built drawings, in accordance with the Employer's Requirements. The relevant work shall not be considered to be completed for the purposes of issuing the Commissioning Certificate under Sub-Clause 11.7 [*Commissioning Certificate*] until the Employer's Representative has received these documents.

5.6
Operation and Maintenance Manuals

Prior to the commencement of the Commissioning Period, the Contactor shall supply to the Employer's Representative two copies of all operation and maintenance manuals in sufficient detail for the Employer to operate, maintain, dismantle, reassemble, adjust and repair the Plant and the Works. The Contractor shall supply the balance of the required operation and maintenance manuals prior to the issue of the Commissioning Certificate. The Works or any Section shall not be considered to be completed for the purposes of issuing the Commissioning Certificate under Sub-Clause 11.7 [*Commissioning Certificate*] until the Employer's Representative has received these documents.

5.7
Design Error

If errors, omissions, ambiguities, inconsistencies, inadequacies or other defects are found in the Contractor's Documents, they and the Works shall be corrected at the Contractor's cost, notwithstanding any consent or approval under this Clause.

6
Staff and Labour

6.1
Engagement of Staff and Labour

Except as otherwise stated in the Employer's Requirements, the Contractor shall make arrangements for the engagement of all staff and labour, local or otherwise, and for their payment, housing, feeding and transport.

6.2
Rates of Wages and Conditions of Employment

The Contractor shall pay rates of wages and observe conditions of labour which are not lower than those established for the trade or industry where the work is carried out. If no established rates or conditions are applicable, the Contractor shall pay rates of wages and observe conditions which are not lower than the general level of wages and conditions observed locally by employers whose trade or industry is similar to that of the Contractor.

5.5 竣工文件

承包商应编制并随时更新一套完整的工程施工"竣工"记录,如实记载竣工的准确位置、尺寸和已实施工作的详细说明。这些记录应保存在**现场**,并仅限用于本款需要。在**设计 - 施工竣工试验**前,应向**雇主代表**提供至少两份副本。

此外,**承包商**应向**雇主代表**提供工程竣工图,表明所有**工程**已实施完毕,提交**雇主代表**根据第 5.2 款 [*承包商文件*] 的规定进行审核。**承包商**应取得**雇主代表**就其尺寸、参考系统和其他相关细节的同意。

在签发**调试证书**前,**承包商**应按照**雇主要求**中规定的数量和类型的副本,向**雇主代表**提供相关竣工图。根据第 11.7 款 [*调试证书*] 的规定签发**调试证书**,在**雇主代表**收到这些文件之前,相关工作不得视为已完成。

5.6 操作和维护手册

在**调试期**开始前,**承包商**应向**雇主代表**提供两套足够详细的操作和维护手册,以便**雇主**操作、维修、拆卸、重新组装、调整和修复**生产设备**和**工程**。在签发**调试运行证书**前,**承包商**应补齐所需的操作和维修手册。根据第 11.7 款 [*调试证书*] 的规定签发**调试证书**,在**雇主代表**收到这些文件之前,**工程**或任何**分项工程**不得视为已完成。

5.7 设计错误

如果在**承包商文件**中发现有错误、遗漏、含糊、不一致、不适当或其他缺陷,尽管根据本**条**的规定做出了任何同意或批准,**承包商**仍应自费对这些缺陷和**工程**进行改正。

6 员工

6.1 员工的雇用

除**雇主要求**中另有说明外,**承包商**应安排从当地或其他地方雇用所有的员工,并负责他们的报酬、住宿、膳食和交通。

6.2 工资标准和劳动条件

承包商所支付的薪酬标准及遵守的劳动条件,应不低于工作所在地该工种或行业制订的标准和条件。如果没有现成的适用标准或条件,**承包商**所付的工资标准和遵守的劳动条件,应不低于当地与**承包商**类似的工种或行业雇主所付的一般工资标准和遵守的劳动条件。

6.3 Persons in the Service of Employer

The Contractor shall not recruit, or attempt to recruit, staff and labour from amongst the Employer's Personnel.

6.4 Labour Laws

The Contractor shall comply with all the relevant labour Laws applicable to the Contractor's Personnel, including Laws relating to their employment, health, safety, welfare, immigration and emigration, and shall allow them all their legal rights.

The Contractor shall require the Contractor's Personnel to obey all applicable Laws, including those concerning safety at work.

6.5 Working Hours

No work shall be carried out on the Site on locally recognised days of rest or outside the normal working hours stated in the Contract Data, unless:

(a) otherwise stated in the Contract;
(b) the Employer's Representative gives consent;
(c) the work is unavoidable, or necessary for the protection of life or property or for the safety of the Works, in which case the Contractor shall immediately advise the Employer's Representative; or
(d) required for the proper fulfilment of the requirements of the Operation Service Period.

6.6 Facilities for Staff and Labour

Except as otherwise stated in the Employer's Requirements, the Contractor shall provide and maintain all necessary accommodation and welfare facilities for the Contractor's Personnel. The Contractor shall also provide facilities for the Employer's Personnel as stated in the Employer's Requirements.

The Contractor shall not permit any of the Contractor's Personnel to maintain any temporary or permanent living quarters within the Site of the Works, save where the Employer has given the Contractor permission in writing.

6.7 Health and Safety

The Contractor shall at all times during the Contract Period take all reasonable precautions to maintain the health and safety of the Contractor's Personnel. In collaboration with local health authorities, the Contractor shall ensure that medical staff, first aid facilities, sick bay and ambulance service are available at all times at the Site and at any accommodation for Contractor's and Employer's Personnel, and that suitable arrangements are made for all necessary welfare and hygiene requirements and for the prevention of epidemics.

The Contractor shall appoint an accident prevention officer at the Site, responsible for maintaining safety and protection against accidents. This person shall be qualified for this responsibility, and shall have the authority to issue instructions and take protective measures to prevent accidents. Throughout the execution and operation of the Works, the Contractor shall provide whatever is required by this person to exercise this responsibility and authority.

The Contractor shall send details of any accident to the Employer's Representative as soon as practicable after its occurrence. The Contractor shall maintain records and make reports concerning health, safety and welfare of persons, and damage to property, as the Employer's Representative may reasonably require.

6.3
为雇主服务的人员   承包商不应从雇主人员中招聘或试图招聘员工。

6.4
劳动法   承包商应遵守所有适用于承包商人员的相关劳动法，包括有关他们的雇用、健康、安全、福利、入境和出境等法律，并应允许他们享有所有合法权利。

承包商应要求承包商人员遵守所有适用的法律，包括有关工作安全的法律。

6.5
工作时间   除非出现下列情况，在当地公认的休息日，或合同数据中规定的正常工作时间以外，不应在现场进行工作：

（a） 合同中另有规定；
（b） 雇主代表同意；
（c） 因保护生命或财产或因工程安全而不可避免或必需的工作，在此情况下，承包商应立即告知雇主代表；（或）

（d） 需要适当满足运营服务期的要求。

6.6
为员工提供设施   除雇主要求中另有说明外，承包商应为承包商人员提供和保持一切必要的食宿和福利设施。承包商还应按照雇主要求中的规定，为雇主人员提供设施。

承包商不应允许任何承包商人员，在工程现场内保留任何临时或永久的居住场所，除非雇主以书面形式许可承包商。

6.7
健康和安全   在合同期内，承包商应始终采取所有合理的预防措施，维护承包商人员的健康和安全。承包商应与当地卫生部门合作，始终确保在现场，以及承包商人员和雇主人员的任何住地，配备医务人员、急救设施、病房及救护车服务，并应对所有必要的福利和卫生要求，以及预防传染病做出适当安排。

承包商应在现场指派一名事故预防员，负责维护安全和事故预防工作。该人员应能胜任此项职责，并应有权发布指示及采取防止事故的保护措施。在工程实施和运营过程中，承包商应提供该人员为履行其职责和权利所需的任何事项。

任何事故发生后，承包商应立即将事故详情通报雇主代表。承包商应按雇主代表可能提出的合理要求，保持记录，并写出关于人员健康、安全和福利，以及财产损害等情况的报告。

6.8
Contractor's Superintendence

For the complete Contract Period, the Contractor shall provide all necessary superintendence to plan, arrange, direct, manage, inspect, test and monitor the design and execution of the Works and the provision of the Operation Service in accordance with his obligations under the Contract.

Superintendence shall be given by a sufficient number of persons having adequate knowledge of the language for communications (defined in Sub-Clause 1.4 [*Law and Language*]) and of the operations to be carried out (including the methods and techniques required, the hazards likely to be encountered and methods of preventing accidents), for the satisfactory and safe execution of the Works and the provision of the Operation Service.

6.9
Contractor's Personnel

The Contractor's Personnel shall be appropriately qualified, skilled and experienced in their respective trades or occupations. The Employer's Representative may require the Contractor to remove (or cause to be removed) any person employed on the Site or Works, including the Contractor's Representative if applicable, who:

(a) persists in any misconduct or lack of care;
(b) carries out duties incompetently or negligently;
(c) fails to conform with any provisions of the Contract; or
(d) persists in any conduct which is prejudicial to safety, health, or the protection of the environment.

If appropriate, the Contractor shall then appoint (or cause to be appointed) a suitable replacement person.

6.10
Records of Contractor's Personnel and Equipment

During the Design-Build Period, the Contractor shall submit, to the Employer's Representative, details showing the number of each class of Contractor's Personnel and of each type of Contractor's Equipment on the Site. Any changes to the Personnel or Equipment shall be notified at the end of each calendar month to the Employer's Representative.

During the Operation Service Period, any changes to the Personnel or Equipment shall be notified at the end of each calendar month to the Employer's Representative.

6.11
Disorderly Conduct

The Contractor shall at all times take all reasonable precautions to prevent any unlawful, riotous or disorderly conduct by or amongst the Contractor's Personnel, and to preserve peace and protection of persons and property on and near the Site.

7 Plant, Materials, and Workmanship

7.1
Manner of Execution

The Contractor shall carry out the manufacture and/or replacement and/or repair of Plant, the production and manufacture of Materials, and all other activities during the execution of the Works and provision of the Operation Service:

(a) in accordance with the applicable Laws in the manner (if any) specified in the Contract;
(b) in a proper workmanlike and careful manner, in accordance with recognised good practice; and

| 6.8 承包商的监督 | 在整个合同期内，**承包商**应根据合同规定的义务，对设计、工程实施和**运营服务**的规划、安排、指导、管理、检验、试验和监测，提供一切必要的监督。

此类监督应由足够数量的人员执行，他们应能掌握（**第1.4款**[*法律和语言*]所规定的）交流语言，以及具有令人满意和安全的，对要实施的**工程**和提供**运营服务**各项作业所需的足够知识（包括所需的方法和技术、可能遇到的危险和预防事故的方法）。|

| 6.9 承包商人员 | **承包商人员**应是在他们各自工种或职业内，具有相应资质、技能和经验的人员。**雇主代表**可要求**承包商**撤换（或敦促撤换）受雇于**现场**或**工程**的，有下列行为的任何人员，也包括**承包商代表**（如果有）：

(a) 经常行为不当，或工作漫不经心；
(b) 无能力履行义务或玩忽职守；
(c) 不遵守**合同**的任何规定；（或）
(d) 坚持任何有损安全、健康或有损环境保护的行为。

如果适宜，**承包商**随后应指派（或敦促指派）合适的替代人员。|

| 6.10 承包商人员和设备的记录 | 在**设计-施工期**间，**承包商**应向**雇主代表**提交说明**现场**各类**承包商人员**的人数和各类**承包商设备**数量的详细资料。**人员**或**设备**的任何变化应在每个日历月底通知**雇主代表**。

在**运营服务期**间，**人员**或**设备**的任何变化应在每个日历月底通知**雇主代表**。|

| 6.11 无序行为 | **承包商**应始终采取各种必要的预防措施，防止**承包商人员**或其内部发生任何非法的、骚动的或无序的行为，以保持安定，保护**现场**及邻近人员和财产的安全。|

7 生产设备、材料和工艺

| 7.1 实施方法 | **承包商**应在**工程**实施和提供**运营服务**期间，按以下方法进行**生产设备**的制造和/或更换和/或维修、**材料**的生产加工，以及所有其他活动：

(a) 按照合同规定的方法（如果有）遵守适用**法律**；

(b) 按照公认的良好惯例，使用恰当、精巧和仔细的方法；（以及）|

(c) with properly equipped facilities and non-hazardous Materials, except as otherwise specified in the Contract.

7.2 Samples

The Contractor shall submit the following samples of Materials, and relevant information, to the Employer's Representative for review in accordance with the procedures for Contractor's Documents described in Sub-Clause 5.2 [*Contractor's Documents*]:

(a) manufacturer's standard samples of Materials and samples specified in the Contract, all at the Contractor's cost; and
(b) additional samples instructed by the Employer's Representative as a Variation.

Each sample shall be labelled as to origin and intended use in the Works.

7.3 Inspection

The Employer's Personnel and other persons authorised by the Employer shall at all reasonable times:

(a) have full access to all parts of the Site and to all places from which natural Materials are being obtained;
(b) during production, manufacture and construction (at the Site and elsewhere), operation and maintenance, be entitled to examine, inspect, measure and test the Materials and workmanship, and to check the progress of manufacture of Plant and production and manufacture of Materials; and
(c) carry out other authorised duties and inspections.

The Contractor shall give the Employer's Personnel and other persons authorised by the Employer full opportunity to carry out these activities, including providing access, facilities, permissions and safety equipment. No such activity shall relieve the Contractor from any obligation or responsibility.

The Contractor shall give Notice to the Employer's Representative whenever any work is ready and before it is covered up, put out of sight, or packaged for storage or transport. The Employer's Representative shall then either carry out the examination, inspection, measurement or testing without unreasonable delay, or promptly give Notice to the Contractor that the Employer's Representative does not require to do so. If the Contractor fails to give the Notice, he shall, if and when required by the Employer's Representative, uncover the work and thereafter reinstate and make good, all at the Contractor's cost.

7.4 Testing

This Sub-Clause shall apply to all tests on Plant, Materials and workmanship specified in the Contract.

The Contractor shall provide all apparatus, assistance, documents and other information, electricity, equipment, fuel, consumables, instruments, labour, materials, and suitably qualified and experienced staff, as are necessary to carry out the specified tests efficiently. The Contractor shall agree, with the Employer's Representative, the time and place for the specified testing of any Plant, Materials and other parts of the Works.

The Employer's Representative may, under Clause 13 [*Variations and Adjustments*], vary the location or details of specified tests, or instruct the Contractor to carry out additional tests. If these varied or additional tests show that the tested Plant, Materials or workmanship is not in accordance with the Contract, the cost of carrying out this Variation shall be borne by the Contractor, notwithstanding other provisions of the Contract.

(c) 除**合同**另有规定外，使用适当配备的设施和无危险的**材料**。

7.2 样品

承包商应按照第 5.2 款[**承包商文件**]中所述的**承包商**文件送审程序，向**雇主代表**提交以下**材料**样品和有关资料，供其审核：

(a) 制造商的**材料**标准样品和**合同**规定的样品，均由**承包商**自费提供；(以及)
(b) **雇主代表**指示的作为**变更**的附加样品。

每种样品均应标明其原产地和在**工程**中的拟定用途。

7.3 检验

雇主人员和**雇主**授权的其他人员应在所有合理的时间内：

(a) 有充分机会进入**现场**的所有部分，以及获得天然**材料**的所有地点；
(b) 有权在生产、加工和施工（在**现场**和其他地方）、操作和维护期间，对**材料**和工艺进行检查、检验、测量和试验，并检查**生产设备**的制造和**材料**的生产加工的进度；(以及)

(c) 执行其他授权任务和检验。

承包商应为**雇主人员**和**雇主**授权的其他人员进行上述活动提供一切机会，包括提供安全进入条件、设施、许可和安全装备。此类活动不应免除**承包商**的任何义务或责任。

每当任何工作已经准备好，在将其覆盖、掩蔽或包装以便储存或运输前，**承包商**应**通知雇主代表**。这时，**雇主代表**应及时进行检查、检验、测量或试验，不得无故拖延，或立即**通知承包商**，**雇主代表**无须进行这些工作。如果**承包商**没有发出此类**通知**，而当**雇主代表**提出要求时，**承包商**应除去物件上的覆盖，并在随后恢复完好，所有费用由**承包商**承担。

7.4 试验

本款适用于**合同**规定的所有**生产设备**、**材料**和工艺试验。

为有效进行规定的试验，**承包商**应提供所需的所有仪器、协助、文件和其他资料、临时供应电力、装备、燃料、消耗品、工具、劳力、材料，以及具有适当资质和经验的工作人员。对任何**生产设备**、**材料**和**工程**其他部分进行规定的试验，其时间和地点，应由**承包商**和**雇主代表**商定。

根据第 13 条[**变更和调整**]的规定，**雇主代表**可以改变进行规定试验的位置或细节，或指示**承包商**进行附加试验。如果这些改变的或附加试验证明，经过试验的**生产设备**、**材料**或工艺不符合**合同**要求，尽管**合同**另有规定，**承包商**应承担进行本项**变更**的费用。

The Employer's Representative shall give Notice to the Contractor not less than 24 hours prior to the tests, of the Employer's Representative's intention to attend the tests. If the Employer's Representative does not attend at the time and place agreed, the Contractor may proceed with the tests, unless otherwise instructed by the Employer's Representative, and the tests shall then be deemed to have been made in the Employer's Representative's presence.

If the Contractor suffers delay in carrying out the tests and/or incurs cost from complying with these instructions or as a result of a delay for which the Employer is responsible, the Contractor shall give Notice to the Employer's Representative and shall be entitled, subject to Sub-Clause 20.1 [Contractor's Claims], to:

(a) an extension of time for any such delay, if completion is or will be delayed, under Sub-Clause 9.3 [Extension of Time for Completion of Design-Build]; and
(b) payment of any such Cost Plus Profit, which shall be included in the Contract Price.

After receiving this Notice, the Employer's Representative shall proceed in accordance with Sub-Clause 3.5 [Determinations] to agree or determine these matters.

The Contractor shall promptly forward to the Employer's Representative duly certified reports of the tests. When the specified tests have been passed, the Employer's Representative shall endorse the Contractor's test certificate, or issue a certificate to him, to that effect. If the Employer's Representative has not attended the tests, he shall be deemed to have accepted the readings as accurate.

7.5 Rejection

If, as a result of an examination, inspection, measurement or testing, any Plant, Materials, or workmanship is found to be defective or otherwise not in accordance with the Contract, the Employer's Representative may reject the Plant, Materials, design or workmanship by giving Notice to the Contractor, with reasons. The Contractor shall then promptly make good the defect at the Contractor's cost and ensure that the rejected item complies with the Contract.

If the Employer's Representative requires this Plant, Materials, or workmanship to be retested, the tests shall be repeated under the same terms and conditions. If the rejection and retesting cause the Employer to incur additional costs, the Contractor shall, subject to Sub-Clause 20.2 [Employer's Claims], pay these costs to the Employer.

7.6 Remedial Work

At any time during the Contract Period, notwithstanding any previous test or certification, the Employer's Representative may instruct the Contractor to:

(a) repair, remove from the Site and replace, any Plant or Materials which is not in accordance with the Contract;
(b) remove and re-execute any other work which is not in accordance with the Contract; and
(c) execute any work which is urgently required for the safety of the Works or the provision of the Operation Service, whether because of an accident, unforeseeable event or otherwise.

The Contractor shall comply with the instruction within a reasonable time, which shall be the time (if any) specified in the instruction, or immediately if urgency is specified under sub-paragraph (c).

雇主代表应至少提前 24 小时将参加试验的意图**通知承包商**。如果**雇主代表**没有在商定的时间和地点参加试验，除非**雇主代表**另有指示，**承包商**可自行进行试验，这些试验应被视为是在**雇主代表**在场情况下进行的。

如果由于遵守这些指示或因**雇主**应负责的延误，使**承包商**在进行试验时遭受延误和／或招致增加费用，**承包商**应向**雇主代表**发出**通知**，并有权根据第 20.1 款［*承包商索赔*］的规定获得：

（a） 根据第 9.3 款［*设计 - 施工竣工时间的延长*］的规定，如果竣工已或将受到延误，对任何此类延误，给予延长期；（以及）

（b） 任何此类**成本加利润**的费用，应计入**合同价格**，给予支付。

雇主代表收到此**通知**后，应按照第 3.5 款［*确定*］的规定，对这些事项进行商定或确定。

承包商应迅速向**雇主代表**提交充分证实的试验报告。当规定的试验通过时，**雇主代表**应在**承包商**的试验证书上签字认可，或向**承包商**签发等效的证书。如果**雇主代表**未参加试验，其应被视为已经认可试验示数是准确的。

| 7.5 拒收 | 如果检查、检验、测量或试验结果，发现任何**生产设备**、**材料**、**工艺**有缺陷，或不符合**合同**要求，**雇主代表**可向**承包商**发出**通知**，并说明理由，拒收该**生产设备**、**材料**、设计或**工艺**。**承包商**应迅速修复缺陷，费用由**承包商**承担，并确保此项拒收**项目**符合**合同**要求。

如果**雇主代表**要求对上述**生产设备**、**材料**或**工艺**重新进行试验，这些试验应按相同的规定和条件重新进行。如果此项拒收和重新试验使**雇主**增加了额外费用，**承包商**应根据第 20.2 款［*雇主索赔*］的规定，向**雇主**支付这些费用。

| 7.6 修补工作 | 在**合同期**内任何时候，尽管已有先前的任何试验或证书，**雇主代表**可指示**承包商**进行以下工作：

（a） 修理、从**现场**移除并更换不符合**合同**要求的任何**生产设备**或**材料**；
（b） 移除并重新实施不符合**合同**规定的任何其他工作；（以及）
（c） 实施因意外、不可预见的事件或其他原因引起的、**工程**安全或提供**运营服务**迫切需要的任何工作。

承包商应在指示中规定的合理时间（如果有）内执行该指示，或在上述（c）段规定的紧急情况下立即实施。

Except to the extent that the Contractor may be entitled to payment for the work required under sub-paragraph (c), the Contractor shall bear the cost of such remedial work.

If the Contractor fails to comply with the instruction, the Employer shall be entitled to employ and pay other persons to carry out the work. Except to the extent that the Contractor would have been entitled to payment for the work, the Contractor shall, subject to Sub-Clause 20.2 [*Employer's Claims*], pay to the Employer all costs arising from this failure.

7.7 Ownership of Plant and Materials

Each item of Plant and Materials shall, to the extent consistent with the Laws of the Country, become the property of the Employer at whichever is the earlier of the following times, free from liens and other encumbrances:

(a) when it is delivered to the Site;
(b) when the Contractor is paid the value of the Plant and Materials under Sub-Clause 9.9 [*Payment for Plant and Materials in Event of Suspension*]; and
(c) when the Contractor is paid the value of the Plant and Materials under Sub-Clause 14.6 [*Payment for Plant and Materials intended for the Works*].

7.8 Royalties

Unless otherwise stated in the Employer's Requirements, the Contractor shall pay all royalties, rents and other payments for:

(a) natural Materials obtained from outside the Site; and
(b) the disposal of material from demolitions and excavations and of other surplus material (whether natural or man-made), except to the extent that disposal areas within the Site are specified in the Contract.

8 Commencement Date, Completion and Programme

8.1 Commencement Date

The Employer's Representative shall give Notice stating the Commencement Date to the Contractor not less than 14 days prior to the Commencement Date. Unless otherwise stated in the Particular Conditions, the Commencement Date shall be within 42 days after the Contractor receives the Letter of Acceptance.

8.2 Time for Completion

The Contractor shall complete the whole of the Design-Build and each Section (if any), in accordance with Sub-Clause 9.2 [*Time for Completion of Design-Build*], or as extended under Sub-Clause 9.3 [*Extension of Time for Completion of Design-Build*], and shall provide the Operation Service for the period stated in the Contract Data.

8.3 Programme

The Contractor shall submit a detailed time programme to the Employer's Representative within 28 days after receiving the Notice under Sub-Clause 8.1 [*Commencement Date*]. The Contractor shall also submit a revised programme whenever the previous programme is inconsistent with actual progress or with the Contractor's obligations. Each programme shall include:

(a) the order in which the Contractor intends to carry out the Works, including the anticipated timing of each stage of design, Contractor's Documents, procurement, manufacture, inspection, delivery to Site, construction, erection, testing, commissioning and trial operation;

除**承包商**有权获得（c）段所要求工程的付款外，**承包商**应承担此类修补工作的费用。

如果**承包商**未能遵从指示，**雇主**有权雇用并付款给他人从事该工作。除**承包商**原有权从该工作所得付款外，**承包商**应按照**第 20.2 款**［*雇主索赔*］的规定，向**雇主**支付因其未履行指示招致的所有费用。

7.7
生产设备和材料的所有权

从下列较早者的时间起，在符合工程所在国法律规定的范围内，每项**生产设备和材料**都应无抵押权和其他阻碍地成为**雇主**的财产：

（a） 当上述**生产设备和材料**运至**现场**时；
（b） 当根据**第 9.9 款**［*暂停时对生产设备和材料的付款*］的规定，**承包商**得到按**生产设备和材料**价值的付款时；（以及）
（c） 当根据**第 14.6 款**［*拟用于工程的生产设备和材料的付款*］的规定，**承包商**得到**生产设备和材料**价值的付款时。

7.8
土地（矿区）使用费

除非**雇主要求**中另有说明，**承包商**应为以下事项支付所有的土地（矿区）使用费、租金和其他款项：

（a） 从**现场**以外地区得到的天然材料；（以及）
（b） 在合同规定的**现场**范围内的弃置地区以外，弃置拆除和开挖的材料和其他剩余材料（不论是天然的或人工的）。

8 开工日期、竣工和进度计划

8.1
开工日期

雇主代表应在开工日期前不少于 14 天向**承包商**发出开工日期的通知。除非**专用条件**中另有说明，开工日期应在**承包商**收到**中标函**后 42 天内。

8.2
竣工时间

承包商应按照**第 9.2 款**［*设计 - 施工竣工时间*］的规定或根据**第 9.3 款**［*设计 - 施工竣工时间的延长*］的规定，完成整个**设计 - 施工**和每个分项工程（如果有），并应在**合同数据**中规定的期限内提供**运营服务**。

8.3
进度计划

承包商应在收到根据**第 8.1 款**［*开工日期*］规定发出的**通知**后 28 天内，向**雇主代表**提交一份详细的时间进度计划。当原进度计划与实际进度，或与**承包商**义务不相符时，**承包商**还应提交一份修订计划。每份进度计划应包括：

（a） **承包商**计划实施工程的工作顺序，包括设计、**承包商文件**、采购、制造、检验、交付到**现场**、施工、安装、试验、调试和试运行等每个阶段的预期时间安排；

(b) the period of Operation Service;
(c) the periods for reviews under Sub-Clause 5.2 [*Contractor's Documents*] and for any other submissions, including the supply of samples in accordance with Sub-Clause 7.2 [*Samples*], approvals and consents specified in the Employer's Requirements;

(d) the sequence and timing of inspections and tests specified in the Contract, and
(e) a supporting report which includes:

  (i) a general description of the methods which the Contractor intends to adopt for both the Design-Build and the Operation Service;
  (ii) details showing the Contractor's reasonable estimate of the number of each class of Contractor's Personnel and of each type of Contractor's Equipment, required on the Site for each major stage; and
  (iii) the Contractor's proposed manning schedule for the Operation Service.

Unless the Employer's Representative, within 21 days after receiving a programme, gives Notice to the Contractor stating the extent to which it does not comply with the Contract, the Contractor shall proceed in accordance with the programme, subject to his other obligations under the Contract. The Employer's Personnel shall be entitled to rely upon the programme when planning their activities.

If, at any time, the Employer's Representative gives Notice to the Contractor that a programme fails (to the extent stated) to comply with the Contract or to be consistent with actual progress and the Contractor's stated intentions, the Contractor shall submit, within 14 days, a revised programme to the Employer's Representative in accordance with this Sub-Clause.

8.4
Advance Warning

Each Party shall endeavour to advise the other Party in advance of any known or probable future events or circumstances which may adversely affect the work, increase the Contract Price or delay the execution of the Works or the Operation Service. The Employer's Representative may require the Contractor to submit an estimate of the anticipated effect of the future events or circumstances, and/or a proposal under Sub-Clause 13.3 [*Variation Procedure*].

8.5
Delay Damages

If the Contractor fails to complete the Design-Build in accordance with the requirements of Sub-Clause 9.2 [*Time for Completion of Design-Build*], he shall pay delay damages as detailed in Sub-Clause 9.6 [*Delay Damages relating to Design-Build*].

If the Contractor fails or is unable to provide the Operation Service for the complete period specified in the Contract, or parts of the Operation Service, and such failure is:

(a) due to a cause for which the Contractor is responsible; and
(b) results in the Employer losing revenue or income which the Employer would normally have expected to receive during the Operation Service Period; or
(c) results in the Employer suffering any other loss which he would not have suffered but for such failure,

(b) 运营服务期；
(c) 根据第5.2款[*承包商文件*]规定的审核期，以及任何其他提交文件的期限，包括根据第7.2款[*样品*]的规定提供样品，**雇主要求**中规定的批准和同意；

(d) 合同中规定的各项检验和试验的顺序和时间安排；（以及）

(e) 一份支持报告，内容包括：

（i）**承包商**在**设计-施工和运营服务**中拟采用的方法的一般描述（说明）；
（ii）**承包商**对各主要阶段**现场**所需各级**承包商人员**和各类**承包商设备**合理估计数量的详细情况；（以及）

（iii）**承包商**建议的**运营服务**人员配备计划。

除非**雇主代表**在收到进度计划后21天内向**承包商**发出**通知**，指出其中不符合**合同**规定的部分，**承包商**应按照进度计划进行工作，并应遵守**合同**规定的**承包商**其他义务。**雇主人员**应有权依照进度计划安排他们的活动。

如果任何时候**雇主代表**向**承包商**发出**通知**，指出进度计划（在规定的范围内）不符合**合同**要求，或与实际进度和**承包商**的意图不一致时，**承包商**应在14天内，按照本款的规定向**雇主代表**提交一份修订的进度计划。

8.4 预先警示

任何一方应尽力在任何已知的或可能将要发生的未来事件或情况之前，将可能对工作产生不利影响、提高**合同价格**或延误**工程**施工或**运营服务**的事件或情况，通知另一方。**雇主代表**可要求**承包商**提交对未来事件或情况预期影响的估算，和/或根据第13.3款[*变更程序*]的规定提交建议书。

8.5 误期损害赔偿费

如果**承包商**未能按照第9.2款[*设计-施工竣工时间*]的要求完成**设计-施工**，**承包商**应按照第9.6款[*设计-施工的误期损害赔偿费*]的规定，支付误期损害赔偿费。

如果**承包商**未能履行或无法在**合同**规定的完整期限内提供**运营服务**或部分**运营服务**，且此类未能履行是：

（a）由于**承包商**负责的原因；（和）
（b）导致**雇主**损失其在**运营服务**期间通常预期会收到的收益或收入；（或）

（c）导致**雇主**遭受任何其他损失，如果没有这种失误，**雇主**是不会遭受损失的；

then the Contractor shall pay to the Employer compensation in accordance with Sub-Clause 10.6 [*Delays and Interruptions during the Operation Service*].

8.6 Contract Completion Certificate

Performance of the Contractor's obligations in respect of the Contract shall not be considered to have been completed until the Contract Completion Certificate has been signed by the Employer's Representative and issued to the Contractor, stating the date on which the Contractor completed his obligations in respect of both the Design-Build and the Operation Service (Contract Completion Date).

The Employer's Representative shall, subject to Sub-Clause 11.8 [*Joint Inspection Prior to Contract Completion*], Sub-Clause 10.8 [*Completion of Operation Service*] and Sub-Clause 4.23 [*Contractor's Operations on Site*], issue the Contract Completion Certificate to the Contractor, with a copy to the Employer, within 21 days after the last day of the Contract Period. No extension of the Operation Service Period shall be allowed except by written agreement between the Parties.

Only the Contract Completion Certificate shall be deemed to constitute the Employer's acceptance of the Contractor's completion of his obligations under the Contract. Following the issue of the Contract Completion Certificate the Employer shall be fully responsible for the care, safety, operation, servicing and maintenance of the Works.

8.7 Handback Requirements

The Contractor shall ensure that the Works comply with the handback requirements specified in the Employer's Requirements prior to the issue of the Contract Completion Certificate.

8.8 Unfulfilled Obligations

After the Contract Completion Certificate has been issued, each Party shall remain liable for the fulfilment of any obligation under the Contract which remains unperformed at that time. For the purposes of determining the nature and extent of unperformed obligations, the Contract shall be deemed to remain in force.

9 Design-Build

9.1 Commencement of Design-Build

The Contractor shall commence the design and execution of the Works within 28 days of the Commencement Date, and shall then proceed with the Design-Build with due expedition and without delay.

9.2 Time for Completion of Design-Build

The Contractor shall complete the whole of the Design-Build of the Works, and each Section (if any), within the Time for Completion of Design-Build of the Works or Section (as the case may be) as set out in the Contract Data, including:

(a) passing the Tests on Completion under Sub-Clause 11.1 [*Testing of the Works*];
(b) completing all work which is stated in the Contract as being required under Sub-Clause 11.5 [*Completion of the Works and Sections*]; and
(c) preparation and delivery to the Employer's Representative of Contractor's Documents required under Sub-Clause 5.2 [*Contractor's Documents*].

则**承包商**应根据第10.6款[*运营服务期间的延误和中断*]的规定，向**雇主**支付赔偿金。

| 8.6 合同完成证书 | 在**雇主代表**签署**合同完成证书**并发给**承包商**之前，**承包商**根据合同中规定履行的义务不得视为已完成，**合同完成证书**说明**承包商**完成**设计-施工**和**运营服务**义务的日期（**合同完成日期**）。

雇主代表应在**合同期**最后一天后的21天内，根据第11.8款[*合同完成前的联合检验*]、第10.8款[*运营服务的完成*]和第4.23款[*承包商的现场作业*]的规定，向**承包商**签发**合同完成证书**，并向**雇主**提供一份副本。**运营服务期**不允许延长，双方有书面协议书除外。

只有**合同完成证书**应被视为构成**雇主**接受**承包商**完成其在合同中规定的义务。签发**合同完成证书**后，**雇主**将对**工程**的照管、安全、运营、服务和维护负全责。

| 8.7 移交要求 | 在签发**合同完成证书**前，**承包商**应确保**工程**符合**雇主要求**中规定的移交要求。

| 8.8 未履行的义务 | **合同完成证书**签发后，各方仍应负责履行合同规定的当时仍未履行的任何义务。为确定未履行义务的性质和范围，本合同应视为继续有效。

9　设计-施工

| 9.1 设计-施工的开始 | **承包商**应在**开工日期**后28天内开始**工程**的设计和实施。然后，应尽快进行**设计-施工**，不得延误。

| 9.2 设计-施工竣工时间 | **承包商**应在**合同数据**中规定的**工程**或**分项工程**（视情况而定）的**设计-施工竣工时间**内，完成整个**工程**的**设计-施工**，以及每个**分项工程**（如果有），包括：

（a）通过第11.1款[*工程试验*]规定的竣工试验；

（b）完成合同中规定的第11.5款[*工程和分项工程的竣工*]要求的所有工作；（以及）

（c）准备并向**雇主代表**提交第5.2款[*承包商文件*]规定的**承包商文件**。

9.3 Extension of Time for Completion of Design-Build

The Contractor shall be entitled, subject to Sub-Clause 20.1 [*Contractor's Claims*], to an extension of the Time for Completion of Design-Build if and to the extent that completion for the purposes of Sub-Clause 11.5 [*Completion of the Works and Sections*] is or will be delayed by any of the following causes:

(a) a Variation (unless an adjustment to the Time for Completion of Design-Build has been agreed under Sub-Clause 13.3 [*Variation Procedure*]);
(b) a cause of delay giving an entitlement to extension of time under a Sub-Clause of these Conditions;
(c) exceptionally adverse climatic conditions;
(d) Unforeseeable shortages in the availability of personnel or Goods caused by epidemic or governmental actions; or
(e) any delay, impediment or prevention caused by or attributable to the Employer, the Employer's Personnel, or the Employer's other contractors on the Site

If the Contractor considers himself to be entitled to an extension of the Time for Completion of Design-Build, the Contractor shall give Notice to the Employer's Representative in accordance with Sub-Clause 20.1 [*Contractor's Claims*]. When determining each extension of time, the Employer's Representative shall review previous determinations and may increase, but shall not decrease, the total extension of time.

If a Dispute regarding an extension of time has been referred to the DAB, the Contractor shall be immediately entitled to any extension of the Time for Completion of Design-Build which is decided by the DAB under Sub-Clause 20.6 [*Obtaining Dispute Adjudication Board's Decision*].

9.4 Delays Caused by Authorities

If the following conditions apply during the Design-Build Period, namely:

(a) the Contractor has diligently followed the procedures laid down by the relevant legally constituted public and/or local authorities in the Country;
(b) these authorities delay or disrupt the Contractor's work; and
(c) the delay or disruption was Unforeseeable,

then this delay or disruption will be considered as a cause of delay under subparagraph (b) of Sub-Clause 9.3 [*Extension of Time for Completion of Design-Build*].

9.5 Rate of Progress

If, in the opinion of the Employer's Representative, at any time during the Design-Build Period:

(a) actual progress is too slow to complete within the Time for Completion of Design-Build; and/or
(b) progress has fallen (or will fall) behind the current programme under Sub-Clause 8.3 [*Programme*],

other than as a result of a cause listed in Sub-Clause 9.3 [*Extension of Time for Completion of Design-Build*], then the Employer's Representative may instruct the Contractor to submit, under Sub-Clause 8.3 [*Programme*], a revised programme and supporting report describing the revised methods which the Contractor proposes to adopt in order to expedite progress and complete within the Time for Completion of Design-Build.

9.3
设计 - 施工竣工时间的延长

如果由于下述任何原因，致使第 11.5 款［*工程和分项工程的竣工*］要求的竣工受到或将受到延误，**承包商**应有权按照第 20.1 款［*承包商索赔*］的规定，获得**设计 - 施工竣工时间**的延长：

(a) **变更**（除非已根据第 13.3 款［*变更程序*］的规定商定调整了**设计 - 施工竣工时间**）；

(b) 根据本**条件**某款，有权获得延长期的原因；

(c) 异常不利的气候条件；

(d) 由于流行病或政府行为造成可用的人员或**货物**的**不可预见**的短缺；（或）

(e) 由**雇主**、**雇主人员**，或在**现场**的雇主的其他承包商造成或引起的任何延误、妨碍或阻碍。

如果**承包商**认为自己有权提出延长**设计 - 施工竣工时间**，**承包商**应按照第 20.1 款［*承包商索赔*］的规定，向**雇主代表**发出**通知**，在确定每次延长时间时，**雇主代表**应对以前所做的确定进行审核，可以增加，但不得减少总的延长时间。

如果有关延长时间的**争端**已提交**争端裁决委员会**，**承包商**应立即有权获得**争端裁决委员会**根据第 20.6 款［*取得争端裁决委员会的决定*］的规定，决定的任何**设计 - 施工竣工时间**的延长。

9.4
部门造成的延误

在**设计 - 施工**期间如果下列条件成立，即：

(a) **承包商**已努力遵守了**工程**所在国依法成立的有关公共和/或地方部门制定的程序；

(b) 这些部门延误或扰乱了**承包商**的工作；（以及）

(c) 延误或中断是**不可预见**的，

则上述延误或中断可视为根据第 9.3 款［*设计 - 施工竣工时间的延长*］(b) 段规定的延误的原因。

9.5
工程进度

如果**雇主代表**认为，在**设计 - 施工**期间的任何时候：

(a) 实际进度过慢，未能在**设计 - 施工竣工时间**内完成；（和/或）

(b) 进度已（或将）落后于根据第 8.3 款［*进度计划*］的规定制订的现行进度计划，

除由于第 9.3 款［*设计 - 施工竣工时间的延长*］中列举的某项原因造成的结果外，**雇主代表**可指示**承包商**根据第 8.3 款［*进度计划*］的规定提交一份修订的进度计划，以及说明**承包商**为加快进度在**设计 - 施工竣工时间**内竣工，而建议采用的修订方法的证明报告。

Unless the Employer's Representative notifies otherwise, the Contractor shall adopt these revised methods, which may require increases in the working hours and/or in the numbers of Contractor's Personnel and/or Goods, at the risk and cost of the Contractor. If these revised methods cause the Employer to incur additional costs, the Contractor shall, subject to Sub-Clause 20.2 [*Employer's Claims*], pay these costs to the Employer, in addition to delay damages (if any) under Sub-Clause 9.6 [*Delay Damages relating to Design-Build*] below.

9.6 Delay Damages relating to Design-Build

If the Contractor fails to comply with Sub-Clause 9.2 [*Time for Completion of Design-Build*], the Contractor shall, subject to Sub-Clause 20.2 [*Employer's Claims*], pay delay damages to the Employer for this default. These delay damages shall be the amount stated in the Contract Data, which shall be paid for every day which shall elapse between the relevant Time for Completion and the date stated in the Commissioning Certificate. However, the total amount due under this Sub-Clause shall not exceed the maximum amount of delay damages (if any) stated in the Contract Data.

These delay damages shall be the only damages due from the Contractor for such default, other than in the event of termination under Clause 15 [*Termination by Employer*] prior to completion of the Works. These damages shall not relieve the Contractor from his obligation to complete the Design-Build and the Operation Service, or from any other duties, obligations or responsibilities which he may have under the Contract.

9.7 Suspension of Work

The Employer's Representative may at any time instruct the Contractor to suspend progress of part or all of the Works. During such suspension, the Contractor shall protect, store, secure and maintain such part or the Works against any deterioration, loss or damage.

The Employer's Representative shall also notify the cause for the suspension. If and to the extent that the cause is the responsibility of the Contractor, the following Sub-Clauses 9.8, 9.9 and 9.10 shall not apply.

9.8 Consequences of Suspension

If, during the Design-Build Period, the Contractor suffers delay and/or incurs cost from complying with the Employer's Representative's instructions under Sub-Clause 9.7 [*Suspension of Work*] and/or from resuming the work, the Contractor shall give Notice to the Employer's Representative and shall be entitled, subject to Sub-Clause 20.1 [*Contractor's Claims*], to:

(a) an extension of time for any such delay, if completion is or will be delayed, under Sub-Clause 9.3 [*Extension of Time for Completion of Design-Build*]; and

(b) payment of any such Cost, which shall be included in the Contract Price.

After receiving this Notice, the Employer's Representative shall proceed in accordance with Sub-Clause 3.5 [*Determinations*] to agree or determine these matters.

The Contractor shall not be entitled to an extension of time for, or to payment of the Cost incurred in, making good the consequences of the Contractor's faulty design, workmanship or materials, or of the Contractor's failure to protect, store or secure in accordance with Sub-Clause 9.7 [*Suspension of Work*].

除非**雇主代表**另有通知，**承包商**应采用这些修订的方法，对可能需要增加工时和 / 或**承包商人员**和 / 或**货物**的数量，**承包商**应自行承担风险和费用。如果这些修订的方法使**雇主**招致额外费用，**承包商**根据第 20.2 款［*雇主索赔*］的规定，连同下述第 9.6 款［*设计 - 施工的误期损害赔偿费*］规定的误期损害赔偿费（如果有），向**雇主**支付这些费用。

9.6 设计 - 施工的误期损害赔偿费

如果**承包商**未能遵守第 9.2 款［*设计 - 施工竣工时间*］的要求，**承包商**应当为其违约行为根据第 20.2 款［*雇主索赔*］的规定，向**雇主**支付误期损害赔偿费。误期损害赔偿费应按**合同数据**中规定的每天应付的金额，以**调试证书**竣工日期超过相应**竣工时间**的天数计算。但按本款计算的赔偿总额不得超过**合同数据**中规定的误期损害赔偿费的最高限额（如果有）。

除在**工程竣工**前根据第 15 条［*由雇主终止*］的规定终止的情况外，这些误期损害赔偿费应是**承包商**为此类违约应付的唯一损害赔偿费。这些误期损害赔偿费不应免除**承包商**完成**设计 - 施工和运营服务**的义务，或**合同**规定的其可能承担的任何其他任务、义务或责任。

9.7 暂时停工

雇主代表可以随时指示**承包商**暂停**工程**某一部分或全部的施工进度，在暂停期间，**承包商**应保护、保管、保证安全并维护该部分或全部**工程**不致产生任何变质、损失或损害。

如果暂停的原因是由于**承包商**的责任造成的，**雇主代表**还应通知暂停的原因，则下列第 9.8 款、第 9.9 款和第 9.10 款应不适用。

9.8 暂停的后果

在**设计 - 施工**期间，如果**承包商**因执行**雇主代表**根据第 9.7 款［*暂时停工*］的规定发出的指示，和 / 或因复工而遭受延误和 / 或招致增加费用，**承包商**应向**雇主代表**发出通知，并有权根据第 20.1 款［*承包商索赔*］的规定，获得：

（a） 根据第 9.3 款［*设计 - 施工竣工时间的延长*］的规定，如竣工已或将受到延误，应对任何此类延误，给予延长期；（以及）

（b） 任何此类**费用**应计入**合同价格**，给予支付。

雇主代表收到此类**通知**后，应按照第 3.5 款［*确定*］的要求，对这些事项进行商定或确定。

为弥补因**承包商**有缺陷的设计、工艺或材料，或因**承包商**未能按照第 9.7 款［*暂时停工*］的规定保护、保管或保证安全的后果，**承包商**无权得到延长期或由其带来的招致**费用**的支付。

9.9 Payment for Plant and Materials in Event of Suspension

The Contractor shall be entitled to payment of the value (as at the date of suspension) of Plant and/or Materials which have not been delivered to Site, if:

(a) the work on Plant or delivery of Plant and/or Materials has been suspended for more than 28 days; and
(b) the Contractor has marked the Plant and/or Materials as the Employer's property in accordance with the Employer's Representative's instructions.

Payment for Plant and/or Materials made pursuant to this Sub-Clause shall, if requested by the Employer's Representative, be subject to the production of satisfactory evidence by the Contractor that the said Plant and/or Materials are fully owned by the Contractor and are not subject to any retention of title by the supplier.

9.10 Prolonged Suspension

If the suspension under Sub-Clause 9.7 [*Suspension of Work*] has continued for more than 84 days, the Contractor may request the Employer's Representative's permission to proceed. If the Employer's Representative does not give permission within 28 days after being requested to do so, the Contractor may, by giving Notice to the Employer's Representative, treat the suspension as an omission under Clause 13 [*Variations and Adjustments*] of the affected part of the Works. If the suspension affects the whole of the Works, the Contractor may give Notice of termination under Sub-Clause 16.2 [*Termination by Contractor*].

9.11 Resumption of Work

After the permission or instruction to proceed is given, the Contractor and the Employer's Representative shall jointly examine the Works and the Plant and Materials affected by the suspension. The Contractor shall make good any deterioration or defect in or loss of the Works or Plant or Materials, which has occurred during the suspension. The Employer's Representative shall make a written record of all making good required to be carried out by the Contractor.

9.12 Completion of Design-Build

The Design-Build shall not be considered as complete until all of the following are achieved:

(a) the Works have been fully designed and executed in accordance with the Employer's Requirements and other relevant provisions of the Contract;
(b) the Works have passed the Tests on Completion of Design-Build in accordance with Sub-Clause 11.1 [*Testing of the Works*];
(c) Contractor's Documents in accordance with Sub-Clause 5.5 [*As-Built Documents*] and Sub-Clause 5.6 [*Operation and Maintenance Manuals*] have been supplied and approved by the Employer's Representative; and
(d) the Commissioning Certificate required under Sub-Clause 11.7 [*Commissioning Certificate*] has been issued stating the date upon which the Design-Build has been completed and the Operation Service shall commence.

9.13 Failure to Complete

Should the Contractor fail to complete the Design-Build prior to the Cut-Off Date, the Employer may, at his sole option, either:

9.9 暂停时对生产设备和材料的付款		承包商应有权获得尚未交付现场的生产设备和/或材料（按暂停的日期时）的价值的付款：

(a) **生产设备**的生产或**生产设备**和/或**材料**的交付被暂停达 28 天以上；（以及）
(b) **承包商**已按**雇主代表**的指示，标明上述**生产设备**和/或**材料**为**雇主**的财产。

如果**雇主代表**要求，根据本款支付的**生产设备**和/或**材料**应以**承包商**提供满意的证据为准，证明上述**生产设备**和/或**材料**完全属于**承包商**所有，且供应商不保留任何所有权。

9.10 拖长的暂停		如果第 9.7 款 [*暂时停工*] 所述的暂停已持续 84 天以上，**承包商**可要求**雇主代表**允许继续施工。如果在提出这一要求后 28 天内，**雇主代表**没有给予许可，**承包商**可以通知**雇主代表**，将工程受暂停影响的部分视为根据第 13 条 [*变更和调整*] 规定的删减项目。如果暂停影响到整个工程，**承包商**可根据第 16.2 款 [*由承包商终止*] 的规定发出终止通知。

9.11 复工		在发出继续施工的许可或指示后，**承包商**和**雇主代表**应共同对受暂停影响的**工程、生产设备**和**材料**进行检查。**承包商**应负责修复暂停期间发生在**工程、生产设备**或**材料**中的任何变质、缺陷或损失。**雇主代表**应书面记录要求**承包商**进行的所有修复工作。

9.12 设计-施工的竣工		在达到以下所有条件之前，**设计-施工**不应认为完成：

(a) 工程已完全按照**雇主要求**和合同其他相关规定进行设计和实施；

(b) 工程已根据第 11.1 款 [*工程试验*] 的规定，通过了**设计-施工竣工试验**；
(c) **雇主代表**已提供并批准了符合第 5.5 款 [*竣工文件*] 和第 5.6 款 [*操作和维护手册*] 规定要求的**承包商文件**；（以及）

(d) 根据第 11.7 款 [*调试证书*] 规定要求的**调试证书**已签发，说明**设计-施工**已完成的日期和**运营服务**应开始。

9.13 未能竣工		如果**承包商**未能在**截止日期**前完成**设计-施工**，**雇主**可自行选择：

(a) permit the Contractor to continue the Design-Build for a further named period, with an absolute right to re-apply this Sub-Clause in the event that the Contractor fails to complete the Design-Build within the extended period; or

(b) terminate the Contract in accordance with Sub-Clause 15.2 [*Termination for Contractor's Default*] and, if he so chooses, complete the work and subsequently execute the Operation Service himself or by engaging others.

In either case, the Employer will be entitled to recover from the Contractor any direct loss incurred, including any loss resulting from the delayed operation of the Works, subject to the limitations contained in Sub-Clause 9.6 [*Delay Damages Relating to Design-Build*] and Sub-Clause 17.8 [*Limitation of Liability*].

10 Operation Service

10.1 General Requirements

The Contractor shall comply with the Operation Management Requirements as provided for in the Contract and any revisions thereof which are agreed during the Contract Period.

The Contractor shall follow the requirements of the Operation and Maintenance Plan and the operation and maintenance manuals. No significant alteration to such arrangements and methods shall be made without the prior approval of the Employer's Representative.

During the Operation Service, the Contractor shall be responsible for ensuring that the Works remain fit for the purposes for which they are intended.

The operators and maintenance personnel for the Works, including Plant operators, shall have the appropriate experience and qualifications to perform the Operation Service. The names, with details of their qualifications and experience, of all operation and maintenance personnel shall be submitted to the Employer for approval, and no such personnel shall be engaged prior to receiving such approval.

10.2 Commencement of Operation Service

Unless otherwise stated in the Employer's Requirements, the commencement of the Operation Service shall be from the date stated in the Commissioning Certificate issued under Sub-Clause 11.7 [*Commissioning Certificate*].

The Operation Service shall not commence until the Design-Build of the Works or any Sections has been completed in accordance with Sub-Clause 9.12 [*Completion of Design-Build*].

Should the Commissioning Certificate, or any Notice attached or pertaining thereto, contain requirements or restrictions over and above those in the Contract, the Contractor shall comply with such requirements and/or restrictions, and, to the extent that the Contractor suffers additional Cost as a result, and subject to the provisions of Sub-Clause 20.1 [*Contractor's Claims*], he shall be reimbursed by the Employer unless such requirements or restrictions were as a result of a fault or failure of the Contractor.

The Contractor shall thereafter provide the Operation Service in compliance with the Operation Management Requirements and in accordance with Sub-Clause 5.5 [*As-Built Documents*] and Sub-Clause 5.6 [*Operation and Maintenance Manuals*].

(a) 允许**承包商**在进一步指定的期限内继续**设计 - 施工**，如果**承包商**未能在延长的期限内完成**设计 - 施工**，则**雇主**有绝对权利重新适用**本款**；（或）

(b) 根据第 15.2 款［*由承包商违约的终止*］的规定终止**合同**，如果**承包商**选择终止**合同**，则完成工作并随后自行或通过雇佣其他人来执行**运营服务**。

在任何一种情况下，**雇主**均有权根据第 9.6 款［*设计 - 施工的误期损害赔偿费*］和第 17.8 款［*责任限度*］中所述的限额，向**承包商**追偿所产生的任何直接损失，包括因**工程**延误运营所造成的任何损失。

10 运营服务

10.1 一般要求

承包商应遵守**合同**中规定的**运营管理要求**以及在**合同期间**商定的任何修订。

承包商应遵守**运营和维护计划**以及**操作和维护手册**的要求。未经**雇主代表**事先批准，不得对此类安排和方法做出重大改变。

在**运营服务**期间，**承包商**应负责确保**工程**符合其预期目的。

工程的运营人员和维护人员，包括**生产设备**运营人员，应具有从事**运营服务**的适当经验和资质。所有运营和维护人员的姓名及其资质和经验详细资料应提交给**雇主**批准，在获得此类批准前，不得雇佣此类人员。

10.2 运营服务的开始

除非**雇主要求**中另有规定，**运营服务**应从根据第 11.7 款［*调试证书*］签发的**调试证书**中规定的日期开始。

在按照第 9.12 款［*设计 - 施工的竣工*］的规定，完成**工程**或任何分项**工程**的**设计 - 施工**之前，**运营服务**不得开始。

如果**调试证书**或随附的或与之相关的任何**通知**中包含超出**合同**规定的要求或限制，**承包商**应遵守此类要求和 / 或限制，并且，在**承包商**因此遭受增加额外**费用**的情况下，除非此类要求或限制是由于**承包商**的过失或失误造成的，否则根据第 20.1 款［*承包商索赔*］的规定，**承包商**有权要求**雇主**补偿增加额外的**费用**。

此后，**承包商**应按照**运营管理要求**和第 5.5 款［*竣工文件*］和第 5.6 款［*操作和维护手册*］的要求提供**运营服务**。

If the Contractor wishes to modify a document which has previously been submitted and approved, the Contractor shall immediately notify the Employer's Representative, and shall subsequently submit revised document(s) to the Employer's Representative for review accompanied by a written explanation of the need for such modification.

The Contractor shall not implement any proposed modification in accordance with subparagraph (d) of Sub-Clause 5.2 [*Contractor's Documents*] until such modification has been reviewed by the Employer's Representative, and consent to proceed has been given in writing. However, any such approval or consent, or any review (under this Sub-Clause or otherwise), shall not relieve the Contractor from any obligation or responsibility.

10.3 Independent Compliance Audit

At least 182 days prior to the commencement of the Operation Service, the Employer and the Contractor shall jointly appoint the Auditing Body to carry out an independent and impartial audit during the Operation Service. The terms of appointment of the Auditing Body shall be included in the Employer's Requirements, and the purpose will be to audit and monitor the performance of both the Employer and the Contractor during the Operation Service in compliance with the Operation Management Requirements. If the Parties cannot agree on the appointment of the Auditing Body, the matter shall be referred to the DAB by the Parties. The DAB shall make the appointment and notify the Parties accordingly.

The Auditing Body shall commence its duties on the same date as the Operation Service commences.

Payment of the Auditing Body shall be made from the Provisional Sum included in the Contract for that purpose.

Both Parties shall cooperate with the Auditing Body and give due regard to the matters raised in each report issued by the Auditing Body.

10.4 Delivery of Raw Materials

The Employer shall be responsible for the free issue and supply and delivery to the Site (or other designated place) of the raw materials, fuels, consumables and other such items specified in the Employer's Requirements. The Employer shall be responsible that all such items are fit for purpose and comply with the requirements of the Contract in respect of quality, purpose and function.

In the event that any such item or product is not delivered in accordance with the agreed delivery programme or deviates from the specified quality, and such delay or deviation causes the Contractor to suffer additional cost, the Contractor shall be entitled to give due notice to the Employer of the nature of the costs which he has incurred and, subject to Sub-Clause 20.1 [*Contractor's Claims*], be entitled to recover his Cost Plus Profit.

The provisions of this Sub-Clause shall not apply in cases where delays are due to:

(a) breakdown, maintenance, repair, replacement or other operational failure under the responsibility of the Contractor;
(b) health, safety and environmental risks carried by the Contractor; or
(c) any act or omission of the Contractor under the Contract.

10.5 Training

The Contractor shall carry out the training of Employer's Personnel in the operation and maintenance of the Works to the extent specified in the Employer's Requirements.

如果**承包商**希望修改先前提交和批准的文件，**承包商**应立即通知**雇主代表**，并随后将修改后的文件提交给**雇主代表**审核，并附上书面说明，说明修改的必要性。

承包商不得按照第 5.2 款 [*承包商文件*]（d）段的规定进行拟议的修改，直到**雇主代表**对此类修改进行了审核，并以书面形式同意继续进行。但是，任何此类批准或同意，或任何审核（根据**本款**或其他规定），不应免除**承包商**的任何义务或责任。

10.3 独立合规审计	在**运营服务**开始前至少 182 天，**雇主**和**承包商**应共同指定**审计机构**在**运营服务**期间进行独立和公正的审计。**审计机构**的任命条款应包括在**雇主要求**中，其目的是根据运营管理要求，对**雇主**和**承包商**在**运营服务**期间的表现进行审计和监督。如果双方不能就**审计机构**的任命达成一致意见，则应将此事提交**争端裁决委员会**。**争端裁决委员会**应做出任命并相应地通知**双方**。 **审计机构**应于**运营服务**开始之日起开始执行其任务。 **审计机构**的付款应从**合同**中为此目的的列入的**暂列金额**中支付。 双方应与**审计机构**合作，并适当考虑**审计机构**出具的每份报告中提出的事项。
10.4 原材料的交付	**雇主**应负责免费发放、供应和交付**雇主要求**中规定的原材料、燃料、消耗品和其他此类物品至**现场**（或其他指定地点）。**雇主**负责所有此类项目符合目的，并符合**合同**关于质量、目的和功能的要求。 如果任何此类事项或产品未能按照商定的交付计划交付或偏离规定的质量，并且此类延误或偏离导致**承包商**承担额外费用，**承包商**应有权根据第 20.1 款 [*承包商索赔*] 的规定，向**雇主**发出其所产生费用性质的适当通知，收回其**成本加利润**。 **本款**的规定不适用于由于下列原因造成的延误： （a） **承包商**负责的故障、维护、修理、更换或其他操作故障； （b） **承包商**承担的健康、安全和环境风险；（或） （c） **承包商**在**合同**中规定的任何作为或不作为。
10.5 培训	**承包商**应按照**雇主要求**中规定的范围，对**雇主人员**进行工程操作和维护培训。

The programme and scheduling of the training shall be agreed with the Employer, and the Contractor shall provide experienced training staff, and all training materials as stated in the Employer's Requirements. The Employer shall be responsible for providing the training facilities and nominating and selecting suitable personnel for training.

10.6 Delays and Interruptions during the Operation Service

Delays and interruptions during the Operation Service shall be agreed and determined as follows:

(a) Delays or Interruptions caused by the Contractor

If there are any delays or interruptions during the Operation Service which are caused by the Contractor or by a cause for which the Contractor is responsible, the Contractor shall compensate the Employer for any losses including loss of revenue, loss of profit and overhead losses. The amount of compensation due shall be agreed or determined according to Sub-Clause 3.5 [*Determinations*], and the Employer shall be entitled to recover the amount due by making a corresponding deduction from the next payment due to the Contractor. However, the total amount of compensation payable by the Contractor to the Employer shall not exceed the amount stated in the Contract Data. There will be no extension of the period of the Operation Service as a result of any such delay or interruption.

(b) Delays or Interruptions caused by the Employer

If there are any delays or interruptions during the Operation Service which are caused by the Employer or by a cause for which the Employer is responsible, the Employer shall compensate the Contractor for any cost and losses including loss of revenue and loss of profit. The amount of compensation due shall be agreed or determined according to Sub-Clause 3.5 [*Determinations*], and the Employer shall pay the amount due by making a corresponding adjustment to the next payment due to the Contractor. In any event other than in the case of election by the Employer to terminate for his convenience pursuant to Sub-Clause 15.5 [*Termination for Employer's Convenience*], the total amount of compensation payable by the Employer to the Contractor shall not exceed the amount stated in the Contract Data. There will be no extension of the period of the Operation Service as a result of any such delay or interruption.

(c) Suspension by the Employer

The Employer's Representative may at any time during the Operation Service instruct the Contractor to suspend progress of the Operation Service. During such suspension, the Contractor shall protect, store, secure and maintain the Plant against any deterioration, loss or damage.

If the need to suspend the Operation Service by the Employer is due to any failure of the Contractor or circumstances for which the Contractor is responsible under the Contract, the provisions of paragraph (a) of this Sub-Clause shall apply.

If the need to suspend the Operation Service is a result neither of any failure by the Contractor nor of circumstances for which the Contractor is responsible under the Contract, the provisions of paragraph (b) of this Sub-Clause shall apply.

培训进度计划和时间表应与**雇主**商定，**承包商**应提供经验丰富的培训人员，以及**雇主要求**中规定的所有培训材料。**雇主**应负责提供培训设施，并提名和选择合适的培训人员。

10.6
运营服务期间的延误和中断

运营服务期间的延误和中断应按以下商定和确定：

(a) 由**承包商**造成的**延误**或**中断**

如果在**运营服务期**间，由于**承包商**或**承包商**负责的原因造成任何延误或中断，**承包商**应赔偿**雇主**的任何损失，包括收入损失、利润损失和管理费损失。应支付的赔偿金，应根据第 3.5 款［*确定*］的规定商定或确定，并且**雇主**有权从应付给**承包商**的下一笔付款中扣除相应金额，以收回应付金额。但是，**承包商**应向**雇主**支付的赔偿总额不应超过**合同数据**中规定的金额。**运营服务**期不会因任何此类延误或中断而延长。

(b) 由**雇主**造成的**延误**或**中断**

如果在**运营服务期**间，由于**雇主**或**雇主**负责的原因造成任何延误或中断，**雇主**应赔偿**承包商**的任何费用和损失，包括收入损失和利润损失。应支付的赔偿金，应根据第 3.5 款［*确定*］的规定商定或确定，**雇主**应通过对应付给**承包商**的下一笔付款做出相应调整来支付应付金额，在任何情况下，除**雇主**根据第 15.5 款［*为雇主便利的终止*］的规定为其便利而选择终止外，**雇主**应向**承包商**支付的赔偿总额不应超过**合同数据**中规定的金额。**运营服务**期不会因任何此类延误或中断而延长。

(c) 由**雇主**暂停

雇主代表可在运营服务期间的任何时候指示**承包商**暂停**运营服务**的进度，在此类暂停期间，**承包商**应保护、保管、保证安全并维护**生产设备**，使其免受任何变质、损失或损害。

如果**雇主**需要暂停**运营服务**是由于**承包商**的任何失误，或**承包商**根据**合同**规定应负责的情况，则本款（a）段的规定应适用。

如果暂停**运营服务**的需要既不是由于**承包商**的任何失误，也不是由于**承包商**根据**合同**规定应负责的情况，则本款（b）段的规定应适用。

If a suspension, which is due neither to any failure by the Contractor nor to circumstances for which the Contractor is responsible under the Contract, has continued for more than 84 days, the Contractor may request the Employer's Representative's permission to proceed. If the Employer's Representative does not give permission within 28 days after being requested to do so, the Contractor may give Notice of termination under Sub-Clause 16.2 [*Termination by Contractor*].

After the permission or instruction to proceed is given, the Contractor and the Employer's Representative shall jointly examine the Works. The Contractor shall make good any deterioration or defect in the Plant and the Employer's Representative shall make a written record of all making good required to be carried out by the Contractor. If the suspension is due neither to any failure by the Contractor nor to circumstances for which the Contractor is responsible under the Contract, the Contractor shall be entitled to be paid the Cost Plus Profit of making good the Works prior to re-commencing the Operation Service.

10.7 Failure to Reach Production Outputs

In the event that the Contractor fails to achieve the production outputs required under the Contract, the Parties shall jointly establish the cause of such failure.

(a) If the cause of the failure lies with the Employer or any of his servants or agents, then, after consultation with the Contractor, the Employer shall give written instruction to the Contractor of the measures which the Employer requires the Contractor to take.

If the Contractor suffers any additional cost as a result of the failure or the measures instructed by the Employer, the Employer, subject to Sub-Clause 3.5 [*Determinations*] and Sub-Clause 20.1 [*Contractor's Claims*], shall pay the Contractor his Cost Plus Profit.

(b) If the cause of the failure lies with the Contractor then, after due consultation with the Employer, the Contractor shall take all steps necessary to restore the output to the levels required under the Contract.

If the Employer suffers any loss as a result of the failure or the measures taken by the Contractor, the Contractor, subject to Sub-Clause 3.5 [*Determinations*], shall pay the Employer the performance damages specified in the Contract Data.

Unless otherwise stated in the Contract Data, if the failure continues for a period of more than 84 days and the Contractor is unable to achieve the required production output, the Employer may either:

(i) continue with the Operation Service at a reduced level of compensation determined in accordance with Sub-Clause 3.5 [*Determinations*]; or,
(ii) if the production outputs fail to reach the minimum values required in the Contract Data, give Notice to the Contractor not less than 56 days prior to terminating the Contract, in accordance with Sub-Clause 15.2 [*Termination for Contractor's Default*]. In such an event, the Employer shall be free to continue the Operation Service himself or by others.

10.8 Completion of Operation Service

Unless the Parties have mutually agreed to prolong the Operation Service, the obligation of the Contractor to operate and maintain the Plant under the Operation Service shall cease at the end of the period stated in the Contract as the Operation Service Period.

如果暂停已经持续 84 天以上，该暂停不是由于**承包商**的任何失误，也不是由于**承包商**根据**合同**规定应负责的情况造成的，则**承包商**可要求**雇主代表**同意继续施工。如果**雇主代表**在收到要求后 28 天内未能给予许可，**承包商**可根据第 16.2 款［*由承包商终止*］的规定，发出**终止通知**。

在发出继续开工许可或指示后，**承包商**和**雇主代表**应联合检验**工程**。**承包商**应修复**生产设备**中的任何损坏或缺陷，**雇主代表**应就**承包商**需要进行的所有修复工作做好书面记录。如果暂停既不是由于**承包商**的任何失误，也不是由于**承包商**根据**合同**规定应负责的情况，**承包商**有权在重新开始**运营服务**之前，获得修复工程的**成本加利润**的支付。

10.7 未能达到产量

如果**承包商**未能达到**合同**要求的产量，双方应共同确定失误的原因。

(a) 如果失误的原因在于**雇主**或其任何雇员或代理人，在与**承包商**协商后，**雇主**应向**承包商**发出书面指示，说明**雇主**要求**承包商**采取的措施。

如果**承包商**因上述失误或**雇主**指示的措施而遭受任何额外费用，**雇主**应根据第 3.5 款［*确定*］和第 20.1 款［*承包商索赔*］的规定，向**承包商**支付其**成本加利润**。

(b) 如果失误原因在于**承包商**，在与**雇主**进行适当协商后，**承包商**应采取一切必要措施，将产量恢复到**合同**要求的水平。

如果**雇主**因**承包商**的失误或采取的措施而遭受任何损失，**承包商**应根据第 3.5 款［*确定*］的规定，向**雇主**支付**合同数据**中规定的**履约损害赔偿费**。

除非**合同数据**中另有规定，如果失误持续超过 84 天，并且**承包商**无法达到所需产量，**雇主**可以：

(i) 按照第 3.5 款［*确定*］的规定，确定以较低补偿水平继续提供**运营服务**；（或）

(ii) 如果产量未能达到**合同数据**中要求的最小值，则应根据第 15.2 款［*由承包商违约的终止*］的规定，在终止合同前至少 56 天**通知承包商**。在这种情况下，**雇主**可自行或由他人继续提供**运营服务**。

10.8 运营服务的完成

除非双方商定延长**运营服务期**，**承包商**负责**运营服务**的运营和维护**生产设备**的义务，应在**合同**规定的**运营服务期**结束时终止。

Notwithstanding the foregoing, other services to be performed by the Contractor must be completed before the Contractor will be entitled to receive the Contract Completion Certificate in accordance with Sub-Clause 8.6 [Contract Completion Certificate].

Pre-conditions which must be fulfilled by the Contractor before the Contract Completion Certificate will be issued are:

(a) Inspection in accordance with Sub-Clause 11.8 [Joint Inspection Prior to Contract Completion];
(b) Testing in accordance with Sub-Clause 11.9 [Procedure for Tests Prior to Contract Completion];
(c) Updating Operation and Maintenance manuals providing performance records and data in accordance with Sub-Clause 5.6 [Operation and Maintenance Manuals]; and
(d) Remedying defects found during inspection in accordance with Sub-Clause 11.8 [Joint Inspection Prior to Contract Completion].

10.9
Ownership of Output and Revenue

During the Operation Service, any production output and revenue shall be the exclusive property of the Employer.

Testing

11.1
Testing of the Works

The Contractor shall carry out the Tests on Completion of Design-Build in accordance with this Clause and Sub-Clause 7.4 [Testing], after providing the documents in accordance with Sub-Clause 5.5 [As-Built Documents] and Sub-Clause 5.6 [Operation and Maintenance Manuals].

The Contractor shall give Notice to the Employer's Representative not less than 21 days prior to the date after which the Contractor will be ready to carry out each of the Tests on Completion of Design-Build. Unless otherwise agreed, Tests on Completion of Design-Build shall be carried out within 14 days after this date, on such day or days as the Employer's Representative shall instruct.

Unless otherwise stated in the Particular Conditions, the Tests on Completion of Design-Build shall be carried out in the following sequence and are further detailed in the Employer's Requirements:

(a) pre-commissioning tests, which shall include the appropriate inspections and ("dry" or "cold") functional tests to demonstrate that each item of Plant can safely undertake the next stage, (b);
(b) commissioning tests, which shall include the specified operational tests to demonstrate that the Works or Section can be operated safely and as specified, under all available operating conditions; and
(c) trial operation, which shall demonstrate that the Works or Section perform reliably and in accordance with the Contract.

The Employer shall be the sole beneficiary of any revenue or benefit resulting from the Tests on Completion of Design-Build.

During trial operation, when the Works are operating under stable conditions, the Contractor shall give Notice to the Employer's Representative that the Works are ready for any other Tests on Completion of Design-Build, including performance tests to demonstrate whether the Works conform with criteria specified in the Employer's Requirements and with the Schedule of Guarantees.

尽管有上述规定，在**承包商**有权根据第 8.6 款［**合同完成证书**］的规定收到**合同完成证书**之前，**承包商**必须完成由其提供的其他服务。

在签发**合同完成证书**之前，**承包商**必须满足的先决条件是：

(a) 根据第 11.8 款［**合同完成前的联合检验**］的规定进行检验；

(b) 根据第 11.9 款［**合同完成前试验程序**］的规定进行试验；

(c) 根据第 5.6 款［**操作和维护手册**］的规定，更新提供性能记录和数据的**操作和维护手册**；（以及）

(d) 按照第 11.8 款［**合同完成前的联合检验**］的规定，修补检验时发现的缺陷。

10.9 产出和收入所有权

在**运营服务**期间，任何生产产出和收入均为**雇主**的专有财产。

11 试验

11.1 工程试验

承包商应在按照第 5.5 款［**竣工文件**］和第 5.6 款［**操作和维护手册**］的规定提供各种文件后，按照本条和第 7.4 款［**试验**］的要求进行**设计 - 施工竣工试验**。

承包商应在其可以进行每项**设计 - 施工竣工试验**的日期前至少 21 天，**通知雇主代表**。除非另有商定，**设计 - 施工竣工试验**应在该日期后 14 天内，在**雇主代表**指示的某日或某几日内进行。

除非**专用条件**中另有规定，**设计 - 施工竣工试验**应按以下顺序进行，并在**雇主要求**中进一步详细说明：

(a) 预调试试验，应包括适当的检验和（"干"或"冷"）性能试验，以证明每项**生产设备**都能安全地承受下一阶段（b）段试验；

(b) 调试试验，应包括规定的运行试验，以证明**工程**或**分项工程**在所有可利用的运行条件下安全运行；（以及）

(c) 试运行，应证明**工程**或**分项工程**根据合同要求可靠运行。

雇主应是**设计 - 施工竣工试验**产生的任何收入或利益的唯一受益人。

在试运行期间，当**工程**在稳定条件下运行时，**承包商**应向**雇主代表**发出**通知**，告知其**工程**已可以进行任何其他**设计 - 施工竣工试验**，包括性能试验，以证明**工程**是否符合**雇主要求**中规定的标准和**保证表**中的标准。

Trial operation shall not constitute a commencement of the Operation Service under Sub-Clause 10.2 [*Commencement of Operation Service*].

In considering the results of the Tests on Completion of Design-Build, the Employer's Representative shall make allowances for the effect of any use of the Works by the Employer on the performance or other characteristics of the Works. As soon as the Works, or a Section, have passed each of the Tests on Completion of Design-Build described in sub-paragraph (a), (b) or (c) above, the Contractor shall submit a report certified by the Contractor of the results of these Tests to the Employer's Representative.

11.2 Delayed Tests on Completion of Design-Build

If the Tests on Completion of Design-Build are being unduly delayed by the Employer Sub-Clause 7.4 [*Testing*] (fifth paragraph) shall be applicable.

If the Tests on Completion of Design-Build are being unduly delayed by the Contractor, the Employer's Representative may by Notice require the Contractor to carry out such Tests within 21 days after receiving the Notice. The Contractor shall carry out such Tests on the day or days within that period as the Contractor may fix and of which he shall give Notice to the Employer's Representative.

If the Contractor fails to carry out the Tests on Completion of Design-Build within the period of 21 days, the Employer's Personnel may proceed with the Tests at the risk and cost of the Contractor. The Tests on Completion shall then be deemed to have been carried out in the presence of the Contractor and the results of the Tests shall be accepted as accurate.

11.3 Retesting of the Works

If the Works, or a Section, fail to pass the Tests on Completion of Design-Build, Sub-Clause 7.5 [*Rejection*] shall apply, and the Employer's Representative or the Contractor may require the failed Tests, and Tests on Completion of Design-Build on any related work, to be repeated under the same terms and conditions.

11.4 Failure to Pass Tests on Completion of Design-Build

If the Works, or a Section, fail to pass the Tests on Completion of Design-Build repeated under Sub-Clause 11.3 [*Retesting of the Works*] the Employer's Representative shall be entitled to:

(a) order further repetition of Tests on Completion of Design-Build under Sub-Clause 11.3 [*Retesting of the Works*]; or
(b) issue a Notice under Sub-Clause 15.1 [*Notice to Correct*].

11.5 Completion of the Works and Sections

Except as stated in Sub-Clause 11.11 [*Failure to Pass Tests Prior to Contract Completion*], the Works shall be deemed by the Employer to be completed when:

(a) the Works have been completed in accordance with the Contract, including the matters described in Sub-Clause 9.2 [*Time for Completion of Design-Build*] and Sub-Clause 5.6 [*Operation and Maintenance Manuals*] and except as allowed in sub-paragraph (i) below; and
(b) a Commissioning Certificate has been issued, or is deemed to have been issued, in accordance with this Sub-Clause.

The Contractor may apply by Notice to the Employer's Representative for a Commissioning Certificate not earlier than 14 days before the Works will, in the Contractor's opinion, be complete and ready for commencement of the Operation Service Period. If the Works are divided into Sections, the Contractor may similarly apply for a Commissioning Certificate for each Section.

试运行，不应构成第 10.2 款［*运营服务的开始*］规定的运营服务的开始。

雇主代表在考虑**设计 - 施工竣工试验**结果时，应考虑到**雇主**对**工程**的任何使用，对**工程**的性能或其他特性的影响。一旦**工程**或**分项工程**通过了上述（a）、（b）或（c）段中的每项**设计 - 施工试验**，**承包商**应向**雇主代表**提交一份经其证实的这些**试验**结果的报告。

11.2 设计 - 施工竣工试验的延误	如果雇主不当地延误**设计 - 施工竣工试验**，第 7.4 款［*试验*］（第 5 段）的规定应适用。 如果**承包商**不当地延误了**设计 - 施工竣工试验**，**雇主代表**可向**承包商**发出**通知**，要求其在接到**通知**后 21 天内进行此类**试验**。**承包商**应在规定的时间内就能确定的某日或某几日内进行此类**试验**，并应将该日期**通知雇主代表**。 如果**承包商**未在规定的 21 天内进行**设计 - 施工竣工试验**，**雇主人员**可以继续进行**试验**，风险和费用由**承包商**承担。这些**竣工试验**应视为是**承包商**在场时进行的，**试验**结果应认为准确，予以认可。
11.3 工程重新试验	如果**工程**或某**分项工程**未能通过**设计-施工竣工试验**，第 7.5 款［*拒收*］应适用，且**雇主代表**或**承包商**可要求按相同的条款和条件，重新进行此项未通过的**试验**和相关**工程**的**设计 - 施工竣工试验**。
11.4 未能通过设计 - 施工竣工试验	如果**工程**或某**分项工程**未能通过根据第 11.3 款［*工程重新试验*］的规定，重新进行的**设计 - 施工竣工试验**，**雇主代表**应有权： （a）下令根据第 11.3 款［*工程重新试验*］再次重复**设计 - 施工竣工试验**；（或） （b）根据第 15.1 款［*通知改正*］的规定发出**通知**。
11.5 工程和分项工程的竣工	除第 11.11 款［*未能通过合同完成前的试验*］中规定的情况外。**雇主**应认为**工程**在下列情况下已竣工： （a）**工程**已按照合同完成，包括第 9.2 款［*设计 - 施工竣工时间*］和第 5.6 款［*操作和维护手册*］所述事项，但下述（i）段允许的情况除外；（以及） （b）根据**本款**规定，已签发或视为已签发**调试证书**。 **承包商**可在其认为**工程**将竣工并准备好开始运营服务期前 14 天，向**雇主代表**发出**通知**，申请**调试证书**。如果**工程**分成若干**分项工程**，**承包商**可类似地为每个**分项工程**申请**调试证书**。

The Employer's Representative shall, within 28 days after receiving the Contractor's application:

(i) issue the Commissioning Certificate to the Contractor, stating the date on which the Works or Section were completed in accordance with the Contract, except for any minor outstanding work and defects which will not substantially affect the use of the Works or Section for their intended purpose (listing such outstanding work and defects which are to be remedied); or

(ii) reject the application, giving reasons and specifying the work required to be done by the Contractor to enable the Commissioning Certificate to be issued.

The Contractor shall then complete the work referred to in sub-paragraph (ii) above before issuing a further Notice under this Sub-Clause.

If the Employer's Representative either fails to issue the Commissioning Certificate or reject the Contractor's application within the period of 28 days, and if the Works or Section (as the case may be) are substantially in accordance with the Contract, the Commissioning Certificate shall be deemed to have been issued on the last day of that period.

11.6 Commissioning of Parts of the Works

The Employer's Representative may, at the request of the Contractor, issue a Section Commissioning Certificate for any part of the Permanent Works.

If a Section Commissioning Certificate has been issued for a part of the Works, the delay damages thereafter for completion of the remainder of the Works shall be reduced. Similarly, the delay damages for the remainder of the Section (if any) in which this part is included shall also be reduced. For any period of delay after the date stated in this Section Commissioning Certificate, the proportional reduction in these delay damages shall be calculated as the proportion which the value of the part so certified bears to the value of the Works or Section (as the case may be) as a whole. The Employer's Representative shall proceed in accordance with Sub-Clause 3.5 [*Determinations*] to agree or determine these proportions. The provisions of this paragraph shall only apply to the daily rate of delay damages under Sub-Clause 9.6 [*Delay Damages relating to Design-Build*], and shall not affect the maximum amount of these damages (if any).

11.7 Commissioning Certificate

Performance of the Contractor's Design-Build obligations, including care of the Works, shall not be considered to have been completed until the Commissioning Certificate has been signed by the Employer's Representative and delivered to the Contractor, stating the date on which the Contractor, in the opinion of the Employer's Representative, completed all such obligations in accordance with the Contract (subject to the outstanding works and defects listed in accordance with Sub-Clause 11.5 [*Completion of the Works and Sections*]).

The Employer's Representative shall issue the Commissioning Certificate to the Contractor within 28 days after the application by the Contractor for the Commissioning Certificate subject to the provisions of Sub-Clause 11.5 [*Completion of the Works and Sections*].

Only the Commissioning Certificate shall be deemed to constitute acceptance of the Works.

雇主代表在收到承包商的申请后28天内，应：

(i) 向承包商签发调试证书，注明工程或分项工程按照合同要求竣工的日期，任何对工程或分项工程预期使用目的没有实质影响的少量扫尾工作和缺陷（列出此类扫尾工作和待修补的缺陷）除外；（或）

(ii) 拒绝申请，说明理由，说明在能签发调试证书前承包商需做的工作。

然后，在再次根据本款发出申请通知前，承包商应完成上述（ii）段所述的工作。

如果雇主代表在28天期限内既未签发调试证书，又未拒绝承包商的申请，而工程或分项工程（视情况而定）实际上符合合同规定，调试证书应视为已在上述期限的最后一日已签发。

11.6 部分工程的调试

应承包商要求，雇主代表可签发永久工程任何部分的调试证书。

如果已签发了部分工程的分项工程调试证书，此后工程剩余部分的竣工误期损害赔偿费应予减少。与此类似，包括该部分的分项工程（如果有）的剩余部分的误期损害赔偿费也应减少。对分项工程调试证书注明日期以后的任何延误期，这些误期损害赔偿费的比例减少额，应按已签发证书部分的价值占整个工程或分项工程（视情况而定）价值的比例计算。雇主代表应按照第3.5款［*确定*］的规定，对这些比例进行商定或确定。本段的规定仅适用于第9.6款［*设计-施工误期损害赔偿费*］规定的误期损害赔偿费的每日费率，不应影响该损害赔偿费的最高限额（如果有）。

11.7 调试证书

在雇主代表签发调试证书并交付给承包商之前，承包商履行设计-施工的义务，包括对工程的照管，不应视为已完成，该证书说明了雇主代表认为承包商根据合同规定完成所有此类义务（根据第11.5款［*工程和分项工程的竣工*］的规定，列出的扫尾工作和缺陷）的日期。

根据第11.5款［*工程和分项工程的竣工*］的规定，雇主代表应在承包商申请调试证书后28天内，向承包商签发调试证书。

只有调试证书应视为构成对工程的接收。

11.8
Joint Inspection Prior to Contract Completion

Not less than two years prior to the expiry date of the Operation Service Period, the Employer's Representative and the Contractor shall carry out a joint inspection of the Works and, within 28 days of the completion of the joint inspection, the Contractor shall submit a report on the condition of the Works identifying maintenance works (excluding routine maintenance works and the correction of defects), replacements and other works required to be carried out to satisfy the requirements of the Operation and Maintenance Plan after the Contract Completion Date.

The Contractor shall submit a programme for carrying out such works over the remainder of the Operation Service Period.

Following receipt of the Contractor's report, the Employer's Representative may, throughout the remainder of the Operation Service Period, instruct the Contractor to carry out all or part of the works identified in the Contractor's report. The quoted sums from the Asset Replacement Fund will be added to the monthly payments upon replacement of items of Plant in accordance with the Schedule of replacement prepared at Tender stage and the provisions of Sub-Clause 14.18 [*Asset Replacement Fund*]. Other works shall be carried out at the Contractor's cost.

Upon satisfactory completion of the items identified in this Sub-Clause the Employer shall instruct the Contractor to commence the Tests Prior to Contract Completion in accordance with Sub-Clause 11.9 [*Procedure for Tests Prior to Contract Completion*].

11.9
Procedure for Tests Prior to Contract Completion

The Tests Prior to Contract Completion ("Tests") are to be carried out by the Contractor who shall provide all necessary labour, materials, electricity, fuel and water, other than items identified as being the responsibility of the Employer under Sub-Clause 10.4 [*Delivery of Raw Materials*], and undertake any required remedial works as may be required. The Tests are to be carried out in accordance with the Employer's Requirements.

The Tests shall be carried out towards the end of the Operation Service Period. The Employer shall give Notice to the Contractor not less than 21 days prior to the date after which the Tests shall be carried out. Unless otherwise agreed, such Tests shall be commenced within 14 days after this date, on the day or days determined by the Employer's Representative.

The results of the Tests shall be compiled and evaluated by the Employer's Representative and the Contractor. The Contractor shall make the results of any tests, inspections or monitoring available to the Employer's Representative within 7 days of their receipt. Any effect on the results of the Tests which can reasonably be shown to be due to prior use of the Works by the Contractor during the Operation Service Period shall be taken into account in assessing such results.

As soon as the Contractor has completed the Tests, the Contractor shall notify the Employer's Representative that the Works are complete and ready for final inspection. Upon the Employer's Representative being satisfied that the Contractor has satisfied the requirements of the Tests regarding such final inspection, the Employer's Representative shall notify the Employer and the Contractor prior to the issue of the Contract Completion Certificate.

11.8		
合同完成前的联合检验		雇主代表和承包商应在运营服务期期满前，至少两年对工程进行联合检验，并在联合检验完成后 28 天内，承包商应提交一份关于工程条件的报告，说明维护工作（不包括日常维护工作和缺陷的纠正）、更换以及合同完成日期后，为满足运营和维护计划的要求而需要进行的其他工作。

承包商应提交在运营服务期剩余时间内执行此类工作的进度计划。

在收到承包商的报告后，雇主代表可在剩余的运营服务期内，指示承包商实施承包商报告中确定的全部或部分工作。根据投标阶段编制的置换计划表和第 14.18 款 [*资产置换基金*] 的规定，资产置换基金中的报价金额将加到生产设备部件更换后的每月付款中。其他工作应由承包商承担费用。

在圆满完成本款中确定的事项后，雇主应指示承包商按照第 11.9 款 [*合同完成前试验程序*] 的规定，开始合同完成前试验。

11.9		
合同完成前试验程序		合同完成前试验（"试验"）应由承包商进行，承包商应提供所有必要的劳动力、材料、电力、燃料和水，但根据第 10.4 款 [*原材料的交付*] 的规定，确定为雇主负责的事项除外，并承担所需的任何补救工程工作。试验应按雇主要求进行。

试验应在运营服务期结束时进行。雇主应在试验开始前至少 21 天通知承包商。除非另有商定，此类试验应在该日期后 14 天内，在雇主代表确定的一个或多个日期开始。

试验结果应由雇主代表和承包商编制和评估。承包商应在收到任何试验、检验或监测结果后 7 天内向雇主代表提供。在评估此类结果时，应考虑到承包商在运营服务期内，提前使用工程而对试验结果造成的任何影响。

一旦承包商完成试验，承包商应通知雇主代表，工程已完成并准备好进行最终检验。在雇主代表确信承包商已满足有关此类最终检验的试验后，雇主代表应在签发合同完成证书之前，通知雇主和承包商。

11.10 Delayed Tests Prior to Contract Completion

If the Employer incurs cost as a result of any unreasonable delay by the Contractor in carrying out the Tests Prior to Contract Completion ("Tests"), the Employer shall be entitled, subject to Sub-Clause 20.2 [*Employer's Claims*], to payment of any such cost which shall be recoverable from the Contractor by the Employer, and may be deducted by the Employer from any monies due, or to become due, to the Contractor.

If the Contractor fails to commence the Tests on the day or days determined under Sub-Clause 11.9 [*Procedure for Tests Prior to Contract Completion*], the Employer's Representative shall give Notice to the Contractor that unless the Tests are commenced within 14 days of this Notice the Employer's Representative may order that the Tests be undertaken by others on behalf of the Employer. In such event, the Contractor shall be bound by the results of such Tests as being accurate and the Employer shall be entitled to deduct the costs associated with the undertaking of the Tests by others from any monies due, or to become due, to the Contractor.

If, for reasons not attributable to the Contractor, the Tests Prior to Contract Completion of the Works, or any Section, cannot be completed during the Contract Period (or any other period agreed upon by both Parties), then the Works or Section shall be deemed to have passed the Tests.

11.11 Failure to Pass Tests Prior to Contract Completion

If the Works or a Section thereof, fails to pass the Tests Prior to Contract Completion ("Tests") under Sub-Clause 11.9 [*Procedure for Tests Prior to Contract Completion*], the Employer's Representative shall be entitled to:

(a) order further repetition of Tests under Sub-Clause 11.12 [*Retesting Prior to Contract Completion*];
(b) reject the Works or a Section thereof (as the case may be), in which event the Employer shall have the same remedies against the Contractor as provided under Clause 15 [*Termination by Employer*]; or
(c) issue a Contract Completion Certificate, if the Employer so requires. The Contract Price shall then be reduced by such an amount as may be agreed by the Employer and the Contractor (in full satisfaction of such failure only),

and the Contractor shall then proceed in accordance with his other obligations under the Contract.

In the event of (c) above, if the Works, or a Section, fail to pass any of the Tests and the Contractor proposes to make adjustments or modifications to the Works or such Section, the Contractor may be instructed by (or on behalf of) the Employer that right of access to the Works or Section cannot be given until a time that is convenient to the Employer. The Contractor shall then remain liable to carry out the adjustments or modifications and to satisfy this Test, within a reasonable period of receiving Notice by (or on behalf of) the Employer of the time that is convenient to the Employer. However, if the Contractor does not receive this Notice during the relevant Contract Period, the Contractor shall be relieved of this obligation and the Works or Section (as the case may be) shall be deemed to have passed the Tests.

If the Contractor incurs additional cost as a result of any unreasonable delay by the Employer in permitting access to the Works or Plant by the Contractor after issue of the Contract Completion Certificate, either to investigate the causes of a failure to pass any of the Tests or to carry out any adjustments or modifications, the Contractor shall be paid the additional Cost Plus Profit, as determined or agreed in accordance with Sub-Clause 3.5 [*Determinations*], caused by such a delay.

11.10 合同完成前试验的延误

如果由于**承包商**在进行**合同完成前试验**("**试验**")的任何不合理延误,导致**雇主**招致费用,**雇主**应有权根据第 20.2 款 [*雇主索赔*] 的规定,从**承包商**处收回任何此类费用,**雇主**可从应付给或即将到期应付给**承包商**的任何款项中扣除。

如果**承包商**未能根据第 11.9 款 [*合同完成前试验程序*] 的规定,在确定的日期或某几日内开始**试验**,**雇主代表**应**通知承包商**,除非**试验**在收到**通知**后 14 天内开始,否则**雇主代表**可命令其他人代表**雇主**进行**试验**。在这种情况下,**承包商**应遵守此类**试验**结果的准确性,**雇主**有权从任何应付或即将到期应付给**承包商**的款项中,扣除与其他人进行**试验**相关的费用。

如果由于不可归责于**承包商**的原因,在合同期内(或双方商定的任何其他期限),**工程**或任何**分项工程**的**合同完成前试验**不能完成,则该**工程**或**分项工程**应被视为已通过**试验**。

11.11 未能通过合同完成前试验

如果**工程**或某**分项工程**,未能通过第 11.9 款 [*合同完成前试验程序*] 规定的合同完成前试验("**试验**"),**雇主代表**应有权:

(a) 下令根据第 11.12 款 [*合同完成前的重新试验*] 规定的重新**试验**;

(b) 拒收**工程**或**分项工程**(视情况而定),在这种情况下,**雇主**应采用与第 15 条 [*由雇主终止*] 规定的,对**承包商**采取相同的补救措施;(或)

(c) 如果**雇主**要求,签发合同完成证书。然后,**合同价格**应按照**雇主**和**承包商**商定的金额(仅在完成满足此类失误要求的情况下)进行扣减,

然后,**承包商**应继续履行其在本合同中规定的其他义务。

在上述(c)段情况下,如果**工程**或某**分项工程**未能通过任何**试验**,并且**承包商**建议对**工程**或该**分项工程**进行调整或修改,**雇主**(或其代表)可指示**承包商**,在**雇主**方便的时间之前,不得给予**承包商**进入**工程**或**分项工程**的权利。然后,**承包商**应在收到**雇主**(或其代表)**通知**的合理时间内,在**雇主**方便的时间进行调整或修改,并满足本**试验**的要求。但是,如果**承包商**在相关合同期内未收到该**通知**,则应免除**承包商**的此项义务,且**工程**或**分项工程**(视情况而定)应视为已通过**试验**。

如果在签发合同完成证书后,**雇主**不合理地延迟允许**承包商**进入**工程**或**生产设备**导致**承包商**招致额外费用,为调查未能通过任何**试验**的原因或进行任何调整或修改,**承包商**应有权获得根据第 3.5 款 [*确定*] 中规定的,确定或商定的由此类延误引起的额外**成本加利润**的支付。

11.12
Retesting Prior to Contract Completion

If the Works, or a Section, fail to pass the Tests Prior to Contract Completion:

(a) sub-paragraph (b) of Sub-Clause 12.1 [*Completion of Outstanding Work and Remedying Defects*] shall apply; and
(b) the Employer may require the failed Tests, and the Tests Prior to Contract Completion on any related work, to be repeated under the same terms and conditions.

If such failure and retesting results from a default of the Contractor and causes the Employer to incur additional costs, such costs shall be recoverable from the Contractor by the Employer, subject to Sub-Clause 20.2 [*Employer's Claims*], and may be deducted by the Employer from any monies due, or to become due, to the Contractor.

The Employer's Representative may carry out such additional tests, inspections and monitoring as he deems necessary. The costs of such tests, except where such tests are carried out for the purpose of remedying any damage, defect or failure to meet standards that are the responsibility of the Contractor under the Contract, shall be borne by the Employer.

Defects 12

12.1
Completion of Outstanding Work and Remedying Defects

The requirements regarding the completion of outstanding work and the remedying of defects are as follows:

(a) Design-Build Period: In order that the Works and Contractor's Documents, and each Section, shall be in the condition required by the Contract, the Contractor shall:

  (i) complete any work which is outstanding on the date stated in the Commissioning Certificate as soon as practicable after such date, and not later than one year after such date; and
  (ii) execute all work required to remedy defects or damage, as may be notified by (or on behalf of) the Employer.

Final payment for the Design-Build Period, in accordance with Clause 14 [*Contract Price and Payment*], will not be certified until the above requirements have, in the opinion of the Employer's Representative, been met.

If a defect appears or damage occurs, the Contractor shall be notified accordingly, by (or on behalf of) the Employer.

(b) Operation Service Period: The Contractor shall be responsible for repairing and making good any damage or defect occurring during the Operation Service Period, whether such defect or damage is notified by the Employer or his Representative, or observed by the Contractor himself.

The Contract Completion Certificate issued under Sub-Clause 8.6 [*Contract Completion Certificate*] will not be issued until all defects and damage and all outstanding work, including all such items identified during the joint inspection made in accordance with Sub-Clause 11.8 [*Joint Inspection Prior to Contract Completion*], have been completed.

11.12 合同完成前的重新试验

如果工程或分项工程未能通过合同完成前试验：

(a) 第12.1款[完成扫尾工作和修补缺陷](b)段应适用；(以及)

(b) **雇主**可要求在相同的条款和条件下，重新进行未通过的**试验**，以及任何相关工程的**合同完成前试验**。

如果此类失误和重新试验是由于**承包商**的失误造成的，并导致**雇主**招致额外费用，**雇主**应有权根据**第20.2款**[*雇主索赔*]的规定，要求**承包商**支付此类费用，并可由**雇主**从应付给或即将到期应付给**承包商**的任何款项中扣除。

雇主代表可进行其认为必要的附加试验、检验和监测。此类试验的费用应由**雇主**承担，但为修补任何损害、缺陷或未能达到合同规定的**承包商**的责任标准而进行的试验除外。

12 缺陷

12.1 完成扫尾工作和修补缺陷

完成扫尾工作和修补缺陷的要求如下：

(a) **设计 - 施工期**：为了使**工程**、**承包商文件**和每个分项工程达到合同要求的条件，**承包商**应：

 (i) 在**调试证书**规定的日期后，在可行的范围，且不迟于该日期后的一年内，尽快完成任何扫尾的工作；(以及)

 (ii) 按照**雇主**(或其代表)可能通知要求，完成修补缺陷或损害所需的所有工作。

根据**第14条**[*合同价格和付款*]的规定，在**雇主代表**认为满足上述要求之前，不会对**设计 - 施工期**的最终付款进行确认。

如果出现缺陷或发生损害，**雇主**(或其代表)应相应地通知**承包商**。

(b) **运营服务期**：**承包商**应负责维修和修复运营服务期间发生的任何损害或缺陷，无论此类缺陷或损害是由**雇主**或其**代表**通知的，还是由**承包商**自己观察到的。

根据**第8.6款**[*合同完成证书*]的规定签发的**合同完成证书**，直到所有缺陷和损害以及所有扫尾工作，包括根据**第11.8款**[*合同完成前的联合检验*]规定的，进行联合检验期间的所有此类事项均已完成，方可签发合同完成证书。

12.2 Cost of Remedying Defects

All work required to repair defects or damage shall be executed at the risk and cost of the Contractor, except:

(a) where it is attributable to any act by the Employer or the Employer's Personnel or agents; or
(b) where it is as a result of an event that is covered under Clause 18 [*Exceptional Risks*].

Where the Contractor is required to remedy a defect or damage to the Works under sub-paragraphs (a) or (b) of this Sub-Clause, the Contractor shall notify the Employer's Representative and shall be entitled to a Variation under Clause 13 [*Variations and Adjustments*].

12.3 Failure to Remedy Defects

If the Contractor fails to remedy any defect or damage arising during either the Design-Build Period or the Operation Service Period within a reasonable time, a date may be fixed by (or on behalf of) the Employer's Representative, on or by which the defect or damage is to be remedied. The Contractor shall be given reasonable Notice of this date.

If the Contractor fails to remedy the defect or damage by such date and the necessity for such work is due to the Contractor subject to Sub-Clause 12.2 [*Cost of Remedying Defects*], the Employer may (at his sole discretion):

(a) require the Employer's Representative to determine and certify a reasonable reduction in the Contract Price or the Rates and Prices submitted for the Operation Service Period in accordance with Sub-Clause 3.5 [*Determinations*];or

(b) if the defect or damage is such that the Contractor has been unable to commission the Works or continue providing the Operation Service and the Employer has been deprived of substantially the whole of the benefit of the Works or parts of the Works, the Employer shall be entitled to terminate the Contract in respect of such parts of the Works as cannot be put to the intended use in accordance with the provisions of Clause 15 [*Termination by Employer*].

In the event of (b) above occurring, the Employer shall, notwithstanding the provisions of Sub-Clause 15.4 [*Payment after Termination for Contractor's Default*]:

(i) during the Design-Build Period, be entitled to recover from the Contractor all sums paid for such parts of the Works plus financing costs together with the cost of dismantling the same, clearing the Site and returning Plant and Materials to the Contractor; or, if the Employer chooses to complete the Works himself or by engaging others, the Employer shall be entitled to recover the extra costs, if any, of completing the Works after allowing for any sum due to the Contractor under Sub-Clause 15.3 [*Valuation at Date of Termination for Contractor's Default*]. If there are no such extra costs, the Employer shall pay any balance to the Contractor; and
(ii) during the Operation Service Period, not be liable to make any further payments to the Contractor until the costs of operation and maintenance, completion and remedying of any defects and all other costs incurred and to be incurred by the Employer have been established.

12.2 修补缺陷的费用

修复缺陷或损害所需的所有工作的风险和费用应由**承包商**承担,但以下情况除外:

(a) 可能由于**雇主**或**雇主人员**或代理人的任何行为所导致的;(或)

(b) 由于**第 18 条** [*例外风险*] 规定的所涵盖的事件造成的。

如果根据本款(a)或(b)段要求**承包商**修补**工程**的缺陷或损害,**承包商**应通知**雇主代表**,并有权根据**第 13 条** [*变更和调整*] 的规定进行变更。

12.3 未能修补缺陷

如果**承包商**未能在合理时间内修补**运营服务期**或**设计-施工期**产生的任何缺陷或损害,**雇主代表**(或其代表)可确定一个日期,要求在该日期或不迟于该日期修补好缺陷或损害。应向**承包商**发出该日期的合理**通知**。

如果**承包商**未能在该日期之前修补好缺陷或损害,并且根据**第 12.2 款** [*修补缺陷的费用*] 的规定,由于**承包商**的原因而需要进行此类工作,**雇主**可以(自行决定):

(a) 要求**雇主代表**根据**第 3.5 款** [*确定*] 的规定,确定并证明**合同价格**或运营服务期提交的**费率和价格**的合理减少额;(或)

(b) 如果缺陷或损害导致**承包商**无法调试**工程**或继续提供**运营服务**,使雇主实质上丧失了**工程**或部分**工程**的整个利益,根据**第 15 条** [*由雇主终止*] 的规定,**雇主**应有权就不能投入预期用途的**工程**部分终止合同。

如果发生上述(b)段的情况,尽管有**第 15.4 款** [*由承包商违约终止后的付款*] 的规定,**雇主**应:

(i) 在**设计-施工期**间,有权向**承包商**收回为该部分**工程**支付的所有款项,加上融资费用和拆除该部分**工程**、清理**现场**,以及将**生产设备**和**材料**退还给**承包商**所支付的费用;或者,如果**雇主**选择自行或聘请他人完成**工程**,根据**第 15.3 款** [*由承包商违约终止日期时的估价*] 的规定,考虑到应付给**承包商**的任何金额后,**雇主**有权收回完成**工程**所需的额外费用,如果有。如果没有此类额外费用,**雇主**应向**承包商**支付任何余款;(以及)

(ii) 在**运营服务期**间,在运营和维护、竣工和修补任何缺陷的费用,以及**雇主**已发生和将要发生的所有其他费用确定之前,不负责向**承包商**支付任何进一步的款项。

12.4
Further Tests

If the work of remedying any defect or damage may affect the performance of the Works, the Employer's Representative may require the repetition of any of the tests described in the Contract. The requirement shall be made by Notice within 28 days after the defect or damage is remedied.

These tests shall be carried out in accordance with the terms applicable to the previous tests, except that they shall be carried out at the risk and cost of the Party liable, under Sub-Clause 12.2 [*Cost of Remedying Defects*], for the cost of the remedial work.

12.5
Removal of Defective Work

If the defect or damage cannot be remedied expeditiously on the Site and the Employer gives consent, the Contractor may remove from the Site for the purposes of repair such items of Plant as are defective or damaged. This consent may require the Contractor to increase the amount of the Performance Security by the full replacement cost of these items, or to provide other appropriate security.

12.6
Contractor to Search

The Contractor shall, if required by the Employer's Representative, search for the cause of any defect, under the direction of the Employer's Representative. Unless the defect is to be remedied at the cost of the Contractor under Sub-Clause 12.2 [*Cost of Remedying Defects*], the Cost Plus Profit of the search shall be agreed or determined by the Employer's Representative in accordance with Sub-Clause 3.5 [*Determinations*] and shall be included in the Contract Price.

13 Variations and Adjustments

13.1
Right to Vary

Variations may be initiated by the Employer's Representative at any time prior to issuing the Commissioning Certificate, either by an instruction to the Contractor by the Employer's Representative or by a request for the Contractor to submit a proposal. A Variation shall not comprise the omission of any work which is to be carried out by others.

The Contractor shall execute and be bound by each Variation; unless the Contractor promptly gives Notice to the Employer's Representative stating (with supporting particulars) that (i) the Contractor cannot readily obtain the Goods required for the Variation, (ii) it will reduce the safety or suitability of the Works for the purposes for which they were intended under the Contract; (iii) it will have an adverse impact on the achievement of the Schedule of guarantees; or (iv) it will have an adverse effect on the provision of the Operation Service under the Contract. Upon receiving this Notice, the Employer's Representative shall cancel, confirm or vary the instruction and the Contractor shall execute and be bound by it.

If the Employer or the Employer's Representative wishes to instruct a Variation during the Operation Service Period, he shall give the Contractor written details of his requirements. The Contractor shall then proceed in accordance with Sub-Clause 13.3 [*Variation Procedure*] sub-paragraphs (a), (b) and (c). However, the Contractor shall not be obliged to proceed with the Variation until the matters covered in Sub-Clause 13.3 [*Variation Procedure*] sub-paragraphs (a), (b) and (c) have been agreed between the Employer and the Contractor.

12.4
进一步试验

如果任何缺陷或损害的修补，可能对工程的性能产生影响，**雇主代表**可要求重新进行**合同**中规定的任何试验。此要求应在缺陷或损害修补后 28 天内以**通知**形式提出。

这些试验，除应根据第 12.2 款 [*修补缺陷的费用*] 的规定，由负责修补工作的一方承担试验的风险和费用外，应按照适用于先前试验的条款进行。

12.5
移出有缺陷的工程

如果缺陷或损害在**现场**无法迅速修复，**承包商**可经**雇主**同意，将有缺陷或损害的各项**生产设备**移出**现场**进行修复。雇主此项同意可要求**承包商**按该项设备的全部重置成本，增加**履约担保**的金额，或提供其他适当的担保。

12.6
承包商调查

如果**雇主代表**要求**承包商**调查任何缺陷的原因，**承包商**应在**雇主代表**的指导下进行调查。除非根据第 12.2 款 [*修补缺陷的费用*] 的规定，应由**承包商**承担修补费用的情况，调查的成本加利润，应由**雇主代表**根据第 3.5 款 [*确定*] 的规定，商定或确定，并计入**合同价格**。

13 变更和调整

13.1
变更权

在签发**调试证书**前的任何时间，**雇主代表**可通过向**承包商**发出指示或要求**承包商**提交建议书的形式，提出**变更**。**变更**不应包括由他人将要进行任何工作的删减。

承包商应遵守并进行每项**变更**；除非**承包商**迅速向**雇主代表**发出**通知**，说明（附详细证明资料）：（i）**承包商**难以取得**变更**所需的**货物**；（ii）将降低工程的安全性或适用性，难以达到合同规定的预期目的；（iii）将对**保证资料表**的实现产生不利影响；或（iv）将对**合同**规定的运营服务提供产生不利影响。收到此通知后，**雇主代表**应取消、确认或更改该指示，**承包商**应执行并受其约束。

如果**雇主**或**雇主代表**希望在**运营服务**期间指示**变更**，他应向**承包商**提供其要求的书面细节。**承包商**应随即按照第 13.3 款 [*变更程序*]（a）、（b）和（c）段的规定进行。但是，在**雇主**和**承包商**就第 13.3 款 [*变更程序*]（a）、（b）和（c）段规定的事项商定一致前，**承包商**没有义务继续进行**变更**。

13.2 Value Engineering

The Contractor may, at any time, submit to the Employer's Representative a written proposal, which (in the Contractor's opinion) will, if adopted:

(a) accelerate completion of the Works;
(b) reduce the cost to the Employer of executing, maintaining or operating the Works;
(c) improve the efficiency or value to the Employer of the completed Works;
(d) improve the efficiency of the Operation Service being provided; or
(e) otherwise be of benefit to the Employer.

The proposal shall be prepared at the cost of the Contractor and shall include the items listed in Sub-Clause 13.3 [*Variation Procedure*].

13.3 Variation Procedure

If the Employer's Representative requests a proposal, prior to instructing a Variation, the Contractor shall respond in writing as soon as practicable, either by giving reasons why he cannot comply (if this is the case) or by submitting:

(a) a description of the proposed design and/or work to be performed and a programme for its execution;
(b) the Contractor's proposal for any necessary modifications to the programme according to Sub-Clause 8.3 [*Programme*] and to the Time for Completion; and
(c) the Contractor's proposal for adjustment to the Contract Price.

The Employer's Representative shall, as soon as practicable after receiving such proposal (under Sub-Clause 13.2 [*Value Engineering*] or otherwise), respond with approval, disapproval or comments. The Contractor shall not delay any work whilst awaiting a response.

Each instruction to execute a Variation, with any requirements for the recording of costs, shall be issued by the Employer's Representative to the Contractor, who shall acknowledge receipt.

Upon instructing or approving a Variation, the Employer's Representative shall proceed in accordance with Sub-Clause 3.5 [*Determinations*] to agree or determine adjustments to the Contract Price and the Schedule of Payments. These adjustments, except adjustments made under Sub-Clause 13.6 [*Adjustments for Changes in Legislation*] and Sub-Clause 13.7 [*Adjustments for Changes in Technology*], shall include reasonable profit, and shall take account of the Contractor's submissions under Sub-Clause 13.2 [*Value Engineering*] if applicable.

13.4 Payment in Applicable Currencies

If the Contract provides for payment of the Contract Price in more than one currency, then whenever an adjustment is agreed, approved or determined as stated above, the amount payable in each of the applicable currencies shall be specified. For this purpose, reference shall be made to the actual or expected currency proportions of the cost of the varied work, and to the proportions of various currencies specified for payment of the Contract Price.

13.5 Provisional Sums

Each Provisional Sum shall only be used, in whole or in part, in accordance with the Employer's Representative's instructions and the Contract Price shall be adjusted accordingly. The total sum paid to the Contractor shall include only such amounts, for the work, supplies or services to which the Provisional Sum relates, as the Employer's Representative shall have instructed. For each Provisional Sum, the Employer's Representative may instruct:

13.2 价值工程

承包商可随时向雇主代表提交书面建议,提出(承包商认为)采纳后将:

(a) 加快工程的竣工;
(b) 降低雇主的工程施工、维护或运行的费用;
(c) 提高雇主的竣工工程的效率或价值;
(d) 提高所提供运营服务的效率;(或)
(e) 给雇主带来其他利益的建议。

此类建议书应由承包商自费编制,并应包括第 13.3 款 [*变更程序*] 所列的事项。

13.3 变更程序

如果雇主代表在发出变更指示前要求承包商提交一份建议书,承包商应尽快做出书面回复,或提出他不能照办的理由(如果情况如此),或提交:

(a) 对建议的设计和/或将要执行的工作的说明,以及实施的进度计划;
(b) 根据第 8.3 款 [*进度计划*] 和竣工时间的要求,承包商对进度计划做出必要修改的建议书;(以及)
(c) 承包商对合同价格调整建议书。

雇主代表收到此类(根据第 13.2 款 [*价值工程*] 的规定或其他规定提出的)建议书后,应尽快给予批准、不批准或提出意见的回复。在等待回复期间,承包商不应延误任何工作。

应由雇主代表向承包商发出执行每项变更,并附做好各项费用记录的任何要求的指示,承包商应确认收到该指示。

指示或批准一项变更时,雇主代表应按照第 3.5 款 [*确定*] 的要求,商定或确定对合同价格和付款计划表的调整。这些调整,除根据第 13.6 款 [*因法律改变的调整*] 和第 13.7 款 [*因技术改变的调整*] 的规定所做的调整外,应包括合理的利润,如果适用,应考虑承包商根据第 13.2 款 [*价值工程*] 提交的建议。

13.4 以适用货币支付

如果合同规定合同价格以一种以上货币支付,在上述商定、批准或确定调整时,应规定以每种适用的货币支付的款项。为此,应参照变更后工作费用的实际或预期的货币比例和规定的合同价格支付中的各种货币比例。

13.5 暂列金额

每笔暂列金额只应按照雇主代表的指示全部或部分地使用,合同价格应相应进行调整。付给承包商的总金额只应包括雇主代表已指示的,与暂列金额有关的工作、供货或服务的应付款项。对于每笔暂列金额,雇主代表可指示用于下列支付:

(a) work to be executed (including Plant, Materials or services to be supplied) by the Contractor and valued under Sub-Clause 13.3 [*Variation Procedure*]; and/or

(b) Plant, Materials or services to be purchased by the Contractor, for which there shall be included in the Contract Price:

  (i) the actual amounts paid (or due to be paid) by the Contractor; and
  (ii) a sum for overhead charges and profit, calculated as a percentage of these actual amounts by applying the relevant percentage rate (if any) stated in the appropriate Schedule. If there is no such rate, the percentage rate stated in the Contract Data shall be applied.

The Contractor shall, when required by the Employer's Representative, produce quotations, invoices, vouchers and accounts or receipts in substantiation.

13.6 Adjustments for Changes in Legislation

Adjustments to the execution of the Works or provision of the Operation Service necessitated by a change in Law shall be dealt with as a Variation and as provided for under Clause 13 [*Variations and Adjustments*]. Either Party may, by written Notice to the other, require that adjustments shall be made to the provision of the Contract as are necessary to enable the Contractor to comply with changes in Law.

The Contract Price and programme for design, execution and operation of the Works shall be adjusted to take account of any increase or decrease in cost resulting from a change in the Laws of the Country (including the introduction of new Laws and the repeal or modification of existing Laws) or in the judicial or official governmental interpretation of such Laws or changes to technical standards and regulations in accordance with Sub-Clause 5.4 [*Technical Standards and Regulations*], made after the Base Date, which affect the Contractor in the performance of obligations under the Contract.

If the Contractor suffers (or will suffer) delay and/or incurs (or will incur) additional cost as a result of these changes in the Laws or in such interpretations, made after the Base Date, the Contractor shall give Notice to the Employer's Representative providing evidence supporting any adjustment, an indication of the nature of change in cost and how the Contractor proposes to implement the necessary change.

The Contractor shall be entitled, subject to Sub-Clause 20.1 [*Contractor's Claims*], to:

(a) an extension of time for any such delay, if completion is or will be delayed, under Sub-Clause 9.3 [*Extension of Time for Completion of Design-Build*]; and

(b) payment of any such additional Cost, which shall be included in the Contract Price.

After receiving this Notice, the Employer's Representative shall proceed in accordance with Sub-Clause 3.5 [*Determinations*] to agree or determine these matters.

13.7 Adjustments for Changes in Technology

The Contract Price and programme for design, execution and operation of the Works shall be adjusted to take into account any increase or decrease in cost resulting from any changes in technology, new materials or products which the Contractor is obliged to adopt, either:

(a) 根据第 13.3 款［*变更程序*］的规定进行估价，要由**承包商**实施的工作（包括要提供的**生产设备**、**材料**或**服务**）；（和／或）

(b) 应包括在**合同价格**中的，要由**承包商**购买的**生产设备**、**材料**或**服务**：

  (i) **承包商**已付（或应付）的实际金额；（以及）
  (ii) 以相应**资料表**规定的有关百分率（如果有）计算的，这些实际金额的一个百分比，作为管理费和利润的金额。如无此类百分比，应采用**合同数据**中的百分比。

当**雇主代表**要求时，**承包商**应出示报价单、发票、凭证以及账单或收据等证明。

13.6 因法律改变的调整

因**法律**改变而对**工程**实施或**运营服务**提供的调整应作为**变更**处理，并按照第 13 条［*变更和调整*］的规定处理。任何一方可通过书面**通知**另一方，要求对合同条款进行必要的调整，以使**承包商**能够遵守**法律**改变。

在**基准日期**后**工程**所在国的**法律**有改变（包括实施新的**法律**，废除或修改现有**法律**），或对此类**法律**的司法或政府官方解释的改变，或根据第 5.4 款［*技术标准和法规*］的规定，对技术标准和规范的改变，影响了**承包商**履行**合同**规定的义务，**工程**设计、施工和运营的**合同价格**和进度计划，应考虑上述改变导致的任何费用增减进行调整。

如果由于这些**基准日期**后做出的**法律**或解释的改变，使**承包商**已（或将）遭受延误和／或已（或将）招致增加**费用**，**承包商**应向**雇主代表**发出**通知**，提供任何调整的证据，说明成本改变的性质，以及**承包商**建议任何实施必要的改变。

根据第 20.1 款［*承包商索赔*］的规定，**承包商**有权获得：

(a) 根据第 9.3 款［*设计－施工竣工时间的延长*］的规定，如果竣工已或将受到延误，对任何此类延误给予延长期；（以及）

(b) 如果此类额外**费用**，应计入**合同价格**，给予支付。

雇主代表在收到此**通知**后，应根据第 3.5 款［*确定*］的规定，对这些事项进行商定或确定。

13.7 因技术改变的调整

考虑到**承包商**有义务采用的技术、新材料或产品的任何改变，所导致的成本增加或减少，应调整**合同价格**和**工程**设计、施工和运营进度计划，或者：

(a) where a proposal from the Contractor under Sub-Clause 13.2 [*Value Engineering*] is accepted by the Employer's Representative;
(b) where the Employer's Representative instructs the Contractor to use new technology or new materials or products; or
(c) there is a statutory requirement for the Contractor to use new technology or new materials or products.

In any such case, the Contractor shall be entitled subject to Sub-Clause 20.1 [*Contractor's Claims*] to:

(i) an extension of time for any such delay, if the events delay the completion of the Design-Build; and
(ii) any additional Cost, subject to an adjustment for any operational or other savings which the Contractor may make as a result of the introduction of such new technology, materials or products.

After receiving a Notice of claim, the Employer's Representative shall proceed in accordance with Sub-Clause 3.5 [*Determinations*] to agree or determine these matters. Where appropriate, the Employer's Representative shall issue a Variation to the Contractor with details of the required changes.

13.8 Adjustments for Changes in Costs

The Contract Price and the Rates and Prices shall be adjusted in accordance with the Schedules of cost indexation as contained in the Schedule of Payments. If there are no such Schedules of cost indexation included in the Contract, this Sub-Clause shall not apply.

14 Contract Price and Payment

14.1 The Contract Price

The Contract Price shall be the amount or amounts submitted by the Contractor for the Design-Build and the Operation Service including the Asset Replacement Fund, priced at the Base Date, and due to be paid to the Contractor in accordance with the Contract together with any adjustments as provided for under Clause 13 [*Variations and Adjustments*] or arising as a result of claims under Clause 20 [*Claims, Disputes and Arbitration*].

The Contractor shall pay all taxes, duties and fees required to be paid by him under the Contract and the Contract Price shall not be adjusted for changes in any of these costs, except as provided for in Sub-Clause 13.6 [*Adjustments for Changes in Legislation*] and to the extent allowed for under Clause 20 [*Claims, Disputes and Arbitration*].

14.2 Advance Payment

The Employer shall make an advance payment, as an interest-free loan for mobilisation and design, when the Contractor submits a guarantee in accordance with this Sub-Clause that shall be based on the sample form included in the tender documents or in another form acceptable to the Employer. The amount of the advance payment and the applicable currencies shall be as stated in the Contract Data.

Unless and until the Employer receives this guarantee, or if no advance payment is stated in the Contract Data, this Sub-Clause shall not apply.

(a) **雇主代表**接受**承包商**根据第 13.2 款［*价值工程*］提出的建议；

(b) **雇主代表**指示**承包商**使用新技术或新材料或新产品；（或）

(c) 法律要求**承包商**使用新技术或新材料或产品。

在任何此类情况下，根据第 20.1 款［*承包商索赔*］的规定，**承包商**有权获得：

（i） 如果事件延误了**设计 - 施工竣工**，对任何此类延误给予延长期；（以及）

（ii） 任何额外**费用**，应根据**承包商**引进此类新技术、材料或产品可能产生的任何运营或其他节省进行调整。

在收到索赔**通知**后，**雇主代表**应按照第 3.5 款［*确定*］的规定，商定或确定这些事项。在适当的情况下，**雇主代表**应向**承包商**发出变更的**通知**，说明所需改变的细节。

13.8
因成本改变的调整

合同价格、**费率**和**价格**应根据**付款计划表**中包括的成本指数表进行调整。如果**合同**中没有此类成本指数表，本款应不适用。

14 合同价格和付款

14.1
合同价格

合同价格应为**承包商**为**设计 - 施工和运营服务**提交的一笔或多笔金额，包括**资产置换基金**、**基准日期**的价格，以及根据合同规定应付给**承包商**的，以及根据第 13 条［*变更和调整*］规定或产生的任何调整，根据第 20 条［*索赔、争端和仲裁*］的规定提出的索赔。

承包商应支付根据合同要求应由其支付的各项税金、关税和费用，并且**合同价格**不应因任何这些费用的改变而进行调整，除第 13.6 款［*因法律改变的调整*］说明的情况外，以及在第 20 条［*索赔、争端和仲裁*］允许的范围内进行调整。

14.2
预付款

当**承包商**根据本款提交保函时，**雇主**应支付一笔预付款，作为用于动员和设计的无息贷款，该保函应以招标文件中的样本格式或**雇主**可接受的其他格式为依据（基础）。预付款的金额和适用货币应按**合同数据**中的规定。

除非并直到**雇主**收到此保函，或如果**合同数据**中没有规定预付款，本**款**应不适用。

The Employer's Representative shall issue an Interim Payment Certificate for the advance payment under Sub-Clause 14.7 [*Issue of Advance and Interim Payment Certificates*] after receiving an application under Sub-Clause 14.3 [*Application for Advance and Interim Payment Certificates*] and after the Employer receives (i) the Performance Security in accordance with Sub-Clause 4.2 [*Performance Security*] and (ii) a guarantee in amounts and currencies equal to the advance payment. This guarantee shall be issued by an entity and from within a country (or other jurisdiction) approved by the Employer, and shall be based on the sample form included in the tender documents or in another form approved by the Employer.

The Contractor shall ensure that the guarantee is valid and enforceable until the advance payment has been repaid, but its amount may be progressively reduced by the amount repaid by the Contractor as indicated in the Interim Payment Certificates. If the terms of the guarantee specify its expiry date, and the advance payment has not been repaid by the date 28 days prior to the expiry date, the Contractor shall extend the validity of the guarantee until the advance payment has been repaid.

The advance payment shall be repaid through percentage deductions in Interim Payment Certificates. Unless other percentages are stated in the Contract Data:

(a) deductions shall commence in the Interim Payment Certificate in which the total of all certified interim payments (excluding the advance payment and deductions and repayments of retention) exceeds ten percent (10%) of the Accepted Contract Amount for the Design-Build less Provisional Sums; and

(b) deductions shall be made at the amortisation rate of one-quarter (25%) of the amount of each Interim Payment Certificate (excluding the advance payment and deductions and repayments of retention) issued during the Design-Build Period.

If the advance payment has not been repaid prior to the issue of the Commissioning Certificate or prior to termination under Clause 15 [*Termination by Employer*], Clause 16 [*Suspension and Termination by Contractor*] or Clause 18 [*Exceptional Risks*] (as the case may be), the whole of the balance then outstanding shall immediately become due and payable by the Contractor to the Employer.

14.3 Application for Advance and Interim Payment Certificates

When submitting the advance payment guarantee required under Sub-Clause 14.2 [*Advance Payment*], the Contractor shall include his application for the advance payment.

The Contractor shall thereafter submit a Statement in one original and five copies to the Employer's Representative after the end of each month (unless otherwise stated in the Contract), in a form approved by the Employer's Representative, showing in detail the amounts to which the Contractor considers himself to be entitled, together with supporting documents.

The Statement shall include the following items, as applicable, which shall be expressed in the various currencies in which the Contract Price is payable:

(a) the estimated contract value of the Works executed and the Contractor's Documents produced up to the end of the month (including Variations but excluding items described in sub-paragraphs (b) to (j) below);

雇主代表在收到根据第 14.3 款［*预付款和期中付款证书的申请*］规定提出的申请，且雇主收到（i）按照第 4.2 款［*履约担保*］要求提交的**履约担保**后，**雇主代表**应根据第 14.7 款［*预付款和期中付款证书的签发*］的规定，签发预付款的期中付款证书，和（ii）金额与货币种类与预付款一致的保函。该保函应由雇主批准的国家（或其他司法管辖区）的实体出具，并应以招标文件中包含的样本格式或雇主批准的其他格式为依据（基础）。

在还清预付款前，**承包商**应确保该保函一直有效并可执行，但其总额可根据**期中付款证书**规定的**承包商**付还的金额逐渐减少。如果保函条款中规定了其期满日期，而在期满日期前 28 天预付款尚未还清时，**承包商**应将保函有效期延至预付款还清为止。

预付款应通过**期中付款证书**中按百分比扣减的方式付（偿）还。除非在**合同数据**中规定了其百分比：

(a) 扣减应从确认的期中付款（不包括预付款、扣减额和保留金的发放）累计额超过以该货币支付的**设计 - 施工中标合同金额**减去**暂列金额**后余额的百分之十（10%）时的**期中付款证书**开始；（以及）

(b) 扣减应按**设计 - 施工期**签发的每次**期中付款证书**中金额（不包括预付款、扣减额和保留金的发放）的四分之一（25%）的摊还比例。

如果在签发**调试证书**前，或根据第 15 条［*由雇主终止*］、第 16 条［*由承包商暂停和终止*］或 18 条［*例外风险*］（视情况而定）的规定终止前，预付款尚未还清，则全部余额应立即成为**承包商**对**雇主**的到期应付款。

14.3 预付款和期中付款证书的申请	在根据第 14.2 款［*预付款*］要求提交的预付款保函时，**承包商**应包括其预付款申请。

此后，**承包商**应按照**雇主代表**批准的格式，在每个月结束后，向**雇主代表**提交一份原件，五份副本**报表**（除非**合同**另有规定），详细说明**承包商**认为其有权得到的款额，连同证明文件。

适用时，该**报表**应包括下列项目，以**合同价格**应付的各种货币表示：

(a) 截至月末已实施的**工程**和已提出的**承包商文件**的估算合同价值（包括各项**变更**，但不包括以下（b）至（j）段所列事项）；

(b) any amounts to be added and deducted for changes in legislation, changes in cost and changes in technology, in accordance with Sub-Clause 13.6 [*Adjustments for Changes in Legislation*], Sub-Clause 13.7 [*Adjustments for Changes in Technology*] and Sub-Clause 13.8 [*Adjustments for Changes in Cost*];

(c) any amount to be deducted for retention, calculated by applying the percentage of retention stated in the Contract Data to the total of the above amounts, until the amount so retained by the Employer's Representative reaches the limit of Retention Money (if any) stated in the Contract Data;

(d) any amounts to be added and deducted for the advance payment and repayments in accordance with Sub-Clause 14.2 [*Advance Payment*];

(e) any amounts to be added and deducted for Plant and Materials in accordance with Sub-Clause 14.6 [*Payment for Plant and Materials intended for the Works*];

(f) any amounts due for Plant, Materials or services purchased by the Contractor under Sub-Clause 13.5 [*Provisional Sums*];

(g) amounts due for the Operation Service;

(h) amounts due from the Asset Replacement Fund;

(i) adjustments due for the Maintenance Retention Fund;

(j) any other additions or deductions which may have become due under the Contract or otherwise, including those under Clause 20 [*Claims, Disputes and Arbitration*]; and

(k) the deduction of amounts certified in all previous Interim Payment Certificates.

14.4 Schedule of Payments

If the Contract includes a Schedule of Payments for the Design-Build Period and/or the Operation Service Period specifying the instalments in which the Contract Price and/or the Rates and Prices will be paid, then, unless otherwise stated in this Schedule:

(a) the instalments quoted in the Schedule of Payments shall be the estimated values for the purposes of Sub-Clause 14.3 [*Application for Advance and Interim Payment Certificates*];

(b) Sub-Clause 14.6 [*Payment for Plant and Materials intended for the Works*] shall not apply; and

(c) if these instalments are not defined by reference to the actual progress achieved in executing the Works, and if actual progress is found to differ from that on which the Schedule of Payments was based, then the Employer's Representative may proceed in accordance with Sub-Clause 3.5 [*Determinations*] to agree or determine revised instalments which shall take account of the extent to which progress differs from that on which the instalments were previously based.

If the Contract does not include a Schedule of Payments for the Design-Build Period and/or the Operation Service Period, the Contractor shall submit non-binding estimates of the payments which he expects to become due during each quarterly period. The first estimate shall be submitted within 42 days after the Commencement Date. Revised estimates shall be submitted at quarterly intervals until the Contract Completion Certificate has been issued.

14.5 Asset Replacement Schedule

Payments from the Asset Replacement Fund shall be made in accordance with the provisions of Sub-Clause 14.18 [*Asset Replacement Fund*].

On no account will payments be made for assets replaced which are not identified in the Asset Replacement Schedule unless they have been instructed as a Variation under Clause 13 [*Variations and Adjustments*].

（b）按照第 13.6 款［*因法律改变的调整*］、第 13.7 款［*因技术改变的调整*］和第 13.8 款［*因成本改变的调整*］的规定，由于法律改变、成本改变和技术改变，应增减的任何款额；

（c）至**雇主代表**提取的保留金额达到**合同数据**中规定的**保留金限额**（如果有）前，用**合同数据**中规定的保留金百分比乘以上述的款项总额计算的应扣减的任何保留金额；

（d）按照第 14.2 款［*预付款*］的规定，因预付款的支付和付还，应增加和 / 或扣减的任何款额；

（e）按照第 14.6 款［*拟用于工程的生产设备和材料的付款*］的规定，为购买**生产设备**和**材料**应增加和扣减的任何款额；

（f）**承包商**根据第 13.5 款［*暂列金额*］规定购买的**生产设备**、**材料**或服务产生的任何款额；

（g）**运营服务**应付款额；

（h）**资产置换基金**应付款额；

（i）应付**维护保留金**的调整；

（j）根据合同或其他规定，包括第 20 条［*索赔、争端和仲裁*］规定的，应付的任何其他增加额或扣减额；

（k）所有以前**期中付款证书**中确认的扣减额。

14.4 付款计划表

如果合同包括一份**设计 - 施工期**和 / 或**运营服务期**的**付款计划表**，其中规定了**合同价格**和 / 或**费率和价格**的分期付款，除非该表中另有规定：

（a）该**付款计划表**所述的分期付款，应是为了应对第 14.3 款［*预付款和期中付款证书的申请*］中所述的估算价值；

（b）第 14.6 款［*拟用于工程的生产设备和材料的付款*］的规定应不适用；以及

（c）如果分期付款额不是参照**工程**实施达到的实际进度确定，且如果发现实际进度与**付款计划表**依据的进度不同，**雇主代表**可按照第 3.5 款［*确定*］的要求进行商定或确定，修改分期付款额，这种修改的分期付款应考虑实际进度与先前分期付款额所依据的进度的不同程度。

如果合同未包括**设计 - 施工期**和 / 或**运营服务期**的**付款计划表**，**承包商**应每 3 个月提交其预计应付的无约束性估算付款额。第一次估算应在**开工日期**后 42 天内提交。直到签发**合同完成证书**前，应按每 3 个月提交一次修正的估算。

14.5 资产置换计划表

资产置换基金的付款应按照第 14.18 款［*资产置换基金*］的规定进行。

除非已根据第 13 条［*变更和调整*］的规定指示为**变更**，否则不得对**资产置换计划表**中未确认的被置换资产进行付款。

If Assets are replaced in advance of the date given in the Asset Replacement Schedule, payment will not be released until the date stated in the Schedule has been reached.

If Assets are not replaced on or before the scheduled date, payment will not be released until such replacements have been effected.

Any monies remaining in the Asset Replacement Fund at the time of issue of the Contract Completion Certificate will be disbursed between the Parties as described in Sub-Clause 14.18 [*Asset Replacement Fund*].

14.6
Payment for Plant and Materials intended for the Works

If this Sub-Clause applies, Interim Payment Certificates shall include, under subparagraph (e) of Sub-Clause 14.3 [*Application for Advance and Interim Payment Certificates*], (i) an amount for Plant and Materials which have been sent to the Site for incorporation in the Permanent Works, and (ii) a reduction when the contract value of such Plant and Materials is included as part of the Permanent Works under subparagraph (a) of Sub-Clause 14.3.

If the lists referred to in sub-paragraphs (b) (i) or (c) (i) below are not included in the Contract Data, this Sub-Clause shall not apply.

The Employer's Representative shall determine and certify each addition if the following conditions are satisfied:

(a) the Contractor has:

  (i) kept satisfactory records (including the orders, receipts, costs and use of Plant and Materials) which are available for inspection; and
  (ii) submitted a statement of the cost of acquiring and delivering the Plant and Materials to the Site, supported by satisfactory evidence; and either:

(b) the relevant Plant and Materials:

  (i) are those listed in the Contract Data for payment when shipped;
  (ii) have been shipped to the Country, en route to the Site, in accordance with the Contract; and
  (iii) are described in a clean shipped bill of lading or other evidence of shipment, which has been submitted to the Employer's Representative together with evidence of payment of freight and insurance, any other documents reasonably required, and a bank guarantee in a form and issued by an entity approved by the Employer in amounts and currencies equal to the amount due under this Sub-Clause. This guarantee may be in a similar form to the form referred to in Sub-Clause 14.2 [*Advance Payment*] and shall be valid until the Plant and Materials are properly stored on Site and protected against loss, damage or deterioration; or

(c) the relevant Plant and Materials:

  (i) are those listed in the Contract Data for payment when delivered to the Site; and
  (ii) have been delivered to and are properly stored on the Site, are protected against loss, damage or deterioration, and appear to be in accordance with the Contract.

如果**资产**在**资产置换计划表**中规定的日期之前被置换，则在该**计划表**中规定的日期之前，付款将不会被发放。

如果**资产**在计划表日期当日或之前未被置换，则在该置换生效之前，付款将不会被发放。

在签发合同完成证书之前，**资产置换基金**中剩余的任何款项，将按照**第 14.18 款**[**资产置换基金**]的规定在双方之间支付。

14.6
拟用于工程的生产设备和材料的付款

如果本款适用，则根据**第 14.3 款**[*预付款和期中付款证书的申请*]（e）段的规定，**期中付款证书**应包括：(i) 已装运至**现场**用于**永久工程**的**生产设备**和**材料**的金额；(以及)(ii) 当此类生产设备和材料的合同价值已根据**第 14.3 款**（a）段的规定，作为**永久工程**一部分包含在内时的减少额。

如果**合同数据**中没有下述（b）(i) 和（c）(i) 段提到的所列内容，本款应不适用。

如满足以下条件，**雇主代表**应确定和确认各项增加金额：

(a) **承包商**已：

    (i) 保存了符合要求、可供检验的（包括**生产设备**和**材料**的订单、收据、费用和使用的）记录；(以及)

    (ii) 提交了购买**生产设备**和**材料**并将其装运至**现场**的费用报表，并附有符合要求的证据；(以及，或)

(b) 有关**生产设备**和**材料**：

    (i) 是**合同数据**中所列装运付费的物品；
    (ii) 按照合同已运到**工程所在国**，在运往**现场**的途中；

    (iii) 已写入清洁装运提单或其他装运证明，此类提单或证明，已连同运费和保费的支付证据、合理要求的任何其他文件，以及由**雇主**批准的实体按**雇主**同意的格式出具、与根据本款规定应付金额和货币一致的银行保函，一起提交给**雇主代表**。此保函可具有与**第 14.2 款**[*预付款*]中提到的格式相类似的格式，并应做到在**生产设备**和**材料**已在**现场**妥善储存并做好防止损失、损害或变质的保护以前，一直有效；(或)

(c) 有关**生产设备**和**材料**：

    (i) 是**合同数据**中所列运到**现场**时付款的物品；(以及)

    (ii) 已运到**现场**和妥善储存，并已做好防止损失、损害或变质的保护，似乎已符合**合同**要求。

The additional amount to be certified shall be the equivalent of eighty percent (80%) of the Employer's Representative determination of the cost of the Plant and Materials (including delivery to Site), taking account of the documents mentioned in this Sub-Clause and of the contract value of the Plant and Materials.

The currencies for this additional amount shall be the same as those in which payment will become due when the contract value is included under sub-paragraph (a) of Sub-Clause 14.3 [*Application for Advance and Interim Payment Certificates*]. At that time, the Interim Payment Certificate shall include the applicable reduction which shall be equivalent to, and in the same currencies and proportions as, this additional amount for the relevant Plant and Materials.

14.7 Issue of Advance and Interim Payment Certificates

No amount will be certified or paid until the Employer has received and approved the Performance Security provided for in Sub-Clause 4.2 [*Performance Security*]. Upon receipt of the Contractor's application for the advance payment, the Employer's Representative shall, within 14 days of receiving the application, issue to the Employer an Interim Payment Certificate in respect of such payment, with a copy to the Contractor. Thereafter, in respect of interim payment applications the Employer's Representative shall, within 28 days after receiving a Statement and supporting documents, issue to the Employer an Interim Payment Certificate which shall state the amount which the Employer's Representative fairly determines to be due, with supporting particulars, and shall include any amounts due to or from the Contractor in accordance with a decision by the DAB made under Sub-Clause 20.6 [*Obtaining Dispute Adjudication Board's Decision*].

However, prior to issuing the Commissioning Certificate, the Employer's Representative shall not be bound to issue an Interim Payment Certificate in an amount which would (after retention and other deductions) be less than the minimum amount of Interim Payment Certificates (if any) stated in the Contract Data. In this event, the Employer's Representative shall give Notice to the Contractor accordingly.

An Interim Payment Certificate shall not be withheld for any other reason, although:

(a) if any thing supplied or work done by the Contractor is not in accordance with the Contract, the cost of rectification or replacement may be withheld until rectification or replacement has been completed; and/or

(b) if the Contractor was or is failing to perform any work or obligation in accordance with the Contract, and had been so notified by the Employer's Representative, the value of this work or obligation may be withheld until the work or obligation has been performed.

The Employer's Representative may in any Payment Certificate make any correction or modification that should properly be made to any previous Payment Certificate. An Interim Payment Certificate shall not be deemed to indicate the Employer's Representative's acceptance, approval, consent or satisfaction of the Works.

14.8 Payment

The Employer shall pay to the Contractor:

(a) the advance payment within 21 days after receiving the documents in accordance with Sub-Clause 4.2 [*Performance Security*] and Sub-Clause 14.2 [*Advance Payment*] and the Payment Certificate for the advance payment issued in accordance with Sub-Clause 14.7 [*Issue of Advance and Interim Payment Certificates*];

要确认的增加金额，应是**雇主代表**考虑本款要求的各项文件及**生产设备**和**材料**的合同价值，确定的**生产设备**和**材料**（包括运送到**现场**）的费用的百分之八十（80%）。

此项增加的货币，应与**第 14.3 款**［*预付款和期中付款证书的申请*］（a）段包括的合同价值应付的货币相同。此时，**期中付款证书**应计入适当的减少额，该减少额应与相关**生产设备**和**材料**的增加额相等，并采用同样的货币和比例。

14.7 预付款和期中付款证书的签发

在雇主收到并确认**第 4.2 款**［*履约担保*］中规定的**履约担保**之前，不确认或支付任何金额。在收到**承包商**的预付款申请后，**雇主代表**应在收到申请后 14 天内，向雇主签发关于此类付款的**期中付款证书**，并向**承包商**提供一份副本。此后，对于期中付款申请，**雇主代表**应在收到**报表**和证明文件后 28 天内，向雇主签发**期中付款证书**，说明**雇主代表**公正确定的应付金额，并附详细证明资料，并应包括根据**争端裁决委员会**，按照**第 20.6 款**［*取得争端裁决委员会的决定*］的规定做出的决定，应付给**承包商**或其应付的任何款额。

但是，在签发**调试证书**前，**雇主代表**无须签发金额（扣除保留金和其他扣减额后）少于**合同数据**中规定的**期中付款证书**的最低额（如果有）的**期中付款证书**。在此情况下，**雇主代表**应相应地**通知承包商**。

虽然存在以下情况，对**期中付款证书**不应因任何其他原因予以扣发：

（a） 如果**承包商**供应的任何物品或完成的工作不符合**合同**要求，在完成修正或更换前，可以扣发该修正或更换所需费用（和／或）

（b） 如果**承包商**未能按照**合同**要求履行任何工作或义务，并已得到**雇主代表**的通知，在该项工作或义务完成前，可以扣留该工作或义务的价值。

雇主代表可在任一次付款证书中，对以前任何**付款证书**做出任何适当的改正或修改。**期中付款证书**不应被视为表明**雇主代表**对工程的接受、批准、同意或满意。

14.8 付款

雇主应向**承包商**支付：

（a） 预付款支付时间，在收到**第 4.2 款**［*履约担保*］和**第 14.2 款**［*预付款*］规定的文件，和按照**第 14.7 款**［*预付款和期中付款证书的签发*］中规定签发的预付款**付款证书**后 21 天内；

(b) the amount certified in each Interim Payment Certificate within 56 days after the Employer's Representative receives the corresponding Statement and supporting documents, including any amounts due in accordance with a decision by the DAB which have been included in the Interim Payment Certificate; and

(c) the amounts certified in the Final Payment Certificate Design-Build and the Final Payment Certificate Operation Service within 56 days after the Employer receives each such Final Payment Certificate, including any amounts due in accordance with a decision by the DAB which have been included in the Final Payment Certificate.

Payment of the amount due in each currency shall be made into the bank account, nominated by the Contractor, in the payment country (for this currency) specified in the Contract.

14.9 Delayed Payment

If the Contractor does not receive payment in accordance with Sub-Clause 14.8 [*Payment*], the Contractor shall be entitled to receive financing charges compounded monthly on the amount unpaid during the period of delay. This period shall be deemed to commence on the date for payment specified in Sub-Clause 14.8 [*Payment*], irrespective (in the case of its sub-paragraph (b)) of the date on which any Interim Payment Certificate is issued.

Unless otherwise stated in the Contract Data, these financing charges shall be calculated at the annual rate of three percentage points above the discount rate of the central bank in the country of the currency (or currencies if more than one) of payment, and shall be paid in such currencies.

The Contractor shall be entitled to this payment without formal Notice or certification, and without prejudice to any other right or remedy.

14.10 Payment of Retention Money

When the Commissioning Certificate has been issued, the first half of the Retention Money shall be certified by the Employer's Representative for payment to the Contractor. If a Section Commissioning Certificate is issued for a Section, the relevant percentage of the first half of the Retention Money shall be certified and paid to the Contractor. Such amount shall be included for payment in the next Interim Payment Certificate following the issue of the Commissioning Certificate.

The Contractor shall be entitled to include the second half of the Retention Money in the Final Statement Design-Build.

14.11 Application for Final Payment Certificate Design-Build

Within 28 days after the end of the Retention Period, the Contractor shall submit to the Employer's Representative one original and five copies of the Final Statement Design-Build with supporting documents showing:

(a) the value of all work done in respect of the Design-Build; and
(b) any further sums which the Contractor considers to be due to him under the Contract in respect of the Design-Build.

Together with the Final Statement Design-Build, the Contractor shall submit a written undertaking that the Statement is in full and final settlement of all matters under or in connection with the Contract relating to the Design-Build.

(b) 各期中付款证书中确认的金额，支付时间在**雇主代表**收到相应的**报表**和证明文件后 56 天内，包括根据**争端裁决委员会**的决定，应支付的已包含在**期中付款证书**中的任何金额；（以及）

(c) **设计-施工最终付款证书**和**运营服务最终付款证书**中确认的金额，支付时间在**雇主**收到每份**最终付款证书**后 56 天内，包括根据**争端裁决委员会**的决定，应支付的已包含在**最终付款证书**中的任何金额。

每种货币的应付款额，应汇入**合同**（为此货币）规定的付款国境内的**承包商**指定的银行账户。

14.9 延误的付款

如果**承包商**没有在按照**第 14.8 款**[*付款*]规定的时间收到付款，**承包商**应有权就未付款额按月计算复利，收取延误期的融资费用。该延误期应视为从**第 14.8 款**[*付款*]规定的支付期限届满时算起，而不考虑[如本款（b）段的情况]签发任何**期中付款证书**的日期。

除非**合同数据**中另有规定，上述融资费用应以高出付款货币（或多种货币）所在国中央银行的贴现率 3% 的年利率进行计算，并应用同种货币支付。

承包商应有权得到此项付款，而无须正式**通知**或证明，以及损害其任何其他权利或补偿。

14.10 保留金的支付

签发**调试证书**后，**雇主代表**应确认**保留金**的前半部分支付给**承包商**。如果为某**分项工程**签发了分项**调试证书**，应确认并向**承包商**支付**保留金**前半部分的相关百分比。此类金额应包括在签发**调试证书**后的下一次**期中付款证书**中。

承包商有权将**保留金**的后半部分包含在**最终设计-施工报表**中。

14.11 设计-施工最终付款证书的申请

在**保留金**期结束后 28 天内，**承包商**应向**雇主代表**提交**设计-施工最终报表**，一份原件和五份副本，并附上证明文件，列出：

（a）与**设计-施工**相关的所有工作的价值；（以及）
（b）**承包商**认为根据合同应向其支付的与**设计-施工**有关的任何其他款额。

承包商应在提交**设计-施工最终报表**的同时，提交一份书面承诺，确认该报表的总额和最终结算代表了**合同规定的**或与**设计-施工**相关的所有事项。

If the Employer's Representative disagrees with or cannot verify any part of the Final Statement Design-Build, the Employer's Representative and the Contractor shall attempt to agree such matters, and the Contractor shall re-submit his Final Statement based on the agreement with the Employer's Representative. The Employer's Representative shall then issue a Final Payment Certificate Design-Build under Sub-Clause 14.12 [*Issue of Final Payment Certificate Design-Build*] for the agreed amount. If the Parties cannot agree on such matters, or if the Contractor has failed to submit his application for payment within the said 28 days, the Employer's Representative shall issue an Interim Payment Certificate under Sub-Clause 14.7 [*Issue of Advance and Interim Payment Certificates*] for the amount which he considers to be due to the Contractor. If the Contractor is dissatisfied with the amount certified, he may refer the matter to the DAB for a decision in accordance with Clause 20.6 [*Obtaining Dispute Adjudication Board's Decision*].

14.12
Issue of Final Payment Certificate Design-Build

Within 28 days of receiving the Final Statement Design-Build, or the re-submitted Final Statement (as the case may be), and the written undertaking from the Contractor in accordance with Sub-Clause 14.11 [*Application for Final Payment Certificate Design-Build*], the Employer's Representative shall issue to the Employer, with a copy to the Contractor, the Final Payment Certificate Design-Build stating:

(a) the amount which is finally due for the Design-Build; and
(b) after giving credit to the Employer for all amounts previously paid by the Employer and all sums to which the Employer is entitled in respect of the Design-Build, the balance (if any) due from the Employer to the Contractor or from the Contractor to the Employer, as the case may be.

Upon receipt of the Final Payment Certificate Design-Build, the Employer shall pay the Contractor the amount, if any, due in accordance with the provisions of Sub-Clause 14.8 [*Payment*].

14.13
Application for Final Payment Certificate Operation Service

Within 56 days after receiving the Contract Completion Certificate, the Contractor shall submit to the Employer's Representative one original and five copies of the Final Statement Operation Service with supporting documents showing:

(a) the value of all work done in respect of the Operation Service including authorised expenditure from the Asset Replacement Fund; and
(b) any further sums which the Contractor considers to be due to him under the Contract including any unused monies from the Maintenance Retention Fund.

Together with the Final Statement Operation Service, the Contractor shall submit a written discharge according to the requirements of Sub-Clause 14.14 [*Discharge*].

14.14
Discharge

When submitting the Final Statement Operation Service, the Contractor shall submit a written discharge which confirms that the total of the Final Statement Operation Service, together with the Final Statement Design-Build submitted according to Sub-Clause 14.11 [*Application for Final Payment Certificate Design-Build*] represents full and final settlement of all monies due to the Contractor under or in connection with the Contract. This discharge may state that it becomes effective only after payment due under the Final Payment Certificate Operation Service has been made and the Performance Security referred to in Sub-Clause 4.2[*Performance Security*] has been returned to the Contractor.

如果**雇主代表**不同意或无法核实**设计-施工最终报表**的任何部分，**雇主代表**和**承包商**应尝试就此类事项商定一致，且**承包商**应根据与**雇主代表**的商定重新提交其**最终报表**。然后，**雇主代表**应根据第 14.12 款 [*设计-施工最终付款证书的签发*] 的规定，就商定的金额签发**设计-施工最终付款证书**。如果双方不能就此类事项商定一致，或如果**承包商**未能在上述 28 天内提交付款申请，**雇主代表**应根据第 14.7 款 [*预付款和期中付款证书的签发*] 的规定，就其认为应支付给**承包商**的金额签发期中付款证书。如果**承包商**对确认的金额不满意，他可将此事项提交给**争端裁决委员会**，由其根据第 20.6 款 [*取得争端裁决委员会的决定*] 的规定做出决定。

14.12 设计-施工最终付款证书的签发

在收到**承包商**根据第 14.11 款 [*设计-施工最终付款证书的申请*] 规定提交的，**设计-施工最终报表**或重新提交的**最终报表**（视情况而定）和书面承诺后 28 天内，**雇主代表**应向**雇主**签发**设计-施工最终付款证书**，并抄送**承包商**，其中说明：

（a） **设计-施工**最终应付款额；（以及）
（b） 在确认**雇主**以前已付的所有款额以及**雇主**有权得到**设计-施工**的全部金额后，**雇主**尚需付给**承包商**，或**承包商**尚需付给**雇主**的余额（如果有），视情况而定。

在收到**设计-施工最终付款证书**后，**雇主**应按照第 14.8 款 [*付款*] 的规定，向**承包商**支付应付的款额。

14.13 运营服务最终付款证书的申请

在收到合同完成证书后 56 天内，**承包商**应向**雇主代表**提交**运营服务最终报表**，一份原件和五份副本，并附上证明文件，列出：

（a） 与**运营服务**相关的所有工作的价值，包括**资产置换基金**的授权支出；（以及）
（b） **承包商**认为根据合同应向其支付的任何其他款额，包括**维护保留金**中未使用的任何款项。

承包商应按照第 14.14 款 [*结清证明*] 的要求，连同**运营服务最终报表**一起提交一份书面结清证明。

14.14 结清证明

承包商在提交**运营服务最终报表**时，应提交一份书面结清证明，确认根据第 14.11 款 [*设计-施工最终付款证书的申请*] 规定提交的**运营服务最终报表**和**设计-施工最终报表**的总额代表了**合同**规定的或与**合同**有关的事项，应付给**承包商**的所有款项的全部和最终的结算总额。该结清证明可注明，只有在**运营服务最终付款证书**规定的款项已支付，且第 4.2 款 [*履约担保*] 中提及的**履约担保**已退还该**承包商**后，该结清证明才生效。

14.15
Issue of Final Payment Certificate Operation Service

Within 28 days of receiving the Final Statement Operation Service and the written discharge from the Contractor in accordance with Sub-Clause 14.13 [*Application for Final Payment Certificate Operation Service*] and Sub-Clause 14.14 [*Discharge*] respectively, the Employer's Representative shall issue to the Employer, with a copy to the Contractor, the Final Payment Certificate Operation Service stating:

(a) the amount which is finally due for the Operation Service; and
(b) the amount which is finally due for the Contract; and
(c) after giving credit to the Employer for all amounts previously paid by the Employer and all sums to which the Employer is entitled in respect of the Contract, the balance (if any) due from the Employer to the Contractor or from the Contractor to the Employer, as the case may be.

If the Employer's Representative disagrees with or cannot verify any part of the Final Statement Operation Service, the Employer's Representative and the Contractor shall attempt to agree such matters, and the Employer's Representative shall issue a Final Payment Certificate Operation Service for the agreed amount. If the Parties cannot agree on such matters, the Employer's Representative shall issue a Final Payment Certificate Operation Service for the amount which he considers to be due to the Contractor. If the Contractor is dissatisfied with the amount certified, he may refer the matter to the DAB for a decision in accordance with Clause 20.6 [*Obtaining Dispute Adjudication Board's Decision*].

Upon receipt of the Final Payment Certificate Operation Service, the Employer shall pay the Contractor in accordance with the provisions of Sub-Clause 14.8 [*Payment*].

14.16
Cessation of Employer's Liability

The Employer shall not be liable to the Contractor for any matter or thing under or in connection with the Contract or execution of the Works, except to the extent that the Contractor shall have included an amount expressly for it in the Final Statement Design-Build or the Final Statement Operation Service.

However, this Sub-Clause shall not limit the Employer's liability under his indemnification obligations, or the Employer's liability in any case of fraud, deliberate default or reckless misconduct by the Employer.

Furthermore, if the Contractor has not submitted any matter to the Dispute Adjudication Board under Sub-Clause 20.6 [*Obtaining Dispute Arbitration Board's Decision*] within 56 days of receiving notification from the Employer's Representative of the amounts included for payment in either the Final Certificate Design-Build or the Final Certificate Operation Service, then he will be deemed to have accepted the amounts so certified, and the Employer shall be deemed to have no further liability to the Contractor, subject only to that payment due under the Final Payment Certificate Operation Service has been made and that the Performance Security referred to in Sub-Clause 4.2 [*Performance Security*] has been returned to the Contractor.

14.17
Currencies of Payment

The Contract Price shall be paid in the currency or currencies named in the Contract Data. Unless otherwise stated in the Particular Conditions, if more than one currency is so named, payments shall be made as follows:

(a) if the Accepted Contract Amount was expressed in Local Currency only:

14.15 运营服务最终付款证书的签发

在收到承包商分别根据第 14.13 款［*运营服务最终付款证书的申请*］和第 14.14 款［*结清证明*］规定提交的，运营服务最终报表和书面结清证明后 28 天内，雇主代表应向雇主签发运营服务最终付款证书，并抄送承包商，其中说明：

(a) 运营服务最终应付款额；(和)
(b) 合同最终应付款额；(以及)
(c) 确认雇主先前已付的所有款额以及雇主有权得到与合同相关的全部款额后，雇主尚需付给承包商，或承包商尚需付给雇主的余额(如果有)，视情况而定。

如果雇主代表不同意或无法核实运营服务最终报表的任何部分，雇主代表和承包商应尝试就此类事项商定一致，且雇主代表应就商定的金额签发运营服务最终付款证书。如果双方不能就此类事项商定一致，雇主代表应就其认为应支付给承包商的金额签发运营服务最终付款证书。如果承包商对确认的金额不满意，他可将此事项提交给争端裁决委员会，由其根据第 20.6 款［*取得争端裁决委员会的决定*］的规定做出决定。

在收到运营服务最终付款证书后，雇主应按照第 14.8 款［*付款*］的规定，向承包商支付应付的款额。

14.16 雇主责任的中止

除了承包商在设计-施工最终报表或运营服务最终报表中，因合同或工程实施造成的或与之有关的任何问题或事项，明确提出款项要求以外，雇主应不再为之对承包商承担责任。

但是，本款不应减少雇主因其保障义务，或因其任何欺骗、重大过失、故意违约或轻率不当行为等情况引起的责任。

此外，如果承包商在收到雇主代表关于设计-施工最终付款证书或运营服务最终付款证书的通知后 56 天内，未能根据第 20.6 款［*取得争端裁决委员会的决定*］的规定，向争端裁决委员会提交任何事项，则承包商应被视为已接受经确认的款项。只有在运营服务最终付款证书规定的款项已支付，且第 4.2 款［*履约担保*］中提及的履约担保已退还给承包商后，雇主被视为不应对承包商承担进一步的责任。

14.17 支付的货币

合同价格应按合同数据中规定的货币或几种货币支付。除非专用条件中另有规定，如果规定了一种以上货币，应按以下办法支付：

(a) 如果中标合同金额只是用当地货币表示的：

(i) the proportions or amounts of the Local and Foreign Currencies, and the fixed rates of exchange to be used for calculating the payments, shall be as stated in the Contract Data, except as otherwise agreed by both Parties;

(ii) payments and deductions under Sub-Clause 13.5 [*Provisional Sums*] and Sub-Clause 13.6 [*Adjustments for Changes in Legislation*] shall be made in the applicable currencies and proportions; and

(iii) other payments and deductions under sub-paragraphs (a) to (d) of Sub-Clause 14.3 [*Application for Advance and Interim Payment Certificates*] shall be made in the currencies and proportions specified in subparagraph (a) (i) above;

(b) payment of the damages specified in the Contract Data shall be made in the currencies and proportions specified in the Contract Data;

(c) other payments to the Employer by the Contractor shall be made in the currency in which the sum was expended by the Employer, or in such currency as may be agreed by both Parties;

(d) if any amount payable by the Contractor to the Employer in a particular currency exceeds the sum payable by the Employer to the Contractor in that currency, the Employer may recover the balance of this amount from the sums otherwise payable to the Contractor in other currencies; and

(e) if no rates of exchange are stated in the Contract Data, they shall be those prevailing on the Base Date and determined by the central bank of the Country.

14.18 Asset Replacement Fund

The Asset Replacement Fund is to provide the necessary funding for the replacement of items of Plant identified in the Asset Replacement Schedule as required for the continued efficient operation of the Works for the duration of the Operation Service Period.

In each application for an Interim Payment Certificate during the Operation Service Period made in accordance with Sub-Clause 14.3 [*Application for Advance and Interim Payment Certificates*], the Contractor shall be entitled to include any monies from the Asset Replacement Fund which, according to the Asset Replacement Schedule, have become due following the replacement of the scheduled items by the Contractor. Under no circumstances will the amount payable from the Asset Replacement Fund be increased from the amount due according to the Asset Replacement Schedule, irrespective of the value or amount of replacements which have been made. For any items which have not been replaced by the date or other operational milestone identified in the Asset Replacement Schedule, payment will not be released until such replacement has been effected.

In the event that there is money remaining in the Asset Replacement Fund upon completion of the Contract due to planned replacements, which by mutual agreement of the Parties, are not required or used, such amount shall be shared equally between the Parties, and the Contractor shall be entitled to include his share of such amount in his Application for Final Payment Certificate Operation Service made in accordance with Sub-Clause 14.13 [*Application for Final Payment Certificate Operation Service*].

The Asset Replacement Fund shall not cover the cost of:

(a) routine maintenance items associated with the correction of defects;
(b) replacement of Plant and Material which have a life expectancy of less than five years;

(i) 当地货币和外币的比例或款额，以及计算付款采用的固定汇率，除双方另有商定外，应按**合同数据**中的规定；

(ii) 根据第 13.5 款 [*暂列金额*] 和第 13.6 款 [*因法律改变的调整*] 规定的付款和扣减，应按适用的货币和比例；（以及）

(iii) 根据第 14.3 款 [*预付款和期中付款证书的申请*]（a）至（b）段做出的其他支付和扣减，应按上述（a）（i）段中规定的货币和比例；

(b) **合同数据**中规定的损害赔偿费的支付，应按**合同数据**中规定的货币和比例；

(c) **承包商**付给**雇主**的其他款额，应以**雇主**支出金额的货币，或双方商定的货币支付；

(d) 如果**承包商**以某种特定货币应付给**雇主**的任何款额，超过**雇主**以该货币应付给**承包商**的款额，**雇主**可从以其他货币应付给**承包商**的款额中收回该项差额；（以及）

(e) 如果**合同数据**中未规定汇率，应采用**基准日期**当天和工程所在国中央银行确定的汇率。

14.18
资产置换基金

资产置换基金旨在为**资产置换计划表**中确认的生产设备部件的更换提供必要的资金，以确保**工程**在**运营服务期**间持续高效运行。

在根据第 14.3 款 [*预付款和期中付款证书的申请*] 的规定，提出**运营服务期**的期中付款证书的每次申请中，**承包商**应有权从**资产置换基金**中提取任何款项，根据**资产置换计划表**，在**承包商**更换计划表中的事项后到期。在任何情况下，**资产置换基金**的应付金额，均不得从**资产置换计划表**规定的到期金额中增加，而不考虑已进行重置的价值或金额。对于在**资产置换计划表**中确认的日期或其他运营里程碑（译注：重要阶段）尚未更换的任何事项，在此类更换生效之前，不会发放付款。

如果**合同**完成后，由于计划更换的事项，**资产置换基金**中有剩余资金，经双方商定不需要或使用后，则应由双方平均分摊该剩余资金，且**承包商**应有权根据第 14.13 款 [*运营服务最终付款证书的申请*] 的规定，在提交**运营服务最终付款证书**申请中，包括其在该资金中的份额。

资产置换基金不包括下列费用：

(a) 与纠正缺陷相关的日常维护事项；
(b) 更换预期寿命低于五年的**生产设备和材料**；

(c) providing spares between scheduled dates for major plant replacement; or
(d) the replacement of Plant and Materials which are not identified in the Asset Replacement Schedule.

The cost of meeting the requirements of sub-paragraphs (a) to (d) above shall be borne by the Contractor and be deemed to be included in the Contract Price.

The Contractor shall give Notice to the Employer's Representative at least 28 days prior to his intention to replace any item of Plant identified in the Asset Replacement Schedule.

The Employer shall authorise release of funds from the Asset Replacement Fund in accordance with the amounts certified by the Employer's Representative in each applicable Interim Payment Certificate. Funds will only be disbursed from the Asset Replacement Fund to the values and in accordance with the time scales for replacement identified in the Asset Replacement Schedule.

Where items of Plant require replacement at times earlier than the scheduled replacement times given in the Asset Replacement Schedule, the appropriate funds shall not be released until the scheduled replacement date has been reached.

If the Contract Price is subject to adjustments for changes in cost according to Sub-Clause 13.8 [*Adjustments for Changes in Cost*], the amounts due from the Asset Replacement Fund shall be adjusted on the same basis as other costs.

In the event of a termination of the Contract under Clause 15 [*Termination by Employer*], or Clause 16 [*Suspension and Termination by Contractor*], any amount remaining in the Asset Replacement Fund, including any accrued interest, shall be deemed to be to the account of the Employer and shall not be disbursed to the Contractor.

14.19 Maintenance Retention Fund

During the Operation Service Period, a Maintenance Retention Fund shall be created by deducting five percent (5%) from the value of each interim payment, determined by the Employer's Representative in accordance with Sub-Clause 14.7 [*Issue of Advance and Interim Payment Certificates*], due to the Contractor, commencing with the first payment following the issue of the Commissioning Certificate, and continuing until the last Interim Payment Certificate is issued or until the amount in the Maintenance Retention Fund has reached the value (if any) stated in the Contract Data, whichever is the earlier. If the Contractor so chooses, the Maintenance Retention Fund may be replaced by a Maintenance Retention Guarantee in a form and with an entity approved by the Employer. However, the value of the Guarantee shall not exceed the maximum amount of the Maintenance Retention Fund stated in the Contract Data. The Contractor shall ensure that the Maintenance Retention Guarantee remains valid and in force until the issue of the Contract Completion Certificate.

If the maintenance required under the Contract has not been carried out, the Employer may, after giving due Notice to the Contractor, carry out such maintenance himself and apply any amounts standing to the credit of the Maintenance Retention Fund in so doing. Where such amounts are insufficient to cover the Employer's whole costs of carrying out the maintenance, the unrecovered costs shall be set off against any payment due to the Contractor under the Contract, or to the extent that no such payment is due, shall become a debt due by the Contractor to the Employer.

(c) 在主要生产设备更换计划日期之间提供的备件；(或)

(d) **资产置换资计划**中未确认的**生产设备**和**材料**的替换。

满足上述（a）至（d）段要求的费用应由**承包商**承担，并视为包含在**合同价格**中。

承包商应在其打算更换**资产置换计划表**中确认的任何**生产设备**部件前，至少 28 天**通知雇主代表**。

雇主应根据**雇主代表**在每份适用**期中付款证书**中确认的金额，授权从**资产置换基金**中发放资金。资金将只从**资产置换基金**中，按照**资产置换计划表**中确认的价值和时间比例进行支付。

如果**生产设备**部件需要在**资产置换计划表**中规定的预定更换时间之前进行更换，则在计划的更换日期之前，不得发放相应的资金。

如果**合同价格**可根据第 13.8 款［*因成本改变的调整*］的规定，因成本变化而进行调整，**资产置换基金**应支付的金额，应按照与其他成本相同的基础进行调整。

如果根据第 15 条［*由雇主终止*］或第 16 条［*由承包商暂停和终止*］的规定终止合同，**资产置换基金**中的任何剩余金额，包括任何应计利息，应视为计入**雇主**的账户，不得支付给**承包商**。

14.19
维护保留金

在**运营服务期**间，应通过从**雇主代表**根据第 14.7 款［*预付款和期中付款证书的签发*］的规定，确认的签发应支付给**承包商**的期中付款的价值中扣除百分之五（5%）的方式，设立**维护保留金**，从签发**调试证书**后的第一次付款开始，一直持续到签发最后一次**期中付款证书**，或直到**维护保留金**的金额达到**合同数据**中规定的价值（如果有）为止，以较早者为准。如果**承包商**如此选择，**维护保留金**可由**雇主**批准的格式和实体的**维护保留金保函**代替。但是，保函的价值不得超过**合同数据**中规定的**维护保留基金**的最高限额。**承包商**应确保**维护保留金保函**在**合同完成证书**签发前保持有效。

如果**合同**要求的维护尚未进行，**雇主**可在向**承包商**发出适当**通知**后，自行进行此类维护，并在**维护保留基金**的贷方支付任何金额。如果此类金额不足以支付**雇主**进行维护的全部费用，则未收回的费用应与根据本**合同**应支付**给承包商**的任何款项相抵消，或在未支付此类款项的情况下，应成为**承包商**欠**雇主**的债务。

Following the issue of the Contract Completion Certificate under Sub-Clause 8.6 [*Contract Completion Certificate*], all funds remaining in the Maintenance Retention Fund shall be included in the Final Payment Certificate Operation Service and paid to the Contractor with the final payment.

15 Termination by Employer

15.1

Notice to Correct

If the Contractor fails to carry out any obligation under the Contract, the Employer's Representative shall by Notice require the Contractor to make good the failure and to remedy it within the time specified in the said Notice.

15.2

Termination for Contractor's Default

The Employer shall be entitled to terminate the Contract if the Contractor:

(a) fails to comply with Sub-Clause 4.2 [*Performance Security*] or with a Notice under Sub-Clause 15.1 [*Notice to Correct*],

(b) abandons the Works or otherwise plainly demonstrates the intention not to continue performance of his obligations under the Contract,

(c) without reasonable excuse fails:

    (i) to proceed with the Works in accordance with Sub-Clause 9.1 [*Commencement of Design-Build*] or Sub-Clause 10.2 [*Commencement of Operation Service*]; or

    (ii) to comply with a Notice issued under Sub-Clause 7.5 [*Rejection*] or Sub-Clause 7.6 [*Remedial Work*], within 28 days after receiving it;

(d) subcontracts the whole of the Works or assigns the Contract without the required agreement or subcontracts the Operation Service or any parts of the Works in breach of Sub-Clause 4.4 [*Subcontractors*];

(e) either gives Notice to the Employer under Sub-Clause 4.25 [*Changes in the Contractor's Financial Situation*] from which the Employer reasonably concludes that the Contractor will be unable to complete or fulfil his obligations under the Contract or, if the Contractor fails to give such a Notice, but the Employer in any event reasonably concludes that the Contractor will be unable to complete or fulfil his obligations under the Contract due to the Contractor's financial situation;

(f) becomes bankrupt or insolvent, goes into liquidation, has a receiving or administration order made against him, compounds with his creditors, or carries on business under a receiver, trustee or manager for the benefit of his creditors, or if any act is done or event occurs which (under applicable Laws) has a similar effect to any of these acts or events;

(g) gives or offers to give (directly or indirectly, either before or during the currency of the Contract) to any person any bribe, gift, gratuity, commission or other thing of value, as an inducement or reward:

    (i) for doing or forbearing to do any action in relation to the Contract; or

    (ii) for showing or forbearing to show favour or disfavour to any person in relation to the Contract;

    or if any of the Contractor's Personnel, agents or Subcontractors gives or offers to give (directly or indirectly) to any person any such inducement or reward as is described in this sub-paragraph (g). However, lawful inducements and rewards to Contractor's Personnel shall not give a right to termination;

根据第 8.6 款［合同完成证书］的规定签发合同完成证书后，**维护保留基金**中的所有剩余资金应包括在**运营服务最终付款证书**中，并应随最终付款一起支付给**承包商**。

15 由雇主终止

15.1
通知改正

如果**承包商**未能根据合同履行任何义务，**雇主代表**可通过向**承包商**发出**通知**，要求其在上述**通知**规定的时间内，纠正并补救上述违约。

15.2
由承包商违约的终止

如果**承包商**有下列行为，**雇主**应有权终止合同：

（a）　未能遵守第 4.2 款［*履约担保*］的规定，或根据第 15.1 款［*通知改正*］的规定发出**通知**的要求；

（b）　放弃工程，或以其他方式明确表现出不愿继续履行合同规定的**承包商**义务的意向；

（c）　在无合理解释，未能：

　　（i）　按照第 9.1 款［*设计 - 施工的开始*］或第 10.2 款［*运营服务的开始*］的规定实施工程；（或）

　　（ii）　在收到按照第 7.5 款［*拒收*］或第 7.6 款［*修补工作*］的规定发出**通知**后的 28 天内，遵守**通知**要求；

（d）　未经要求同意，将全部工程分包或转让**合同**，或违反第 4.4 款［*分包商*］的规定，将运营服务或工程的任何部分分包出去；

（e）　根据第 4.25 款［*承包商资金状况的改变*］的规定向**雇主**发出**通知**，**雇主**据此合理地认为，**承包商**将无法完成或履行其在**合同**中规定的义务，或如果**承包商**未能发出此类**通知**，但**雇主**在任何情况下合理地断定，由于**承包商**的资金状况，**承包商**将无法完成或履行其在**合同**中规定的义务；

（f）　破产或无力偿债，进入清算、对其发出接管令或管理令，与债权人达成和解，或为其债权人的利益在接管人、委托人或管理人的监督下开展业务，或如果采取任何行为或发生的任何事件（根据适用法律）具有与上述行为或事件类似的效果；

（g）　给予或提议给予（直接或间接，在**合同**生效之前或期间）任何人贿赂、礼物、酬金、佣金或其他有价物品，作为引诱或报酬：

　　（i）　采取或不采取与**合同**有关的任何行动；（或）

　　（ii）　对与**合同**有关的任何人做出或不做有利或不利的表示；

或如果任何**承包商人员**、代理人或**分包商**（直接或间接）向任何人给予或提议给予本款（g）段所述的任何此类引诱或报酬。但是，对**承包商人员**的合法奖励和报酬不应给予终止合同的权利。

(h) fails to complete the Design-Build by the Cut-Off Date stated in the Contract Data or, if no such date is given, then a period of 182 days after the Time for Completion of Design-Build.

In any of these events or circumstances, the Employer may, not less than 14 days after giving Notice to the Contractor, terminate the Contract and expel the Contractor from the Site unless the Contractor cures the event or circumstance within the said 14 days. However, in the case of sub-paragraph (f) or (g), the Employer may by Notice terminate the Contract immediately.

The Employer's election to terminate the Contract shall not prejudice any other rights of the Employer, under the Contract or otherwise.

The Contractor shall then leave the Site and deliver any required Goods, all Contractor's Documents, and other design documents made by or for him, to the Employer's Representative. However, the Contractor shall use his best efforts to comply immediately with any reasonable instructions included in the Notice (i) for the assignment of any subcontract, and (ii) for the protection of life or property or for the safety of the Works.

After termination, the Employer may complete the Works and/or arrange for any other entities to do so. The Employer and these entities may then use any Goods, Contractor's Documents and other design documents made by or on behalf of the Contractor.

The Employer shall then give Notice that the Contractor's Equipment and Temporary Works will be released to the Contractor at or near the Site. The Contractor shall promptly arrange their removal, at the risk and cost of the Contractor. However, if by this time the Contractor has failed to make a payment due to the Employer, these items may be sold by the Employer in order to recover this payment. Any balance of the proceeds shall then be paid to the Contractor.

15.3 Valuation at Date of Termination for Contractor's Default

As soon as practicable after a Notice of termination under Sub-Clause 15.2 [*Termination for Contractor's Default*] has taken effect, the Employer's Representative shall proceed in accordance with Sub-Clause 3.5 [*Determinations*] to agree or determine the value of the Works, Goods and Contractor's Documents, and any other sums due to the Contractor for work executed in accordance with the Contract.

15.4 Payment after Termination for Contractor's Default

After a Notice of termination under Sub-Clause 15.2 [*Termination for Contractor's Default*] has taken effect, the Employer may:

(a) proceed in accordance with Sub-Clause 20.2 [*Employer's Claims*];
(b) withhold further payments to the Contractor until the costs of design, execution, completion and remedying of any defects, damages for delay in completion (if any), and all other costs incurred by the Employer, have been established; and/or
(c) recover from the Contractor any losses and damages incurred by the Employer and any extra costs of completing the Works, after allowing for any sum due to the Contractor under Sub-Clause 15.3 [*Valuation at Date of Termination for Contractor's Default*]. After recovering any such losses, damages and extra costs, the Employer shall pay any balance to the Contractor.

(h) 未能在**合同数据**中规定的**截止日期**前完成**设计 - 施工**，或，如果没有给出此日期，则为**设计 - 施工竣工时间**后的 182 天。

在出现任何上述事件或情况时，**雇主**可在向**承包商**发出**通知**后不少于 14 天，终止**合同**，并要求其离开**现场**除非**承包商**在上述 14 天内纠正了该事件或情况。但在（f）或（g）段情况下，**雇主**可发出**通知**立即终止**合同**。

雇主做出终止**合同**的选择，不应损害其根据**合同**或其他规定所享有的其他任何权利。

此时，**承包商**应撤离**现场**，并将任何需要的**货物**、所有**承包商文件**、以及由或为其编制的其他设计文件交给**雇主代表**。但**承包商**应尽最大努力立即遵守**通知**中关于：(i) 转让任何分包合同，以及 (ii) 保护生命或财产或**工程**安全的任何合理指示。

终止后，**雇主**可以继续完成**工程**，和 / 或安排任何其他实体完成。这时**雇主**和这些实体可使用任何**货物**、**承包商文件**和由**承包商**或以其名义编制的其他设计文件。

雇主随后应发出**通知**，将在**现场**或其附近的**承包商设备**和**临时工程**放还给**承包商**。**承包商**应迅速安排移除，风险和费用由**承包商**承担。但如果此时**承包商**还有应付**雇主**的款项未付清，**雇主**可出售这些物品，以收回欠款。收益的余款应付给**承包商**。

15.3
由承包商违约终止日期时的估价

在根据**第 15.2 款**［*由承包商违约的终止*］的规定发出的终止**通知**生效后，**雇主代表**应在切实可行的范围内，尽快按照**第 3.5 款**［*确定*］的规定，继续商定或确定**工程**、**货物**和**承包商文件**的价值，以及**承包商**按照**合同**实施的工作应得的任何其他款项。

15.4
由承包商违约终止后的付款

在按照**第 15.2 款**［*由承包商违约的终止*］规定发出的终止**通知**生效后，**雇主**可以：

（a） 按照**第 20.2 款**［*雇主索赔*］的规定进行；
（b） 在确定设计、施工、竣工和修补任何缺陷的费用，延误竣工（如果有）的损害赔偿费，以及**雇主**负担的所有其他费用前，暂不向**承包商**支付进一步款项；(和 / 或)

（c） 根据**第 15.3 款**［*由承包商违约终止日期时的估价*］的规定，考虑到应付给**承包商**的任何款额后，从**承包商**处收回**雇主**遭受的任何损失和损害赔偿费，以及完成**工程**所需的任何额外费用。在收回任何此类损失、损害赔偿费和额外费用后，**雇主**应将任何余额支付给**承包商**。

15.5 Termination for Employer's Convenience

If at any time the Employer elects to terminate the Contract for reasons other than those specified in Sub-Clause 15.2 [*Termination for Contractor's Default*], and subject to the applicable Law of the Contract, he shall notify the Contractor in writing, with a copy to the Employer's Representative. Such termination shall be deemed to be termination for the convenience of the Employer.

Upon issuing a Notice to terminate under this Sub-Clause, the Employer shall immediately make arrangements to return the Performance Security to the Contractor, and the termination shall take effect 28 days after the date the Contractor receives the Notice, or 28 days after he receives the Performance Security, whichever is the later. Upon issuing the Notice, the Employer shall immediately cease to have any right of use of any of the Contractor's Documents, and shall forthwith return all and any such Contractor's Documents to the Contractor.

The Employer shall not terminate the Contract under this Sub-Clause in order to execute or operate the Works (or any part thereof) himself, or arrange for the Works (or any part thereof) to be executed by another contractor.

15.6 Valuation at Date of Termination for Employer's Convenience

As soon as practicable after a Notice of termination under Sub-Clause 15.5 [*Termination for Employer's Convenience*] has taken effect, the Employer's Representative shall proceed in accordance with Sub-Clause 3.5 [*Determinations*] to agree or determine the value of the Works, Goods and Contractor's Documents, and any other sums due to the Contractor for work executed in accordance with the Contract.

15.7 Payment after Termination for Employer's Convenience

After termination for the Employer's convenience under Sub-Clause 15.5 [*Termination for Employer's Convenience*], the Contractor shall proceed in accordance with Sub-Clause 16.3 [*Cessation of Work and Removal of Contractor's Equipment*] and shall be paid in accordance with Sub-Clause 16.4 [*Payment on Termination*].

16 Suspension and Termination by Contractor

16.1 Contractor's Entitlement to Suspend Work

If the Employer's Representative fails to certify in accordance with Sub-Clause 14.7 [*Issue of Advance and Interim Payment Certificates*], or the Employer fails to comply with Sub-Clause 2.4 [*Employer's Financial Arrangements*] or Sub-Clause 14.8 [*Payment*], the Contractor may, not less than 21 days after giving Notice to the Employer, suspend work (or reduce the rate of work) unless and until the Contractor has received the Interim Payment Certificate, reasonable evidence or payment, as the case may be and as described in the Notice.

The Contractor's action shall not prejudice his entitlements to financing charges under Sub-Clause 14.9 [*Delayed Payment*] and to termination under Sub-Clause 16.2 [*Termination by Contractor*].

If the Contractor subsequently receives such Interim Payment Certificate, evidence or payment (as described in the relevant Sub-Clause and in the above Notice) before giving a Notice of termination, the Contractor shall resume normal working as soon as is reasonably practicable.

15.5 为雇主便利的终止

如果雇主在任何时候出于第 15.2 款 [*由承包商违约的终止*] 中规定以外的原因,选择终止合同,并遵守合同的适用**法律**,雇主应书面通知**承包商**,并向**雇主代表**提供一份副本。此类终止应视为是为雇主便利的终止。

根据本款发出终止**通知**后,雇主应立即安排将**履约担保**退还给**承包商**,且该终止应在**承包商**收到该**通知**或雇主退还**履约担保**,两者中较晚的日期后第 28 天生效。发出**通知**后,雇主应立即停止对任何**承包商文件**的使用权,并应将所有此类**承包商文件**退还给**承包商**。

雇主不应为了自己实施或运营**工程**(或其任何部分),或安排另外的**承包商**实施**工程**(或其任何部分),而根据本款终止合同。

15.6 为雇主便利终止日的估价

当按照第 15.5 款 [*为雇主便利的终止*] 的规定发出终止**通知**生效后,**雇主代表**应在切实可行的范围内,尽快按照第 3.5 款 [*确定*] 的规定,商定或确定**工程**、**货物**和**承包商文件**的价值,以及根据合同规定工程施工应支付给**承包商**的任何其他款项。

15.7 为雇主便利终止后的付款

按照第 15.5 款 [*为雇主便利的终止*] 的规定,为雇主的便利终止合同后,**承包商**应按照第 16.3 款 [*停止工作和承包商设备的撤离*] 的规定执行,并按照第 16.4 款 [*终止时的付款*] 的规定获得付款。

16 由承包商暂停和终止

16.1 承包商暂停工作的权利

如果**雇主代表**未按照第 14.7 款 [*预付款和期中付款证书的签发*] 的规定确认发证,或雇主未能按照第 2.4 款 [*雇主的资金安排*] 或第 14.8 款 [*付款*] 的规定,**承包商**可以在向雇主发出**通知**后不少于 21 天,暂停工作(或放慢工作进度),除非并直到**承包商**根据情况和**通知**中所述,收到**期中付款证书**、合理证据或付款为止。

承包商的上述行动不应影响其根据第 14.9 款 [*延误的付款*] 的规定获得融资费,以及按照第 16.2 款 [*由承包商终止*] 的规定提出终止的权利。

如果在发出终止**通知**前,**承包商**随后收到了上述**期中付款证书**、证据或付款(如有关**条款**和上述**通知**中所述),则**承包商**应在合理可行的范围内尽快恢复正常工作。

If the Contractor suffers delay and/or incurs cost as a result of suspending work (or reducing the rate of work) in accordance with this Sub-Clause, the Contractor shall give Notice to the Employer's Representative and shall be entitled, subject to Sub-Clause 20.1 [*Contractor's Claims*], to:

(a) an extension of time for any such delay, if completion is or will be delayed, under Sub-Clause 9.3 [*Extension of Time for Completion of Design-Build*]; and
(b) payment of any such Cost Plus Profit, which shall be included in the Contract Price.

After receiving this Notice, the Employer's Representative shall proceed in accordance with Sub-Clause 3.5 [*Determinations*] to agree or determine these matters.

16.2
Termination by Contractor

The Contractor shall be entitled to terminate the Contract if:

(a) the Contractor does not receive the reasonable evidence within 42 days after giving Notice under Sub-Clause 16.1 [*Contractor's Entitlement to Suspend Work*] in respect of a failure to comply with Sub-Clause 2.4 [*Employer's Financial Arrangements*];
(b) the Employer's Representative fails, within 56 days after receiving a Statement and supporting documents, to issue the relevant Payment Certificate;
(c) the Contractor does not receive the amount due under an Interim Payment Certificate within 42 days after the expiry of the time stated in Sub-Clause 14.8 [*Payment*] within which payment is to be made (except for deductions in accordance with Sub-Clause 20.2 [*Employer's Claims*]);
(d) the Employer substantially fails to perform his obligations under the Contract,
(e) the Employer fails to comply with Sub-Clause 1.6 [*Contract Agreement*] or Sub-Clause 1.8 [*Assignment*];
(f) a prolonged suspension affects the whole of the Works as described in Sub-Clause 9.10 [*Prolonged Suspension*]; or
(g) the Employer becomes bankrupt or insolvent, goes into liquidation, has a receiving or administration order made against him, compounds with his creditors, or carries on business under a receiver, trustee or manager for the benefit of his creditors, or if any act is done or event occurs which (under applicable Laws) has a similar effect to any of these acts or events.

In any of these events or circumstances, the Contractor may, not less than 14 days after giving Notice to the Employer, terminate the Contract unless the Employer cures the event or circumstance within the said 14 days. However, in the case of subparagraph (f) or (g), the Contractor may by Notice terminate the Contract immediately.

The Contractor's election to terminate the Contract shall not prejudice any other rights of the Contractor, under the Contract or otherwise.

16.3
Cessation of Work and Removal of Contractor's Equipment

After a Notice of termination under Sub-Clause 16.2 [*Termination by Contractor*] or Sub-Clause 18.5 [*Optional Termination, Payment and Release*] has taken effect, the Contractor shall, unless the Employer cured the event or circumstance within the 14days' Notice period, promptly:

如果因按照本款暂停工作（或放慢工作进度），使**承包商**遭受延误和／或招致增加费用，**承包商**应向**雇主代表**发出**通知**，有权根据第 20.1 款 [*承包商索赔*] 的规定，要求：

（a）根据第 9.3 款 [*设计－施工竣工时间的延长*] 的规定，如果竣工已或将受到延误，对任何此类延误给予延长期；（以及）

（b）任何此类**成本加利润**的费用应计入**合同价格**，给予支付。

雇主代表收到此**通知**后，应按照第 3.5 款 [*确定*] 的规定，对这些事项进行商定或确定。

| 16.2
由承包商终止 | 如果出现下列情况，**承包商**应有权终止合同：

（a）**承包商**在根据第 16.1 款 [*承包商暂停工作的权利*] 的规定，就未能遵守第 2.4 款 [*雇主的资金安排*] 规定的事项发出**通知**后 42 天内，仍未收到合理的证据；

（b）**雇主代表**未能在收到**报表**和证明文件后 56 天内签发有关**付款证书**；

（c）在第 14.8 款 [*付款*] 规定的付款时间到期后 42 天内，**承包商**仍未收到期中付款证书规定的应付款额（根据第 20.2 款 [*雇主索赔*] 规定的扣除额除外）；

（d）雇主实际上未能根据合同履行其义务；

（e）雇主未遵守第 1.6 款 [*合同协议书*] 或第 1.8 款 [*权益转让*] 的规定；

（f）第 9.10 款 [*拖长的暂停*] 所述的拖长的暂停影响了整个工程；或

（g）雇主破产或无力偿债，进入清算、对其发出接管令或管理令，与债权人达成和解，或为其债权人的利益在接管人、委托人或管理人的监督下开展业务，或如果采取任何行为或发生的任何事件（根据适用**法律**）具有与上述行为或事件类似的效果。

在出现任何上述事件或情况时，**承包商**可在向**雇主**发出**通知**后不少于 14 天终止**合同**，除非**雇主**在上述 14 天内纠正了该事件或情况。但在（f）或（g）段情况下，**承包商**可通过发出**通知**立即终止合同。

承包商做出终止合同的选择，不应损害其根据合同或其他规定所享有的其他任何权利。

| 16.3
停止工作和承包商设备的撤离 | 根据第 16.2 款 [*由承包商终止*] 或第 18.5 款 [*自主选择终止、付款和解除*] 的规定发出的终止**通知**生效后，除非**雇主**在 14 天的**通知**期内纠正了该事件或情况，否则**承包商**应立即：

(a) cease all further work, except for such work as may have been instructed by the Employer's Representative for the protection of life or property or for the safety of the Works or protection of the environment. For all such instructed work, the Contractor shall be entitled to be paid Cost Plus Profit and shall be relieved of further liabilities under Sub-Clauses 4.8 [*Safety Procedures*] and 4.18 [*Protection of the Environment*];

(b) hand over to the Employer the Contractor's Documents, Plant, Materials and other work, for which the Contractor has received payment; and

(c) remove all other Goods from the Site, except as necessary for safety, and leave the Site.

16.4
Payment on Termination

After a Notice of termination under Sub-Clause 16.2 [*Termination by Contractor*] has taken effect, the Employer shall promptly:

(a) return the Performance Security to the Contractor;
(b) pay the Contractor in accordance with Sub-Clause 18.5 [*Optional Termination, Payment and Release*]; and
(c) pay to the Contractor the amount of any loss of profit or other loss or damage sustained by the Contractor as a result of this termination.

Risk Allocation 17

17.1
The Employer's Risks during the Design-Build Period

Subject to the provisions of Sub-Clause 17.8 [*Limitation of Liability*], the risks allocated to the Employer and for which the Employer is liable during the Design-Build Period are divided into:

(a) The Employer's Commercial Risks, which are:

(i) the financial loss, delay or damage allocated to the Employer under the Contract or for which the Employer is liable by law, unless otherwise modified under the Contract;
(ii) the right of the Employer to construct the Works or any part thereof on, over, under, in or through the Site;
(iii) the use or occupation of the Site by the Works or any part thereof, or for the purpose of design, construction or completion of the Works other than the abusive or wrongful use by the Contractor; and
(iv) the use or occupation by the Employer of any part of the Permanent Works, except as may be specified in the Contract;

and

(b) The Employer's Risks of Damage, which are:

(i) damage due to any interference, whether temporary or permanent, with any right of way, light, air, water or other easement (other than that resulting from the Contractor's method of construction) which is the unavoidable result of the construction of the Works in accordance with the Contract;
(ii) fault, error, defect or omission in any element of the design of the Works by the Employer or which may be contained in the Employer's Requirements, other than design carried out by the Contractor pursuant to his obligations under the Contract;

(a) 停止所有进一步的工作,但**雇主代表**为保护生命或财产或**工程**安全或保护环境可能指示的工作除外。对于所有此类指示的工作,**承包商**应有权获得**成本加利润**的支付,并应免除**第 4.8 款**[*安全程序*]和**第 4.18 款**[*环境保护*]规定的进一步责任;

(b) 将**承包商**已得到付款的**承包商文件**、**生产设备**、**材料**和其他工作移交给**雇主**;(以及)

(c) 从**现场**运走除安全需要以外的所有其他**货物**,并撤离**现场**。

16.4 终止时的付款

根据**第 16.2 款**[*由承包商终止*]的规定发出终止**通知**生效后,**雇主**应立即:

(a) 将**履约担保**退还**承包商**;
(b) 按照**第 18.5 款**[*自主选择终止、付款和解除*]的规定,向**承包商**付款;(以及)
(c) 付给**承包商**因此项终止而遭受的任何利润损失,或其他损失或损害的款额。

17 风险分配

17.1 设计 - 施工期间雇主的风险

根据**第 17.8 款**[*责任限度*]的规定,在**设计 - 施工**期间,分配给**雇主**并由**雇主**负责的风险分为:

(a) **雇主**的商业风险,包括:

 (i) **合同**规定分配给**雇主**的或**雇主**依法应承担的资金(财务)损失、延误或损害赔偿,除非**合同**另有修改;

 (ii) **雇主**在**现场**上、上方、下方、内部或穿过**现场**施工**工程**或其任何部分的权利;

 (iii) **工程**或其任何部分对**现场**的使用或占用,或为**工程**的设计、施工或竣工而使用或占用,但**承包商**滥用或不当使用除外;(以及)

 (iv) **雇主**使用或占用**永久工程**的任何部分,除非**合同**另有规定;

以及

(b) **雇主**的损害风险,包括:

 (i) 由于任何通行权、光线、空气、水或其他地役权(**承包商**施工方法造成的除外)的任何干扰造成的损害,无论是临时的还是永久的,这是根据**合同**进行**工程**的施工所不可避免的结果;

 (ii) **雇主**对**工程**设计的任何部分或**雇主要求**中可能包含的缺点、错误、缺陷或遗漏,**承包商**根据**合同**规定的义务进行的设计除外;

(iii) any operation of the forces of nature (other than those allocated to the Contractor in the Contract Data) against which an experienced contractor could not reasonably have been expected to have taken adequate preventative precautions; and

(iv) The Exceptional Risks under Clause 18 [*Exceptional Risks*].

17.2 The Contractor's Risks during the Design-Build Period

Subject to the provisions of Sub-Clause 17.8 [*Limitation of Liability*], the risks allocated to the Contractor and for which the Contractor is liable during the Design-Build Period are all the risks other than those listed under Sub-Clause 17.1 [*The Employer's Risks during the Design-Build Period*], including the care of both the Works and the Goods.

17.3 The Employer's Risks during the Operation Service Period

Subject to the provisions of Sub-Clause 17.8 [*Limitation of Liability*], the risks allocated to the Employer and for which the Employer is liable during the Operation Service Period are divided into:

(a) The Employer's Commercial Risks, which are:

(i) the financial loss, delay or damage allocated to the Employer under the Contract or for which the Employer is liable by law, unless otherwise modified under the Contract;

(ii) the use or occupation by the Employer of any part of the Permanent Works, except as may be specified in the Contract; and

(iii) the use or occupation of the Site by the Works or any part thereof, or for the purpose of operating and maintaining the Permanent Works;

and

(b) The Employer's Risks of Damage, which are:

(i) damage due to any interference, whether temporary or permanent, with any right of way, light, air, water or other easement (other than that resulting from the Contractor's methods of operation and maintenance) which is the unavoidable result of operating and maintaining the Permanent Works in accordance with the Contract;

(ii) fault, error, defect or omission in any element of the design of the Works by the Employer or which may be contained in the Employer's Requirements, other than design carried out by the Contractor pursuant to his obligations under the Contract;

(iii) any operation of the forces of nature against which an experienced contractor could not reasonably have been expected to have taken adequate preventative precautions; and

(iv) The Exceptional Risks under Clause 18 [*Exceptional Risks*].

17.4 The Contractor's Risks during the Operation Service Period

Subject to the provisions of Sub-Clause 17.8 [*Limitation of Liability*], the risks allocated to the Contractor and for which the Contractor is liable during the Operation Service Period are:

(a) all risks resulting or arising from the design (excluding any design allocated to the Employer under Sub-Clauses 17.1 (b) (ii) and 17.3 (b) (ii)) or construction of the Works, or the Materials used therein, notwithstanding any testing carried out by or approved or witnessed by the Employer or the Employer's Representative during the Design-Build Period; and

(iii) 一个有经验的承包商无法合理地预期其采取适当预防措施的任何自然力的作用（**合同数据**中分配该**承包商**的除外）；（以及）

(iv) 第18条［*例外风险*］规定的**例外风险**。

17.2 设计-施工期间承包商的风险

根据第17.8款［*责任限度*］的规定，在**设计-施工**期间，分配给**承包商**并由**承包商**负责的风险，是除第17.1款［*设计-施工期间雇主的风险*］中所列风险以外的所有风险，包括**工程**和**货物**的照管。

17.3 运营服务期间雇主的风险

根据第17.8款［*责任限度*］的规定，在**运营服务**期间，分配给**雇主**并由**雇主**负责的风险分为：

（a）**雇主**的**商业风险**，包括：

(i) **合同**规定分配给**雇主**的或**雇主**依法应承担的资金（财务）损失、延误或损害，除非**合同**另有修改；

(ii) **雇主**使用或占用**永久工程**的任何部分，除非**合同**另有规定；（以及）

(iii) **工程**或其任何部分对**现场**的使用或占用，或为运营和维护**永久工程**而使用或占用；

以及

（b）**雇主**的**损害风险**，包括：

(i) 由于任何通行权、光线、空气、水或其他地役权（**承包商**运营和维护**永久工程**方法造成的除外）的任何干扰造成的损害，无论是临时的还是永久的，这是根据**合同**进行运营和维护**永久工程**所不可避免的结果；

(ii) **雇主**对工程设计的任何部分或**雇主要求**中可能包含的缺点、错误、缺陷或遗漏，**承包商**根据合同规定的义务进行的设计除外；

(iii) 一个有经验的承包商无法合理地预期其采取适当预防措施的任何自然力的作用；（以及）

(iv) 第18条［*例外风险*］规定的**例外风险**。

17.4 运营服务期间承包商的风险

根据第17.8款［*责任限度*］的规定，在**运营服务**期间，分配给**承包商**并由**承包商**负责的风险为：

（a）由于设计（不包括根据**第17.1款（b）(ii)段**和**第17.3款（b）(ii)段**中分配给**雇主**的任何设计），或工程施工或其中使用的**材料**导致或产生的所有风险，尽管在**设计-施工**期间，**雇主**或**雇主代表**进行了任何试验，或经**雇主**或**雇主代表**批准或见证的；（以及）

(b) all risks resulting or arising from the operation and maintenance of the Permanent Works and the care of the Works excluding the Employer's Risks listed under Sub-Clause 17.3 [*The Employer's Risks during the Operation Service Period*].

17.5 Responsibility for Care of the Works

Unless the Contract is terminated in accordance with these Conditions, the Contractor shall take full responsibility for the care of the Works and Goods from the Commencement Date until the Commissioning Certificate for the whole of the Works is issued pursuant to Sub-Clause 11.7 [*Commissioning Certificate*]. If the Contract is terminated in accordance with these Conditions, the Contractor shall cease to be responsible for the care of the Works from the date of expiry of the Notice of termination.

The Contractor shall also be responsible for the care of the Permanent Works during the Operation Service Period in accordance with the requirements of the Operating Licence pursuant to Sub-Clause 1.7 [*Operating Licence*].

The Contractor shall also be responsible for the care of any part of the Permanent Works for which a Section Commissioning Certificate has been issued.

The Contractor shall also take full responsibility for any outstanding work which he shall have undertaken to complete during the Operation Service Period until all such outstanding work is completed.

17.6 Consequences of the Employer's Risks of Damage

Subject to the provisions of Sub-Clause 18.4 [*Consequences of an Exceptional Event*], if any of the risks allocated as an Employer's Risk under Sub-Clause 17.1 [*The Employer's Risks during the Design-Build Period*] and 17.3 [*The Employer's Risks during the Operation Service Period*] occurs and results in damage to the Works or other property or Goods or Contractor's Documents, the Contractor shall promptly give Notice to the Employer's Representative, and shall thereafter rectify such loss and/or damage to the extent required by instruction of the Employer's Representative. Such instruction shall be deemed a Variation.

In the event of the allocation of the risk not being governed by any other term of the Contract, and such risk occurs during the Design-Build Period and the Contractor is delayed and/or incurs cost from rectifying this damage, the Contractor shall give a further Notice to the Employer's Representative and shall be entitled to:

(a) an extension of time for any such delay, if completion is or will be delayed, under Sub-Clause 9.3 [*Extension of Time for Completion of Design-Build*]; and
(b) payment of Cost Plus Profit, which shall be included in the Contract Price.

If the event occurs during the Operation Service Period, sub-paragraph (b) of this Sub-Clause shall apply, but sub-paragraph (a) of this Sub-Clause shall not apply.

The Employer's Representative shall proceed in accordance with Sub-Clause 3.5 [*Determinations*] to determine the amounts due.

17.7 Consequences of the Contractor's Risks resulting in Damage

If any of the risks allocated as a Contractor's risk under Sub-Clause 17.2 [*The Contractor's Risks during the Design-Build Period*] and 17.4 [*The Contractor's Risks during the Operation Service Period*] occurs and results in damage to the Works or other property or Goods, the Contractor shall promptly give Notice to the Employer's Representative, and shall

（b） 由**永久工程**的运营和维护以及对**工程**的照管而导致或产生的所有风险，不包括第 17.3 款［*运营服务期间雇主的风险*］中所列的**雇主风险**。

17.5 工程照管的职责

除非根据本**条件**终止**合同**，否则**承包商**应自**开工日期**起，直至根据第 11.7 款［*调试证书*］的规定签发整个**工程**的**调试证书**止，承担对**工程**和**货物**的全部照管责任。如果根据本**条件**终止了**合同**，则**承包商**应自终止**通知**期满之日起不再负责**工程**的照管。

承包商还应根据第 1.7 款［*运营执照*］规定的**运营执照**要求，负责照管**运营服务期间**的**永久工程**。

承包商还应负责照管已签发**分项工程调试证书**的**永久工程**的任何部分。

承包商还应对其在**运营服务期间**内完成的任何扫尾工作承担全部责任，直到完成所有此类扫尾工作。

17.6 雇主损害风险的后果

按照第 18.4 款［*例外事件的后果*］的规定，如果根据第 17.1 款［*设计-施工期间雇主的风险*］和第 17.3 款［*运营服务期间雇主的风险*］所述的，任何属于**雇主**的风险，发生并导致**工程**或其他财产、**货物**或**承包商文件**的损害，**承包商**应立即通知**雇主代表**，并应在**雇主代表**的指示要求范围内，纠正此类损失和/或损害。该指示应视**为变更**。

如果风险分配不受**合同**任何其他条款的约束，以及此类风险发生在**设计-施工期**间，因纠正此类损害使**承包商**遭受延误和/或招致增加费用，**承包商**应进一步**通知雇主代表**，并应有权获得：

（a） 根据第 9.3 款［*设计-施工竣工时间的延长*］的规定，如果竣工已或将受到延误，对此类延误给予延长期；

（b） **成本加利润**的费用应计入**合同价格**，给予支付。

如果事件发生在**运营服务期**间，本款（b）段应适用，但本款（a）段应不适用。

雇主代表应按照第 3.5 款［*确定*］的规定确定应付款额。

17.7 承包商损害风险的后果

如果根据第 17.2 款［*设计-施工期间承包商的风险*］和第 17.4 款［*运营服务期间承包商的风险*］所述的，任何分配给**承包商**承担的风险，发生并导致**工程**或其他财产或**货物**的损害，**承包商**应立即**通知雇主代表**，并应

thereafter rectify such damage to the extent required by the Employer's Representative. All such work of replacement, repair or rectification shall be carried out by the Contractor at his own cost.

17.8 Limitation of Liability

Neither Party shall be liable to the other Party for any loss of use of any Works, loss of profit, loss of contract or for any other indirect loss or damage which may be suffered by the other Party in connection with the Contract, other than under Sub-Clause 10.6 [*Delays and Interruptions during the Operation Service*], Sub-Clause 16.4 [*Payment on Termination*], Sub-Clause 17.9 [*Indemnities by the Contractor*], Sub-Clause 17.10 [*Indemnities by the Employer*] and Sub-Clause 17.12 [*Risk of Infringement of Intellectual and Industrial Property Rights*].

The total liability of the Contractor to the Employer, under or in connection with the Contract, shall not exceed the sum stated in the Contract Data or (if a sum is not so stated) the Accepted Contract Amount.

This Sub-Clause shall not limit any liability in any case of fraud, deliberate default or reckless misconduct by the defaulting Party.

17.9 Indemnities by the Contractor

The Contractor shall indemnify and hold harmless the Employer, the Employer's Personnel, and their respective agents, against and from all claims, damages, losses and expenses (including legal fees and expenses) in respect of:

(a) bodily injury, sickness, disease or death, of any person whatsoever arising out of or in the course of or by reason of the Contractor's design, execution, completion or operation and maintenance of the Works, unless attributable to any negligence, wilful act or breach of the Contract by the Employer, the Employer's Personnel, or any of their respective agents; and

(b) damage to or loss of any property, real or personal (other than the Works), to the extent that such damage or loss;

　(i) arises out of or in the course of or by reason of the Contractor's design, execution and completion or operation and maintenance of the Works, or

　(ii) is attributable to any negligence, wilful act or breach of the Contract by the Contractor, the Contractor's Personnel, their respective agents, or anyone directly or indirectly employed by any of them.

The Contractor shall also indemnify the Employer against all errors in the Contractor's design of the Works and other professional services which result in the Works not being fit for purpose or result in any loss and/or damage for the Employer.

17.10 Indemnities by the Employer

The Employer shall indemnify and hold harmless the Contractor, the Contractor's Personnel, and their respective agents, against and from all claims, damages, losses and expenses (including legal fees and expenses) in respect of:

(a) bodily injury, sickness, disease or death, or loss of or damage to any property other than the Works, which is attributable to any negligence, wilful act or breach of the Contract by the Employer, the Employer's Personnel, or any of their respective agents; and

在**雇主代表**要求的范围内，纠正此类损害。所有此类更换、修理或纠正工作，应由**承包商**自费进行。

17.8 **责任限度**	除根据第 10.6 款［*运营服务期间的延误和中断*］、第 16.4 款［*终止时的付款*］、第 17.9 款［*由承包商保障*］、第 17.10 款［*由雇主保障*］和第 17.12 款［*知识产权和工业产权侵权风险*］的规定外，任何一方不应对另一方使用任何**工程**中的损失、利润损失、合同损失或对另一方可能遭受的与**合同**有关的任何其他间接损失或损害负责。 根据**合同**或与**合同**有关的规定，**承包商**对**雇主**的全部责任不应超过**合同数据**中规定的总额，或（任何未规定总额）**中标合同金额**。 本**款**不应限制违约方的欺骗、有意违约或轻率不当行为等任何情况的责任。
17.9 **由承包商保障**	**承包商**应保障和保持使**雇主**、**雇主人员**及其各自的代理人免受以下所有索赔、损害赔偿费、损失和开支（包括法律费用和开支）带来的损害： （a） 任何人员的人身伤害、患病、疾病或死亡，不论是由于**承包商**的设计、施工、竣工或运营和维护**工程**引起，或在其过程中，或因其原因产生的，**雇主**、**雇主人员**或他们各自的任何代理人的任何疏忽、故意行为或违反**合同**造成的情况除外；（以及） （b） 由下列情况造成的对任何财产、不动产或人员（**工程**除外）的损害或损失： 　　（i） 由于**承包商**的设计、施工和竣工或运营和维护**工程**引起，或在其过程中或因其原因产生的；（或） 　　（ii） 由**承包商**、**承包商人员**、他们各自的代理人，或由他们中任何人员直接或间接雇用的任何人员的疏忽、故意行为或违反**合同**造成的。 **承包商**应保障**雇主**免受**承包商**在其**工程**设计和其他专业服务方面的所有错误，这些错误会导致**工程**不符合预期目的，或给**雇主**造成任何损失和/或损害。
17.10 **由雇主保障**	**雇主**应保障和保持使**承包商**、**承包商人员**以及他们各自的代理人免受以下所有索赔、损害赔偿费、损失和开支（包括法律费用和开支）带来的损害： （a） 由于**雇主**、**雇主人员**或他们各自的任何代理人的任何疏忽、故意行为或违反**合同**造成的除**工程**以外的人身伤害、患病、疾病或死亡或任何财产的损失或损害赔偿费；（以及）

(b) the Employer's Risks as set out in Sub-Clauses 17.1 [*The Employer's Risks during the Design-Build Period*] and 17.3 [*The Employer's Risks during the Operation Service Period*].

17.11 Shared Indemnities

The Contractor's liability to indemnify the Employer, as aforesaid, shall be reduced proportionately to the extent that the Employer's Risks may have contributed to the said damage, loss or injury. Similarly, the Employer's liability to indemnify the Contractor, as aforesaid, shall be reduced proportionately to the extent that the Contractor's risks may have contributed to the said damage, loss or injury.

17.12 Risk of Infringement of Intellectual and Industrial Property Rights

In this Sub-Clause, "infringement" means an infringement (or alleged infringement) of any patent, registered design, copyright, trademark, trade name, trade secret or other intellectual or industrial property right relating to the Works; and "claim" means a claim (or proceedings pursuing a claim) alleging an infringement.

Whenever a Party does not give Notice to the other Party of any claim within 28 days of receiving the claim, the first Party shall be deemed to have waived any right to indemnity under this Sub-Clause.

The Employer shall indemnify and hold the Contractor harmless against and from any claim alleging an infringement which is or was:

(a) an unavoidable result of the Contractor's compliance with the Employer's Requirements; or
(b) a result of any Works being used by the Employer:

  (i) for a purpose other than that indicated by, or reasonably to be inferred from, the Contract; or
  (ii) in conjunction with any thing not supplied by the Contractor, unless such use was disclosed to the Contractor prior to the Base Date or is stated in the Contract.

The Contractor shall indemnify and hold the Employer harmless against and from any other claim which arises out of or in relation to (i) the Contractor's design, manufacture, construction or execution of the Works, (ii) the use of Contractor's Equipment, or (iii) the proper use of the Works.

If a Party is entitled to be indemnified under this Sub-Clause, the indemnifying Party may (at its cost) conduct negotiations for the settlement of the claim, and any litigation or arbitration which may arise from it. The other Party shall, at the request and cost of the indemnifying Party, assist in contesting the claim. This other Party (and its Personnel) shall not make any admission which might be prejudicial to the indemnifying Party, unless the indemnifying Party failed to take over the conduct of any negotiations, litigation or arbitration upon being requested to do so by the other Party.

18 Exceptional Risks

18.1 Exceptional Risks

An exceptional risk is a risk arising from an Exceptional Event which includes, but is not limited to:

(a) war, hostilities (whether war be declared or not), invasion, act of foreign enemies;

(b) 第 17.1 款［*设计 - 施工期间雇主的风险*］和第 17.3 款［*运营服务期间雇主的风险*］中规定的雇主风险。

17.11 保障分担

承包商对**雇主**的赔偿责任，应按如上所述**雇主**风险可能造成上述损害、损失或伤害的程度按比例减少。同样，**雇主**对**承包商**的赔偿责任，应按如上所述**承包商**风险可能造成上述损害、损失或伤害的程度按比例减少。

17.12 知识产权和工业产权侵权风险

本**款**中，"侵权"系指对与**工程**有关的任何专利权、注册设计、版权、商标、商品名称、商业秘密或其他知识产权和工业产权的侵权行为（或涉嫌侵权）；以"索赔"系指声称侵权的索赔（或索赔诉讼）。

当一方在收到索赔后 28 天内，未向另一方发出索赔**通知**，则该方应被认为已放弃根据本**款**规定获得的任何赔偿权利。

雇主应保障和保持**承包商**免受以下情况提出的指称侵权的任何索赔引起的损害，该索赔是或曾经是：

(a) 因**承包商**遵从**雇主**要求而造成的不可避免的结果；（或）

(b) 因**雇主**为以下原因使用任何**工程**的结果：

 (i) 为了**合同**中指明的或根据**合同**可合理推断的事项以外的目的；（或）
 (ii) 与非**承包商**提供的任何物品联合使用，除非此类使用已基**准日期**前向**承包商**透露，或**合同**中有规定。

承包商应保障并保持**雇主**免受因下述情况引起的或与之相关的任何索赔引起的伤害：(i) **承包商**的设计、制造、施工或**工程**实施，(ii) 使用的**承包商设备**，或 (iii) **工程**的正确使用。

如果一方有权根据本款获得赔偿，则赔偿方可（自费）就索赔的解决进行谈判，以及由此产生的任何诉讼和仲裁。另一方应在赔偿方请求并承担费用的情况下，协助对索赔进行抗辩。该另一方（及其**人员**）不应做出可能损害赔偿**方不利**的任何承认，除非赔偿方未能在另一方要求下接管任何谈判、诉讼或仲裁。

18 例外风险

18.1 例外风险

例外风险是由**例外事件**引起的风险，包括但不限于：

(a) 战争、敌对行动（无论宣战与否）入侵、外敌行为；

(b) rebellion, terrorism, revolution, insurrection, military or usurped power, or civil war, within the Country;
(c) riot, commotion or disorder within the Country by persons other than the Contractor's Personnel and other employees of the Contractor and Subcontractors;
(d) strike or lockout not solely involving the Contractor's Personnel and other employees of the Contractor and Subcontractors;
(e) munitions of war, explosive materials, ionising radiation or contamination by radio-activity, within the Country, except as may be attributable to the Contractor's use of such munitions, explosives, radiation or radio-activity; and
(f) natural catastrophes such as earthquake, hurricane, typhoon or volcanic activity which are Unforeseeable or against which an experienced contractor could not reasonably have been expected to have taken adequate preventative precautions.

18.2 Notice of an Exceptional Event

If a Party is or will be prevented from performing any of its obligations under the Contract due to an Exceptional Event, then it shall give Notice to the other Party of such event or circumstance and shall specify the obligations, the performance of which is or will be prevented. The Notice shall be given within 14 days after the Party became aware, or should have become aware, of the event or circumstance constituting an Exceptional Event.

The Party shall, having given Notice, be excused performance of such obligations for so long as such Exceptional Event prevents it from performing them.

Notwithstanding any other provision of this Clause, the obligations of either Party to make payments to the other Party under the Contract shall not be excused by an Exceptional Event.

18.3 Duty to Minimise Delay

Each Party shall at all times use all reasonable endeavors to minimise any delay in the performance of the Contract as a result of an Exceptional Event.

A Party shall give Notice to the other Party when it ceases to be affected by an Exceptional Event.

18.4 Consequences of an Exceptional Event

If the Contractor is prevented from performing any of his obligations under the Contract due to an Exceptional Event of which Notice has been given under Sub-Clause 18.2 [*Notice of an Exceptional Event*] and suffers delay and/or incurs cost by reason of such Exceptional Event, the Contractor shall be entitled, subject to Sub-Clause 20.1 [*Contractor's Claims*], to:

(a) an extension of time for any such delay, if completion is or will be delayed, under Sub-Clause 9.3 [*Extension of Time for Completion of Design-Build*]; and
(b) if the event or circumstance is of the kind described in sub-paragraphs (a) to (e) of Sub-Clause 18.1 [*Exceptional Risks*] and, in the case of sub-paragraphs (b) to (e), occurs in the Country, payment of any such Cost.

If the Exceptional Event occurs during the Operation Service Period, sub-paragraph (a) of this Sub-Clause 18.4 will not apply.

After receiving this Notice, the Employer's Representative shall proceed in accordance with Sub-Clause 3.5 [*Determinations*] to agree or determine these matters.

(b) 工程所在国的叛乱、恐怖主义、革命、暴动、军事政变或篡夺政权，或内战；

(c) 承包商人员和承包商及其分包商的其他雇员以外的人员的骚动、喧闹或混乱；

(d) 不仅仅涉及承包商人员和承包商及其分包商的其他雇员的罢工或停工；

(e) 工程所在国的战争军火、爆炸物资、电离辐射或放射性污染，但可能因承包商使用此类军火、炸药、辐射或放射性引起的除外；（以及）

(f) 不可预见的或有经验的承包商无法合理地采取预防措施的自然灾害，如地震、飓风、台风或火山活动。

18.2 例外事件的通知

如果一方因例外事件已或将无法履行根据合同规定其的任何义务，则应将此类事件或情况通知另一方，并应明确说明已或将受到阻止履行的各项义务。此通知应在该方觉察或应已觉察构成例外事件的事件或情况后14天内发出。

在发出通知后，只要此例外事件阻止该方履行义务，则该方可免除履行被阻止的义务。

尽管本款有任何其他规定，任一方根据合同向另一方支付款项的义务不得因例外事件而免除。

18.3 将延误减至最小的义务

各方都应在任何时间尽所有合理的努力，使例外事件对履行合同造成的任何延误减至最小。

当一方不再受例外事件影响时，应通知另一方。

18.4 例外事件的后果

如果承包商由于根据第18.2款［例外事件的通知］的规定发出通知的例外事件，而无法履行其合同规定的任何义务，并因此遭受延误和/或招致增加费用，承包商应有权根据第20.1款［承包商索赔］的规定，要求：

(a) 根据第9.3款［设计－施工竣工时间的延长］的规定，如果竣工已或将受到延误，对任何此类延误给予延长期；（以及）

(b) 如果该事件或情况属于第18.1款［例外风险］（a）至（e）段所述的类型，且该款（b）至（e）段所述情况发生在工程所在国，获得任何此类费用的支付。

如果例外事件发生在运营服务期间，则第18.4款（a）段将不适用。

雇主代表收到此通知后，应按照第3.5款［确定］的规定，对这些事项进行商定或确定。

18.5 Optional Termination, Payment and Release

If the execution of substantially all the Works in progress is prevented for a continuous period of 84 days by reason of an Exceptional Event of which Notice has been given under Sub-Clause 18.2 [*Notice of an Exceptional Event*], or for multiple periods which total more than 140 days due to the same notified Exceptional Event, then either Party may give to the other Party a Notice of termination of the Contract. In this event, the termination shall take effect 7 days after the Notice is given, and the Contractor shall proceed in accordance with Sub-Clause 16.3 [*Cessation of Work and Removal of Contractor's Equipment*].

Upon such termination, the Employer's Representative shall determine the value of the work done and issue a Payment Certificate which shall include:

(a) the amounts payable for any work carried out for which a price is stated in the Contract;

(b) the Cost of Plant and Materials ordered for the Works which have been delivered to the Contractor, or of which the Contractor is liable to accept delivery. This Plant and Materials shall become the property of (and be at the risk of) the Employer when paid for by the Employer, and the Contractor shall place the same at the Employer's disposal;

(c) any other Cost or liability which in the circumstances was reasonably incurred by the Contractor in the expectation of completing the Works;

(d) the Cost of removal of Temporary Works and Contractor's Equipment from the Site and the return of these items to the Contractor's works in his country (or to any other destination at no greater cost); and

(e) the Cost of repatriation of the Contractor's staff and labour employed wholly in connection with the Works at the date of termination.

18.6 Release from Performance under the Law

Notwithstanding any other provision of this Clause, if any event arises outside the control of the Parties (including, but not limited to, an Exceptional Event) which makes it impossible or unlawful for either or both Parties to fulfil its or their contractual obligations or which, under the law governing the Contract, entitles the Parties to be released from further performance of the Contract, then upon Notice by either Party to the other Party of such event:

(a) the Parties shall be discharged from further performance, without prejudice to the rights of either Party in respect of any previous breach of the Contract; and

(b) the sum payable by the Employer to the Contractor shall be the same as would have been payable under Sub-Clause 18.5 [*Optional Termination, Payment and Release*] if the Contract had been terminated under that Sub-Clause.

Insurance

19.1 General Requirements

Without limiting his or the Employer's obligations or responsibilities under the Contract, the Contractor shall effect and maintain all insurances for which he is responsible with insurers and in terms, both of which shall be subject to approval by the Employer, such approval shall not be unreasonably withheld or delayed.

18.5 自主选择终止、付款和解除

如果由于已根据第 18.2 款 [*例外事件的通知*] 的规定发出**通知**的**例外事件**，导致进行中的全部**工程**的实施连续 84 天受阻，或由于同一**例外事件**导致多个时段累计受阻超过 140 天，任一方可向另一方发出**通知**，终止**合同**。在此情况下，终止应在发出**通知** 7 天后生效，**承包商**应按照第 16.3 款 [*停止工作和承包商设备的撤离*] 的规定继续进行。

此类终止后，**雇主代表**应确定已完成工作的价值，并签发**支付证书**，其中包括：

（a） 已完成的、**合同**中有价格规定的任何工作的应付款额；

（b） 为**工程**订购的、已交付给**承包商**或**承包商**有责任接受交付的**生产设备和材料**的**费用**。当**雇主**支付上述费用后，此项**生产设备和材料**应成为**雇主**的财产（风险也由其承担），**承包商**应将其交由**雇主**处理；

（c） 在**承包商**原预期要完成**工程**的情况下，合理产生的任何其他**费用**或债务；

（d） 将**临时工程**和**承包商设备**撤离**现场**，并运回**承包商**本国工作地点的**费用**（或运往任何其他目的地，但其费用不得超过）；（以及）

（e） 将终止日期时完全为**工程**雇用的**承包商**的员工送返回国的**费用**。

18.6 依法解除履约

尽管有**本条**的任何其他规定，如果发生双方不能控制的任何事件（包括但不限于**例外事件**），使任一方或双方完成其**合同**义务成为不可能的或非法的，或根据**合同**管辖法律规定，双方有权解除进一步履行**合同**的义务，则在任一方将此类事件**通知**另一方后：

（a） 在不损害任一方任何先前违反**合同**的权利的情况下，**双方**应解除进一步履约的义务；（以及）

（b） **雇主**应付给**承包商**的款额，应与第 18.5 款 [*自主选择终止、支付和解除*] 规定的应付款额相同，该款额是**合同**已根据**本款**终止。

19 保险

19.1 一般要求

在不限制其或**雇主**在**合同**规定义务或责任的情况下，**承包商**应在保险人处按条款办理并保持其负责的所有保险项目，保险人及条款应征得**雇主**的批准，此类批准不得无理拒绝或延误。

The insurances required to be provided herein are the minimum required by the Employer, and the Contractor may, at his own cost, add such other insurances that he may deem prudent.

Whenever required by the Employer, the Contractor shall produce the insurance policies which he is required to effect under the Contract. As each premium is paid, the Contractor shall send a copy of each receipt of payment to the Employer.

If the Contractor fails to effect and keep in force any of the insurances required under Sub-Clause 19.2 [*Insurances to be provided by the Contractor during the Design-Build Period*], or fails to provide the policies or receipts as aforementioned, then, and in any such case, the Employer may effect and keep in force such insurances and pay any premium as may be necessary and recover the same from the Contractor from time to time by deducting the amount (s) so paid from any monies due to the Contractor or otherwise recover the same as a debt from the Contractor.

If either the Contractor or the Employer fails to comply with the conditions attaching to the insurances effected pursuant to the Contract, the Party so failing to comply as aforesaid shall indemnify the other Party against all losses and claims arising from such failure.

The Contractor shall also be responsible for the following:

(a) notifying the insurers of any changes in the nature, extent or programme for the execution of the Works;
(b) notifying the insurers of any changes in the nature, extent or programme for the provision of the Operation Service; and
(c) the adequacy and validity of the insurances in accordance with the Contract at all times during the performance of the Contract.

The permitted deductible limits allowed in any policy shall not exceed the amounts stated in the Contract Data.

Where there is a shared liability the loss shall be borne by each Party in proportion to its liability under Clause 17 [*Risk Allocation*] or Clause 18 [*Exceptional Risks*], provided the non-recovery from insurers has not been caused by a breach of this Clause by the Contractor. In the event that non-recovery from insurers has been caused by such a breach of Contract by the Contractor, the Contractor shall bear the loss suffered.

19.2
Insurances to be provided by the Contractor during the Design-Build Period

The Contractor shall provide the following insurances during the Design-Build Period:

(a) The Works

The Contractor shall insure and keep insured in the joint names of the Contractor and the Employer from the Commencement Date until the date of issue of the Commissioning Certificate:

(i) the Works, together with Materials and Plant for incorporation therein, for their full replacement value with deductible limits not exceeding those stated in the Contract Data. The insurance cover shall extend to include loss and damage of any part of the Works as a consequence of failure of elements defectively designed or constructed with defective material or workmanship; and

此款规定的应提供的保险是雇主的最低要求，承包商可自费增加其认为必要的保险。

无论任何时候，只要雇主提出要求，承包商应投保合同要求的其应投保的保险。每一笔保费支付后，承包商应将每一份付款收据的复印件发送雇主。

如果承包商未能按照第19.2款［承包商在设计-施工期间提供的保险］规定的要求办理保险，或未能提供前面提到的保单或收据，并使之保持有效，则在任何情况下，雇主均可办理此类保险并使之保持有效，或支付任何有必要支付的保险费，并可以随时在给承包商的任何到期应付款中扣除上述金额，或将上述金额作为承包商的债务。

如果承包商或雇主中的任一方未能遵守合同规定的保险的附加条件，未遵守前面提到的规定的一方应赔偿另一方因这种不当而造成的所有直接损失和索赔。

承包商还应对以下事项负责：

（a）通知保险人工程实施的性质、范围或程序的任何改变；

（b）通知保险人提供运营服务的性质、范围或进度计划的任何改变；（以及）

（c）履行合同期间的任何时候，根据合同规定保证保险的充分性和有效性。

任何保单中允许的可扣减额不应超过合同数据中规定的金额。

如果损失未能从保险人处获得补偿，且未获得补偿不是因承包商违反此条规定造成的，对于共同责任的损失，应由各方按照其在第17条［风险分配］或第18条［例外风险］的规定按比例分担。如果未能从保险人处获得补偿是由于承包商违反本条款造成的，则承包商应承担所有遭受的损失。

19.2 承包商在设计-施工期间提供的保险	承包商应在设计-施工期间提供以下保险：

（a）工程

承包商应从开工日期至调试证书的签发日期，以雇主和承包商的共同名义投保并保持保险：

（i）工程，连同所含的材料和生产设备，保险金额为其全部重置价值，免赔限额不超过合同数据中规定的限额。保险范围应扩大到由于设计缺陷或使用有缺陷的材料或工艺导致的部件故障而造成的工程任何部分的损失和损害；（以及）

(ii) an additional sum of fifteen percent (15%) of such replacement value (or such sum as may be specified in the Contract Data) to cover any additional costs incidental to the rectification of loss or damage, including professional fees and the cost of demolition and removal of debris.

The insurance cover shall cover the Employer and the Contractor against all loss or damage from whatever cause arising until the Commissioning Certificate is issued. Thereafter, the insurance shall continue until the date of issue of the Final Payment Certificate Design Build in respect of any incomplete work for loss or damage arising from any cause occurring prior to the date of the Commissioning Certificate, and for any loss or damage occasioned by the Contractor in the course of any operation carried out by him for the purpose of complying with his obligations under Clause 12 [*Defects*].

The insurance cover provided by the Contractor for the Works may exclude any of the following:

(1) the cost of making good any part of the Works which is defective (including defective material and workmanship) or otherwise does not comply with the Contract, provided that it does not exclude the cost of making good any loss or damage to any other part of the Works attributable to such defect or non-compliance.
(2) indirect or consequential loss or damage including any reductions in the Contract Price for delay.
(3) wear and tear, shortages and pilferages.
(4) the Employer's Risks set out in Sub-Clause 17.1 [*Employer's Risks during the Design-Build Period*] unless otherwise stated in the Contract Data regarding the risks in sub-paragraph (b) (iii) thereof.
(5) the Exceptional Risks set out in Sub-Clause 18.1 [*Exceptional Risks*] unless, otherwise stated in the Contract Data regarding the risks in subparagraph (f) thereof.

(b) Contractor's Equipment

The Contractor shall insure in the joint names of the Employer and the Contractor the Contractor's Equipment and other things brought onto Site by the Contractor to the extent specified in the Contract Data.

(c) Liability for breach of professional duty

The Contractor shall insure the legal liability of the Contractor arising out of the negligent fault, defect, error or omission of the Contractor or any person for whom the Contractor is responsible in the carrying out their professional duties in an amount not less than that stated in the Contract Data.

Such insurance shall contain an extension indemnifying the Contractor for his liability arising out of negligent fault, defect, error or omission in the carrying out his professional duties which result in the Works not being fit for the purpose specified in the Contract and resulting in any loss and/or damage to the Employer.

The Contractor shall maintain this insurance for the period specified in the Contract Data.

(d) Injury to persons and damage to property

（ii） 此重置价值增加 15% 的附加金额（或**合同数据**中规定的金额），以涵盖修复损失或损害的额外费用，包括专业费用以及拆除和移除废弃物的费用。

保险范围应涵盖**雇主**和**承包商**，以防止在签发**调试证书**之前因任何原因造成的所有损失或损害。此后，对于因签发**调试证书**之前发生的任何原因造成的任何损失或损害，任何未完成的工作，以及**承包商**为履行**第 12 条**［**缺陷**］规定的**承包商**义务，**承包商**作业过程中造成的任何损失或损坏，保险应持续到签发**设计 - 施工最终付款证书**之日。

承包商为**工程**提供的保险范围可不包括以下任何一项：

（1） 修复有缺陷的（包括有缺陷的材料和工艺）或不符合**合同**规定的**工程**任何部分的费用，但前提是不排除修复由于上述缺陷或不合规导致**工程**其他任何部分的损失或损害的费用。

（2） 间接或结果性损失或损害，包括因延误而扣减的**合同价格**。

（3） 磨损、短缺和盗窃。

（4） **第 17.1 款**［**设计-施工期间雇主的风险**］中规定的**雇主风险**，除非**合同数据**中对（b）（iii）段中所述的风险另有说明。

（5） **第 18.1 款**［**例外风险**］中规定的**例外风险**，除非**合同数据**中对（f）段中所述的风险另有说明。

（b） **承包商设备**

承包商应以**雇主**和**承包商**的共同名义，在**合同数据**中规定的范围内，为**承包商**交运到**现场**的**承包商设备**和其他物品投保。

（c） 违反职业职责的责任

承包商应对其或任何人员在履行职业职责时，因疏忽、缺陷、错误或遗漏而产生的法律责任投保，其金额不少于**合同数据**中规定的金额。

此类保险应包括对**承包商**在履行其职业职责时的疏忽、缺陷、错误或遗漏而导致**工程**不能符合**合同**规定的目的，以及对**雇主**造成任何损失和 / 或损害而产生的责任进行延期赔偿。

承包商应在**合同数据**规定的期限内，保持此保险。

（d） 人员伤害和财产损害

The Contractor shall insure, in the joint names of the Contractor and the Employer, against liabilities for death or injury to any person, or loss of or damage to any property (other than the Works) arising out of the performance of the Contract and occurring before the issue of the Final Payment Certificate Design-Build, other than loss or damage caused by any event covered under Sub-Clause 17.1 [*Employer's Risks during the Design-Build Period*] or Sub-Clause 18.1 [*Exceptional Risks*].

The insurance policy shall include a cross liability clause such that the insurance shall apply to the Contractor and the Employer as separate insureds.

Such insurance shall be effected before the Contractor begins any work on the Site and shall remain in force until the issue of the Final Payment Certificate Design-Build and shall be for not less than the amount specified in the Contract Data.

(e) Injury to employees

The Contractor shall effect and maintain insurance against liability for claims, damages, losses and expenses (including legal fees and expenses) arising from injury, sickness, disease or death of any person employed by the Contractor or any other of the Contractor's Personnel.

The Employer and the Employer's Representative shall also be indemnified under the policy of insurance, except that this insurance may exclude losses and claims to the extent that they arise from any act or neglect of the Employer or of the Employer's Personnel.

The insurance shall be maintained in full force and effect during the whole time that the Contractor's Personnel are assisting in the execution of the Works. For any person employed by a Subcontractor, the insurance may be effected by the Subcontractor, but the Contractor shall be responsible for the Subcontractor's compliance with this Sub-Clause.

(f) Other insurances required by Law and by local practice

Other insurances required by Law and by local practice (if any) shall be detailed in the Contract Data and the Contractor shall provide such other insurances in compliance with the details given, at his own cost.

19.3 Insurances to be provided by the Contractor during the Operation Service Period

The Contractor shall provide the following insurances during the Operation Service Period:

(a) Fire extended cover for the Works

The Contractor shall provide, in the joint names of the Employer and the Contractor, fire extended cover insurance for the Works as specified in the Contract Data for the Operation Service Period. Notwithstanding any other provision in the Contract, the Operation Service shall not commence until the fire extended cover insurance is effected and the terms and details have been approved by the Employer.

The terms of the policy shall be submitted to the Employer for his approval no later than 28 days before the date upon which the Commissioning Certificate is due to be issued, and shall come into force on the date stated in the Commissioning Certificate.

(b) Injury to any person and damage to property

承包商应以承包商和雇主的共同名义，对因履行合同而产生的以及在签发设计 - 施工最终付款证书之前发生的，任何人员的死亡或伤害，或任何财产（而非工程）的损失或损害等责任投保，由第17.1款［设计-施工期间的雇主风险］或第18.1款［例外风险］中所涵盖的任何事件导致的损失或损害除外。

保单应包括交叉责任条款，以便保险应适用于作为单独被保险人的承包商和雇主。

此类保险应在承包商开始在现场进行任何工作之前投保，并直至签发设计 - 施工最终付款证书为止保持有效，且保险金额不得少于合同数据中规定的金额。

(e) 雇员的人身伤害

承包商应对其雇用的任何人员或任何其他承包商人员发生的伤害、患病、疾病或死亡而引起的索赔、损害、损失和开支（包括法律费用和开支）的责任办理并维持保险。

除该保险可不包括由雇主或雇主人员的任何行为或疏忽引起的损失和索赔的情况以外，雇主和雇主代表也应由该项保单得到保障。

此保险应在承包商人员参加工程实施的整个期间保持全面实施和有效。对于分包商雇用的任何人员，此类保险可以由分包商投保，但承包商应对分包商符合本条规定的保险负责。

(f) 法律和当地惯例要求的其他保险

法律和当地惯例要求的其他保险（如果有）应在合同数据中详细说明，承包商应根据给出的详细信息提供此类保险，费用由承包商承担。

19.3 承包商在运营服务期间提供的保险

承包商应在运营服务期间提供以下保险：

(a) 工程防火延长险

承包商应以雇主和承包商的共同名义，按照合同数据的规定为运营服务期的工程提供防火延长险。尽管合同中有任何其他规定，在防火延长险生效且条款和细节得到雇主批准之前，运营服务将不得开始。

应在签发调试证书日期前28天，将保险单的条款提交给雇主批准，并应在调试证书中规定的日期生效。

(b) 任何人员伤害和财产损害

The Contractor shall ensure that an insurance as required under Sub-Clause 19.2 (d) [*Injury to any person and damage to property*] be effected prior to the issue of the Commissioning Certificate and maintained until the issue of the Contract Completion Certificate. Such insurance shall be for an amount and in terms as specified in the Contract Data.

(c) Injury to employees

The Contractor shall ensure that an insurance as required under Sub-Clause 19.2 (e) [*Injury to employees*] be effected prior to the issue of the Commissioning Certificate and maintained until the issue of the Contract Completion Certificate, or the last of his or any of his Subcontractors' employees have left the Site, whichever is the later.

(d) Other insurances required by Law and by local practice

Other insurances required by Law and by local practice (if any) shall be detailed in the Contract Data and the Contractor shall provide such insurances in compliance with the details given, at his own cost.

(e) Other optional operational insurances

Other optional insurances required (if any) shall be detailed in the Contract Data and the Contractor shall provide such other insurances in compliance with the details given, at his own cost.

20 Claims, Disputes and Arbitration

20.1 Contractor's Claims

If the Contractor considers himself to be entitled to any extension of the Time for Completion of Design-Build and/or any additional payment, under any Clause of these Conditions or otherwise in connection with the Contract, he must comply with the following procedures:

(a) Notices

The Contractor shall give Notice to the Employer's Representative, describing the event or circumstance giving rise to the claim as soon as practicable, and not later than 28 days after the Contractor became aware, or should have become aware, of the event or circumstance. The Notice shall state that it is given under this Sub-Clause.

If the Contractor fails to give Notice of a claim within such period of 28 days, the Time for Completion of Design-Build shall not be extended, the Contractor shall not be entitled to additional payment, and the Employer shall be discharged from all liability in connection with the claim. However, if the Contractor considers there are circumstances which justify the late submission, he may submit the details to the DAB for a ruling. If the DAB considers that, in all the circumstances, it is fair and reasonable that the late submission be accepted, the DAB shall have the authority to overrule the relevant 28-day limit and, if it so decides, it shall advise the Parties accordingly.

If the Contractor has submitted his Notice of claim within the 28-day limit or the DAB has ruled that the late Notice was acceptable, then the Contractor shall proceed in accordance with the provisions of this Sub-Clause.

承包商应确保根据第 19.2 款（d）段［*人员伤害和财产损害*］要求的保险，在签发**调试证书**之前生效，并在**合同完成证书**签发之前保持有效。此类保险的金额和条款应符合**合同数据**的规定。

(c) 雇员的人身伤害

承包商应确保根据**第 19.2 款**（e）段［*雇员伤害*］要求的保险，在签发**调试证书**之前生效，并在**合同完成证书**签发之前保持有效，或**承包商**或其**分包商**的最后一名雇员离开**现场**，以较晚者为准。

(d) **法律和当地惯例要求的其他保险**

法律和当地惯例要求的其他保险（如果有）应在**合同数据**中详细说明，**承包商**应根据给出的详细信息提供此类保险，费用由**承包商**承担。

(e) 其他可选择运营保险

所需的其他可选择保险（如果有）应在**合同数据**中详细说明，**承包商**应根据给出的详细信息提供此类其他保险，费用由**承包商**承担。

20 索赔、争端和仲裁

20.1 承包商索赔

如果**承包商**认为，根据本**条件**的任何**条款**或与合同有关的其他规定，自己有权获得任何**设计－施工竣工时间**的延长和／或任何额外付款，其必须遵守以下程序：

(a) 通知

承包商应向**雇主代表**发出**通知**，说明引起索赔的事件或情况，该**通知**应尽快在**承包商**觉察或应已觉察该事件或情况后 28 天内发出。**通知**应说明是根据本**款**规定发出的。

如果**承包商**未能在上述 28 天期限内发出索赔**通知**，**设计－施工竣工时间**不得延长，**承包商**应无权得到追加付款，而**雇主**应免除有关该索赔的全部责任。但是，如果**承包商**认为有理由推迟提交，其可将详细资料提交给**争端裁决委员会**裁决。如果**争端裁决委员会**认为，在所有情况下，接受迟交的资料是公平和合理的，**争端裁决委员会**有权否决有关的 28 天期限，如果如此决定的话，应相应地告知双方。

如果**承包商**在 28 天期限内提交了索赔**通知**，或**争端裁决委员会**裁定可以接受迟交的**通知**，则**承包商**应按照本**款**的规定进行。

(b) Contemporary records

Following the giving of Notice, the Contractor shall keep such contemporary records as may be necessary to substantiate any claim. Contemporary records shall be kept on Site unless agreed otherwise with the Employer's Representative. Without admitting the Employer's liability, the Employer's Representative may, after receiving any Notice under this Sub-Clause, monitor the record-keeping and/or instruct the Contractor to keep additional contemporary records. The Contractor shall permit the Employer's Representative to inspect all these records, and shall (if instructed) submit copies to the Employer's Representative.

(c) Details and particulars

With 42 days after the Contractor became aware (or should have become aware) of the event or circumstance giving rise to the claim, or within such other period as may be allowed by the DAB under paragraph (a) above, or proposed by the Contractor and approved by the Employer's Representative, the Contractor shall send to the Employer's Representative a fully detailed claim which includes full supporting particulars of the contractual or other basis of the claim and of the extension of time and/or additional payment claimed. The Contractor shall also provide the Employer's Representative with any additional particulars which the Employer's Representative may reasonably require.

If the Contractor fails to provide the contractual or other basis of the claim within the said 42 days or other time allowed or approved, the Notice given under paragraph (a) above shall be deemed to have lapsed and shall no longer be considered as a valid Notice. If the Contractor considers there are circumstances which justify a late submission, he may submit the details to the DAB for a ruling. If the DAB considers that, in all the circumstances, it is fair and reasonable that the late submission be accepted, the DAB shall have the authority to overrule the given 42-day limit and, if it so decides, it shall advise the Parties accordingly.

If the event or circumstance giving rise to the claim has a continuing effect:

(i) the fully detailed claim shall be considered as interim;
(ii) the Contractor shall send further interim claims at 28-day intervals, giving the accumulated delay and/or amount claimed, and such additional particulars as the Employer's Representative may reasonably require; and
(iii) the Contractor shall send a final claim within 28 days after the end of the effects resulting from the event or circumstance, or within such other period as may be proposed by the Contractor and approved by the Employer's Representative.

(d) Employer's Representative's response

Within 42 days after receiving a fully detailed claim or any further particulars requested by the Employer's Representative, or within such other period as may be agreed by the Employer's Representative and the Contractor, the Employer's Representative shall proceed in accordance with Sub-Clause 3.5 [*Determinations*] to agree or determine (i) the extension (if any) of the Time for Completion of Design-Build (before or after its expiry) in accordance with Sub-Clause 9.3 [*Extension of Time for Completion for Design-Build*], and/or (ii)

(b) 同期记录

在发出**通知**后，**承包商**应保存必要的同期记录，以证明任何索赔。除非与**雇主代表**另有商定，否则应在**现场**保存同期记录。在不承认**雇主**责任的情况下，**雇主代表**可在收到本**款**规定的任何**通知**后，监督记录的保存和／或指示**承包商**保存额外的同期记录。**承包商**应允许**雇主代表**检验所有这些记录，并应向**雇主代表**（如有指示）提供复印件。

(c) 详细资料和依据（证据）

在**承包商**觉察（或应已觉察）引起索赔的事件或情况后 42 天内，或在**争端裁决委员会**根据上述（a）段可能允许的，或**承包商**建议并经**雇主代表**认可的其他期限内，**承包商**应向**雇主代表**提交一份充分详细的索赔报告，包括索赔的合同依据或其他依据以及要求延长的时间和／或追加付款的全部详细资料。**承包商**还应向**雇主代表**提供**雇主代表**可能合理要求的任何附加资料。

如果**承包商**未能在上述 42 天或其他允许或批准的时间内，提供索赔的合同依据或其他依据，则根据上述（a）段规定发出的**通知**应视为已失效，不再视为有效**通知**。如果**承包商**认为有理由推迟提交，其可将证明资料提交给**争端裁决委员会**裁决。如果**争端裁决委员会**认为，在所有情况下，接受迟交的资料是公平和合理的，**争端裁决委员会**有权否决有关的 42 天期限，如果如此决定，应相应地告知双方。

如果引起索赔的事件和情况具有连续影响，则：

(i) 上述充分详细的索赔应被认为是临时的；
(ii) **承包商**应每隔 28 天提交进一步的临时索赔**报告**，说明累计索赔的延误时间和／或款额，以及**雇主代表**可能合理要求的此类附加证明资料；（以及）
(iii) **承包商**应在引起索赔的事件或情况所产生的影响结束后 28 天，或在**承包商**可能建议并经**雇主代表**认可的此类其他期限内，递交一份最终索赔报告。

(d) **雇主代表**的响应

在收到充分详细的索赔报告或**雇主代表**要求的进一步证明资料后 42 天内，或**雇主代表**和**承包商**商定的其他期限内，**雇主代表**应按照**第 3.5 款**［*确定*］的规定，就以下事项商定或确定（i）根据**第 9.3 款**［*设计-施工竣工时间的延长*］的规定，应给予设计-施工竣工时间（在其期满之前或之后）的延长期（如果有）。和／或（ii）

the additional payment (if any) to which the Contractor is entitled under the Contract with detailed comments. He may also request any necessary additional particulars, but shall nevertheless give his response on the contractual or other aspects of the claim within the 42 days after receiving the fully detailed claim from the Contractor.

If the Employer's Representative does not respond in accordance with the foregoing procedures and timetable, either Party may consider that the claim has been rejected by the Employer's Representative and either Party may refer the matter to the DAB in accordance with Sub-Clause 20.6 [*Obtaining Dispute Adjudication Board's Decision*].

Each Payment Certificate shall include such amounts for any claim as have been reasonably substantiated as due under the relevant provision of the Contract. Unless and until the particulars supplied are sufficient to substantiate the whole of the claim, the Contractor shall only be entitled to payment for such part of the claim as he has been able to substantiate.

If either Party is dissatisfied with the determination of the Employer's Representative, either Party may, within 28 days after receiving the determination, issue to the Employer's Representative and the other Party, a Notice of dissatisfaction, and thereafter proceed in accordance with Sub-Clause 20.6 [*Obtaining Dispute Adjudication Board's Decision*]. If no Notice of dissatisfaction is issued by either Party within the said 28 days, the determination of the Employer's Representative shall be deemed to have been accepted by both Parties.

The requirements of this Sub-Clause are in addition to those of any other Sub-Clause which may apply to a claim. If the Contractor fails to comply with this or another Sub-Clause in relation to any claim, any extension of time and/or additional payment shall take account of the extent (if any) to which the failure has prevented or prejudiced proper investigation of the claim, unless the claim is excluded under the paragraph (a) of this Sub-Clause.

20.2 Employer's Claims

If the Employer considers himself to be entitled to any payment under any Clause of these Conditions or otherwise in connection with the Contract, the Employer or the Employer's Representative shall give Notice and particulars to the Contractor.

The Notice shall be given as soon as practicable after the Employer becomes aware, or should have become aware, of the event or circumstances giving rise to the claim.

The particulars shall specify the Clause or other basis of the claim, and shall include substantiation of the amount to which the Employer considers himself to be entitled in connection with the Contract. The Employer's Representative shall then proceed in accordance with Sub-Clause 3.5 [*Determinations*] to agree or determine the amount (if any) which the Employer is entitled to be paid by the Contractor.

If either Party is dissatisfied with the determination of the Employer's Representative, either Party may, within 28 days after receiving the determination, issue to the Employer's Representative and the other Party, a Notice of dissatisfaction, and thereafter proceed in accordance with Sub-Clause 20.6 [*Obtaining Dispute Adjudication Board's Decision*]. If no Notice of dissatisfaction is issued by either Party within the said 28 days, the determination of the Employer's Representative shall be deemed to have been accepted by both Parties.

根据**合同**，**承包商**有权获得的追加付款（如果有），并附上详细意见。**承包商**也可要求提供任何必要的附加证明资料，但应在收到**承包商**的充分详细的索赔报告后 42 天内，就索赔的合同或其他方面做出答复。

如果**雇主代表**没有按照前述程序和时间表做出答复，任何一方均可认为该索赔已被**雇主代表**拒绝，并且任何一方均可根据**第 20.6 款**［*取得争端裁决委员会的决定*］的规定，将该事项提交给**争端裁决委员会**。

每份**付款证书**应包括已根据**合同**有关规定，合理证明的任何此类索赔的款额。除非并直到所提供的证明资料足以证实全部的索赔，否则**承包商**只有权就其已能证实的部分索赔获得付款。

如果任何一方对**雇主代表**的确定不满意，任何一方可在收到该确定后 28 天内，向**雇主代表**和另一方发出不满意**通知**，并随后按照**第 20.6 款**［*取得争端裁决委员会的决定*］的规定进行。如果任何一方未能在所述的 28 天内发出不满意**通知**，则**雇主代表**的确定应被视为已被双方所接受。

本**款**的各项要求是对适用于索赔的任何其他**条款**的补充要求。如果**承包商**未能达到本**款**或有关任何索赔的其他**条款**的要求，除非该索赔根据本**款**（a）段的规定被拒绝，在给予任何延长期和／或追加付款时，应考虑到此项未达到要求在多大的程度上（如果有）阻止或妨碍了对索赔的适当调查。

20.2 雇主索赔

如果**雇主**认为其有权根据本**条件**的任何**条款**或与本合同有关的其他规定获得任何付款，**雇主**或**雇主代表**应向**承包商**发出**通知**并提供证明资料。

在**雇主**觉察或应已觉察引起索赔的范围或情况后，应尽快发出**通知**。

详细资料应说明索赔的**条款**或其他依据，并应包括**雇主**认为其根据合同有权获得金额的证明。然后，**雇主代表**应按照**第 3.5 款**［*确定*］的规定，商定或确定**雇主**有权由**承包商**支付的金额（如果有）。

如果任何一方对**雇主代表**的确定不满意，任何一方可在收到该确定后 28 天内，向**雇主代表**和另一方发出不满意**通知**，并随后按照**第 20.6 款**［*取得争端裁决委员会的决定*］的规定进行。如果任何一方未能在所述的 28 天内发出不满意**通知**，则**雇主代表**的确定应被视为已被双方所接受。

The amount determined by the DAB may be included as a deduction in the Contract Price and Payment Certificates. The Employer shall only be entitled to set off against or make any deduction from an amount certified in a Payment Certificate, or to otherwise claim against the Contractor, in accordance with this Sub-Clause.

20.3 Appointment of the Dispute Adjudication Board

Disputes arising during the Design-Build Period shall be adjudicated by a DAB in accordance with Sub-Clause 20.6 [*Obtaining Dispute Adjudication Board's Decision*]. The Parties shall jointly appoint a DAB by the date stated in the Contract Data.

The DAB shall comprise, as stated in the Contract Data, either one or three suitably qualified persons ("the members"). If the number is not so stated and the Parties do not agree otherwise, the DAB shall comprise three persons.

If the DAB is to comprise three persons, each Party shall nominate one member for the approval of the other Party. The Parties shall consult both these members and shall agree upon the third member, who shall be appointed to act as chairman.

However, if a list of potential members is included in the Contract, the members shall be selected from those on the list, subject to their being able and willing to accept appointment to the DAB.

The agreement between the Parties and either the sole member ("adjudicator") or each of the three members shall incorporate by reference the General Conditions of Dispute Adjudication Agreement in these General Conditions, with such amendments as are agreed between them.

The terms of the remuneration of either the sole member or each of the three members shall be mutually agreed upon by the Parties when agreeing the terms of appointment. Each Party shall be responsible for paying one-half of this remuneration.

If at any time the Parties so agree, they may appoint a suitably qualified person or persons to replace any one or more members of the DAB. Unless the Parties agree otherwise, the appointment will come into effect if a member declines to act or is unable to act as a result of death, disability, resignation or termination of appointment. The replacement shall be appointed in the same manner as the replaced person was required to have been nominated or agreed upon, as described in this Sub-Clause. However the appointment of any member may only be terminated by mutual agreement of both Parties, and not by the Employer or the Contractor acting alone.

Unless otherwise agreed by both Parties, the appointment of the DAB (including each member) shall expire upon the issue of the Commissioning Certificate under Sub-Clause 9.12 [*Completion of Design-Build*] or 28 days after the DAB has given its decision to a Dispute under Sub-Clause 20.6 [*Obtaining Dispute Adjudication Board's Decision*], whichever is the later.

20.4 Failure to Agree Dispute Adjudication Board

If any of the following conditions apply, namely:

(a) the Parties fail to agree upon the appointment of the sole member of the DAB by the date stated in the first paragraph of Sub-Clause 20.3 [*Appointment of the Dispute Adjudication Board*];

争端裁决委员会确定的金额可作为扣减额列入合同价格和付款证书中。雇主根据本款规定，只有权从付款证书中确认的金额中抵消或扣减，或以其他方式向承包商提出索赔。

20.3 争端裁决委员会的任命

在设计 - 施工期间发生的争端，应按照第 20.6 款［*取得争端裁决委员会的决定*］的规定，由争端裁决委员会裁决。双方应在合同数据中规定的日期前，共同任命争端裁决委员会。

争端裁决委员会应按合同数据中的规定，由具有适当资格的一名人员或三名人员（"成员"）组成。如果对委员会人数没有规定，且双方未另行商定，争端裁决委员会应由三人组成。

如果争端裁决委员会由三名成员组成，每方均应推荐一名成员供另一方认可。双方应与这些成员协商，并商定第三名成员，该成员应任命为主席。

但是，如果合同中包括一份备选成员名单，除非有人不能或不愿意接受争端裁决委员会的任命，这些成员应从名单上的人员中选择。

双方与该名唯一成员（"裁决人"）或三名成员中的每一个成员之间的协议书，应参考本通用条件的争端裁决协议书一般条件，并按他们商定的此类修订意见修改。

唯一成员或三名成员中每一名成员的报酬条款，应由双方在商定任命条款时共同商定。各方应负责支付该报酬的一半。

如经双方商定，可在任何时候任命一名或几名有适当资格的人员，替代争端裁决委员会的任何一名或几名成员。除非双方另有商定，在某一成员拒绝履行职责，或因其死亡、无行为能力、辞职或任命期满而不能履行职责时，上述替代任命即告生效。替代任命应按本款规定的要求任命或认可被替代成员的方式一致。但是，任何成员的任命，可经双方商定终止，但雇主或承包商都不能单独采取行动。

除非双方另有商定，争端裁决委员会（包括每名成员）的任期，应在根据第 9.12 款［*设计 - 施工的竣工*］规定的签发调试证书之日起，或在争端裁决委员会根据第 20.6 款［*取得争端裁决委员会的决定*］对争议做出决定后 28 天到期，以较晚者为准。

20.4 对争端裁决委员会未能取得一致

如下列任何情况适用，即：

(a) 双方未能在第 20.3 款［*争端裁决委员会的任命*］第一段所述日期前，就争端裁决委员会唯一成员的任命达成一致；

(b) either Party fails to nominate a member (for approval by the other Party), or fails to approve a member nominated by the other Party, of a DAB of three persons by such date;
(c) the Parties fail to agree upon the appointment of the third member (to act as chairman) of the DAB by such date, or
(d) the Parties fail to agree upon the appointment of a replacement person within 42 days after the date on which the sole member or one of the three members declines to act or is unable to act as a result of death, disability, resignation or termination of appointment,

then the appointing entity or official named in the Contract Data shall, upon the request of either or both of the Parties and after due consultation with both Parties, appoint this member of the DAB. This appointment shall be final and conclusive. Each Party shall be responsible for paying one-half of the remuneration of the appointing entity or official.

20.5 Avoidance of Disputes

If at any time the Parties so agree, they may jointly refer a matter to the DAB in writing with a request to provide assistance and/or informally discuss and attempt to resolve any disagreement that may have arisen between the Parties during the performance of the Contract. Such informal assistance may take place during any meeting, Site visit or otherwise. However, unless the Parties agree otherwise, both Parties must be present at such discussions. The Parties are not bound to act upon any advice given during such informal meetings, and the DAB shall not be bound in any future Dispute resolution process and decision by any views given during the informal assistance process, whether provided orally or in writing.

If a Dispute of any kind whatsoever arises between the Parties, whether or not any informal discussions have been held under this Sub-Clause, either Party may refer the Dispute in writing to the DAB according to the provisions of Sub-Clause 20.6 [*Obtaining Dispute Adjudication Board's Decision*].

20.6 Obtaining Dispute Adjudication Board's Decision

If a Dispute (of any kind whatsoever) arises between the Parties in connection with, or arising out of, the Contract or the execution of the Works during the Design-Build Period, including any Dispute as to any certificate, determination, instruction, opinion or valuation of the Employer's Representative, either Party may, within 28 days of issuing a Notice of dissatisfaction under Sub-Clause 20.1 (d) [*Contractor's Claims*] or Sub-Clause 20.2 [*Employer's Claims*], refer the Dispute in writing to the DAB for its decision, with copies to the other Party and the Employer's Representative. Such reference shall state that it is given under this Sub-Clause. The other Party shall then have 21 days to send a response to the DAB with copies to the referring Party and the Employer's Representative. If the dissatisfied Party has not formally referred the matter to the DAB within the said 28-day period, the Notice of dissatisfaction shall be deemed to have lapsed and no longer be considered to be valid.

For a DAB of three persons, the DAB shall be deemed to have received such submissions on the date when they are received by the chairman of the DAB.

Both Parties shall promptly make available to the DAB all information, access to the Site, and appropriate facilities, as the DAB may require for the purposes of making a decision on such Dispute. The DAB shall not act as arbitrator (s).

(b) 到规定的日期之前，任一方未能提名**争端裁决委员会**的三名成员中的一人（经另一方认可），或未能批准另一方提名的成员；

(c) 双方未能就**争端裁决委员会**第三名成员（担任主席）的任命达成一致；（或）

(d) 在唯一成员或三名成员中的一人拒绝履行职责，或因其死亡、无行为能力、辞职或任命期满而不能履行职责后 42 天内，双方未能就任命一位替代人员达成一致。

然后，**合同数据**中指定的实体或官员，应根据一方或双方的要求，在与双方进行适当协商后，任命**争端裁决委员会**的成员。此任命应是最终的和决定性的。每一方应负责支付任命实体或官员的一半报酬。

20.5 避免争端

如双方在任何时候同意，其可共同以书面形式向**争端裁决委员会**提出请求，要求提供协助和 / 或非正式讨论并试图解决双方在履行**合同**期间可能出现的任何分歧。此类非正式协助可在任何会议、**现场**考察或其他期间进行。但是，除非双方另有商定，否则双方应出席此类讨论。双方没有义务按照非正式会议期间提供的任何建议采取措施，**争端裁决委员会**在今后的任何**争端**解决过程中，不受非正式协助过程中提供的任何意见的约束，无论是口头的还是书面的。

如果双方间发生了任何种类的**争端**，无论是否根据本款进行了任何非正式讨论，任一方可根据第 20.6 款［*取得争端裁决委员会的决定*］的规定，将该争端以书面形式提交**争端裁决委员会**决定。

20.6 取得争端裁决委员会的决定

如果双方之间在**设计 - 施工**期间因合同或工程实施发生了**争端**（任何种类），包括对**雇主代表**的任何证书、确定、指示、意见或估价有关的任何争端，在根据第 20.1 款［*承包商索赔*］（d）段或第 20.2 款［*雇主索赔*］的规定，发出不满意**通知**后 28 天内，任何一方均可以书面形式将**争端**提交给**争端裁决委员会**裁决，并抄送其他各方和**雇主代表**。此类提交应说明是根据本款规定发出的。然后，另一方应有 21 天的时间向**争端裁决委员会**提交一份答复，并抄送提交方和**雇主代表**。如果不满意的一方未能在所述的 28 天期限内，正式将此事项提交给**争端裁决委员会**，则不满意**通知**应视为已失效，不再视为有效。

对于三名成员组成的**争端裁决委员会**，在**争端裁决委员会**主席收到此类提交之日即视为**争端裁决委员会**已收到。

双方应立即向**争端裁决委员会**提供其对**争端**做出决定而可能需要的所有信息、**现场**进入权和相应设施。**争端裁决委员会**不应担任仲裁员。

Within 84 days after receiving the other Party's response or, if no such response is received, within 105 days after receiving the reference, or within such other period as may be proposed by the DAB and approved by both Parties, the DAB shall give its decision in writing to both Parties and the Employer's Representative, which shall be reasoned and shall state that it is given under this Sub-Clause. The decision shall be binding on both Parties and the Employer's Representative, who shall promptly comply with it notwithstanding that a Party gives a Notice of dissatisfaction with such decision as described below. Unless the Contract has already been abandoned, repudiated or terminated, the Contractor shall continue to proceed with the Works in accordance with the Contract.

If either Party is dissatisfied with the DAB's decision, then either Party may, within 28 days after receiving the decision, give Notice to the other Party of its dissatisfaction. If the DAB fails to give its decision within the period prescribed in this Sub-Clause, then either Party may, within 28 days after this period has expired, give Notice to the other Party of its dissatisfaction. In either case, the dissatisfied Party shall send a copy of the Notice to the chairman of the DAB.

In either event, this Notice of dissatisfaction shall state that it is given under this Sub-Clause, and shall set out the matter in Dispute and the reason (s) for dissatisfaction. Except as stated in Sub-Clause 20.9 [*Failure to Comply with Dispute Adjudication Board's Decision*], neither Party shall be entitled to commence arbitration of a Dispute unless a Notice of dissatisfaction with respect to that Dispute has been given in accordance with this Sub-Clause.

If the decision of the DAB requires a payment by one Party to the other Party, the DAB may require the payee to provide an appropriate security in respect of such payment.

If the DAB has given its decision as to a matter in Dispute to both Parties, and no Notice of dissatisfaction has been given by either Party within 28 days after it received the DAB's decision, then the decision shall become final and binding upon both Parties.

20.7 Amicable Settlement

Where Notice of dissatisfaction has been given under Sub-Clause 20.6 [*Obtaining Dispute Adjudication Board's Decision*], both Parties shall attempt to settle the Dispute amicably before the commencement of arbitration. However, unless both Parties agree otherwise, arbitration may be commenced on or after the twenty-eighth day after the day on which Notice of dissatisfaction was given, even if no attempt at amicable settlement has been made.

20.8 Arbitration

Unless settled amicably, and subject to Sub-Clause 20.9 [*Failure to Comply with Dispute Adjudication Board's Decision*], any Dispute in respect of which the DAB's decision (if any) has not become final and binding shall be finally settled by international arbitration. Unless otherwise agreed by both Parties:

(a) the Dispute shall be finally settled under the Rules of Arbitration of the International Chamber of Commerce;
(b) the Dispute shall be settled by three arbitrators appointed in accordance with these Rules; and
(c) the arbitration shall be conducted in the language for communications defined in Sub-Clause 1.4 [*Law and Language*] unless otherwise stated in the Contract Data.

在收到另一方的答复后 84 天内，或如果没有收到答复，则在收到答复后 105 天内，或**争端裁决委员会**可能提议并经双方认可的其他期限内，**争端裁决委员会**应向双方和**雇主代表**做出书面决定，该决定应是合理的并应说明是根据本款规定做出的。该决定对双方和**雇主代表**均具有约束力，即使一方发出了对下述决定不满意**通知**，**雇主代表**应立即遵守。除非**合同**已被放弃、拒绝或终止，**承包商**应继续按照**合同**进行**工程**。

如果任一方对**争端裁决委员会**的决定不满意，任何一方可在收到该决定后 28 天内，将其不满意**通知**发给另一方。如果**争端裁决委员会**未能在本款规定的期限内做出决定，则任一方均可在该期限届满后的 28 天内，将其不满意**通知**发给另一方。在任何一种情况下，不满意的一方应将**通知**抄送给**争端裁决委员会**主席。

在上述任一情况下，不满意通知应说明是根据本款发出的，并应说明**争端**事项和不满意理由。除第 20.9 款 [*未能遵守争端裁决委员会的决定*] 所述情况外，除非根据本款就该**争端**发出了不满意**通知**，任何一方都无权着手**争端**的仲裁。

如果**争端裁决委员会**的决定，要求一方向另一方付款，**争端裁决委员会**可要求收款人就付款提供适当的担保。

如果**争端裁决委员会**已就**争端**事项向双方提出其决定，而任一方均在收到**争端裁决委员会**决定后 28 天内，未发出不满意**通知**，则该决定应成为最终的，并对双方具有约束力。

20.7 友好解决

如果已按照第 20.6 款 [*取得争端裁决委员会的决定*] 发出了不满意**通知**，双方应在仲裁开始前，设法友好解决**争端**。但是，除非双方另有商定，即使没有设法友好解决，也可在发出不满意**通知**第 28 天或其后开始仲裁。

20.8 仲裁

除非友好解决，并根据第 20.9 款 [*未能遵守争端裁决委员会的决定*] 的规定，**争端裁决委员会**的决定（如果有）尚未成为最终和具有约束力的任何**争端**，应通过国际仲裁最终解决。除非双方另有商定：

(a) **争端**应根据**国际商会仲裁规则**最终解决；

(b) **争端**应由按上述**规则**任命的三位仲裁员负责解决；（以及）

(c) 仲裁应根据第 1.4 款 [*法律和语言*] 规定的交流语言进行除非**合同数据**中另有规定。

The arbitrator (s) shall have full power to open up, review and revise any certificate, determination, instruction, opinion or valuation of the Employer's Representative, and any decision of the DAB, relevant to the Dispute. Nothing shall disqualify the Employer's Representative from being called as a witness and giving evidence before the arbitrator (s) on any matter whatsoever relevant to the Dispute.

Neither Party shall be limited in the proceedings before the arbitrator (s) to the evidence or arguments previously put before the DAB to obtain its decision, or to the reasons for dissatisfaction given in its Notice of dissatisfaction. Any decision of the DAB shall be admissible in evidence in the arbitration.

Arbitration may be commenced prior to or after completion of the Works. The obligations of the Parties, the Employer's Representative and the DAB shall not be altered by reason of any arbitration being conducted during the progress of the Works.

20.9 Failure to Comply with Dispute Adjudication Board's Decision

In the event that a Party fails to comply with any decision of the DAB, whether binding or final and binding, then the other Party may, without prejudice to any other rights it may have, refer the failure itself to arbitration under Sub-Clause 20.8 [*Arbitration*] for summary or other expedited relief, as may be appropriate. Sub-Clause 20.6 [*Obtaining Dispute Adjudication Board's Decision*] and Sub-Clause 20.7 [*Amicable Settlement*] shall not apply to this reference.

20.10 Disputes Arising during the Operation Service Period

Disputes arising during the Operation Service Period which cannot be resolved between the Parties shall be settled by a one-person DAB ("Operation Service DAB"). Such person shall be jointly agreed and appointed by the Parties at the time of issue of the Commissioning Certificate.

If the Parties cannot agree on the person who shall be the Operation Service DAB, then the person shall be appointed according to the provisions of Sub-Clause 20.4 [*Failure to Agree Dispute Adjudication Board*].

Such person shall be appointed for a term of five years. At the end of each five-year period, a new Operation Service DAB shall be agreed and appointed. If both Parties and the previously appointed person agree, the same Operation Service DAB may be re-appointed for a second (or third or fourth, as the case may be) five-year term.

The agreement between the Parties and the Operation Service DAB shall incorporate by reference the General Conditions of Dispute Adjudication Agreement contained in these General Conditions, with such amendments as are agreed between them.

The terms of remuneration of the Operation Service DAB shall be mutually agreed upon by the Parties when agreeing the terms of appointment. Each Party shall be responsible for paying one-half of this remuneration.

The procedure for obtaining a decision from the Operation Service DAB shall be in accordance with the provisions of Sub-Clause 20.6 [*Obtaining Dispute Adjudication Board's Decision*], and the DAB shall give its decision no later than 84 days after receiving the other Party's response or, if no such response is received, within 105 days after receiving the reference and the supporting documentation from the Party referring the Dispute.

仲裁员应有充分的权利公开、审查和修改与该**争端**有关的**雇主代表**的任何证书、确定、指示、意见或估价，以及**争端裁决委员会**的任何决定。**雇主代表**被传为证人，并向仲裁员就任何与**争端**有关的事项提供证据的资格不受任何影响。

在仲裁员面前的程序中，任一方都不应局限于先前为取得**争端裁决委员会**的决定而向**争端裁决委员会**提供的证据或论据，或该方在其不满意**通知**中提出的不满意理由。**争端裁决委员会**的任何决定均应在仲裁中被接受为证据。

仲裁在**工程**竣工前或竣工后均可开始。双方、**雇主代表**和**争端裁决委员会**的义务，不得因在**工程**进行中正在执行的任何仲裁而改变。

20.9 未能遵守争端裁决委员会的决定

在一方未能遵守**争端裁决委员会**的任何决定的情况下，无论是具有约束力的或最终且具有约束力的，另一方可以在不损害其可能拥有的其他权利的情况下，根据第 20.8 款［*仲裁*］的规定，将上述未遵守决定的事项提交仲裁，在此情况下，以获得简易或其他快速救济。第 20.6 款［*取得争端裁决委员会的决定*］和第 20.7 款［*友好解决*］的规定应不适用于此参考。

20.10 运营服务期间发生的争端

在**运营服务**期间内发生的双方无法解决的**争端**，应由一人**争端裁决委员会**（"**运营服务争端裁决委员会**"）裁决。此类人员应由双方在签发**调试证书**时共同商定和任命。

如果双方不能就**运营服务争端裁决委员会**的人选商定一致，则应根据**第 20.4 款**［*对争端裁决委员会未能取得一致*］的规定，任命该人员。

该人员任期应为 5 年。在每 5 年期结束时，应商定并任命一个新的**运营服务争端裁决委员会**。如果双方和先前指定的人员均同意，同一**运营服务争端裁决委员会**，可重新任命为第二届 5 年任期（或第三届或第四届，视情况而定）。

双方与**运营服务争端裁决委员会**之间的协议，应参考**通用条件**附录中的**争端裁决协议书一般条件**，以及双方商定的修改意见。

运营服务争端裁决委员会的报酬条款，应由双方在商定任命条款时共同商定。各方应负责支付该报酬的一半。

从**运营服务争端裁决委员会**获得决定的程序，应符合第 20.6 款［*取得争端裁决委员会的决定*］的规定，并且**争端裁决委员会**应在收到另一方的答复后 84 天内，或如果没有收到此类答复，在收到提交**争端**的一方提交的参考资料和证明文件后 105 天内，做出决定。

The appointment of the Operation Service DAB shall expire five years after the date of its appointment unless such appointment is extended for a further five years as aforementioned.

If either Party is dissatisfied with the decision of the Operation Service DAB, the provisions of Sub-Clauses 20.6 [*Obtaining Dispute Adjudication Board's Decision*], 20.7 [*Amicable Settlement*], 20.8 [*Arbitration*] and 20.9 [*Failure to Comply with Dispute Adjudication Board's Decision*] shall apply.

20.11 Expiry of Dispute Adjudication Board's Appointment

If a Dispute arises between the Parties in connection with, or arising out of, the Contract or the execution of the Works and there is no DAB in place, whether by reason of the expiry of the DAB's appointment or otherwise:

(a) Sub-Clause 20.6 [*Obtaining Dispute Adjudication Board's Decision*] and Sub-Clause 20.7 [*Amicable Settlement*], or Sub-Clause 20.10 [*Disputes Arising during the Operation Service Period*], as the case may be, shall not apply; and

(b) the Dispute may be referred directly to arbitration under Sub-Clause 20.8 [*Arbitration*].

运营服务争端裁决委员会的任命应在其任命之日起 5 年后到期，除非如前所述任命再延长 5 年。

如果任何一方对**运营服务争端裁决委员会**的决定不满意，第 20.6 款 [*取得争端裁决委员会的决定*]、第 20.7 款 [*友好解决*]、第 20.8 款 [*仲裁*] 和第 20.9 款 [*未能遵守争端裁决委员会的决定*] 的规定应适用。

20.11 争端裁决委员会任命期满	如果双方之间发生与合同或工程实施有关或产生的**争端**，且未设立**争端裁决委员会**，无论是由于**争端裁决委员会**的任命到期还是其他原因，则：

（a） 第 20.6 款 [*取得争端裁决委员会的决定*] 和第 20.7 款 [*友好解决*]，或第 20.10 款 [*运营服务期间发生的争端*] 的规定，视情况而定，应不适用；（以及）

（b） 此项争端可根据第 20.8 款 [*仲裁*] 的规定，直接提交仲裁。

INDEX OF CLAUSES AND SUB-CLAUSES

This index shows all the Clauses and Sub-Clauses in the General Conditions in alphabetical order.

	CLAUSE/Sub-Clause
Access Route	4.15
Adjustments for Changes in Legislation	13.6
Adjustments for Changes in Technology	13.7
Adjustments for Changes in Cost	13.8
Advance Payment	14.2
Advance Warning	8.4
Amicable Settlement	20.7
Application for Advance and Interim Payment Certificates	14.3
Application for Final Payment Certificate Design-Build	14.11
Application for Final Payment Certificate Operation Service	14.13
Appointment of the Dispute Adjudication Board	20.3
Arbitration	20.8
As-Built Documents	5.5
Asset Replacement Fund	14.18
Asset Replacement Schedule	14.5
Assignment	1.8
Avoidance of Disputes	20.5
Avoidance of Interference	4.14
Care and Supply of Documents	1.9
Cessation of Work and Removal of Contractor's Equipment	16.3
Cessation of Employer's Liability	14.16
Changes in the Contractor's Financial Situation	4.25
CLAIMS, DISPUTES AND ARBITRATION	20
COMMENCEMENT DATE, COMPLETION AND PROGRAMME	8
Commencement Date	8.1
Commencement of Design-Build	9.1
Commencement of Operation Service	10.2
Commissioning Certificate	11.7
Commissioning of Parts of the Works	11.6
Completion of Design-Build	9.12
Completion of Operation Service	10.8
Completion of Outstanding Work and Remedying Defects	12.1
Completion of the Works and Sections	11.5
Compliance with Laws	1.14
Confidential Details	1.13
Consequences of the Contractor's Risks resulting in Damage	17.7
Consequences of the Employer's Risks of Damage	17.6
Consequences of an Exceptional Event	18.4
Consequences of Suspension	9.8
Contract Agreement	1.6
Contract Completion Certificate	8.6
CONTRACT PRICE AND PAYMENT	14
Contract Price The	14.1

条目和条款索引

本索引按字母顺序列出了**通用条件**中的所有**条目**和**条款**

	条目/条款
进场通路	4.15
因法律改变的调整	13.6
因技术改变的调整	13.7
因成本改变的调整	13.8
预付款	14.2
预先警示	8.4
友好解决	20.7
预付款和期中付款证书的申请	14.3
设计-施工最终付款证书的申请	14.11
运营服务最终付款证书的申请	14.13
争端裁决委员会的任命	20.3
仲裁	20.8
竣工文件	5.5
资产置换基金	14.18
资产置换计划表	14.5
权益转让	1.8
避免争端	20.5
避免干扰	4.14
文件的照管和提供	1.9
停止工作和承包商设备的撤离	16.3
雇主责任的中止	14.16
承包商资金(财务)状况的改变	4.25
索赔、争端和仲裁	20
开工日期、竣工和进度计划	8
开工日期	8.1
设计-施工的开始	9.1
运营服务开始	10.2
调试证书	11.7
部分工程的调试	11.6
设计-施工的竣工	9.12
运营服务的完成	10.8
完成扫尾工作和修补缺陷	12.1
工程和分项工程竣工	11.5
遵守法律	1.14
保密事项	1.13
承包商损害风险的后果	17.7
雇主损害风险的后果	17.6
例外事件的后果	18.4
暂停的后果	9.8
合同协议书	1.6
合同完成证书	8.6
合同价格和付款	14
合同价格	14.1

CONTRACTOR, THE	4
Contractor's Claims	20.1
Contractor's Documents	5.2
Contractor's Entitlement to Suspend Work	16.1
Contractor's Equipment	4.17
Contractor's General Obligations	4.1
Contractor's Operations on Site	4.23
Contractor's Personnel	6.9
Contractor's Representative	4.3
Contractor's Risks during the Design-Build Period	17.2
Contractor's Risks during the Operation Service Period	17.4
Contractor's Superintendence	6.8
Contractor's Undertaking	5.3
Contractor's Use of Employer's Documents	1.12
Contractor to Search	12.6
Co-operation	4.6
Cost of Remedying Defects	12.2
Currencies of Payment	14.17
DEFECTS	12
Definitions	1.1
Delays Caused by Authorities	9.4
Delay Damages	8.5
Delay Damages relating to Design-Build	9.6
Delayed Payment	14.9
Delayed Tests on Completion of Design-Build	11.2
Delayed Tests Prior to Contract Completion	11.10
Delays and Interruptions during the Operation Service	10.6
Delegation by the Employer's Representative	3.2
Delivery of Raw Materials	10.4
DESIGN	5
DESIGN-BUILD	9
Design Error	5.7
Determinations	3.5
Discharge	14.14
Disorderly Conduct	6.11
Disputes Arising during the Operation Service Period	20.10
Duty to Minimise Delay	18.3
Electricity, Water and Gas	4.19
EMPLOYER, THE	2
Employer's Claims	20.2
Employer's Financial Arrangements	2.4
Employer's Personnel	2.3
EMPLOYER'S REPRESENTATIVE, THE	3
Employer's Equipment and Free-Issue Materials	4.20
Employer's Representative's Duties and Authority	3.1
Employer's Risks during the Design-Build Period	17.1
Employer's Risks during the Operation Service Period	17.3
Employer's Use of Contractor's Documents	1.11
Engagement of Staff and Labour	6.1
Errors in the Employer's Requirements	1.10
EXCEPTIONAL RISKS	18
Exceptional Risks	18.1
Expiry of Dispute Adjudication Board's Appointment	20.11
Extension of Time for Completion of Design-Build	9.3

承包商	4
承包商索赔	20.1
承包商文件	5.2
承包商暂停工作的权利	16.1
承包商设备	4.17
承包商的一般义务	4.1
承包商的现场作业	4.23
承包商人员	6.9
承包商代表	4.3
设计-施工期间承包商的风险	17.2
运营服务期间承包商的风险	17.4
承包商的监督	6.8
承包商的承诺	5.3
承包商使用雇主文件	1.12
承包商调查	12.6
合作	4.6
修补缺陷的费用	12.2
支付的货币	14.17
缺陷	12
定义	1.1
部门造成的延误	9.4
误期损害赔偿费	8.5
设计-施工的误期损害赔偿费	9.6
延误的付款	14.9
设计-施工竣工试验的延误	11.2
合同完成前试验的延误	11.10
运营服务期间的延误和中断	10.6
由雇主代表付托	3.2
原材料交付	10.4
设计	5
设计-施工	9
设计错误	5.7
确定	3.5
结清证明	14.14
无序行为	6.11
运营服务期间发生的争端	20.10
将延误减至最小的义务	18.3
电、水和燃气	4.19
雇主	2
雇主索赔	20.2
雇主的资金安排	2.4
雇主人员	2.3
雇主代表	3
雇主设备和免费提供的材料	4.20
雇主代表的任务和权利	3.1
设计-施工期间雇主的风险	17.1
运营服务期间雇主的风险	17.3
雇主使用承包商文件	1.11
员工的雇用	6.1
雇主要求中的错误	1.10
例外风险	18
例外风险	18.1
争端裁决委员会任命期满	20.11
设计-施工竣工时间的延长	9.3

Facilities for Staff and Labour	6.6
Failure to Agree Dispute Adjudication Board	20.4
Failure to Complete	9.13
Failure to Comply with Dispute Adjudication Board's Decision	20.9
Failure to Pass Tests on Completion of Design-Build	11.4
Failure to Pass Tests Prior to Contract Completion	11.11
Failure to Reach Production Outputs	10.7
Failure to Remedy Defects	12.3
Fossils	4.24
Further Tests	12.4
GENERAL PROVISIONS	1
General Design Obligations	5.1
General Requirements (Operation Service)	10.1
General Requirements (Insurance)	19.1
Handback Requirements	8.7
Health and Safety	6.7
Indemnities by the Contractor	17.9
Indemnities by the Employer	17.10
Independent Compliance Audit	10.3
Inspection	7.3
Instructions of the Employer's Representative	3.3
INSURANCE	19
Insurances to be provided by the Contractor during the Design-Build Period	19.2
Insurances to be provided by the Contractor during the Operation Service Period	19.3
Interpretation	1.2
Issue of Advance and Interim Payment Certificates	14.7
Issue of Final Payment Certificate Design-Build	14.12
Issue of Final Payment Certificate Operation Service	14.15
Joint Inspection Prior to Contract Completion	11.8
Joint and Several Liability	1.15
Labour Laws	6.4
Law and Language	1.4
Limitation of Liability	17.8
Maintenance Retention Fund	14.19
Manner of Execution	7.1
Materials, Free Issue	4.20
Nominated Subcontractors	4.5
Notices and Other Communications	1.3
Notice to Correct	15.1
Notice of an Exceptional Event	18.2
Obtaining Dispute Adjudication Board's Decision	20.6
Operating Licence	1.7
Operation and Maintenance Manuals	5.6
OPERATION SERVICE	10
Optional Termination, Payment and Release	18.5
Ownership of Output and Revenue	10.9
Ownership of Plant and Materials	7.7

为员工提供设施	6.6
对争端裁决委员会未能取得一致	20.4
未能竣工	9.13
未能遵守争端裁决委员会的决定	20.9
未能通过设计 - 施工竣工试验	11.4
未能通过合同完成前试验	11.11
未能达到产量	10.7
未能修补缺陷	12.3
化石	4.24
进一步试验	12.4
一般规定	1
设计义务一般要求	5.1
一般要求（运营服务）	10.1
一般要求（保险）	19.1
移交要求	8.7
健康和安全	6.7
由承包商保障	17.9
由雇主保障	17.10
独立合规审计	10.3
检验	7.3
雇主代表的指示	3.3
保险	19
承包商在设计 - 施工期间提供的保险	19.2
承包商在运营服务期间提供的保险	19.3
解释	1.2
预付款和期中付款证书的签发	14.7
设计 - 施工最终付款证书的签发	14.12
运营服务最终付款证书的签发	14.15
合同完成前的联合检验	11.8
共同的和各自的责任	1.15
劳动法	6.4
法律和语言	1.4
责任限度	17.8
维护保留金	14.19
实施方法	7.1
材料、免费提供	4.20
指定分包商	4.5
通知和其他通信交流	1.3
通知改正	15.1
例外事件的通知	18.2
取得争端裁决委员会的决定	20.6
运营执照	1.7
操作和维护手册	5.6
运营服务	10
自主选择终止、付款和解除	18.5
产出和收入所有权	10.9
生产设备和材料的所有权	7.7

Payment	14.8
Payment in Applicable Currencies	13.4
Payment for Plant and Materials in Event of Suspension	9.9
Payment for Plant and Materials intended for the Works	14.6
Payment of Retention Money	14.10
Payment after Termination for Contractor's Default	15.4
Payment after Termination for Employer's Convenience	15.7
Payment on Termination	16.4
Performance Security	4.2
Permits, Licences or Approvals	2.2
Persons in the Service of Employer	6.3
PLANT, MATERIAL AND WORKMANSHIP	7
Priority of Documents	1.5
Procedure for Tests Prior to Contract Completion	11.9
Programme	8.3
Progress Reports	4.21
Prolonged Suspension	9.10
Protection of the Environment	4.18
Provisional Sums	13.5
Quality Assurance	4.9
Rate of Progress	9.5
Rates of Wages and Conditions of Employment	6.2
Records of Contractor's Personnel and Equipment	6.10
Rejection	7.5
Release from Performance under the Law	18.6
Remedial Work	7.6
Removal of Defective Work	12.5
Replacement of the Employer's Representative	3.4
Responsibility for Care of the Works	17.5
Resumption of Work	9.11
Retesting of the Works	11.3
Retesting Prior to Contract Completion	11.12
Right of Access to the Site	2.1
Rights of Way and Facilities	4.13
Right to Vary	13.1
RISK ALLOCATION	17
Risk of Infringement of Intellectual and Industrial Property Rights	17.12
Royalties	7.8
Safety Procedures	4.8
Samples	7.2
Schedule of Payments	14.4
Security of the Site	4.22
Setting Out	4.7
Shared Indemnities	17.11
Site Data	4.10
STAFF AND LABOUR	6
Subcontractors	4.4
SUSPENSION AND TERMINATION BY CONTRACTOR	16
Suspension of Work	9.7
Sufficiency of the Accepted Contract Amount	4.11
Termination by Contractor	16.2
Termination for Contractor's Default	15.2

付款	14.8
以适用货币支付	13.4
暂停时对生产设备和材料的付款	9.9
拟用于工程的生产设备和材料的付款	14.6
保留金的支付	14.10
由承包商违约终止后的付款	15.4
为雇主便利终止后的付款	15.7
终止时的付款	16.4
履约担保	4.2
许可、执照或批准	2.2
为雇主服务的人员	6.3
生产设备、材料和工艺	7
文件优先次序	1.5
合同完成前试验程序	11.9
进度计划	8.3
进度报告	4.21
拖长的暂停	9.10
环境保护	4.18
暂列金额	13.5
质量保证	4.9
工程进度	9.5
工资标准和劳动条件	6.2
承包商人员和设备的记录	6.10
拒收	7.5
依法解除履约	18.6
修补工作	7.6
移出有缺陷的工程	12.5
雇主代表的替代	3.4
工程照管的职责	17.5
复工	9.11
工程重新试验	11.3
合同完成前的重新试验	11.12
现场进入权	2.1
道路通行权和设施	4.13
变更权	13.1
风险分配	17
知识产权和工业产权侵权风险	17.12
土地（矿区）使用费	7.8
安全程序	4.8
样品	7.2
付款计划表	14.4
现场安保	4.22
放线	4.7
保障分担	17.11
现场数据	4.10
员工	6
分包商	4.4
由承包商暂停和终止	16
暂时停工	9.7
中标合同金额的充分性	4.11
由承包商终止	16.2
由承包商违约的终止	15.2

TERMINATION BY EMPLOYER	15
Termination for Employer's Convenience	15.5
TESTING	11
Testing of the Works	11.1
Training	10.5
Transport of Goods	4.16
Technical Standards and Regulations	5.4
Testing	7.4
Time for Completion	8.2
Time for Completion of Design-Build	9.2
Unforeseeable Physical Conditions	4.12
Unfulfilled Obligations	8.8
Valuation at Date of Termination for Contractor's Default	15.3
Valuation at Date of Termination for Employer's Convenience	15.6
Value Engineering	13.2
VARIATIONS AND ADJUSTMENTS	13
Variation Procedure	13.3
Working Hours	6.5

由雇主终止	15
为雇主便利的终止	15.5
试验	11
工程试验	11.1
培训	10.5
货物运输	4.16
技术标准和法规	5.4
试验	7.4
竣工时间	8.2
设计 - 施工竣工时间	9.2
不可预见的物质条件	4.12
未履行的义务	8.8
由承包商违约终止日期时的估价	15.3
为雇主便利终止日的估价	15.6
价值工程	13.2
变更和调整	13
变更程序	13.3
工作时间	6.5

INDEX OF PRINCIPAL TERMINOLOGY

This index shows all the Sub-Clauses where the terminology which has been defined in Sub-Clause 1.1 occurs. For commonly used words such as 'Employer', 'Contractor', 'day', 'Cost', etc, only the principal Clauses have been indicated.

	Sub-Clause
"Accepted Contract Amount"	1.1.1, 4.11, 14.2, 14.17, 17.8
"Asset Replacement Fund"	1.1.2, 11.8, 14.1, 14.3, 14.5
	14.13, 14.18
"Asset Replacement Schedule"	1.1.3, 14.5, 14.18
"Auditing Body"	1.1.4, 10.3
"Base Date"	1.1.5, 4.10, 5.4, 13.6, 14.1
	14.17 , 17.12
"Commencement Date"	1.1.6, 4.3, 4.19, 4.21, 5.1, 8.1
	9.1, 14.4, 17.5, 19.2
"Commercial Risk"	1.1.7, 17.1, 17.3
"Commissioning Certificate"	1.1.8, 1.7, 4.23, 5.4, 5.5, 5.6
	9.6, 9.12, 10.2, 11.5, 11.6
	11.7, 12.1, 13.1, 14.2, 14.7
	14.10 , 14.19,17.5, 19.2, 19.3
	20.3, 20.10
"Commissioning Period"	1.1.9, 5.6
"Contract"	1.1.10
"Contract Agreement"	1.1.11, 1.5, 1.6, 16.2
"Contract Completion Certificate"	1.1.12, 1.7, 4.2, 4.21, 4.23, 8.6
	8.7, 8.8, 10.8, 11.9, 11.11, 12.1
	14.4,14.13, 14.19, 19.3
"Contract Completion Date"	1.1.13, 8.6, 11.8
"Contract Data"	1.1.14
"Contract Period"	1.1.15, 6.7, 6.8, 7.6, 8.6, 10.1
	11.10, 11.11
"Contract Price"	1.1.16, 14.1
"Contractor"	1.1.17
"Contractor's Equipment"	1.1.18, 2.2, 4.6, 4.17, 4.23, 6.10
	8.3, 15.2, 15.7, 17.12, 18.5
"Contractor's Documents"	1.1.19, 1.9, 1.11, 2.1, 4.1, 4.6
	4.21, 5.2, 5.3, 5.4, 5.5, 5.7, 7.2
	8.3, 12.1, 15.2, 15.3, 15.6, 16.3
"Contractor's Proposal"	1.1.20, 1.5, 4.1, 13.3
"Contractor's Personnel"	1.1.21, 6.9
"Contractor's Representative"	1.1.22, 4.3
"Cost"	1.1.23
"Cost Plus Profit"	1.1.24, 1.10, 2.1, 4.7, 7.4, 10.4
	10.6, 10.7, 11.11, 12.6, 16.1
	16.3, 17.6
"Country"	1.1.25, 1.4, 2.2, 4.10, 5.3, 5.5, 7.7
	9.4, 13.6, 14.6, 14.17, 18.1, 18.4
"Cut-Off Date"	1.1.26, 9.13, 15.2

主要术语索引

本索引表明了第 1.1 款中定义的术语出现的所有**条款**。对于常用词，如"雇主""承包商""日""费用"等，仅注明了主要**条款**。

术语	条款
"中标合同金额"	1.1.1，4.11，14.2，14.17，17.8
"资产置换基金"	1.1.2，11.8，14.1，14.3，14.5
	14.13，14.18
"资产置换计划表"	1.1.3，14.5，14.18
"审计机构"	1.1.4，10.3
"基准日期"	1.1.5，4.10，5.4，13.6，14.1
	14.17，17.12
"开工日期"	1.1.6，4.3，4.19，4.21，5.1，8.1
	9.1，14.4，17.5，19.2
"商业风险"	1.1.7，17.1，17.3
"调试证书"	1.1.8，1.7，4.23，5.4，5.5，5.6
	9.6，9.12，10.2，11.5，11.6
	11.7，12.1，13.1，14.2，14.7
	14.10，14.19，17.5，19.2，19.3
	20.3，20.10
"调试期"	1.1.9，5.6
"合同"	1.1.10
"合同协议书"	1.1.11，1.5，1.6，16.2
"合同完成证书"	1.1.12，1.7，4.2，4.21，4.23，8.6
	8.7，8.8，10.8，11.9，11.11，12.1
	14.4，14.13，14.19，19.3
"合同完成日期"	1.1.13，8.6，11.8
"合同数据"	1.1.14
"合同期"	1.1.15，6.7，6.8，7.6，8.6，10.1
	11.10，11.11
"合同价格"	1.1.16，14.1
"承包商"	1.1.17
"承包商设备"	1.1.18，2.2，4.6，4.17，4.23，6.10
	8.3，15.2，15.7，17.12，18.5
"承包商文件"	1.1.19，1.9，1.11，2.1，4.1，4.6
	4.21，5.2，5.3，5.4，5.5，5.7，7.2
	8.3，12.1，15.2，15.3，15.6，16.3
"承包商建议书"	1.1.20，1.5，4.1，13.3
"承包商人员"	1.1.21，6.9
"承包商代表"	1.1.22，4.3
"成本（费用）"	1.1.23
"成本加利润"	1.1.24，1.10，2.1，4.7，7.4，10.4
	10.6，10.7，11.11，12.6，16.1
	16.3，17.6
"工程所在国"	1.1.25，1.4，2.2，4.10，5.3，5.5，7.7
	9.4，13.6，14.6，14.17，18.1，18.4
"截止日期"	1.1.26，9.13，15.2

"DAB"	1.1.27
"day"	1.1.28
"Design-Build"	1.1.29
"Design-Build Period"	1.1.30, 4.1, 4.21, 5.5, 6.10, 9.4, 9.5
	9.8, 12.1, 12.3, 14.2, 14.4, 17.1
	17.2, 17.4, 17.6, 19.2, 20.3, 20.6
"Dispute"	1.1.31, 3.5
"Employer"	1.1.32, 20
"Employer's Equipment"	1.1.33
"Employer's Personnel"	1.1.34
"Employer's Representative"	1.1.35
"Employer's Requirements"	1.1.36
"Exceptional Event"	1.1.37, 18
"facility"	1.1.56, 1.1.57, 1.1.82, 1.7
"FIDIC"	1.1.38
"Final Payment Certificate Design-Build"	1.1.39, 14.8, 14.10
	14.11, 14.12, 14.14
"Final Payment Certificate Operation Service"	1.1.40, 14.8, 14.13, 14.14
	14.15, 14.16, 14.18, 14.19
"Final Statement Design-Build"	1.1.41, 14.11, 14.12, 14.14, 14.16
"Final Statement Operation Service"	1.1.42, 14.13, 14.14, 14.15
"Financial Memorandum"	1.1.43, 2.4
"Foreign Currency"	1.1.44
"Goods"	1.1.45, 2.2, 4.1, 4.10, 4.16
	4.17, 9.2, 9.5
	13.1, 15.2, 15.3, 15.6, 16.3, 17.2
	17.5, 17.6, 17.7
"Interim Payment Certificate"	1.1.46, 14.2, 14.7, 14.8, 14.9
	14.10, 14.11, 14.18, 14.19, 16.2
"Laws"	1.1.47, 1.14, 1.15, 2.2, 3.3, 4.10
	4.18, 5.3, 5.4, 6.4, 7.1, 7.7
	13.6, 15.2
"Letter of Acceptance"	1.1.48, 1.5, 1.6, 1.7, 4.2, 8.1
"Letter of Tender"	1.1.49, 1.5
"Local Currency"	1.1.50, 14.17
"Maintenance Retention Fund" and	
"Maintenance Retention Guarantee"	1.1.51, 14.3
	14.13, 14.19
"Materials"	1.1.52
"Notice"	1.1.53, 1.3
"Operating Licence"	1.1.54, 1.7, 17.5
"Operation Management Requirements"	1.1.55, 10.1, 10.2, 10.3
"Operation and Maintenance Plan"	1.1.56, 10.1, 11.8
"Operation Service"	1.1.57
"Operation Service Period"	1.1.58, 1.7, 4.1, 4.21, 6.5, 6.10, 8.5
	8.6, 10.8, 11.5, 11.8, 11.9, 12.1, 12.3
	13.1, 14.4, 14.18, 14.19, 17.3, 17.4
	17.5, 17.6, 17.10, 18.4, 19.3, 20.10
"Party"	1.1.59
"Performance Security"	1.1.60, 2.1, 4.2, 12.5, 14.2, 14.7
	14.8, 14.14, 14.16, 15.2, 15.5, 16.4
"Permanent Works"	1.1.61, 1.14, 11.6, 14.6, 17.1, 17.3
	17.4, 17.5
"Plant"	1.1.62
"Provisional Sum"	1.1.63, 10.3, 13.5
"Rates and Prices"	1.1.64

术语	条款
"争端裁决委员会"	1.1.27
"日"	1.1.28
"设计 - 施工"	1.1.29
"设计 - 施工期"	1.1.30，4.1，4.12，5.5，6.10，9.4，9.5，9.8，12.1，12.3，14.2，14.4，17.1，17.2，17.4，17.6，19.2，20.3，20.6
"争端"	1.1.31，3.5
"雇主"	1.1.32，20
"雇主设备"	1.1.33
"雇主人员"	1.1.34
"雇主代表"	1.1.35
"雇主要求"	1.1.36
"例外事件"	1.1.37，18
"设施"	1.1.56，1.1.57，1.1.82，1.7
"国际咨询工程师联合会"	1.1.38
"设计 - 施工最终付款证书"	1.1.39，14.8，14.10，14.11，14.12，14.14
"运营服务最终付款证书"	1.1.40，14.8，14.13，14.14，14.15，14.16，14.18，14.19
"设计 - 施工最终报表"	1.1.41，14.11，14.12，14.14，14.16
"运营服务最终报表"	1.1.42，14.13，14.14，14.15
"（财务）备忘录"	1.1.43，2.4
"外币"	1.1.44
"货物"	1.1.45，2.2，4.1，4.10，4.16，4.17，9.2，9.5，13.1，15.2，15.3，15.6，16.3，17.2，17.5，17.6，17.7
"期中付款证书"	1.1.46，14.2，14.7，14.8，14.9，14.10，14.11，14.18，14.19，16.2
"法律"	1.1.47，1.14，1.15，2.2，3.3，4.10，4.18，5.3，5.4，6.4，7.1，7.7，13.6，15.2
"中标函"	1.1.48，1.5，1.6，1.7，4.2，8.1
"投标函"	1.1.49，1.5
"当地货币"	1.1.50，14.17
"维护保留金"和	1.1.51，14.3
"维护保留金保函"	14.13，14.19
"材料"	1.1.52
"通知"	1.1.53，1.3
"运营执照"	1.1.54，1.7，17.5
"运营管理要求"	1.1.55，10.1，10.2，10.3
"运营和维护计划"	1.1.56，10.1，11.8
"运营服务"	1.1.57
"运营服务期"	1.1.58，1.7，4.1，4.21，6.5，6.10，8.5，8.6，10.8，11.5，11.8，11.9，12.1，12.3，13.1，14.4，14.18，14.19，17.3，17.4，17.5，17.6，17.10，18.4，19.3，20.10
"当事方（一方）"	1.1.59
"履约担保"	1.1.60，2.1，4.2，12.5，14.2，14.7，14.8，14.14，14.16，15.2，15.5，16.4
"永久工程"	1.1.61，1.14，11.6，14.6，17.1，17.3，17.4，17.5
"生产设备"	1.1.62
"暂列金额"	1.1.63，10.3，13.5
"费率和价格"	1.1.64

"Retention Money"	1.1.65, 14.3, 14.10
"Retention Period"	1.1.66, 4.2, 14.11
"Risk of Damage"	1.1.67
"Schedules"	1.1.68
"Schedule of Payments"	1.1.69, 13.3, 14.4
"Section"	1.1.70
"Section Commissioning Certificate"	1.1.71, 11.6, 14.10, 17.5
"Site"	1.1.72
"Statement"	1.1.73, 14, 16.2
"Subcontractor"	1.1.74, 4.4, 4.5, 5.1, 15.2 18.1, 19.3,
"Tender"	1.1.75, 1.5, 4.10, 4.12 5.1, 11.8
"Tests on Completion of Design-Build"	1.1.76, 5.5, 9.12, 11.1, 11.2 11.3, 11.4
"Tests Prior to Contract Completion"	1.1.77, 11.5, 11.8, 11.9, 11.10 11.11, 11.12
"Time for Completion of Design-Build "	1.1.78, 1.10, 2.1, 4.7, 4.12, 4.24 7.4, 8.2, 8.5, 9.2, 9.3, 9.4, 9.5 9.6, 9.8, 11.5, 13.6, 15.2, 16.1 17.6, 18.4
"Temporary Works"	1.1.79, 4.6, 4.8, 4.23, 15.2, 18.5
"Unforeseeable"	1.1.80, 4.6, 4.12, 7.6, 9.3, 9.4, 18.1
"Variation"	1.1.81, 13
"Works"	1.1.82
"year"	1.1.83

"保留金"	1.1.65，14.3，14.10
"保留期"	1.1.66，4.2，14.11
"损害风险"	1.1.67
"资料表"	1.1.68
"付款计划表"	1.1.69，13.3，14.4
"分项工程"	1.1.70
"分项工程调试证书"	1.1.71，11.6，14.10，17.5
"现场"	1.1.72
"报表"	1.1.73，14，16.2
"分包商"	1.1.74，4.4，4.5，5.1，15.2 18.1，19.3
"投标书"	1.1.75，1.5，4.10，4.12 5.1，11.8
"设计 - 施工竣工试验"	1.1.76，5.5，9.12，11.1，11.2 11.3，11.4
"合同完成前试验"	1.1.77，11.5，11.8，11.9，11.10 11.11，11.12
"设计 - 施工竣工时间"	1.1.78，1.10，2.1，4.7，4.12，4.24 7.4，8.2，8.5，9.2，9.3，9.4，9.5 9.6，9.8，11.5，13.6，15.2，16.1 17.6，18.4
"临时工程"	1.1.79，4.6，4.8，4.23，15.2，18.5
"不可预见的"	1.1.80，4.6，4.12，7.6，9.3，9.4，18.1
"变更"	1.1.81，13
"工程"	1.1.82
"年"	1.1.83

GENERAL CONDITIONS OF DISPUTE ADJUDICATION AGREEMENT

for the Dispute Adjudication Board and the Operation Service Dispute Adjudication Board

1 Definitions

Each "Dispute Adjudication Agreement" is a tripartite agreement by and between:

(a) the "Employer";
(b) the "Contractor"; and
(c) the "Member" who is defined in the Dispute Adjudication Agreement as being:

  (i) the sole adjudicator or sole Member of the DAB ("Dispute Adjudication Board") or the Operation Service DAB (as appropriate), and where this is the case, all references to the "Other Members" hereinafter do not apply; or
  (ii) one of the three persons who are jointly called the DAB and, where this is the case, the other two persons are called the "Other Members".

The Employer and the Contractor have entered (or intend to enter) into a contract, which is called the "Contract" and is defined in the Dispute Adjudication Agreement. In the Dispute Adjudication Agreement, words and expressions which are not otherwise defined shall have the meanings assigned to them in the Contract.

2 General Provisions

Unless otherwise stated in the Dispute Adjudication Agreement, the Agreement shall take effect on the latest of the following dates:

(a) the Commencement Date defined in the Contract;
(b) when the Employer, the Contractor and the Member have each signed the Dispute Adjudication Agreement; or
(c) when the Employer, the Contractor and each of the Other Members (if any) have respectively each signed a dispute adjudication agreement.

This employment of the Member is a personal appointment. At any time, the Member may give not less than 70-days' Notice of resignation to the Employer and to the Contractor, and the Dispute Adjudication Agreement shall terminate upon the expiry of this period.

The language to be used in all communications, reports, decisions and during all meetings and hearings relating to the business of either the DAB or the Operation Service DAB shall be the language for communications stated in the Contract Data.

3 Warranties

The Member warrants and agrees that he/she is and shall be impartial and independent of the Employer, the Contractor and the Employer's Representative. The Member shall promptly disclose, to each of them and to the Other Members (if any), any fact or circumstance which might appear inconsistent with his/her warranty and agreement of impartiality and independence.

争端裁决协议书一般条件

用于争端裁决委员会和运营服务争端裁决委员会

| 1
定义 | 每份"争端裁决协议书"是由下列三方之间签订的三方协议书：

(a) "雇主"；
(b) "承包商"；（以及）
(c) "成员"，在争端裁决协议书中定义为：

　　(i) "DAB"（"争端裁决委员会"）或运营服务争端裁决委员会（视情况而定）的唯一裁决员或唯一成员，在此情况下，下面提及所有"其他成员"的说法均不适用；（或）

　　(ii) 联合被称为"争端裁决委员会"的三名成员之一的人，在此情况下，另外两人称为"其他成员"。

雇主和承包商已（或将）签署一份合同，在争端裁决协议书中称为"合同"，其含义是确定的。争端裁决协议书中的词语和措辞，除另有规定外，应具有合同赋予它们的含义。

| 2
一般规定 | 除非争端裁决协议书中另有规定，否则协议书应在以下最迟日期生效：

(a) 合同规定的开工日期；
(b) 在雇主、承包商和成员各自签署了争端裁决协议书；（或）
(c) 在雇主、承包商和每位其他成员（如果有）分别签署了争端裁决协议书。

这种对成员的聘任属对个人的任命。成员可随时向雇主和承包商发出不少于70天的辞职通知，争端裁决协议书应在该期限届满时终止。

在与争端裁决委员会或运营服务争端裁决委员会的业务有关的所有通信交流、报告、决定，以及所有会议和意见听取会期间使用的交流语言，应为合同数据中规定的交流语言。

| 3
保证 | 成员保证并同意，其对雇主、承包商、雇主代表保持公正和独立。成员应将看来可能与其公正和独立的保证和同意不相符的任何事实或情况，立即告知其各方和其他成员（如果有）。

When appointing the Member, the Employer and the Contractor relied upon the Member's representations that he/she is:

(a) experienced in the work which the Contractor is to carry out under the Contract;
(b) experienced in the interpretation of contract documentation; and
(c) fluent in the language for communications which is stated in the Contract Data.

If there is a challenge of a DAB Member by either Party or, in the case of a three-person DAB, jointly by the other Members, for lack of independence, notwithstanding any disclosure made or not made by that Member under Clause 4 [*General Obligations of the Member*] of these General Conditions of Dispute Adjudication Agreement, the challenging Party or Members (as the case may be) may refer the alleged lack of independence to the appointing entity named in the Contract Data under Sub-Clause 20.4 [*Failure to Agree Dispute Adjudication Board*] of the General Conditions of Contract. If the appointing entity considers it to be prudent or necessary, it may refer the matter to an independent professional person or body (such as the International Chamber of Commerce) to review and assess the challenge. If such person or body is of the opinion that the Member in question is no longer independent as required by the terms of the Dispute Adjudication Agreement, the Member shall be removed from the DAB and the appointing entity shall, without delay, appoint a new Member. Any costs or fees due to the independent person or body shall be shared equally between the Parties.

4
General Obligations of the Member

The Member shall:

(a) have no interest, financial or otherwise, in the Employer, the Contractor or Employer's Representative, nor any financial interest in the Contract except for payment under the Dispute Adjudication Agreement;
(b) not previously have been employed as a consultant or otherwise by the Employer, the Contractor or the Employer's Representative, except in such circumstances as were disclosed in writing to the Employer and the Contractor before they signed the Dispute Adjudication Agreement;
(c) have disclosed in writing to the Employer, the Contractor and the Other Members (if any), before entering into the Dispute Adjudication Agreement and to his/her best knowledge and recollection, any professional or personal relationships with any director, officer or employee of the Employer, the Contractor or the Employer's Representative, and any previous involvement in the overall project of which the Contract forms part;
(d) not, for the duration of the Dispute Adjudication Agreement, be employed as a consultant or otherwise by the Employer, the Contractor or the Employer's Representative, except as may be agreed in writing by the Employer, the Contractor and the Other Members (if any);
(e) comply with the annexed "Procedural Rules for Dispute Adjudication Board Members" ("Rules") and with Sub-Clause 20.5 [*Avoidance of Disputes*] of the General Conditions of Contract;
(f) not give advice to the Employer, the Contractor, the Employer's Personnel or the Contractor's Personnel concerning the conduct of the Contract, other than in accordance with the Rules;
(g) not, while a Member, enter into discussions or make any agreement with the Employer, the Contractor or the Employer's Representative regarding employment by any of them, whether as a consultant or otherwise, after ceasing to act under the Dispute Adjudication Agreement;
(h) ensure his/her availability for all Site visits and hearings as are necessary;
(i) become conversant with the Contract and with the progress of the Works (and of any other parts of the project of which the Contract forms part) by studying all documents received which shall be maintained in a current working file;

任命**成员**时，**雇主**和**承包商**依据**成员**的下列表现：

(a) 具有**承包商**根据合同要进行的工作经验；

(b) 具有解释合同文件的经验；（以及）
(c) 能流利地使用**合同数据**中规定的交流语言。

如果**争端裁决委员会成员**因缺乏独立性而受到任何一方或三人**争端裁决委员会**其他**成员**的联合质疑，尽管该**成员**根据**争端裁决协议书**一般条件中第 4 条 [*成员的一般义务*] 的规定，做出或未做出任何披露，提出质疑的一方或**成员**（视情况而定）可根据合同通用条件第 20.4 款 [*对争端裁决委员会未能取得一致*] 的规定，将所称缺乏独立性的问题提交给**合同数据**中确定的指定实体。如果指定的实体认为这是慎重的或必要的，可将此事项提交独立的专业人员或机构（如**国际商会**）审查和评估该质疑。如果该人员或机构认为该**成员**不再是**争端裁决协议书**条款中所要求的独立成员，则该**成员**应从**争端裁决委员会**中除名，指定的实体应立即任命一名新**成员**。应向独立人员或机构支付的任何成本或费用，应由双方平均分摊。

4

成员的一般义务

成员应：

(a) 除根据**争端裁决协议书**规定的付款外，与**雇主、承包商**或**雇主代表**没有资金（财务）或其他利益关系，在合同中没有任何资金（财务）利益；

(b) 以前未曾被**雇主、承包商**或**雇主代表**聘任咨询顾问和其他职位，在签订**争端裁决协议书**前，已书面告知**雇主**和**承包商**的情况除外；

(c) 签署**争端裁决协议书**之前，已就其了解和记忆所及，将其与**雇主、承包商**或**雇主代表**的任何董事、职员或雇员之间的任何业务或个人关系，以及以前在**合同**为其组成部分的全部项目中的任何参与情况，书面告知**雇主、承包商**和**其他成员**（如果有）；

(d) 在执行**争端裁决协议书**期间，除经**雇主、承包商**和**其他成员**（如果有）的书面同意外，不接受**雇主、承包商**或**雇主代表**的聘任，担任咨询顾问或其他职位；

(e) 遵守所附"**争端裁决委员会成员程序规则**"（"**规则**"）和合同通用条件第 20.5 款 [*避免争端*] 的规定；

(f) 除按照**规则**办事外，不向**雇主、承包商、雇主人员**或**承包商人员**提供有关执行**合同**的建议；

(g) 在担任**成员**期间，不与**雇主、承包商**或**雇主代表**，就其停止按**争端裁决协议书**任职后，受聘于他们中任一方的咨询顾问或其他职位问题，进行讨论或达成任何协议；

(h) 保证出席任何必要的**现场**视察和意见听取会；
(i) 通过研究收到的保存在当时工作文件中的所有文件，熟悉**合同**和工程进度（以及**合同**所属项目的任何其他部分）；

(j) treat the details of the Contract and all the DAB's activities and hearings as private and confidential, and not publish or disclose them without the prior written consent of the Employer, the Contractor and the Other Members (if any); and

(k) be available to give advice and opinions, on any matter relevant to the Contract when requested by both the Employer and the Contractor, subject to the agreement of the Other Members (if any).

5 General Obligations of the Employer and the Contractor

The Employer, the Contractor, the Employer's Personnel and the Contractor's Personnel shall not request advice from or consultation with the Member regarding the Contract, otherwise than in the normal course of the DAB's activities under the Contract and the Dispute Adjudication Agreement, or when both Parties jointly agree to refer a matter to the DAB in accordance with Sub-Clause 20.5 [*Avoidance of Disputes*] of the General Conditions of Contract. The Employer and the Contractor shall be responsible for compliance with this provision by the Employer's Personnel and the Contractor's Personnel respectively.

The Employer and the Contractor undertake to each other and to the Member that the Member shall not, except as otherwise agreed in writing by the Employer, the Contractor, the Member and the Other Members (if any):

(a) be appointed as an arbitrator in any arbitration under the Contract;

(b) be called as a witness to give evidence concerning any Dispute before arbitrator(s) appointed for any arbitration under the Contract; or

(c) be liable for any claims for anything done or omitted in the discharge or purported discharge of the Member's functions, unless the act or omission is shown to have been in bad faith.

The Employer and the Contractor hereby jointly and severally indemnify and hold the Member harmless against and from claims from which he/she is relieved from liability under the preceding paragraph.

Whenever the Employer or the Contractor refers a Dispute to the DAB or the Operation Service DAB under Sub-Clause 20.6 [*Obtaining Dispute Adjudication Board's Decision*] or Sub-Clause 20.10 [*Disputes Arising during the Operation Service Period*] of the General Conditions of Contract, which will require the Member to make a Site visit and attend a hearing, the referring Party shall provide appropriate security for a sum equivalent to the reasonable expenses to be incurred by the Member. No account shall be taken of any other payments due or paid to the Member.

6 Payment

The Member shall be paid as follows, in the currency named in the Dispute Adjudication Agreement:

(a) a retainer fee per calendar month, which shall be considered as payment in full for:

(i) being available on 28-days' notice for all Site visits and hearings;

(ii) becoming and remaining conversant with all project developments and maintaining relevant files, files in accordance with sub-paragraph (i) of Clause 4 hereof [*General Obligations of the Member*];

(iii) all office and overhead expenses including secretarial services, photocopying and office supplies incurred in connection with his/her duties; and

(iv) all services performed hereunder except those referred to in subparagraphs (b) and (c) of this Clause.

(j) 将合同的所有细节及**争端裁决委员会**的所有活动和意见听取会,视为私人和机密事项,未经**雇主**、**承包商**和**其他成员**(如果有)的事先书面同意,不将前述各事项公开发表或向外披露;(以及)

(k) 应**雇主**和**承包商**的要求,在**其他成员**(如果有)同意的情况下,就与合同有关的任何事项提供建议和意见。

| 5 雇主和承包商的一般义务 | 除在合同和**争端裁决协议书**规定的**争端裁决委员会**正常活动过程中,或当双方共同商定提交某一事项时,**雇主**、**承包商**、**雇主人员**和**承包商人员**不应就合同有关问题要求**成员**提供建议或与其协商,根据合同通用条件第 20.5 款 [*避免争端*] 的规定,提交给**争端裁决委员会**。**雇主**和**承包商**应分别对**雇主人员**和**承包商人员**遵守此规定负责。 |

除另经**雇主**、**承包商**、**成员**以及**其他成员**(如果有)书面同意外,**雇主**和**承包商**应互相并向**成员**承诺,**成员**不应:

(a) 在根据**合同**进行的任何仲裁中,被任命为仲裁员;
(b) 在根据**合同**进行的任何仲裁中指定的仲裁员面前,被请来作为证人,就任何**争端**提供证据;或
(c) 对因执行或声称执行**成员**任务中的任何行为或不作为提出的任何索赔负责,除非该行为或不作为表明是不诚实的。

雇主和**承包商**在此共同并各自负责保障和保持**成员**免受上段所述因免除其责任引起索赔带来的损害。

当**雇主**或**承包商**根据合同通用条件第 20.6 款 [*取得争端裁决委员会的决定*] 或第 20.10 款 [*运营服务期间发生的争端*] 的规定,将**争端**提交给**争端裁决委员会**或运营服务争端裁决委员会,要求**成员**进行**现场**视察并参加意见听取会时,提交方应提供适当的担保,保证一笔相当于该**成员**所发生的合理开支的款项。任何其他应付或支付给该**成员**的款项,均不得计算在内。

| 6 报酬 | **成员**应按**争端裁决协议书**中规定的货币,按以下方式获得报酬: |

(a) 每个日历月费,此项费用应视为对下列事项的全额支付:

 (i) 可以参加所有提前 28 天通知的**现场**视察和意见听取会;
 (ii) 根据本协议第 4 条 [*成员的一般义务*](i) 段的规定,提交文件的工作档案,熟悉所有项目开发并维护相关文件的工作档案;
 (iii) 与其职责相关的所有办公及管理费用,包括秘书服务、复印和办公用品;(以及)
 (iv) 除本条(b)和(c)段所述的服务外,根据本**协议**提供的所有服务。

During the periods when each Operation Service DAB is acting, the retainer fee shall be paid monthly until the end of the month in which the appointment expires or is otherwise terminated, or the Member resigns.

(b) a daily fee which shall be considered as payment in full for:

(i) each day or part of a day up to a maximum of two days' travel time in each direction for the journey between the Member's home and the Site, or another location of a meeting with the Other Members (if any);
(ii) each working day on Site visits, hearings or preparing decisions; and
(iii) each day spent reading submissions in preparation for a hearing.

(c) all reasonable expenses including necessary travel expenses (air fare in less than first class, hotel and subsistence and other direct travel expenses, including visa charges) incurred in connection with the Member's duties, as well as the cost of telephone calls, courier charges, faxes and telexes: a receipt shall be required for each item in excess of five percent (5%) of the daily fee referred to in sub-paragraph (b) of this Clause.
(d) any taxes properly levied in the Country on payments made to the Member (unless a national or permanent resident of the Country) under this Clause 6.

The retainer and daily fees shall be as specified in the Dispute Adjudication Agreement. Unless it specifies otherwise, these fees shall remain fixed for the first 24 calendar months, and shall thereafter be adjusted by agreement between the Employer, the Contractor and the Member, at each anniversary of the date on which the Dispute Adjudication Agreement became effective.

If the parties fail to agree on the retainer fee or the daily fee, the appointing entity or official named in the Contract Data shall determine the amount of the fees to be used.

The Member shall submit invoices for payment of the monthly retainer and air fares quarterly in advance. Invoices for other expenses and for daily fees shall be submitted following the conclusion of a Site visit or hearing. All invoices shall be accompanied by a brief description of activities performed during the relevant period and shall be addressed to the Contractor.

The Contractor shall pay each of the Member's invoices in full within 56 days after receiving each invoice and shall apply to the Employer (in the Statements under the Contract) for reimbursement of one-half of the amounts of these invoices. The Employer shall then pay the Contractor in accordance with the Contract.

If the Contractor fails to pay to the Member the amount to which he/she is entitled under the Dispute Adjudication Agreement, the Employer shall pay the amount due to the Member and any other amount which may be required to maintain the function of the DAB, and without prejudice to the Employer's rights or remedies. In addition to all other rights arising from this default, the Employer shall be entitled to reimbursement of all sums paid in excess of one-half of these payments, plus all costs of recovering these sums and financing charges calculated at the rate specified in Sub-Clause 14.9 [*Delayed Payment*] of the General Conditions of Contract.

If the Member does not receive payment of the amount due within 70 days after submitting a valid invoice, the Member may (i) suspend his/her services (without Notice) until the payment is received, and/or (ii) resign his/her appointment by giving Notice under Clause 7 hereof.

7 Default and Termination

At any time: (i) the Employer and the Contractor may jointly terminate the Dispute Adjudication Agreement by giving 42-days' Notice to the Member; or (ii) the Member may resign as provided for in Clause 2 hereof.

在各**运营服务争端裁决委员会**行事期间，聘请费应按月支付，直至任期届满，或其以其他方式终止等原因，或**成员**辞职当月月底为止。

（b） 日费，应视为全额支付：

（i） **成员**的住所与**现场**之间的旅程，或与**其他成员**（如果有）进行的会议的其他地点之间不足一天单程旅行，最多两天的旅程时间；

（ii） **现场**视察、意见听取会或准备决策的每个工作日；（以及）

（iii） 为准备意见听取会，每天都在阅读提交的材料。

（c） 与**成员**职责相关所有合理支出，包括必要的差旅费用（低于头等舱的机票费、酒店和生活补贴以及其他直接的差旅费用，包括签证费用），以及电话费、快递费、传真和电传的费用：对于超过本**条**（b）段所述每日费用百分之五（5%）的每项支出，均应提供收据；

（d） 根据第 6 条向**工程所在国成员**（**工程所在国**的国民或永久居民除外）支付后，应在该国适当征收的任何税款。

聘请费和日常费用应在**争端裁决协议书**中规定。除非另有规定，此类费用应在前 24 个日历月内保持固定不变。此后，应在**争端裁决协议书**生效之日的每个周年日，由**雇主**、**承包商**和**成员**协商调整。

如果双方未能就聘请费或日常费用商定一致，则**合同数据**中指定的任命实体或官员应确定拟使用的费用金额。

成员应每季度提前提交支付每月聘请费和机票的发票。其他费用和日常费用的发票，应在**现场**视察或意见听取会结束后提交。所有发票应附有相关期间所开展活动的简要说明，并应寄给**承包商**。

承包商应在收到每份发票后 56 天内，按每位**成员**的发票全额支付，并应向**雇主**（在根据合同提交的**报表**中）申请付还这些发票款额的一半。然后，**雇主**应按照**合同**向**承包商**付款。

如果**承包商**未能向**成员**支付其根据**争端裁决协议书**的规定应得的款项，**雇主**应向**成员**支付其应得款额，以及维持**争端裁决委员会**运行所需的任何其他款项，此项支付不应损害**雇主**的权利或应得补偿。除因该违约引起的所有其他权利外，**雇主**有权获得超过这些付款一半的所有支付款额的补偿，还应加上收回这些款项的全部费用和按照合同通用条件第 14.9 款 [*延误的付款*] 规定的费率计算的融资费。

如果**成员**在提交有效发票后 70 天内未收到应付款，**成员**可以：（i）暂停其服务（不需**通知**），直到收到付款为止；和 / 或（ii）根据本**协议**第 7 条发出**通知**，辞去其任命。

7	
违约与终止	在任何时候：（i）**雇主**和**承包商**可提前 42 天**通知成员**，共同终止**争端裁决协议书**；或（ii）**成员**可根据本协议第 2 条的规定辞职。

If the Member fails to comply with the Dispute Adjudication Agreement, the Employer and the Contractor may, without prejudice to their other rights, terminate the Agreement by Notice to the Member. The Notice shall take effect when received by the Member.

If the Employer or the Contractor fails to comply with the Dispute Adjudication Agreement, the Member may, without prejudice to his/her other rights, terminate the Agreement by Notice to the Employer and the Contractor. The Notice shall take effect when received by them both.

Any such Notice, resignation and termination shall be final and binding on the Employer, the Contractor and the Member. However, a Notice by the Employer or the Contractor, but not by both, shall be of no effect.

If the Member fails to comply with any of his/her obligations under Clause 4 (a) to (d) above, he/she shall not be entitled to any fees or expenses hereunder and shall, without prejudice to the Employer's and the Contractor's other rights, reimburse each of the Employer and the Contractor for any fees and expenses received by the Member and the Other Members (if any), for proceedings or decisions (if any) of the DAB or the Operation Service DAB which are rendered void or ineffective by the said failure to comply.

If the Member fails to comply with any of his obligations under Clause 4 (e) to (k) above, he shall not be entitled to any fees or expenses hereunder from the date and to the extent of the non-compliance and shall, without prejudice to their other rights, reimburse each of the Employer and the Contractor for any fees and expenses already received by the Member, for proceedings or decisions (if any) of the DAB or the Operation Service DAB which are rendered void or ineffective by the said failure to comply.

8 Disputes

Any Dispute or claim arising out of or in connection with this Dispute Adjudication Agreement, or the breach, termination or invalidity thereof, shall be finally settled by institutional arbitration. If no other arbitration institute is agreed, the arbitration shall be conducted under the Rules of Arbitration of the International Chamber of Commerce by one arbitrator appointed in accordance with these Rules of Arbitration.

如果**成员**未能遵守**争端裁决协议书**，**雇主**和**承包商**可在不损害其其他权利的情况下，通过**通知成员**终止协议书。该通知从**成员**收到时生效。

如果**雇主**或**承包商**未能遵守**争端裁决协议书**，**成员**可以在不损害他/她的其他权利的情况下，**通知雇主**和**承包商**终止协议书。该**通知**在其双方收到后生效。

任何此类**通知**、辞职和终止应为终止**通知**，并对**雇主**、**承包商**和**成员**均具有约束力。但是，由**雇主**或**承包商**组成的**成员**，而不是由双方组成的**成员**应无效。

如果**成员**未能遵守上述**第 4 条**（a）至（d）段规定的任何义务，则其应无权获得在此所述的任何费用或开支，并应在不损害**雇主**和**承包商**其他权利的情况下，向**雇主**和**承包商**偿还其和**其他成员**（如果有）因上述不遵守而导致**争端裁决委员会**或运营服务**争端裁决委员会**的工作或决定（如果有）作废或无效，而产生的任何费用和开支。

如果该**成员**未能遵守上述**第 4 条**（e）至（k）段规定的任何义务，则自违约之日起，该**成员**应无权获得在此所述的任何费用或开支，并应在不损害其其他权利的情况下，向**雇主**和**承包商**偿还**成员**（如果有）因上述不遵守而导致**争端裁决委员会**或运营服务**争端裁决委员会**的工作或决定（如果有）作废或无效，而产生的任何费用和开支。

8 争端	由本**争端裁决协议书**或与之有关的，或因对其违反或其终止或无效而引起的任何**争端**或索赔，应最终通过机构仲裁解决。如果未商定其他仲裁机构，仲裁应根据**国际商会仲裁规则**，由按照这些**仲裁规则**任命的一位仲裁员解决。

PROCEDURAL RULES FOR DISPUTE ADJUDICATION BOARD MEMBERS

1. Unless otherwise agreed by the Employer and the Contractor, the DAB shall visit the Site at intervals of not more than 140 days, including times of critical construction events, at the request of either the Employer or the Contractor. Unless otherwise agreed by the Employer, the Contractor and the DAB, the period between consecutive visits shall not be less than 70 days, except as required to convene a hearing as described below.

2. The timing of and agenda for each Site visit shall be as agreed jointly by the DAB, the Employer and the Contractor, or in the absence of agreement, shall be decided by the DAB. The purpose of Site visits is to enable the DAB to become and remain acquainted with the progress of the Works and of any actual or potential problems or claims, and, as far as reasonable, to endeavour to prevent potential problems or claims from becoming Disputes.

3. Site visits shall be attended by the Employer, the Contractor and the Employer's Representative and shall be co-ordinated by the Employer in co-operation with the Contractor. The Employer shall ensure the provision of appropriate conference facilities and secretarial and copying services. At the conclusion of each Site visit and before leaving the Site, the DAB shall prepare a report on its activities during the visit and shall send copies to the Employer and the Contractor.

4. The Employer and the Contractor shall furnish to the DAB one copy of all documents which the DAB may request, including Contract documents, progress reports, variation instructions, certificates and other documents pertinent to the performance of the Contract. All communications between the DAB and the Employer or the Contractor shall be copied to the other Party. If the DAB comprises three persons, the Employer and the Contractor shall send copies of these requested documents and these communications to each of these persons.

5. If any Dispute is referred to the DAB in accordance with Sub-Clause 20.6 [*Obtaining Dispute Adjudication Board's Decision*] or Sub-Clause 20.10 [*Disputes Arising during the Operation Service Period*] of the General Conditions of Contract, the DAB shall proceed in accordance with the said Sub-Clauses 20.6 and 20.10, and these Rules, or as otherwise agreed by the Employer and the Contractor in writing. Subject to the time allowed to give Notice of a decision and other relevant factors, the DAB shall:

    (a) act fairly and impartially as between the Employer and the Contractor, giving each of them a reasonable opportunity of putting his case and responding to the other's case; and
    (b) adopt procedures suitable to the Dispute, avoiding unnecessary delay or expense.

6. The DAB may conduct a hearing on the Dispute, in which event it will decide on the date and place for the hearing and may request that written documentation and arguments from the Employer and the Contractor be presented to it prior to or at the hearing.

7. If, within 14 days after giving its decision, the members of the DAB find and agree that such decision contained errors of fact or principle, the Chairman of the DAB (or the sole Member if applicable) shall advise the Employer and the Contractor of the error and issue an addendum to its decision in writing to both Parties.

争端裁决委员会成员程序规则

1　除非**雇主**和**承包商**另有商定，否则**争端裁决委员会**应每隔不超过 140 天的时间视察**现场**，包括**雇主**或**承包商**请求的重大施工事件发生时。除非**雇主**、**承包商**和**争端裁决委员会**另有商定，否则连续视察的间隔时间不得少于 70 天，除非需要召开下述意见听取会。

2　每次**现场**视察的时间和议程应由**争端裁决委员会**、**雇主**和**承包商**共同商定，或如无商定，则由**争端裁决委员会**决定。**现场**视察的目的，是使**争端裁决委员会**能够了解并保持对**工程**进度和任何实际或潜在的问题或索赔的知晓，并尽可能合理地努力防止潜在的问题或索赔成为**争端**。

3　**现场**视察应由**雇主**、**承包商**和**雇主代表**参加，并由**雇主**与**承包商**协调。**雇主**应确保提供适当的会议设施、秘书和复印服务。在每次**现场**视察结束后和在离开**现场**之前，**争端裁决委员会**应就其在视察期间的活动编写一份报告，并将副本送交**雇主**和**承包商**。

4　**雇主**和**承包商**应向**争端裁决委员会**提供一份其可能要求的所有文件，包括**合同**文件、进度报告、变更指示、证书和与履行**合同**有关的其他文件。**争端裁决委员会**和**雇主**或**承包商**之间的所有通信函件，应抄送给另一方。如果**争端裁决委员会**由三人组成，**雇主**和**承包商**应将这些要求的文件和这些通信函件抄送给三人中的每位成员。

5　如果根据合同通用条件第 20.6 款［*取得争端裁决委员会的决定*］或第 20.10 款［*运营服务期间发生的争端*］的规定，将任何**争端**提交给**争端裁决委员会**，**争端裁决委员会**应按照所述的第 20.6 款和第 20.10 款和本规则的规定进行工作，或**雇主**和**承包商**以书面形式另有商定。在发出决定和其他有关因素的**通知**所允许的时间，**争端裁决委员会**应：

（a）在**雇主**和**承包商**之间公平、公正地行事，给予每**方**一个合理的机会陈述己方的论据，并回应他方的论据；（以及）

（b）采取适合该**争端**的程序，避免不必要的延误或开支。

6　**争端裁决委员会**可就**争端**召开意见听取会，在此情况下，**争端裁决委员会**将决定意见听取会的日期和地点，并可要求**雇主**和**承包商**在意见听取会之前或在会上提交书面文件和论据。

7　如果在做出决定后 14 天内，**争端裁决委员会**成员发现并同意该决定包含事实或原则上的错误，则**争端裁决委员会主席**（或唯一**成员**，如适用）应将错误告知**雇主**和**承包商**，并以书面形式向双方发出其决定的附录。

8   If, within 14 days of receiving a decision from the DAB, either Party believes that such decision contains an ambiguity, that Party may seek clarification from the DAB in writing with a copy of such request to the other Party. Within 14 days of receiving such a request, the DAB shall respond with a copy to the other Party, and if the DAB is of the opinion that the decision did contain an error or ambiguity, it may correct its decision by issuing an addendum to its original decision.

9   Except as otherwise agreed in writing by the Employer and the Contractor, the DAB shall have power to adopt an inquisitorial procedure, to refuse admission to hearings or audience at hearings to any persons other than representatives of the Employer, the Contractor and the Employer's Representative, and to proceed in the absence of any party who the DAB is satisfied received Notice of the hearing; but shall have discretion to decide whether and to what extent this power may be exercised.

10   The Employer and the Contractor empower the DAB, among other things, to:

(a) establish the procedure to be applied in deciding a Dispute;
(b) decide upon the DAB's own jurisdiction, and as to the scope of any Dispute referred to it;
(c) conduct any hearing as it thinks fit, not being bound by any rules or procedures other than those contained in the Contract and these Rules;
(d) take the initiative in ascertaining the facts and matters required for a decision,
(e) make use of its own specialist knowledge, if any;
(f) decide upon the payment of financing charges in accordance with the Contract;
(g) decide upon any provisional relief such as interim or conservatory measures; and
(h) open up, review and revise any certificate, decision, determination, instruction, opinion or valuation of the Employer's Representative, relevant to the Dispute.

11   The DAB shall not express any opinions during any hearing concerning the merits of any arguments advanced by the Parties. Thereafter, the DAB shall make and give its decision in accordance with Sub-Clause 20.6 [*Obtaining Dispute Adjudication Board's Decision*] of the General Conditions of Contract, or as otherwise agreed by the Employer and the Contractor in writing.

12   If the DAB comprises three persons:

(a) it shall convene in private after a hearing, in order to have discussions and prepare its decision;
(b) it shall endeavour to reach a unanimous decision: if this proves impossible the applicable decision shall be made by a majority of the Members, who may require the minority Member to prepare a written report for submission to the Employer and the Contractor; and
(c) if a Member fails to attend a meeting or hearing, or to fulfil any required function, the other two Members may nevertheless proceed to make a decision, unless:

(i) either the Employer or the Contractor does not agree that they do so; or
(ii) the absent Member is the chairman and he/she instructs the other Members not to make a decision.

8　　如果任一方在收到**争端裁决委员会**的决定后 14 天内，认为该决定含糊不清，则该方可要求**争端裁决委员**以书面形式做出澄清，并向另一方提交该请求的副本。**争端裁决委员会**应在收到此类请求后 14 天内，向另一方提供一份副本，如果**争端裁决委员会**认为该决定确实存在错误或含糊不清，则可以通过签发原始决定的附录更正其决定。

9　　除**雇主**和**承包商**另有书面商定外，**争端裁决委员会**应有权采取询问调查程序，拒绝除**雇主**、**承包商**和**雇主代表**的代表以外的任何人参加或旁听意见听取会，并有权在任一方缺席，且**争端裁决委员会**确信其已收到意见听取会**通知**的情况下，继续进行会议；但对是否行使这一权利和可能实施的范围，应有权自主做出决定。

10　　在其他方面，**雇主**和**承包商**给予**争端裁决委员会**以下权利：

（a）　制定在确定**争端**中应用的程序；
（b）　确定**争端裁决委员会**自身的管辖权，以及提交给**争端裁决委员会**的任何**争端**的范围；
（c）　召开其认为适当的任何意见听取会，除包括在**合同**和本**规则**中的规定外，不受任何规则或程序的约束；
（d）　主动查明决定所需的事实和事项；
（e）　利用自身的专业知识，如果有；
（f）　根据**合同**规定决定融资费的支付；
（g）　决定任何临时性救济事项，如临时性或保全性措施；（以及）
（h）　开启、审核并修改与**争端**相关的**雇主代表**的任何证书、决定、确定、指示、意见或估价。

11　　**争端裁决委员会**在任何意见听取会期间，不应就各方提出的任何论据的是非表示任何意见。此后，**争端裁决委员会**应按照合同通用条件第 **20.6** 款［*取得争端裁决委员会的决定*］，或**雇主**和**承包商**以书面形式商定的其他规定做出决定。

12　　如果**争端裁决委员会**是由三人组成，则：

（a）　为了进行讨论并做出其决定，在意见听取会之后，应召开非公开会议；

（b）　应努力达成一致决定；如果这不可能的话，应由多数**成员**做出适用的决定，并可要求少数**成员**编写一份书面报告，提交给**雇主**和**承包商**；（以及）

（c）　如果一名**成员**未能参加会议或意见听取会，或未能履行其任何要求的职能，其他两名**成员**仍应继续做出决定，除非：

（i）　**雇主**或**承包商**不同意他们这样做；（或）
（ii）　缺席的**成员**是主席，并且其指示其他**成员**不要做出决定。

设计、施工和运营合同条件

Conditions of Contract for
DESIGN, BUILD AND OPERATE PROJECTS

专用条件
PARTICULAR CONDITIONS

引言
INTRODUCTION

通用条件
GENERAL CONDITIONS

专用条件
PARTICULAR CONDITIONS

样本格式
SAMPLE FORMS

Particular Conditions

CONTENTS

PREAMBLE

PART A – CONTRACT DATA 216

    Introduction

    Contract Data

PART B – SPECIAL PROVISIONS 226

    Introduction

    Notes on the Preparation of Tender Documents

    Notes on the Preparation of Special Provisions

专用条件

目　录

序言

A 部分——合同数据 ··· 217

　　引言

　　合同数据

B 部分——特别规定 ··· 227

　　引言

　　编写招标文件注意事项

　　编写特别规定注意事项

Preamble

It is recommended that the following statement is included in the Tender Documents:

The Conditions of Contract comprise the "General Conditions", which form part of the "Conditions of Contract for Design, Build and Operate Projects First Edition 2008" published by the Fédération Internationale des Ingénieurs¬Conseils (FIDIC), "Particular Conditions Part A – Contract Data" and (where applicable) "Particular Conditions Part B – Special Provisions", which include amendments and additions to such General Conditions.

序言

建议在**招标文件**中包括以下内容：

合同条件包括"**通用条件**"，构成国际咨询工程师联合会（FIDIC，菲迪克）出版的"2008年第1版设计、施工和运营合同条件"的一部分，"**专用条件 A 部分**——合同数据"和（如适用）"**专用条件 B 部分**——特别规定"，包括对此类**通用条件**的修改和补充。

Particular Conditions Part A - Contract Data

INTRODUCTION

The following Sub-Clauses in the General Conditions make direct reference to the Contract Data and require that specific information is provided.

The document assumes that all information in the Contract Data will be provided by the Employer and included in the tender documents. If the Employer requires tenderers to provide any of the information required in the Contract Data, this must be clearly stated in the tender documents.

The Conditions of Contract comprise, as a minimum, the General Conditions and the Particular Conditions Part A – Contract Data, and failure by the Employer to provide the information and details required in the Contract Data will mean that either the Contract Documents are incomplete with vital information missing, or that the fall-back provisions to be found in some of the Sub-Clauses in the General Conditions will automatically take effect.

专用条件 A 部分——合同数据[一]

引言

以下**通用条件**中的**条款**直接引用**合同数据**，并要求提供具体信息。

本文件假定**合同数据**中的所有信息将由**雇主**提供，并包含在招标文件中。如果**雇主**要求投标人提供**合同数据**中要求的任何信息，则必须在投标文件中明确说明。

合同条件至少包括**通用条件**和**专用条件 A 部分——合同数据**，如果**雇主**未提供**合同数据**中要求的信息和细节，可能意味着构成**合同文件**的不完整，缺少重要信息，或意味着**通用条件**的某些**条款**中的兜底条款（后备条款）将自动生效。

[一] 此处按英文版翻译——译者注

CONTRACT DATA

Sub-Clause	Data to be given	Data
1.1.24	Where the Contract allows for Cost Plus Profit, percentage profit to be added to the Cost:	_____%
1.1.26	Cut-Off Date (number of days after the Time for Completion of Design-Build):	_____days
1.1.32	Employer's name and address:	
1.1.35	Employer's Representative's name and address:	
1.1.70	Parts of the Works that shall be designated a Section for the purposes of the Contract:	
1.1.78	Time for Completion of Design-Build:	_____days
1.3	Agreed methods of electronic transmission:	
1.3	Address of Employer for communications:	
1.3	Address of Employer's Representative for communications:	
1.3	Address of Contractor for communications:	
1.4	Contract shall be governed by the law of:	
1.4	Ruling language:	
1.4	Language for communications:	
2.1	After receiving the Letter of Acceptance, the Contractor shall be given right of access to all or part of the Site within:	_____days

合同数据

条款	需提供的数据	数据
1.1.24	如果合同允许成本加利润，百分比的利润应加到成本中：	_____%
1.1.26	截止日期（设计 - 施工竣工时间后的天数）：	_____天
1.1.32	雇主的姓名和地址：	
1.1.35	雇主代表的姓名和地址：	
1.1.70	为了合同的目的，应指定为分项工程的部分工程：	
1.1.78	设计 - 施工竣工时间：	_____天
1.3	商定的电子传输方式：	
1.3	雇主的通信地址：	
1.3	雇主代表的通信地址：	
1.3	承包商的通信地址：	
1.4	合同应由 …… 法律管辖：	
1.4	主导语言：	
1.4	交流语言：	
2.1	收到中标函后，承包商应在 …… 天内有权进入全部或部分现场：	_____天

Sub-Clause	Data to be given	Data
4.2	Performance Security (as percentages of the Accepted Contract Amount in Currencies):	
	Percent:	_____%
	Currency:	_____
	Percent:	_____%
	Currency:	_____
4.2	Reduction in Performance Security at the end of the Retention Period:	_____%
5.1	Period for notification of errors, faults and other defects is:	_____days
5.2	Contractor's Documents requiring approval:	_____
		_____
		_____
6.5	Normal working hours on the Site:	_____
8.2	Period of the Operation Service:	_____years
9.2	Time for Completion of Design-Build:	_____days
9.2	Time for Completion of each Section:	
	Section	_____
	Time for Completion	_____days
	Section	_____
	Time for Completion	_____days
9.6	Delay damages (percent of final Contract Price per day of delay):	_____%
9.6	Maximum amount of delay damages (percent of final Contract Price):	_____%
10.6a	Maximum compensation payable by Contractor:	_____
10.6b	Maximum compensation payable by Employer:	_____
10.7	Performance damages:	
	Failure:	_____
	Damages:	_____
	Failure:	_____
	Damages:	_____
10.7	Rights of Employer if failure continues for more than 84 days:	_____

条款	需提供的数据	数据
4.2	履约保函（以货币表示的中标合同金额的百分比）：	
	百分比：	_____%
	货币：	_____
	百分比：	_____%
	货币：	_____
4.2	保留期结束时履约保函的减少：	_____%
5.1	错误、故障和其他缺陷的通知期限为：	_____天
5.2	需要批准的承包商文件：	_____
		_____
		_____
6.5	在现场的正常工作时间：	_____
8.2	运营服务期限：	_____年
9.2	设计 - 施工竣工时间：	_____天
9.2	各分项工程竣工时间：	
	分项工程	_____
	竣工时间	_____天
	分项工程	_____
	竣工时间	_____天
9.6	误期损害赔偿费（每延误一天支付最终合同价格的比例）：	_____%
9.6	误期损害赔偿费的最高金额（每延误一天支付最终合同价格的比例）：	_____%
10.6a	承包商支付的最高赔偿金：	_____
10.6b	雇主支付的最高赔偿金：	_____
10.7	履约损害赔偿费：	
	故障	_____
	损害赔偿费	_____
	故障	_____
	损害赔偿费	_____
10.7	如果故障持续超过84天，雇主的权利：	_____

Sub-Clause	Data to be given	Data
10.7	Minimum production outputs required (give details):	
13.5	Percentage rate to be applied to Provisional Sums:	_____%
14.2	Amount of Advance Payment (percent of Accepted Contract Amount):	_____%
14.2	Currencies of payment if different to the currencies quoted in the Contract:	
14.2	Percentage deductions for the repayment of the Advance Payment:	_____%
14.3	Percentage of Retention:	_____%
14.3	Limit of Retention Money:	_____%
14.6 (b) (i)	Plant and Materials for payment when shipped:	
14.6 (c) (i)	Plant and Materials for payment when delivered to the Site:	
14.7 (b)	Minimum Amount of Interim Payment Certificate:	
14.9	Financing charges for delayed payment (percent points above discount rate):	_____%
14.17	Currencies for payment of Contract Price:	
14.17	Proportions of Local and Foreign Currencies are: Local Foreign	
14.17	Rate of Exchange	
14.17	Payment of damages shall be: Currency Proportion Currency Proportion	
14.19	Amount of Maintenance Retention Fund:	
17.1	Operation of forces of nature allocated to the Contractor:	

条款	需提供的数据	数据
10.7	所需最低产量（给出详细信息）：	_____
13.5	暂列金额使用的百分比：	_____%
14.2	预付款金额（占中标合同金额的比例）：	_____%
14.2	付款的币种，如果与合同中报价的币种不同：	_____
14.2	预付款再支付的扣减比例：	_____%
14.3	保留金比例：	_____%
14.3	保留金限额：	_____%
14.6（b）（i）	运输时应支付的生产设备和材料：	_____
14.6（c）（i）	发运到现场时应支付的生产设备和材料：	_____
14.7（b）	期中付款证书的最小金额：	_____
14.9	延误付款的融资费用（高于折现率的百分点）：	_____%
14.17	合同价格支付的币种：	_____
14.17	当地和外国货币的比例是：	
	当地	_____
	外国	_____
14.17	汇率	_____
14.17	损害赔偿费的支付：	
	货币	_____
	比例	_____
	货币	_____
	比例	_____
14.19	维护保留基金金额：	_____
17.1	分配给承包商的运营自然力：	_____

Sub-Clause	Data to be given	Data
17.8	Total liability of the Contractor shall not exceed:	_____
19.2 (a) (i)	Permitted deductible limits:	_____%
19.2 (a) (ii)	Additional sum to be insured:	_____
19.2 (a)4	Additional sum to be insured:	_____
19.2 (a)5	Employer's Risks to be insured if different to Sub-Clause 17.1:	_____
19.2 (b)	Exceptional Risks to be insured if different to Sub-Clause 18.1:	_____
19.2 (c)	Insurance of Contractor's Equipment (amount required):	_____
19.2 (c)	Amount of professional liability insurance required:	_____
19.2 (d)	Period for which professional liability insurance required:	_____
19.2 (f)	Amount of insurance required for injury to persons and damage to property:	_____ _____
19.3 (a)	Other insurances required from the Contractor (give details):	_____
19.3 (d)	Amount of fire extended cover insurance required:	_____
19.3 (e)	Other insurances required by law from the Contractor (give details):	_____ _____
20.3	Other optional insurances required from the Contractor (give details):	_____ _____
20.3	Date for appointment of DAB:	_____
20.4	The DAB shall comprise:	_____members
20.8	Appointing entity (official) for DAB members, if not agreed, shall be the President of FIDIC or a person appointed by him. Language of arbitration:	_____

条款	需提供的数据	数据
17.8	承包商的总责任不得超过：	_____
19.2（a）（i）	允许的免赔额度：	_____%
19.2（a）（ii）	投保的附加金额：	_____
19.2（a）4	投保的附加金额：	_____
19.2（a）5	雇主投保的风险如果与第17.1款不同：	_____
19.2（b）	投保的例外风险如果与第18.1款的不同：	_____
19.2（c）	承包商设备保险（所需金额）：	_____
19.2（c）	所需职业责任保险金额：	_____
19.2（d）	职业责任要求的保险期限：	_____
19.2（f）	人身伤害和财产损害要求的保险金额：	_____
19.3（a）	承包商要求的其他保险（详细情况）：	_____
19.3（d）	所需火灾延长保险金额：	_____
19.3（e）	法律要求承包商提供的其他保险（详细情况）：	_____
20.3	承包商要求的其他可选保险（详细情况）：	_____
20.3	任命争端裁决委员会的日期：	_____
20.4	争端裁决委员会应由……组成：	_____
20.8	争端裁决委员会成员的任命实体（官方），如未能商定一致，将是菲迪克（FIDIC）主席或其任命的人员。	
	仲裁语言：	_____

Particular Conditions Part B – Special Provisions

INTRODUCTION

The terms of the Conditions of Contract for Design, Build and Operate (DBO) Projects have been prepared by the Fédération Internationale des Ingénieurs-Conseils (FIDIC) and are recommended where one entity takes total responsibility for an engineering project which incorporates the design, manufacture, delivery and installation of a facility, and the long-term operation and maintenance of that facility on behalf of the Employer. The DBO form is most suitable where tenders are invited on an international basis. Modifications to the Conditions of Contract may be required in some legal jurisdictions, particularly if they are to be used on domestic contracts.

One of the main objectives of the DBO contract format is to ensure the full commitment of the Contractor not only to design and build the facility, but also to operate the facility under licence from the Employer, for a period of 20 years, before returning the facility to the Employer for his continued operation. With the various skills and expertise required to cover all aspects of a DBO project, it is expected that the Contractor will be a consortium of several contractors covering all the required disciplines, and it is important that the joint and several liability provisions to be found in General Conditions are properly reflected in any new provisions prepared under Particular Conditions Part B – Special Provisions.

Before incorporating any new or changed clauses, the wording must be carefully checked to ensure that it is wholly suitable for the particular circumstances and that it does not unintentionally alter the meaning or operation of other clauses in the Contract, and does not inadvertently change the obligations assigned to the Parties or the balance of risks shared between them. Furthermore, it is important that new clauses do not create any ambiguity or misunderstanding in the rest of the document.

There are a number of Sub-Clauses in the General Conditions which require data to be provided by the Employer and inserted in the Particular Conditions Part A – Contract Data. However, there are no Sub-Clauses in the General Conditions which require data or information to be included in the Particular Conditions Part B – Special Provisions. Any provisions found in the tender documents and/or Contract Documents under Particular Conditions Part B – Special Provisions indicate that the General Conditions have been amended or supplemented.

Note that the provisions of the Particular Conditions Part B – Special Provisions will always overrule and supersede the equivalent provisions in the General Conditions of Contract, and it is important that the changes are easily identifiable by using the same clause numbers and titles as appear in the General Conditions. Furthermore, it is necessary to add a statement in the tender document and Contract Document that:

> "The provisions to be found in the Particular Conditions Part B – Special Provisions take precedence over the equivalent provisions found under the same Sub-Clause number (s) in the General Conditions, and the provisions of the Particular Conditions Part A – Contract Data take preference over the Particular Conditions Part B – Special Provisions."

Users of the DBO form of contract who wish to amend and use the document for a 'brown field' scenario for the operation and refurbishment of an existing facility, or where an operation period significantly different to the 20-year period assumed in this document, are referred to the forthcoming *FIDIC DBO Contract Guide* (planned for publication by FIDIC at a later date), for guidance and assistance in identifying those clauses and procedures which may need amending.

专用条件 B 部分——特别规定[一]

引言

国际咨询工程师联合会（FIDIC，菲迪克）已编制了《**设计、施工和运营合同条件**》（DBO）的条款，建议用于当一个实体代表**雇主**对包括设施设计、制造、交付和安装，以及该设施的长期运营和维护负全部责任时。在国际招标的情况下，DBO 格式最为适合。如果用于国内的合同时，在某些法律管辖区，可能需要对**合同条件**做些修改。

DBO 合同格式的主要目标之一是确保**承包商**不仅充分承诺对设施的设计和施工，而且在将设施归还给**雇主**继续运营之前，在**雇主**的许可下运营该设施 20 年。凭借涵盖 DBO 项目所有方面所需的各种技能和专业知识，预计**承包商**将是涵盖所有所需专业的多个承包商的联营体，并且重要的是，**通用条件**中共同的和各自的责任条款应适当反映在根据**专用条件 B 部分——特别规定**编制的任何新条款中。

在吸收任何新的或修改的条款前，必须认真核实措辞，以确保其完全适用于特定的情况，并不会无意中改变**合同**中其他条款的含义或使用，并不会无意中改变分配给双方的义务或其之间风险的平衡分担。此外，重要的是，新条款不会与文件的其他部分产生任何歧义或误解。

很多**通用条件**的条款要求雇主提供数据，并将数据插入**专用条件 A 部分——合同数据**。但是，**通用条件**中没有**条款**要求将数据或信息包括在**专用条件 B 部分——特别规定**中。招标文件和/或合同文件中**专用条件 B 部分——特别规定**中的任何规定均表示，**通用条件**已修改或补充。

请注意，**专用条件 B 部分——特别规定**的规定，将始终优先于并取代合同**通用条件**的同等条款，并且重要的是，通过使用**通用条件**中出现的相同条款编号和标题，可以很容易识别出修改之处。此外，有必要在招标文件和**合同文件**中增加以下说明：

"在**专用条件 B 部分——特别规定**中的规定优先于**通用条件**中相同**条款**编号的同等条款的情况下，**专用条件 A 部分——合同数据**的规定优先于**专用条件 B 部分——特别规定**。"

DBO 合同格式的用户，如果希望修改和使用本文件作为设施运营和翻新的"棕地"方案，或者运营期与本文件中假设的 20 年期有很大不同，请参考即将出版的《*菲迪克（FIDIC）设计、施工和运营合同指南*》（FIDIC 计划在以后出版），以指导和帮助确定可能需要修改的条款和程序。

[一] 此处按英文版翻译——译者注

NOTES ON THE PREPARATION OF TENDER DOCUMENTS

When preparing the tender documents and planning the tendering process, Employers are recommended to read the publication *FIDIC Procurement Procedures* which gives invaluable help and advice on the contents of the tender documents, and the procedures for receiving and evaluating tenders.

The tender documents should be prepared by suitably qualified engineers who are familiar with the technical aspects of the required works and the particular requirements and contractual provisions of a DBO project. Furthermore, a review by suitably qualified lawyers may be advisable.

The tender documents issued to tenderers should normally include the following:

- Letter of invitation to tender
- Instructions to Tenderers
- Tender form and required appendices
- Employer's Requirements
- Conditions of Contract: General and Particular
- General information and data
- Technical information and data
- Schedules and drawings from Employer
- Details of schedules and drawings and other information required from tenderers
- Required forms of agreement, licence, securities and guarantees.

The publication *FIDIC Procurement Procedures* referred to above provides useful guidance as to the content and format of each of the above sections.

In particular, the Employer's Requirements should specify the particular requirements for the completed Works, including functional and operational requirements, quality and scope. If the Contractor is required to supply certain items, such as consumables or spare parts, etc., these should be listed in a Schedule. Drafters of the Employer's Requirements must remember that if any matters are not referred to or covered, the Contractor may well be relieved of any responsibility in respect of such matters.

The following Sub-Clauses make specific reference to matters which may be included in the Employer's Requirements. However, it may also be necessary under other Sub-Clauses for the Employer to give specific information in the Employer's Requirements:

1.9	Publications to be kept on Site
1.12	Intellectual property rights retained by Employer
1.14	Permissions being obtained by the Employer
4.1	Intended purposes for which the Works are required
4.5	Details of required nominated Subcontractors
4.6	Other contractors (and others) on the Site
	Documents required by Employer
4.18	Environmental constraints
4.19	Electricity, water, gas and other services available on the Site
4.20	Employer's Equipment and free-issue material
5.1	Criteria for design personnel
5.2	Contractor's Documents required, and whether for approval Period for review
5.4	Technical standards and building regulations
5.5	As-built drawings and other records of the Works
6.1	Engagement of Staff
6.6	Facilities for Personnel
7.8	Payment of Royalties
10.5	Training required
11.1	Testing criteria.

编写招标文件注意事项

编写招标文件并设计招标程序时，**雇主**应阅读出版物《**菲迪克（FIDIC）采购程序**》，该程序对招标文件的内容以及接受和评估投标的程序提供了有价值的帮助和建议。

招标文件应由具备适当资质、熟悉要建工程技术情况，以及 **DBO** 工程特别要求和合同条款的工程师编写。此外，建议由具有适当资质的律师进行审核。

发给投标人的招标文件通常应包括以下内容：

- 招标书；
- **投标人须知**；
- **标书格式**及规定的附录；
- **雇主要求**；
- **合同条件：通用条件和专用条件**；
- 一般信息和数据；
- 技术信息和数据；
- **雇主的资料表**和图纸；
- 招标人要求的详细资料表和图纸以及其他信息；
- 所需的协议书、执照、担保和保函格式。

上述出版物《**菲迪克（FIDIC）采购程序**》对以上各部分的内容和格式提供了有用的指南。

尤其是，**雇主要求**应规定竣工工程的特别要求，包括功能和操作要求、质量和范围。如果要求**承包商**提供某些物品，如消耗品或备件等，则应将这些物品列在**资料表**中。**雇主要求**的起草者必须记住，如果没有提及或未涵盖任何事项，则**承包商**完全可以免除与此类事项相关的任何责任。

下列**条款**具体参考了**雇主要求**中规定的事项。但是，**雇主**也有必要根据其他**条款**，在**雇主要求**中提供具体信息：

1.9	**现场**保存的出版物
1.12	**雇主**保留的知识产权
1.14	获得**雇主**的批准
4.1	工程所需的预期目标
4.5	指定**分包商**所需的详细资料
4.6	**现场**的其他承包商（以及其他人）
	雇主所需的文件
4.18	环境限制
4.19	**现场**可提供的电、水、燃气和其他服务
4.20	**雇主设备**和免费提供的材料
5.1	设计人员标准
5.2	所需的**承包商**文件，以及是否在批准**期**内进行审核
5.4	技术标准和施工法规
5.5	竣工图和其他**工程**记录
6.1	员工的雇用
6.6	人员设施
7.8	**土地（矿区）使用费**的支付
10.5	所需培训
11.1	试验标准

Many Sub-Clauses in the General Conditions make reference to data being contained in the Particular Conditions Part A – Contract Data. This is data which must be provided in the tender documents, and these Conditions of Contract assume that all such Contract Data will be provided by the Employer. If the Employer requires tenderers to provide any of the information required in the Contract Data, the tender documents must make this quite clear.

If the Employer requires tenderers to provide additional data or information, a convenient way of doing this is to provide a suitably worded questionnaire with the tender documents.

If selected tenderers are required to carry out any preliminary design or study prior to deciding on the award, Employers should also consider remunerating the tenderers involved for such work.

It is important for the Parties to understand which of the documents included in the tender dossier, and which of the documents submitted by tenderers, will form a part of the Contract to be awarded by the Employer. For example, the Instructions to Tenderers are not, by definition, a part of the Contract. They are simply instructions and information on the preparation and submission of the tender, and they should not contain anything of a binding or contractual nature.

Finally, when planning the overall programme, Employers must remember to allow a realistic time for tenderers to prepare and submit a responsive tender. Too short a time, and experienced contractors will not be prepared to tender, and too long a time will not be required and will be wasted.

Employers should also allow a realistic time for the review and evaluation of tenders and the award of the Contract to the successful tenderer. This will be the minimum time which tenderers should be asked to hold their tenders valid and open to acceptance.

很多**通用条件**中的**条款**都引用**专用条件**A部分——**合同数据**中的数据。招标文件必须提供该合同数据，并且**合同条件**认为所有此类**合同数据**将由雇主提供。如果**雇主**要求投标人提供**合同数据**需要的任何其他信息，则投标文件必须对此予以明确。

如果**雇主**要求投标人提供其他数据或信息，一种简便的方法是在提供招标文件时，也同时提供适当措辞的问卷。

如果选定的投标人需要在决定授予合同之前进行任何初步设计和研究，**雇主**还应考虑对参与此类工作的投标人给予报酬。

对双方而言，重要的是要了解招标文件中包含哪些文件，以及投标人提交的哪些文件将构成**雇主**授予**合同**的一部分。例如，根据定义，**投标人须知**不构成**合同**的一部分。它们只是有关投标准备和提交的须知和信息，不应包含任何具有约束力或合同性质的内容。

最后，在设计项目的总体进度计划时，**雇主**必须记住给投标人留出实际时间用于编写并提交响应性投标书。时间太短，经验丰富的承包商将不准备投标；而时间过长，就不需要了，会造成浪费。

雇主还应留出实际的时间对投标书进行评审，并将**合同**授予中标人。这将是要求投标人保持其投标书有效并接受的最短时间。

NOTES ON THE PREPARATION OF SPECIAL PROVISIONS

The following references and examples show some of the Sub-Clauses in the General Conditions which may need amending to suit the needs of the project or the requirements of the Employer. The selected Sub-Clauses and the example wording are included as examples only. They also include, as an aide-memoire, references to other documents such as the Employer's Requirements and Contract Data, where particular issues may need to be addressed.

The selected Sub-Clauses do not necessarily require changing and the example wording may not suit the particular needs of the project or the Employer. It is the responsibility of the drafter of the Special Provisions to ensure that the selection of the Clauses and the choice of wording is appropriate to fulfill the new requirements. Furthermore, there may be other Sub-Clauses, not mentioned below, which need to be amended. Great care must be taken when amending the wording of Sub-Clauses from the General Conditions, or adding new provisions, to ensure that the balance of obligations and rights of the Parties is not unintentionally compromised.

编写特别规定注意事项

以下引用和示例展示了**通用条件**中一些需要修改的**条款**,以满足项目需要或**雇主**要求。选定的**条款**和范例措辞仅作为示例提供。作为辅助备忘录,它们还包括对其他文件,如**雇主要求**和**合同数据**,其中可能需要解决特定问题。

选定的**条款**不一定需要修改,并且范例措辞可能不适合特定项目或**雇主**的需求。**特别规定**的起草者有责任保证,**条款**的选定和措辞的选择适合于满足新的要求。此外,可能还有下述未提到其他的**条款**需要修改。在修改**通用条件**中**条款**措辞或增加新的规定时,必须格外小心,以确保双方的义务和权利的平衡不会被无意损害。

Clause 1   General Provisions

Sub-Clause 1.1   Definitions

It is not recommended that any changes are made to the Definitions. This could have serious consequences on the interpretation of the document.

There are limited circumstances where some definitions may not be appropriate and may need changing or developing. For example, if the Site extends over two countries, the following changes could be considered.

EXAMPLE   1.1.25

                             "Country" means either xxxxx or yyyyy depending on the location to which the reference will apply.

EXAMPLE   1.1.50

                             "Local Currency" means the currency of (name of country) or (name of country).

If it is necessary to introduce new terminology into the text of the Special Provisions, this should be carefully and properly defined, commencing with Sub-Clause 1.1.84, for example:

EXAMPLE   1.1.84

                             "Safety Regulations" means the Employer's safety regulations existing on the Site which the Contractor is required to follow.

Sub-Clause 1.5   Priority of Documents

An order of precedence is usually necessary, in case a conflict is subsequently found among the contract documents. If no order of precedence is to be prescribed, this Sub-Clause may be varied:

EXAMPLE

                             Delete Sub-Clause 1.5 and substitute:

                             The documents forming the Contract are to be taken as mutually explanatory of one another. If an ambiguity or discrepancy is found, the priority shall be such as may be accorded by the governing law. The Employer's Representative has authority to issue any instruction which he considers necessary to resolve an ambiguity or discrepancy.

Sub-Clause 1.6   Contract Agreement

Entry into a formal Contract Agreement may be mandatory under the applicable law. In such a case, the words "unless they agree otherwise" should be deleted from the text.

第1条　　一般规定

第1.1款　　定义

不建议对**定义**进行任何修改，这可能对文件的解释产生严重影响。

在少数情况下，有些定义可能不适用，可能需要修改或延展。例如，如果**现场**跨越两国，建议考虑做以下修改。

范例　　　　1.1.25

"**工程所在国**"即可以指 X 国又可以指 Y 国，取决于引用适用的处所。

范例　　　　1.1.50

"**当地货币**"指（工程所在国名称）或（工程所在国名称）的货币。

如果有必要把新术语引入**特别规定**的文本，从**第1.1.84项**开始，应进行仔细、适当的定义，例如：

范例　　　　1.1.84

"**安全守则**"系指**承包商**必须遵守的**雇主**制订的**现场**安全规程。

第1.5条　　文件优先次序

如果随后发现合同文件之间存在冲突，通常需要优先顺序。如未规定优先顺序，则本**款**可修改为：

范例

删除**第1.5款**，代之以：

组成**合同**的各项文件将被认为是互作说明的。如出现模糊或歧义时，应按管辖法律确定先后顺序。**雇主代表**有权发出其认为必要的任何指示，解决此模糊或歧义。

第1.6款　　合同协议书

根据适用法律，签订正式**合同协议书**可能是强制性的。在这种情况下，"除非另有协议"的词句应该从文本中删除。

Sub-Clause 1.7 **Operating Licence**

If the required authorization is not in the form of an Operating Licence, or the terms according to the applicable law differ to the details given in the General Conditions, it may be necessary to provide more specific details regarding the form and nature of the authorization which the Employer will provide.

Sub-Clause 1.11 **Employer's Use of Contractor's Documents**

Additional provisions may be required, if all rights to particular items of computer software (for example) are to be assigned to the Employer. The provisions should take account of the applicable laws.

Sub-Clause 1.15 **Joint and Several Liability**

For a major contract, detailed requirements for the joint venture may need to be specified. These requirements, which tenderers will need to know when preparing their tenders, should be included in the Instructions to Tenderers. The Employer will wish the leader of the joint venture to be appointed at an early stage, providing a single point of contact thereafter, and will not wish to be involved in a dispute between the members of a joint venture. The Employer should scrutinise the joint venture agreement carefully, and it may have to be approved by the project's financing institutions.

Clause 2 The Employer

Sub-Clause 2.1 **Right of Access to the Site**

If right of access and possession of the Site cannot be granted in the normal way, details should be given in the Employer's Requirements.

Sub-Clause 2.3 **Employer's Personnel**

The provisions concerning cooperation between contractors should be reflected in the Employer's contracts with any other contractors on the Site.

Clause 3 The Employer's Representative

Sub-Clause 3.1 **Employer's Representative's Duties and Authority**

Any requirements for Employer's approval should be set out in these Special Conditions:

EXAMPLE

>The Employer's Representative shall obtain the specific approval of the Employer before taking action under the following Sub-Clauses of these Conditions:
>
>(a) Sub-Clause_____ *
>
>(b) Sub-Clause_____ *

* [*Insert number and describe specific procedure, where appropriate*]

If the obligation to obtain the approval of the Employer only applies beyond certain limits, financial or otherwise, the example wording should be varied accordingly.

This requirement should not be applied to Sub-Clause 3.5 [*Determinations*], where the Employer's Representative is required to act fairly.

第 1.7 款　　　　运营执照

如果所需的授权不是以**运营执照**的形式提供，或根据适用法律的条款与**通用条件**中给出的细节不同，可能有必要提供有关**雇主**将提供的授权形式和性质的更具体的详细情况。

第 1.11 款　　　　雇主使用承包商文件

如果要将计算机软件（比如说）的特定项目的所有权利都分配给**雇主**，可能需要附加规定。这些规定应考虑适用法律。

第 1.15　　　　共同的和各自的责任

对于重大合同，可能需要对联营体规定一些具体要求。投标人在编制投标书时需要了解这些要求，应包含在**投标人须知**中。**雇主**将希望早期指定联营体的负责方，以便此后有一个单独的联系方，避免卷入联营体成员间的争端。**雇主**应仔细审核联营体协议书，可能需要项目的融资机构批准。

第 2 条　　　　雇主

第 2.1 款　　　　现场进入权

如果**雇主**不能以正常方式赋予**现场**进入权和占有权，应在**雇主要求**中列出详情。

第 2.3 款　　　　雇主人员

承包商之间合作的有关规定，应反映在**雇主**与**现场**任何其他承包商的合同中。

第 3 条　　　　雇主代表

第 3.1 款　　　　雇主代表的任务和权利

任何需经**雇主**批准的要求应在**特别条件**中规定：

范例

　　　　　　　　雇主代表在根据本**条件**的以下各款采取措施前，应获得**雇主**的专门批准：

　　　　　　　　（a）　第 _____ * 款

　　　　　　　　（b）　第 _____ * 款

---
　　　　　　　　*［插入各款款号并在适用情况下，说明特别程序］

如果取得**雇主**同意的义务只适用于超出某些限制的范围，无论是资金（财务）上的还是其他方面的，则应相应地改变范例措辞。

这一要求不适用于**第 3.5 款**［*确定*］的规定，要求**雇主代表**公平行事。

Schedule of Meetings

It can be useful to give information in the Employer's Requirements of the planned schedule of meetings such as Management Meetings, Site Meetings, Technical Meetings, Progress Meetings, etc.

Clause 4   The Contractor

Sub-Clause 4.1   Contractor's General Obligations

The Employer's Requirements must contain a clear and specific purpose for which the facility will be used when complete, in order that the Contractor can comply with his obligation to provide Works which are 'fit for purpose'.

Sub-Clause 4.2   Performance Security

The acceptable form (s) of Performance Security should be included in the tender documents. Example forms are included in the section "Sample Forms" of this document. They incorporate two sets of Uniform Rules published by the International Chamber of Commerce (the "ICC", which is based at 38 Cours Albert 1er, 75008 Paris, France), which also publishes guides to these Uniform Rules. These example forms and the wording of the Sub-Clause may have to be amended to comply with applicable law.

EXAMPLE

> At the end of the second paragraph of Sub-Clause 4.2, insert:
>
> If the Performance Security is in the form of a bank guarantee, it shall be issued either (a) by a bank located in the Country, or (b) directly by a foreign bank acceptable to the Employer. If the Performance Security is not in the form of a bank guarantee, it shall be furnished by a financial entity registered, or licensed to do business, in the Country.

The tender documents should make it quite clear how the reduction in the amount of the Performance Security at the end of the Design-Build Period will be managed.

If separate, or staged, Performance Securities are required during the Operation Service Period, this Sub-Clause will need amending to reflect the appropriate requirements.

Sub-Clause 4.12   Unforeseeable Physical Conditions

In the case of major sub-surface works, the allocation of the risk of sub-surface conditions is an aspect which should be considered when tender documents are being prepared.

If this risk is to be shared between the Parties, the Sub-Clause may be amended:

EXAMPLE

> Delete sub-paragraph (b) of Sub-Clause 4.12 and substitute:
>
> (b) payment for any such Cost,_____percent (_____%) of which shall be included in the Contract Price (the balance _____percent (_____%) of the Cost shall be borne by the Contractor).

Sub-Clause 4.16   Transport of Goods

In some cases, the Contractor may be required to get permission prior to delivery. In such cases the following wording could be added:

会议时间计划表

雇主要求中提供会议时间计划表信息，如**管理会议、现场会议、技术会议和进度会议**等可能会很有益处。

第 4 条 承包商

第 4.1 款 承包商的一般义务

雇主要求中必须包含明确和特定目的以及竣工后设施的使用，以便**承包商**能够履行其提供本"适合预期目的"的工程的义务。

第 4.2 款 履约担保

招标文件中应包括可接受的**履约担保**格式。范例格式包括在"**格式**"一节。它们体现**国际商会**（"ICC"，总部位于法国巴黎 38 Cours Albert ler，75008 Paris，France）出版的两套**统一规则**，**国际商会**还出版了这些**统一规则**的指南。这些范例格式及**条款**的措辞可能需要进行修改，以符合适用法律。

范例

在**第 4.2 款**第二段末尾插入：

如果**履约担保**是银行保函的形式，它应（a）由**工程所在国**的银行，或（b）直接由雇主认可的外国银行出具。如**履约担保**不是银行保函的形式，应由在**工程所在国**注册或取得营业执照的金融实体提供。

招标文件应明确规定在**设计 - 施工期**结束时，如何减少**履约担保**的数额。

如果在**运营服务期**间内需要单独的或分阶段的**履约担保**，则需要修改本款以反映适当的要求。

第 4.12 款 不可预见的物质条件

对于涉及重大地下工程，地下条件的风险分配是编写招标文件时应考虑的一个方面。

如果双方分担这种风险，则该**款**可修改为：

范例

删除**第 4.12 款**（b）段，代之以：

（b）任何此类费用的支付，百分之＿＿＿＿（＿＿＿＿%）将计入**合同价格**[此费用剩余的百分之＿＿＿＿（＿＿＿＿%）应由**承包商**承担]。

第 4.16 款 货物运输

某些情况下，**承包商**把**货物**运到**现场**之前可能需要事先获得许可。在这种情况下，可以增加以下措辞：

EXAMPLE

>Insert at the end of Sub-Clause 4.16:
>
>The Contractor shall obtain permission in writing from the Employer's Representative prior to delivering any item of Goods to the Site. No Goods shall be delivered without this permission, which shall not relieve the Contractor from any obligation.

Clause 5   Design

Sub-Clause 5.1   General Design Obligations

If the Employer's Requirements include an outline design, tenderers should be advised of the extent to which the Employer's outline design is a suggestion or a requirement, and which parts, if any, are immutable.

Sub-Clause 5.2   Contractor's Documents

The Employer's Requirements should specify the extent to which Contractor's Documents are required, which of them are required for approval (not just review), and the submission procedures.

If different "review periods" are considered necessary, taking account of the time required to review the different types of drawing, and/or of the possibility of substantial submissions at particular stages of the design-build process, details should be given in these Particular Conditions.

Clause 6   Staff and Labour

Sub-Clause 6.6   Facilities for Staff and Labour

If the Employer plans to make office accommodation available for the Contractor, for example, during the Operation Service Period, details should be given in the Employer's Requirements.

See also Clause 17 [*Risk Allocation*] for suggested provisions regarding care of such facilities.

Sub-Clause 6.8   Contractor's Superintendence

If the ruling language is not the same as the language for day-to-day communications (under Sub-Clause 1.4 [*Law and Language*]), or if for any other reason it is necessary to stipulate that the Contractor's superintending staff shall be fluent in a particular language, the following sentence may be added.

EXAMPLE

>Insert at the end of Sub-Clause 6.8:
>
>A reasonable proportion of the Contractor's superintending staff shall have a working knowledge of
>
>[*Insert name of language*],
>
>or the Contractor shall have a sufficient number of competent interpreters available on Site during working hours.

范例

在**第 4.16 款**末尾插入：

任何**货物**在运到**现场**之前，**承包商**应获得**雇主代表**的事先的书面许可。没有这样的许可，不得发运任何**货物**，这些均不应减轻**承包商**的任何义务。

第 5 条　　　　设计

第 5.1 款　　　设计义务一般要求

如果**雇主要求**包括框架设计，投标人应被告知**雇主**的框架设计范围是建议还是要求，以及哪些部分，如果有，是不可变的。

第 5.2 款　　　承包商文件

雇主要求应明确规定**承包商文件**的要求范围，哪些文件需要批准（不仅是审核），以及提交程序。

如果考虑到审核不同类型的图纸所需的时间和/或设计-施工过程中特定阶段的实质性提交的可能性，如果认为有必要设定不同的"审核期"，应在**专用条件**中详细说明。

第 6 条　　　　员工

第 6.6 款　　　为员工提供设施

如果**雇主**计划向**承包商**提供办公室住所，例如在**运营服务期**间，应在**雇主要求**中提供详细信息。

有关照管此类设施的建议规定，请参见**第 17 条**［*风险分配*］。

第 6.8 款　　　承包商的监督

如果主导语言与日常交流语言不同（根据**第 1.4 款**［*法律和语言*］的规定），或由于任何其他原因，有必要规定**承包商**的监督人员应能流利使用某种特定语言，则应增加以下词句。

范例

在**第 6.8 款**末尾，插入：

合理比例的**承包商**的监督人员应具备

［*插入语言名称*］的工作知识，

或，**承包商**应在所有工作时间在**现场**有足够数量胜任的翻译。

Clause 7 — Plant, Materials and Workmanship

Additional Sub-Clause

If the Contract is being financed by an institution whose rules or policies require a restriction on the use of its funds, a further sub-clause may be added:

EXAMPLE SUB-CLAUSE

> All Goods shall have their origin in eligible source countries as defined in
>
> [*Insert name of published guidelines for procurement*].
>
> Goods shall be transported by carriers from these eligible source countries, unless exempted by the Employer in writing on the basis of potential excessive costs or delays. Surety, insurance and banking services shall be provided by insurers and bankers from the eligible source countries.

Clause 8 — Commencement, Delays and Suspension

Sub-Clause 8.2 — Time for Completion

If the Works are to be commissioned in stages, these stages should be defined as Sections, in the Contract Data.

Sub-Clause 8.5 — Delay Damages

Under many legal systems (notably in common law jurisdictions), the amount of these pre-defined damages must represent a reasonable pre-estimate of the Employer's probable loss in the event of delay. If the Accepted Contract Amount is to be quoted as the sum of figures in more than one currency, it may be preferable to define these damages (per day) as the percentage reduction which would be applied to each of these figures.

If the Accepted Contract Amount is expressed in the Local Currency, the damages per day may either be defined as a percentage or be defined as a figure in Local Currency: see Sub-Clause 14.17 (b).

Clause 10 — Operation Service

Sub-Clause 10.2 — Commencement of Operation Service

If there are known reasons why the Operation Service Period cannot commence upon the issue of the Commissioning Certificate, the first paragraph may deleted and replaced by the following:

EXAMPLE

> Notwithstanding the issue of the Commissioning Certificate, the Operation Service shall not commence until the Contractor receives a written instruction to commence from the Employer's Representative. Such instruction shall be issued within 28 days of the date of issue of the Commissioning Certificate.

第 7 条　　生产设备、材料和工艺

附加条款

如果合同由规则或政策要求限制其资金使用的机构提供资金，可以增加以下条款：

范例条款

> 所有**货物**应来源于
>
> *[插入已发布的采购指南名称]*。
>
> 除**雇主**基于潜在的超额费用或延误而书面豁免外，**货物**应由合法来源国的承运人运输。保证金、保险和银行服务应由合法来源国的保险公司和银行提供。

第 8 条　　开工日期、竣工和进度计划

第 8.2 款　　竣工时间

如果**工程**要分阶段进行调试，这些阶段应在**合同数据**中规定为**分项工程**。

第 8.5 款　　误期损害赔偿费

根据许多法律体系（特别是在普通司法管辖区），这些事先规定的损害赔偿费的数额，必须是在延误情况下给雇主造成的预期损失的合理估算。如果**中标合同金额**是多种货币的总和，最好将这些损害赔偿费（按天）确定为适用于每个货币数字的百分比。

如果**中标合同金额**以当地货币表示，每天的损害赔偿费可确定为百分比，也可确定为**当地货币**中的数字：请参阅**第 14.17 款**（b）段。

第 10 条　　运营服务

第 10.2 款　　运营服务的开始

如果有已知原因无法在签发**调试证书**后开始**运营服务**期，可删除第一段，并替换为以下内容：

范例

> 尽管已签发**调试证书**，但在**承包商**收到**雇主代表**的书面开工指示之前，不应开始**运营服务**。此类指示应在**调试证书**签发之日起 28 天内发出。

Clause 11 Testing

Sub-Clause 11.4 **Failure to Pass Tests on Completion of Design-Build**

If the failure is such that the facility can still be operated and used, the Employer may choose to accept the failure and impose non-performance damages. These damages can be tabulated against the required performance criteria in the Contract Data, and a sub-paragraph (c) could be added to Sub-Clause 11.4 [*Failure to Pass Tests on Completion of Design-Build*] as follows:

EXAMPLE

> (c) issue the Commissioning Certificate to the Contractor subject to the payment of the non-performance damages specified in the Contract Data.

Clause 13 Variations and Adjustments

Sub-Clause 13.5 **Provisional Sums**

Provisional Sums may be required for parts of the Works which are not required to be priced at the risk of the Contractor. For example, a Provisional Sum may be necessary to cover goods which the Employer wants to select, or to deal with a major uncertainty regarding sub-surface conditions. It is essential to define the scope of each Provisional Sum (possibly in a Schedule prepared by the Employer), since the defined scope will then be excluded from the other elements of the Accepted Contract Amount.

Clause 14 Contract Price and Payment

The provisions of Clause 14 [*Contract Price and Payment*] should be carefully studied to see that they are acceptable to both the Employer and any financing institution he may be using to fund the project. In particular the Employer's procedures and timing for making payments should be checked to see that they comply within the wording in Clause 14. If they do not, the wording in Clause 14 may need to be changed. For example if the times for payment given in Sub-Clause 14.8 [*Payment*] cannot be met, it will be necessary to change the times given.

If expatriate staff are exempted from paying local income tax, a suitable sub-clause will need adding. However, advice should be sought from a qualified tax expert before drafting any such sub-clause.

Additional Sub-Clause

EXAMPLE SUB-CLAUSE

> Expatriate (foreign) personnel shall not be liable for income tax levied in the Country on earnings paid in any foreign currency, or for income tax levied on subsistence, rentals and similar services directly furnished by the Contractor to Contractor's Personnel, or for allowances in lieu. If any Contractor's Personnel have part of their earnings paid in the Country in a foreign currency, they may export (after the conclusion of their term of service on the Works) any balance remaining of their earnings paid in foreign currencies.
>
> The Employer shall seek exemption for the purposes of this Sub-Clause. If it is not granted, the relevant taxes paid shall be reimbursed by the Employer.

第 11 条　　试验

第 11.4 款　　未能通过设计 - 施工竣工试验

如果违约导致设施仍能运营和使用，**雇主**可选择接受违约并对其处以违约赔偿金。这些损害赔偿金可根据**合同数据**中要求的性能标准制成表格，并可在**第 11.4 款**[*未能通过设计 - 施工竣工试验*]中增加（c）段，如下所示：

范例

（c）向**承包商**签发调试证书，但须支付**合同数据**中规定的违约赔偿金。

第 13 条　　变更和调整

第 13.5 款　　暂列金额

工程的某些部分可能需要**暂列金额**，**暂列金额**不要求**承包商**承担定价风险。例如，**暂列金额**可能是必要的，以涵盖**雇主**想要选择的货物，或应对地下条件的重大不确定性。规定每项**暂列金额**的范围是非常重要的（可能在雇主编制的**资料表**中），因为规定范围的每项**暂定余额**的数额将从**中标合同金额**的其他要素中排除。

第 14 条　　合同价格和付款

应仔细研究检查**第 14 条**[*合同价格和付款*]的规定，以确保**雇主**和雇主可能用于资助项目的任何融资机构都可以接受。特别应检查**雇主**的付款程序和时间安排，以确保其符合**第 14 条**的措辞。如果未能符合，**第 14 条**中的措辞可能需要修改。例如，如果不能满足**第 14.8 款**[*付款*]中规定的付款时间安排，则有必要改变规定的时间安排。

如果外籍员工免缴当地所得税，则应增加适当条款。但是，在起草任何此类条款前，应咨询合格的税务专家。

附加条款

范例条款

外籍（外国）人员不应对在**工程所在国**以任何外币支付的收入缴纳所得税，也不应对**承包商**直接向**承包商人员**提供的生活、租金和类似服务以及补贴缴纳所得税。如果**承包商人员**在**工程所在国**的收入中有一部分是以外币支付的，则他们可以（在其工程服务期限结束后）输出以外币支付的任何余额。

就本**款**而言，**雇主**应寻求豁免。如果不予批准，则相关税款应由**雇主**报销。

Clause 15 — Termination by Employer

Sub-Clause 15.2 — Termination by Employer

Before inviting tenders, the Employer should verify that the wording of this Sub-Clause, and each anticipated ground for termination, is consistent with the law governing the Contract.

Clause 16 — Suspension and Termination by Contractor

Sub-Clause 16.2 — Termination by Contractor

Before inviting tenders, the Employer should verify that the wording of this Sub-Clause is consistent with the law governing the Contract. The Contractor should verify that each anticipated ground for termination is consistent with such law.

Clause 17 — Risk Allocation

Additional Sub-Clause — Use of Employer's Accommodation/Facilities

If the Contractor is to occupy the Employer's facilities and/or accommodation during the Operation Service Period or any other period during the Contract, it may be necessary to add an additional sub-clause to cover his responsibilities for care.

EXAMPLE SUB-CLAUSE

> The Contractor shall take full care of the items listed below from the date of use or occupation by the Contractor until the date on which such use or occupation is re-vested in the Employer.
>
> [List of items and details]
>
> If any loss or damage happens to any of the above items whilst the Contractor is responsible for their care, arising from any cause other than a cause for which the Employer is responsible or liable, the Contractor shall, at his own cost, rectify such loss or damage to the condition prior to such loss or damage occurring.

Clause 19 — Insurance

If the Employer wishes to change the insurance provisions – for example by providing some of the insurance cover himself – it will be necessary to review and revise some of the provisions in Clause 19 [Insurance]. If this is the case, it is strongly recommended that a professional with extensive experience in construction insurance and liability should prepare the revised sub-clauses. If the insurance provisions are changed without due care and attention, there is a risk that the Employer will find himself carrying liabilities for which he is neither prepared nor covered.

Clause 20 — Claims, Disputes and Arbitration

Sub-Clause 20.3 — Appointment of the Dispute Adjudication Board

The adjudication procedure depends for its success on, amongst other things, the Parties' confidence in the agreed individual (s) who will serve on the DAB. Therefore, it is essential that candidates for this position are not imposed by either Party on the other Party. Furthermore, if the individual is selected under Sub-Clause 20.4 [Failure to Agree Dispute Adjudication Board], the selection should be made by a wholly impartial entity with an understanding of the nature and purpose of a DAB. FIDIC is prepared to perform this role, and maintains a list of approved and experienced adjudicators.

第 15 条   由雇主终止

第 15.2 款   由承包商违约的终止

邀标前，**雇主**应保证，本**款**的措辞以及终止的预期理由均符合管辖**合同**的法律。

第 16 条   由承包商暂停和终止

第 16.2 款   由承包商终止

邀标前，**雇主**应保证，本**款**的措辞以及终止的预期理由均符合管辖**合同**的法律。**承包商**应核实每个终止的预期理由是否符合此类法律。

第 17 条   风险分配

附加条款   使用雇主住所 / 设施

如果**承包商**在**运营服务**期间或**合同**期间的任何其他期间占用**雇主**的设施和 / 或住所，则可需要增加一项附加条款，以包括其照管责任。

范例条款

> 从**承包商**使用或占有之日起至**雇主**收回使用或占有权为止，**承包商**应对下列物品负全责。
>
> ［项目清单和详细信息］
>
> **承包商**负责照管期间，如因**雇主**负责以外的原因而使上述任何物品发生任何损失或损害，**承包商**应自费在此类损失或损害发生前纠正此类损失或损害。

第 19 条   保险

如果**雇主**希望修改保险条款——例如，**雇主**提供某些保险——则有必要审核和修订**第 19 条**［*保险*］中的一些规定。在此情况下，强烈建议应由施工保险和责任方面具有丰富经验的专业人员，编制修改的条款。如果在没有适当注意和关注的情况下修改保险条款，**雇主**有可能会发现其承担了未提供也未投保的责任。

第 20 条   索赔、争端和仲裁

第 20.3 款   争端裁决委员会的任命

争端程序的成功，在许多因素中取决于双方对商定的、将在**争端裁决委员会**任职的个人的信心。因此，至关重要的是，任何一方都不得将这一职位的候选人强加给另一方。此外，如果该人员是根据**第 20.4 款**［*对争端裁决委员会未能取得一致*］的规定选定的，应由了解**争端裁决委员会**性质和目的、完全公正的实体进行选择。菲迪克（FIDIC）准备履行这一职责，并保留有一份经批准的且经验丰富的裁决员名单。

Sub-Clause 20.3 [*Appointment of the Dispute Adjudication Board*] provides for two alternative arrangements for the Dispute Adjudication Board.

(a) one person, who acts as the sole member of the DAB, having entered into a tripartite agreement with both Parties; or

(b) a DAB of three persons, each of whom has entered into a tripartite agreement with both Parties.

A recommended form of this tripartite agreement is shown at the end of this document (in the section "Sample Forms"). This agreement incorporates (by reference) the General Conditions of Dispute Adjudication Agreement, which are included in this document (in the section "General Conditions"). They are also incorporated by reference in Sub-Clause 20.3 [*Appointment of the Dispute Adjudication Board*] of the General Conditions.

Before the Contract is entered into, consideration should be given as to whether a one-person or three-person DAB is preferable for a particular project, taking account of its size, duration and the fields of expertise which will be involved.

Sub-Clause 20.4   Failure to Agree Dispute Adjudication Board

It is essential that any entity or official named in the Contract as the 'appointing entity' is suitably qualified and willing to act in that capacity, and accepts to do so prior to naming them in the Contract. Examples of suitable persons able to fill this role include the President of FIDIC and the International Chamber of Commerce.

Sub-Clause 20.8   Arbitration

The Contract should include provisions for the resolution by international arbitration of any Disputes which are not resolved amicably. In international engineering contracts, international commercial arbitration has numerous advantages over litigation in national courts, and may be more acceptable to the Parties.

Careful consideration should be given to ensuring that the international arbitration rules chosen are compatible with the provisions of Clause 20 [*Claims, Disputes and Arbitration*] and with the other elements to be set out in the Contract Data. The Rules of Arbitration of the International Chamber of Commerce (the "ICC", which is based at 38 Cours Albert 1er, 75008 Paris, France) are frequently included in international contracts.

It is important that the Parties agree upon the number of arbitrators and the language of arbitration. If these are not stipulated by the Parties in the Contract, the International Court of Arbitration of the ICC will decide on these issues.

If the UNCITRAL (or other non-ICC) arbitration rules are preferred, it may be necessary to designate, in the Contract Data, an institution to appoint the arbitrators or to administer the arbitration, unless the institution is named (and its role is specified) in the arbitration rules.

For major projects tendered internationally, it is desirable that the place of arbitration be situated in a country other than that of the Employer or the Contractor. This country should have a modern and liberal arbitration law and should have ratified a bilateral or multilateral convention (such as the 1958 *New York Convention on the Recognition and Enforcement of Foreign Arbitral Awards*), or both, that would facilitate the enforcement of an arbitral award in the states of the Parties.

It may be considered desirable in some cases for other parties to be joined into any arbitration between the Parties, thereby creating a multi-party arbitration. While this may be feasible, multi-party arbitration clauses require skilful drafting, and usually need to be prepared on a case-by-case basis by a suitably qualified lawyer.

第 20.3 款［*争端裁决委员会的任命*］规定了**争端裁决委员会**的两种备选安排：

（a） 一人，作为**争端裁决委员会**的唯一成员，已与双方签订了三方协议书；（或）

（b） 由三人组成的**争端裁决委员会**，其中每个人都与双方签订了三方协议书。

该三方协议书的推荐格式见本文件最后（见"**样本格式**"一节）。本协议书纳入（参考）**争端裁决协议书一般条件**，这些条款包含在本文件（在"**一般条件**"一节中）中。它们也通过引用纳入**通用条件**第 20.3 款［*争端裁决委员会的任命*］中。

在签订**合同**之前，应根据每个项目的规模、期限和所涉及的专业技术领域，考虑选用由一人或三人组成的**争端裁决委员会**。

第 20.4 款　　　　对争端裁决委员会未能取得一致

合同中指名为"**任命实体**"的任何实体或官员，必须具备适当的资格并愿意以这种身份行事，并在**合同**中指定他们之前接受这样做。能够胜任这一角色的合适人选的例子，包括**菲迪克（FIDIC）主席**和**国际商会主席**。

第 20.8 款　　　　仲裁

合同应包括通过国际仲裁解决任何未能友好解决的**争端**的规定。在国际工程合同中，与国家法院的诉讼相比，国际商事仲裁具有很多优势，并更可能被双方接受。

应仔细考虑确保选择的国际仲裁规则与**第 20 条**［*索赔、争端和仲裁*］的规定以及**合同数据**中列出的其他要素相一致。**国际商会**（"**ICC**"，其总部位于法国巴黎 38 Cours Albert ler，75008 Paris，France）发布的**仲裁规则**，通常会包含在国际合同中。

双方必须就仲裁员人数和仲裁语言达成一致，这一点很重要。如果双方在**合同**中未规定，**国际商会**的**国际仲裁法院**将决定这些事项。

如果采用**联合国国际贸易法委员会**（**UNCITRAL**）（或其他非**国际商会**）仲裁规则，可能有必要在**合同数据**中指定一家机构任命仲裁员或管理仲裁，除非仲裁规则中提名该机构（并规定其职能）。

对于国际招标的重大项目，仲裁地最好位于**雇主**或**承包商**以外的国家。该国应有一部现代自由的仲裁法，并应已经批准了一项双边或多边公约（例如 1958 年《*承认和执行外国仲裁裁决的纽约公约*》），或者同时批准了这两项公约，这将有利于仲裁裁决在双方所在国的执行。

某些情况下，其他方可能更希望参加双方之间的任何仲裁，从而形成多方仲裁。尽管这可能是可行的，但多方当事方仲裁条款起草需要技巧，通常需要由具有适当资格的律师逐案进行起草。

Sub-Clause 20.10   Disputes Arising during the Operation Service Period

As an alternative to the five-year appointment envisaged in Sub-Clause 20.10 [*Disputes Arising during the Operation Service Period*], the Operation Service DAB could be appointed on an ad-hoc basis, if and when any Dispute arises during this period. In such a case, the DAB would be appointed when a Dispute arises, and would cease its appointment on the issue of its decision in respect of such Dispute. Should a new Dispute arise, a new ad-hoc DAB would be appointed.

The wording of Sub-Clause 20.10 to reflect this could be along the following lines:

EXAMPLE

> Disputes arising during the Operation Service Period which cannot be resolved between the Parties shall be settled by a one person ad-hoc DAB ("Operation Service DAB"). Such person shall be jointly agreed and appointed by the Parties by the date 28 days after one Party has given Notice to the other Party of its intention to refer a Dispute to a DAB in accordance with Sub-Clause 20.10 [*Disputes Arising during the Operation Service Period*].
>
> If the Parties cannot agree on the person who shall be the Operation Service DAB, then the person shall be appointed according to the provisions of Sub-Clause 20.4 [*Failure to Agree Dispute Adjudication Board*].
>
> The agreement between the Parties and the Operation Service DAB shall incorporate by reference the General Conditions of Dispute Adjudication Agreement contained in the General Conditions odf Contract, with such amendments as are agreed between them.
>
> The terms of remuneration of the Operation Service DAB shall be mutually agreed upon by the Parties when agreeing the terms of appointment. Each Party shall be responsible for paying one-half of this remuneration.
>
> The procedure for obtaining a decision from the Operation Service DAB shall be in accordance with the provisions of Sub-Clause 20.6 [*Obtaining Dispute Adjudication Board's Decision*], and the DAB shall give its decision no later than 84 days after receiving the response or, if no response is submitted, 105 days after receiving the reference and the supporting documentation from the Parties.
>
> The appointment of the Operation Service DAB shall expire 28 days after it has given its decision in writing to both Parties.
>
> If either Party is dissatisfied with the decision of the Operation Service DAB, the provisions of Sub-Clauses 20.6 [*Obtaining Dispute Adjudication Board's Decision*], 20.7 [*Amicable Settlement*], 20.8 [*Arbitration*] and 20.9 [*Failure to Comply with Dispute Adjudication Board's Decision*] shall apply.

第 20.10 款　　　　运营服务期间发生的争端

作为**第 20.10 款**[*运营服务期间发生的争端*]中所设想的 5 年任期的替代方案，如果在此期间发生任何**争端**，**运营服务争端裁决委员会**可临时任命。在这种情况下，在**争端**发生时将任命**争端裁决委员会**，并将在其就该**争端**做出决定的问题上停止其任命。如果出现新的**争端**，将任命一个新的临时**争端裁决委员会**。

为反映这一点，**第 20.10 款**的措辞可大致如下：

范例

在**运营服务期**间发生的双方无法解决的**争端**，应由一人组成的临时**争端裁决委员会**（"**运营服务争端裁决委员会**"）解决。根据**第 20.10 款**[*运营服务期间发生的争端*]的规定，在一方向另一方发出将**争端**提交**争端裁决委员会**的**通知**后 28 天内，双方应共同商定和任命该人员。

如果双方不能就**运营服务争端裁决委员会**的人选商定一致，则应根据**第 20.4 款**[*对争端裁决委员会未能取得一致*]的规定任命该人员。

双方与**运营服务争端裁决委员会**之间的协议书，应采用**合同通用条件**中包含的**争端裁决协议书一般条件**，以及双方商定的修正案。

运营服务争端裁决委员会的报酬条款，应由双方在商定任命条款时共同商定。各方应负责支付一半的报酬。

从**运营服务争端裁决委员会**取得决定的程序，应符合**第 20.6 款**[*取得争端裁决委员会的决定*]的规定，并且**争端裁决委员会**应在收到答复后 84 天内做出决定，或如果没有提交答复，在收到双方提供的参考和证明文件后 105 天内做出决定。

运营服务争端裁决委员会的任命，应在其以书面形式向双方做出决定后 28 天期满。

如果任何一方对**运营服务争端裁决委员会**的决定不满意，**第 20.6 款**[*取得争端裁决委员会的决定*]、**第 20.7 款**[*友好解决*]、**第 20.8 款**[*仲裁*]和**第 20.9 款**[*未能遵守争端裁决委员会的决定*]的规定应适用。

设计、施工和运营合同条件

Conditions of Contract for
DESIGN, BUILD AND OPERATE PROJECTS

样本格式
Sample Forms

引言
INTRODUCTION

通用条件
GENERAL CONDITIONS

专用条件
PARTICULAR CONDITIONS

样本格式
SAMPLE FORMS

Sample Forms

CONTENTS

INTRODUCTION 256

SAMPLE FORMS OF TENDER AND AGREEMENT 258

    Letter of Tender

    Letter of Acceptance

    Contract Agreement

    Agreement for Dispute Adjudication Board Members

    Agreement for Operation Service Dispute Adjudication Board

    Operating Licence (Aide Memoire)

SAMPLE FORMS OF SECURITY AND GUARANTEE 274

    Tender Security

    Parent Company Guarantee

    Performance Security - Demand Guarantee

    Performance Security - Surety Bond

    Advance Payment Guarantee

    Maintenance Retention Guarantee

样本格式

目　　录

引言 ··· 257
投标函和协议书样本格式 ··· 259
　　投标函
　　中标函
　　合同协议书
　　争端裁决委员会成员协议书
　　运营服务争端裁决委员会协议书
　　运营执照（许可证）
担保和保函样本格式 ·· 275
　　投标保函
　　母公司保函
　　履约担保——即付保函
　　履约担保——担保保证书
　　预付款保函
　　维护保留金保函

Introduction

The following Sample Forms are the forms referred to in the Contract documents and show formats which are acceptable under most jurisdictions.

The proposed forms should be included in the tender documents so that tenderers know what is required from them.

The sample forms of security (other than the form of Parent Company Guarantee) incorporate Uniform Rules published by the International Chamber of Commerce (the ICC, which is based at 38 Cours Albert 1er, 75008 Paris, France).

The attached sample forms of Security are prepared to cover the Design-Build Period. The provisions of Sub-Clause 4.2 [*Performance Security*] require a performance security to cover the full Contract Period. However it is recognized that this requirement may vary considerably from project to project and from Employer to Employer.

- Some Employers may not require a Performance Security during the Operation Service Period.
- Some Employers may require an on-going Security with a reduced value.
- Some Employers may require a new Security for the full Operation Service Period.
- Some Employers may require a short term renewable Security to cover the Operation Service Period.

There are many options and alternatives.

For this reason, the sample forms included in this section only cover the Design-Build Period, and it is up to the drafter of the tender and contract documents to prepare appropriate provisions to suit the needs of the Employer and, where required, the financial institution which is funding the project. It is essential when preparing extended securities to obtain professional help to ensure that the proposed form is secure and binding on the parties, and it is recommended that all securities and guarantees shall incorporate, and be subject to the applicable Uniform Rules published by the International Chamber of Commerce.

When using or amending any of these sample forms, care must be taken to ensure that the format and wording of the forms to be incorporated into the Contract are not only appropriate, but also comply with the applicable laws.

It is recommended that professional and legal advice should be taken before incorporating or amending any of the sample forms provided.

The Operating Licence is in the form of a short aide memoire since the Licence Agreement itself will need to reflect not only the particular requirements of the Employer, but also the legal requirements to ensure that the Contractor has the continuing right of lawful entry and use during the Operation Service Period.

引言

以下**样本格式**是**合同**文件中提及的格式，表明了大多数司法管辖区都可接受的格式。

建议的格式应包括在投标文件中，以便投标人知道他们从中需要得到什么。

担保函样本格式（**母公司保函**除外），采用了**国际商会**（ICC，总部位于法国巴黎 38 Cours Alber 1er，75008 Paris，France）发布的**统一规则**。

所附的**保函**样本格式用于涵盖**设计 - 施工期**。第 4.2 款 [*履约担保*] 的规定要求履约担保涵盖整个**合同期**。可是人们认识到，这一要求可能因项目到另一个项目，因**雇主**到另一个**雇主**会有很大的不同。

- 一些**雇主**可能不要求在**运营服务期**间提供**履约担保**。

- 一些**雇主**可能会要求一份价值较低的长期**保函**。
- 一些**雇主**可能要求在整个**运营服务期**提供新的**保函**。
- 一些**雇主**可能要求短期可续保的**保函**以涵盖**运营服务期**。

有很多的选项和备选方案。

由于这个原因，本节包含的样本格式仅涵盖**设计 - 施工期**，由招标和合同文件的起草者决定适当的规定，以满足**雇主**和（如有需要）为项目提供资金的金融机构的需要。在准备延长担保时，必须获得专业人员的帮助，以确保拟用的格式是安全的，并对双方具有约束力，建议所有担保和保函应采纳并遵守**国际商会**公布的适用**统一规则**。

在使用或修改任何此类样本格式时，必须注意确保拟采纳**合同表格**的格式和措辞不仅适当，而且符合适用法律。

建议在采纳或修改所提供的任何样本格式之前，应咨询专业和法律意见。

运营执照采用简短备忘录的形式，因为**执照协议书**本身不仅需要反映**雇主**的特殊要求，还需要反映法律的要求，以确保**承包商**在**运营服务期**间拥有持续的合法进入和使用权。

Sample Forms of Tender and Agreement

LETTER OF TENDER

Name of Contract: _____

Contract No.: _____

To: _____

We have examined the Conditions of Contract, Employer's Requirements, Schedules, Contract Data, and the attached Appendices and Addenda Nos _____
for the above-named Contract. We have understood and checked these documents and have ascertained that they contain no errors or other defects except as identified in our Tender. We accordingly offer to design, execute and complete the Works and remedy any defects therein so that they are fit for the purposes defined in the Contract, and to operate and maintain the facility under licence from the Employer for the period and in conformity with the terms and conditions contained in the Contract for the lump sum amount of

_____
(*currency and amount in figures*)

_____
(*currency and amount in words*)

or such other amount as may be determined in accordance with the Contract.

This amount is made up of the following components:

For the Design-Build of the Works, the amount of: _____

_____
(*currency and amount in figures*)

_____
(*currency and amount in words*)

For the Operation Service, the amount of: _____

_____
(*currency and amount in figures*)

_____
(*currency and amount in words*)

For the Asset Replacement Fund, the amount of: _____

_____
(*currency and amount in figures*)

_____
(*currency and amount in words*)

We agree to abide by this Tender until _____ (*date*) and it shall remain binding upon us and may be accepted at any time before that date.

If this offer is accepted, we will provide the required Performance Security, and commence and complete the Works, and provide the Operation Service, in accordance with the above-named documents and the agreed programme.

We further undertake, together with the Employer, to jointly appoint the DAB and the Auditing Body in accordance with the requirements of the Contract.

投标函和协议书样本格式

投标函

合同名称：_____

合同编号：_____

致：_____

我方已研究了上述合同的**合同条件、雇主要求、资料表、合同数据**及第 _____ 号**补充文件**。我方已理解和检查了这些文件，除我方**投标书**中确定的文件外，并确定它们没有错误或其他缺陷。我方因此提议设计、施工和**工程**竣工并修补其中的任何缺陷，使其适合**合同**规定的目的，并在按照**雇主**的执照运营和维护设施，期限和条件符合**合同**中的条款和条件，总价为

                 _____

                 的总额（*货币和用数字表示的金额*）

                 _____

                    （*货币和用文字表示的金额*）

或按照**合同**可能确定的另外金额。

该金额由以下部分组成：

对于**工程**的**设计 - 施工**，金额为： _____

                  （*货币和用数字表示的金额*）

                 _____

                  （*货币和用文字表示的金额*）

对于**运营服务**，金额为：   _____

                  （*货币和用数字表示的金额*）

                 _____

                  （*货币和用文字表示的金额*）

对于**资产置换基金**，金额为： _____

                  （*货币和用数字表示的金额*）

                 _____

                  （*货币和用文字表示的金额*）

我方同意遵守本**投标书**直至_____（*日期*），在该日期前，本**投标书**对我方一直具有约束力，随时可接受中标。

如果我方中标，我方将提供所需的**履约担保**，并按照上述文件和商定的计划，开工和**工程**竣工，并提供**运营服务**。

我方进一步承诺，将根据合同要求，与**雇主**共同任命**争端裁决委员会**和**审计机构**。

Unless and until a formal Contract Agreement is prepared and executed, this Letter of Tender, together with your written acceptance thereof, shall constitute a binding Contract between us.

We understand that you are not bound to accept the lowest or any tender you may receive.

Signed by: ....
(*signature*)

in the capacity of: ....

duly authorised to sign tenders for and on behalf of: ....

Address: ....
....
....

Date: ....

除非并直到制定正式**合同协议书**和实施，本**投标函**以及你方书面中标通知，应构成你我双方间具有约束力的**合同**。

我方理解你方没有必须接受你方可能收到的最低标或任何投标的义务。

签字人：　　　　　_____
　　　　　　　　　　　　　　　　（签字）

职务：　　　　_____

正式授权签署投标书代表：_____

地址：　　　　_____
　　　　　　　_____
　　　　　　　_____

日期：　　　　_____

LETTER OF ACCEPTANCE

Name of Contract: ....

Contract Number.: ....

To: ....

Date:

Your Reference: ....

Our Reference: ....

We thank you for your Tender dated .... for the design, execution and completion of the Works comprising the above-named Contract and remedying of defects therein so that they are fit for the purposes defined in the Contract, and for the operation and maintenance thereof under licence for the period of .... years, all in conformity with the terms and conditions contained in the Contract as amended by the attached Memorandum, signed by you and ourselves.

We have pleasure in accepting your Tender (as corrected/adjusted in accordance with the Memorandum) for the Accepted Contract Amount of:

....
(*currency and amount in figures*)

....
(*currency and amount in words*)

This amount is made up of the following components:

For the Design-Build of the Works, the amount of:

....
(*currency and amount in figures*)

....
(*currency and amount in words*)

For the Operation Service, the amount of:

....
(*currency and amount in figures*)

....
(*currency and amount in words*)

For the Asset Replacement Fund, the amount of:

....
(*currency and amount in figures*)

....
(*currency and amount in words*)

In consideration of you properly and truly performing the Contract, we agree to pay you the Accepted Contract Amount or such other sums to which you may become entitled under the terms of the Contract, at such times and as prescribed by the Contract.

中标函

合同名称： _____

合同编号： _____

致： _____

日期：

贵方函件编号： _____

我方函件编号： _____

我方感谢贵方于 _____（日期）提交的**投标书**，该**投标书**就上述合同所组成**工程**设计、施工和竣工，对其中的缺陷进行修补，以使其满足**合同**规定的目的，并按照执照运营和维护，有效期为 _____ 年，均符合**合同**中的条款以及由贵方和我方签署的随附**备忘录**修订的**合同**中包含的条件。

我方高兴地接受贵方的**投标书**（根据**备忘录**进行改正/调整），**中标合同金额**为：

_____
（货币及用数字表示的金额）

_____
（货币及用文字表示的金额）

该金额由以下部分组成：

对于工程的设计-施工，金额为：

_____
（货币和用数字表示的金额）

_____
（货币和用文字表示的金额）

对于运营服务，金额为：

_____
（货币和用数字表示的金额）

_____
（货币和用文字表示的金额）

对于资产置换基金，金额为：

_____
（货币和用数字表示的金额）

_____
（货币和用文字表示的金额）

考虑到贵方正确而真实地履行**合同**，我方同意按合同规定的时间和次数向贵方支付**中标合同金额**，或**合同**条款规定的贵方可能有权获得的其他此类金额。

We acknowledge that this Letter of Acceptance creates a binding Contract between us, and we undertake to fulfil all our obligations and duties in accordance with the terms of this Contract.

Signed by: ....
(*signature*)

For and behalf of: ....

Date: ....

我方承认，本**中标函**在你我双方之间建立了具有约束力的**合同**，并且我方承诺根据本合同的条款履行我方的所有义务和责任。

签字人：　　　　--
　　　　　　　　　　　　　　（签字）

授权代表：　　　--

日期：　　　　　--

CONTRACT AGREEMENT

This Agreement made the .... day of ...., 20............,
between .... (*name of Employer*)
of .... (*address of Employer*)
(herein called "the Employer"), of the one part,

and .... (*name of Contractor*)
of .... (*address of Contractor*)
(herein called "the Contractor"), of the other part:

Whereas the Employer desires that the Works known as ....
.... (*name of Contract*)

should be designed, executed and operated by the Contractor and has accepted a Tender from the Contractor for the design, execution, completion and operation and maintenance of these Works, and the remedying of any defects therein,

The Employer and the Contractor agree as follows:

1. In this Agreement, the words and expressions shall have the same meanings as are respectively assigned to them in the Conditions of Contract hereinafter referred to.

2. The following documents shall be deemed to form and be read and construed as a part of this Agreement:

    (a) The Letter of Acceptance dated ....
    (b) The Letter of Tender dated ....
    (c) The Addenda Nos. ....
    (d) The Conditions of Contract
    (e) The Employer's Requirements
    (f) The completed Schedules
    (g) The Operating Licence, and
    (h) The Contractor's Proposal

3. In consideration of the payments to be made by the Employer to the Contractor as hereinafter mentioned, the Contractor hereby covenants with the Employer to design, execute, complete, operate and maintain the Works and remedy any defects therein in conformity with the provisions of the Contract and the Operating Licence granted by the Employer.

4. The Employer hereby covenants to pay the Contractor, in consideration of the design, execution, completion, operation and maintenance of the Works and the remedying of defects therein, the Contract Price at the times and in the manner prescribed by the Contract, and to grant the Contractor a royalty-free licence to enable him to operate and maintain the Works during the Operation Service Period.

In witness whereof the Parties hereto have caused this Agreement to be executed on the day and year first above written.

Signed by: .... Signed by: ....
(*signature*)   (*signature*)

for and on behalf of the Employer in the presence   for and on behalf of the contractor in the presence
of Witness .... of Witness ....
(*signature*)   (*signature*)

Name: .... Name: ....
Address: .... Address: ....
Date: .... Date: ....

合同协议书

本协议书于 20_____年_____月_____日

由 _____的 _____（雇主名称）
为一方 _____（雇主地址）
（以下简称"雇主"），为另一方协商签订，

和 _____的 _____（承包商名称）
的 _____（承包商地址）
（以下简称"承包商"），为另一方协商签订：

鉴于雇主愿将名称为_____
_____（合同名称）

的**工程**交由**承包商**设计、施工和运营，并已接受了**承包商**提交的关于设计、施工、竣工、运营和维护这些**工程**及修补其中任何缺陷的**投标书**，

雇主和承包商达成协议如下：

1. **本协议书**中的词语和措辞的含义，应与下文提到的**合同条件**中分别赋予它们的含义相同。

2. 下列文件应被视为**本协议书**的组成部分，并应作为其一部分阅读和解释。

  （a）　中标函日期　_____
  （b）　投标函日期　_____
  （c）　补充文件编号　_____
  （d）　合同条件
  （e）　雇主要求
  （f）　完成的**资料表**
  （g）　运营执照，（以及）
  （h）　承包商建议书

3. 鉴于**雇主**将按下文所述付给**承包商**各项款项，**承包商**特此与**雇主**签约，保证遵守合同各项规定和**雇主**授予的**运营执照**，设计、施工、竣工、运营和维护这些**工程**及修补其任何缺陷。

4. 鉴于**承包商**将承担上述**工程**的设计、施工、竣工、运营和维护及修补其任何缺陷，**雇主**特此立约，保证按合同规定的时间和方式，向**承包商**支付**合同价格**，并授予**承包商**免版税执照，使其能够在**运营服务期**间运营和维护**工程**。

本协议书由双方签字之日起生效，**特立此据**。

签字人：_____　　签字人：_____
　　　　　　　　（签字）　　　　　　　　　　　　　（签字）

在下列证人在场下，代表**雇主**签字　　在下列证人在场下，代表**承包商**签字
见证人：_____　　见证人：_____
　　　　　　　　（签字）　　　　　　　　　　　　　（签字）

姓名：_____　　姓名：_____
地址：_____　　地址：_____
日期：_____　　日期：_____

AGREEMENT FOR DISPUTE ADJUDICATION BOARD MEMBERS

[*All italicised text and any enclosing square brackets is for use in preparing the form and should be deleted from the final product.*]

Name of Contract: ....

This Agreement made the .... day of ...., 20........., between

Name and address of Employer: ....
Name and address of Contractor: ....
Name and address of DAB Member: ....

Whereas the Employer and the Contractor have entered into a Contract and desire jointly to appoint the above-named Member to act on the DAB as [*delete where not applicable*] sole adjudicator/one of three adjudicators/chairman of the DAB,

And whereas the Member accepts the appointment.

The Employer, Contractor and Member jointly agree as follows:

1. The conditions of this Dispute Adjudication Agreement comprise the "General Conditions of Dispute Adjudication Agreement" which are appended hereto, and the following provisions. In these provisions, which include amendments and additions to the "General Conditions of Dispute Adjudication Agreement", words and expressions shall have the same meanings as are assigned to them in the "General Conditions of Dispute Adjudication Agreement".

2. [*Details of any amendments or additions or deletions from the "General Conditions of Dispute Adjudication Agreement" should be given here or in an attachment hereto.*]

3. In accordance with Clause 6 of the "General Conditions of Dispute Adjudication Agreement", the Member shall be paid as follows: A retainer fee of .... per calendar month, and A daily fee of .... per day spent on Site visits, hearings, and other time in connection with submissions to the DAB made in accordance with the provisions of the Contract between the Employer and the Contractor.

4. In consideration of these fees and other payments to be made by the Employer and the Contractor in accordance with Clause 6 of the "General Conditions of Dispute Adjudication Agreement", the Member undertakes to act as the DAB Member in the capacity abovementioned in accordance with the terms of this Dispute Adjudication Agreement.

5. The Employer and the Contractor jointly and severally undertake to pay the Member in consideration for his acting as the DAB Member as aforementioned in accordance with this Dispute Adjudication Agreement.

6. This Dispute Adjudication Agreement shall be governed by the law of: ....

Signed by: .... Signed by: .... Signed by: ....
    (*signature*)   (*signature*)   (*signature*)

for and on behalf of the Employer   for and on behalf of the Contractor   The Member in the presence of
in the presence of   in the presence of
Witness: ....   Witness: ....   Witness: ....
    (*signature*)   (*signature*)   (*signature*)

Name: Name: Name:
Address: Address: Address:
Date: Date: Date:

争端裁决委员会成员协议书

[*所有斜体文本和任何方括号均用于编写格式，应从最终文本中删除。*]

合同名称：_____

本协议书于 20____ 年____ 月____ 日由**雇主**、**承包商**和**争端裁决委员会成员**订立。

雇主名称和地址：_____
承包商名称和地址：_____
争端裁决委员会成员名称和地址：_____

鉴于**雇主**和**承包商**已签订**合同**，并希望共同任命上述**成员**为 [*在不适用的情况下删除*] **争端裁决委员会**的唯一裁决员 / 三名裁决员之一 / **争端裁决委员会**主席，

鉴于该**成员**接受任命。

雇主、**承包商**和该**成员**共同达成协议如下：

1. 本**争端裁决协议书**条件包括本**协议书**所附的"**争端裁决协议书一般条件**"和下列规定。这些规定，包括对"**争端裁决协议书一般条件**"的修改和补充，其词语和措辞应与其在"**争端裁决协议书一般条件**"中赋予相同的含义。

2. [*对"争端裁决协议书一般条件"中的任何修改或增补或删除的细节，应在此处或本协议书的附件中给出。*]

3. 根据"**争端裁决协议书一般条件**"第 6 条的规定，
   成员应按如下方式支付：聘请费_____ 每日历月，以及
   　　　　　　　　　　　　每日费用_____ 根据**雇主**和**承包商**的**合同**规定，
   每日用于**现场**视察、意见听取会和其他与提交给**争端裁决委员会**的文件有关的时间。

4. 考虑到**雇主**和**承包商**将根据"**争端裁决协议书一般条件**"第 6 条的规定，支付这些费用和其他款项，**成员**承诺按照本**争端裁决协议书**的条款，以上述身份担任**争端裁决委员会成员**。

5. 鉴于**雇主**和**承包商**共同并各自承诺，按照本**争端裁决协议书**，向该**成员**支付作为上述**争端裁决委员会成员**的报酬。

6. 本**争端裁决协议书**应受_____ 法律管辖。

签字人：_____　　　签字人：_____　　　签字人：_____
　　　（签字）　　　　　　　（签字）　　　　　　　（签字）

在下列证人在场下，　　　在下列证人在场下，　　　在下列证人在场下，
代表**雇主**签字　　　　　代表**承包商**签字　　　　**成员**本人签字
见证人：_____　　　见证人：_____　　　见证人：_____
　　　（签字）　　　　　　　（签字）　　　　　　　（签字）

姓名：_____　　　　姓名：_____　　　　姓名：_____
地址：_____　　　　地址：_____　　　　地址：_____
日期：_____　　　　日期：_____　　　　日期：_____

AGREEMENT FOR OPERATION SERVICE DISPUTE ADJUDICATION BOARD

[*All italicised text and any enclosing square brackets is for use in preparing the form and should be deleted from the final product.*]

Name of Contract: ....

This Agreement made the .... day of ...., 20........., between

Name and address of Employer: ....
Name and address of Contractor: ....
Name and address of DAB Member: ....

Whereas the Employer and the Contractor have entered into a Contract and desire jointly to appoint the above-named Member to act as the sole adjudicator on the Operation Service DAB for a period of five (5) years from the date of this Agreement,

And whereas the Member accepts the appointment.

The Employer, Contractor and Member jointly agree as follows:

1. The conditions of this Dispute Adjudication Agreement comprise the "General Conditions of Dispute Adjudication Agreement" which are appended hereto, and the following provisions. In these provisions, which include amendments and additions to the "General Conditions of Dispute Adjudication Agreement", words and expressions shall have the same meanings as are assigned to them in the "General Conditions of Dispute Adjudication Agreement".

2. [*Details of any amendments or additions or deletions from the "General Conditions of Dispute Adjudication Agreement" should be given here or in an attachment hereto.*]

3. In accordance with Clause 6 of the "General Conditions of Dispute Adjudication Agreement", the Member shall be paid as follows: A retainer fee of .... per calendar month, and A daily fee of .... per day spent on Site visits, hearings, and other time in connection with submissions to the DAB made in accordance with the provisions of the Contract between the Employer and the Contractor.

4. In consideration of these fees and other payments to be made by the Employer and the Contractor in accordance with Clause 6 of the "General Conditions of Dispute Adjudication Agreement", the Member undertakes to act as the DAB Member in the capacity abovementioned in accordance with the terms of this Dispute Adjudication Agreement.

5. The Employer and the Contractor jointly and severally undertake to pay the Member in consideration for his acting as the DAB Member as aforementioned in accordance with this Dispute Adjudication Agreement.

6. This Dispute Adjudication Agreement shall be governed by the law of: ....

Signed by:	Signed by:	Signed by: ....
(*signature*)	(*signature*)	(*signature*)
for and on behalf of the Employer in the presence of	for and on behalf of the Contractor in the presence of	for and behalf of the Member in the presence of
Witness:	Witness:	Witness: ....
(*signature*)	(*signature*)	(*signature*)
Name:	Name:	Name: ....
Address:	Address:	Address: ....
Date:	Date:	Date: ....

运营服务争端裁决委员会协议书

[*所有斜体文本和任何方括号均用于编写格式，应从最终文本中删除。*]

合同名称：_____

本协议书于 20____年____月____日由**雇主**、**承包商**和**争端裁决委员会成员**订立。

雇主名称和地址：_____
承包商名称和地址：_____
争端裁决委员会成员名称和地址：_____

鉴于**雇主**和**承包商**已签订**合同**，并希望共同任命上述**成员**为**运营服务争端裁决委员会**的唯一裁决员，自本协议书签订之日起五（5）年，

鉴于该**成员**接受任命。

雇主、**承包商**和该**成员**共同达成协议如下：

1. 本**争端裁决协议书**条件包括本协议书所附的"**争端裁决协议书一般条件**"和下列规定。这些规定，包括对"**争端裁决协议书一般条件**"的修改和补充，其词语和措辞应与其在"**争端裁决协议书一般条件**"中赋予相同的含义。

2. [*对"争端裁决协议书一般条件"中的任何修改或增补或删除的细节，应在此处或本协议书的附件中给出。*]

3. 根据"**争端裁决协议书一般条件**"第 6 条的规定，
   成员应按如下方式支付：聘请费_____每日历月，以及
   每日费用_____根据**雇主**和**承包商**的合同规定，
   每日用于**现场**视察、意见听取会和其他与提交给**争端裁决委员会**的文件有关的时间。

4. 考虑到**雇主**和**承包商**将根据"**争端裁决协议书一般条件**"第 6 条的规定，支付这些费用和其他款项，**成员**承诺按照本**争端裁决协议书**的条款，以上述身份担任**争端裁决委员会成员**。

5. 鉴于**雇主**和**承包商**共同并各自承诺，按照本**争端裁决协议书**，向该**成员**支付作为上述**争端裁决委员会成员**的报酬。

6. 本**争端裁决协议书**应受_____法律管辖。

签字人：_____   签字人：_____   签字人：_____
　　　　（签字）　　　　　　（签字）　　　　　　（签字）

在下列证人在场下，　　在下列证人在场下，　　在下列证人在场下，
代表雇主签字　　　　　代表承包商签字　　　　成员本人签字
见证人：_____   见证人：_____   见证人：_____
　　　　（签字）　　　　　　（签字）　　　　　　（签字）

姓名：_____   姓名：_____   姓名：_____
地址：_____   地址：_____   地址：_____
日期：_____   日期：_____   日期：_____

OPERATING LICENCE

Aide Memoire

The Operating Licence is a document which is issued by the Employer to the Contractor at the time of issuing the Letter of Acceptance in accordance with Sub-Clause 1.7 [*Operating Licence*] of the Conditions of Contract, although it will not come into effect until the issue of the Commissioning Certificate.

The purpose of the Operating Licence is to give the Contractor unhindered legal access to the Works and the facility, and the legal right to operate the facility during the Operation Service Period in compliance with his obligations under his Contract with the Employer.

The terms of the licence must ensure that it is royalty-free and is issued without cost to the Contractor. It will automatically come into full force and effect upon the issue of the Commissioning Certificate, and it shall remain in full force and effect until the issue of the Contract Completion Certificate.

The proposed format and wording of the licence should be included in the tender documents so that tenderers know how it will function during the Operation Service Period.

The nature and format of the Operating Licence must clearly define the requirements of the Employer and must be a legally secure commitment from the Employer to allow the Contractor unhindered access to the facility for the duration of the Operation Service Period. Whatever the name or status of the document which the Employer provides for this purpose, all references in the Contract to Operating Licence shall be deemed to refer to that document.

运营执照（许可证）

备忘录

运营执照是雇主根据合同（通用）条件中第 1.7 款 [运营执照] 的规定，在签发中标函时向承包商签发的文件，尽管在签发调试证书之前其不会生效。

运营执照的目的是使承包商能够不受阻碍地合法进入工程和设施，并在运营服务期间根据其与雇主签订的合同规定的义务运营设施的合法权利。

执照的条款必须确保其是免版税的，并且是免费签发给承包商的。其将在签发调试证书后自动完全生效，并在合同完成证书签发之前保持完全效力。

执照的拟定格式和措辞应包含在投标文件中，以便投标人了解其在运营服务期间的作用。

运营执照的性质和格式必须明确规定雇主的要求，以及必须是雇主的合法安全承诺，允许承包商在运营服务期间不受阻碍地进入设施。无论雇主为其目的提供的文件名称或状态如何，合同中提及的所有运营执照均应视为参考该文件。

Sample Forms of Security and Guarantee

TENDER SECURITY

Name of Contract/Contract No.: ....

Name and address of Beneficiary (the Employer): ....

We have been informed that : ....
(name of Tenderer)
(herinafter called the "Principal") is submitting an offer for the above-named Contract in response to your invitation, and the conditions of your invitation require that his offer is supported by a tender security.

At the request of the Principal, we : ....
(name of Bank)
hereby irrevocably undertake to pay you, the Beneficiary/Employer, any sum or sums not exceeding in total the amount of .... (in words: ....) upon receipt by us of your demand in writing and your written statement (in the demand) stating that:

(a) the Principal has, without your agreement, withdrawn his offer after the latest time specified for its submission and before the expiry of its period of validity, or

(b) the Principal has refused to accept the correction of errors in his offer in accordance with the conditions of your invitation, or

(c) you awarded the Contract to the Principal and he has failed to comply with Sub-Clause 1.6 [*Contract Agreement*] of the Conditions of Contract, or

(d) you awarded the Contract to the Principal and he has failed to comply with Sub-Clause 4.2 [*Performance Security*] of the Conditions of Contract.

Any demand for payment must contain your signature (s) which must be authenticated by your bankers or by a notary public. The authenticated demand and statement must be received by us at this office on or before ....(the date 35 days after the expiry of the validity of the Letter of Tender)..,when this guarantee shall expire and shall be returned to us.

This guarantee is subject to the Uniform Rules for Demand Guarantees, published as number 458 by the International Chamber of Commerce, except as stated above.

Signed by: .... Signed by: ....
(*signature*)   (*signature*)

....
(*name*)   (*name*)

Date: ....

担保和保函样本格式

投标保函

合同名称/合同编号：_____

受益人（雇主）名称和地址：_____

我方已获知：_____
（**投标人名称**）
（以下称"**委托人**"）正响应你方邀请对上述**合同**提交一份报价，你方邀请条件要求其报价要有一份投标保函支持。

应**委托人**请求，我方_____（**银行**名称）在此不可撤销地承诺，在我方收到你方的书面要求和关于（在要求中的）下列情况的书面说明后，向你方，**受益人/雇主**，支付总额不超过_____（文字表述：_____）的任何一笔或几笔款额：

(a) **委托人**未经你方同意，在规定的提交报价的最终时间后和其有效期限期满前，已撤回其报价；（或）

(b) **委托人**已拒绝接受对其按照你方邀请条件所做报价中的错误的改正；（或）

(c) 你方将**合同**授予了**委托人**，但**委托人**未能遵守**合同**通用条件第1.6款[*合同协议书*]；（或）

(d) 你方将**合同**授予了**委托人**，但**委托人**未能遵守**合同**通用条件第4.2款[*履约担保*]的规定。

任何付款的要求，都必须有经你方银行或公证人确证的你方签字。经确证的要求和说明必须在_____（*投标函有效期期满后35天的日期*）或其以前，由我方在本办公地点收到_____，届时本保函应期满，应返还我方。

本保函除上述要求外，应遵守**国际商会**以458号文公布的**即付保函统一规则**的规定。

签字人：_____   签字人：_____
　　　　　（签字）　　　　　　　　　　　（签字）

　　_____　　　　　　_____
　　　（姓名）　　　　　　　　　　　（姓名）

日期：　_____

PARENT COMPANY GUARANTEE

Name of Contract/Contract No.: ....

Name and address of Employer: ....
....(together with successors and assigns).

We have been informed that ....
(name of Contractor)
(hereinafter called the "Contractor") is submitting an offer for such Contract in response to your invitation, and that the conditions of your invitation require his offer to be supported by a parent company guarantee.

In consideration of you, the Employer, awarding the Contract to the Contractor, we..........................
....
(name of parent company)

irrevocably and unconditionally guarantee to you, as a primary obligation, the due performance of all the Contractor's obligations and liabilities under the Contract, including the Contractor's compliance with all its terms and conditions according to their true intent and meaning.

If the Contractor fails to so perform his obligations and liabilities and comply with the Contract, we will indemnify the Employer against and from all damages, losses and expenses (including legal fees and expenses) which arise from any such failure for which the Contractor is liable to the Employer under the Contract.

This guarantee shall come into full force and effect when the Contract comes into full force and effect. If the Contract does not come into full force and effect within a year of the date of this guarantee, or if you demonstrate that you do not intend to enter into the Contract with the Contractor, this guarantee shall be void and ineffective. This guarantee shall continue in full force and effect until all the Contractor's obligations and liabilities under the Contract have been discharged, when this guarantee shall expire and shall be returned to us, and our liability hereunder shall be discharged absolutely.

This guarantee shall apply and be supplemental to the Contract as amended or varied by the Employer and the Contractor from time to time. We hereby authorise them to agree any such amendment or variation, the due performance of which and compliance with which by the Contractor are likewise guaranteed hereunder. Our obligations and liabilities under this guarantee shall not be discharged by any allowance of time or other indulgence whatsoever by the Employer to the Contractor, or by any variation or suspension of the works to be executed under the Contract, or by any amendments to the Contract or to the constitution of the Contractor or the Employer, or by any other matters, whether with or without our knowledge or consent.

This guarantee shall be governed by the law of the same country (or other jurisdiction) as that which governs the Contract and any dispute under this guarantee shall be finally settled under the Rules of Arbitration of the International Chamber of Commerce by one or more arbitrators appointed in accordance with such Rules. We confirm that the benefit of this guarantee may be assigned subject only to the provisions for assignment of the Contract.

Signed by: ....   Signed by: ....
(signature)   *(signature)*

....
(name)   *(name)*

....
(position in parent company)   *(position in parent company)*

Date: ....

母公司保函

合同名称／合同编号：_____

雇主名称和地址：_____
_____（连同继承人和受让人）。

我方已获知_____
                                                （**承包商**名称）
（以下称"**承包商**"）正响应你方邀请对上述**合同**提交报价，你方邀请条件要求报价要有一份母公司保函支持。

考虑到你方，**雇主**，将向**承包商**授予**合同**，我方_____
_____
                                                （母公司名称）

不可撤销和无条件地，作为一项首要义务向你方保证，**承包商**根据**合同**规定的所有应履行的义务和责任，包括**承包商**按照其真实意图和含义遵守所有条款和条件。

如果**承包商**未能如上履行其义务和责任，未能遵守**合同**，我方将保障**雇主**免受因**承包商**根据合同应对**雇主**负责的任何该类违约造成的所有损害赔偿费、损失和开支（包括法律费用和开支）。

本保函将在**合同**全面实施和生效时，完全实施和生效。如果在本保函日期一年内，合同没有全面实施和生效，或如果你方表明不想与**承包商**签订**合同**，本保函将作废和无效。本保函将持续全面实施和有效直到**承包商**根据**合同**规定的义务和责任全部解除为止，届时本保函将期满，应退还我方，我方在其下的责任应完全解除。

雇主和**承包商**有时对**合同**进行修改或变更时，本保函仍适用并作为**合同**的补充。我方在此授权他们商定任何此类修改或变更，对**承包商**应履行和应遵守的修改或变更在此同样予以保证。我方根据本保函应负的义务和责任，不应因**雇主**对**承包商**做出的任何时限允许或其他宽让，或根据**合同**要实施的工程的任何变更或暂停，或对**合同**、**承包商**或**雇主**的组成的任何修改，或任何其他事项而解除，不论这些事项是否经我方知晓或同意。

本保函应由管辖**合同**的同一国家（或其他司法管辖区）的法律管辖，关于本保函的任何争端，应根据**国际商会仲裁规则**，由按该**规则**任命的一位或几位仲裁员最终解决。我方确认，本保函的权益仅可按照**合同**转让的条款进行转让。

签字人：_____   签字人：_____
          （签字）   （签字）

_____   _____
          （姓名）   （姓名）

_____   _____
      （在母公司的职位）   （在母公司的职位）

日期：_____

PERFORMANCE SECURITY – DEMAND GUARANTEE

NOTE: This form is suitable during the Design-Build Period. If a security is required during the Operation Service Period (either in the form envisaged in the Contract, or in another form), this must be carefully prepared with professional and legal help.

Name of Contract/Contract No.: ....

Name and address of Beneficiary ("the Employer"): ....

We have been informed that : ....
(name of Contractor)
(hereinafter called the "Principal") is your contractor for the above-named Contract which requires him to obtain a performance security.

At the request of the Principal, we : ....
(name of bank)
undertake to pay you, the Beneficiary/Employer, any sum or sums not exceeding in total the amount of ....(amount in words...................................) (the "guaranteed amount") upon receipt by us of your demand in writing with your written statement stating:

(a) that the Principal is in breach of his obligations under the Contract, and

(b) the respect in which the Principal is in breach.

Any demand for payment must contain your signature (s) which must be authenticated by your bankers or by a notary public. The authenticated demand and statement must be received by us at this office on or before .... (*the date 70 days after the expected date issue o the Commissioning Certificate*) (the "expiry date"), when this guarantee shall expire and shall be returned to us.

We have been informed that the Beneficiary may require the Principal to extend this guarantee if the Commissioning Certificate has not been issued 28 days prior to such expiry date and we hereby undertake to extend this guarantee until the date 70 days after the actual date of issue of the Commissioning Certificate upon receipt of your written statement advising us of the actual date of issue, and that the late issue was for reasons attributable to the Principal. In such a case, the expiry date shall be adjusted accordingly.

This guarantee shall be governed by the laws of ...., and shall be subject to the Uniform Rules for Demand Guarantees, published as number 458 by the International Chamber of Commerce, except as stated above.

Signed by: ....   Signed by: ....
                            (signature)   (signature)

....
                                (name)   (name)

Date: ....

履约担保——即付保函

注:本表格适用于设计-施工期间。如果在**运营服务期**间需要担保(无论是以**合同**规定的格式,还是其他格式),必须在专业人员和法律人员的帮助下精心准备。

合同名称/合同编号:_____

受益人("**雇主**")名称和地址:_____

我方已获知:_____

                       (*承包商*名称)

(以下称"**委托人**")是上述**合同**的承包商,**合同**要求其取得一份履约担保函。

应**委托人**请求,我方:_____

                       (*银行名称*)

承诺,在我方收到你方的书面要求以及书面说明后,向你方,**受益人/雇主**,支付全部总额不超过_____(文字表述":_____")("保证金额")的任何一笔或几笔款额:

(a) **委托人**违反**合同**规定的义务;(以及)

(b) **委托人**违约的方面(委托人的违约行为)。

任何付款的要求,都必须有经你方银行或公证人确证的你方的签字。经确证的要求和说明必须在_____(预定**调试证书**签发日期后 70 天的日期)("期满日期")或其以前,由我方在办公地点收到,届时本保函将期满,应退还我方。

我方已获知,如果到上述期满日期 28 天前,还没有签发**调试证书**,**受益人**可要求**委托人**延长此保函,且我方在此承诺,在收到你方告知我方实际签发**调试证书**日期的书面说明后,将本保函延长到实际签发日期后的 70 天,以及延迟签发是由于**委托人**的原因。在这种情况下。到期日期应做相应的调整。

本保函除上述要求外,应受_____法律管辖,并应遵守**国际商会**以 458 号文公布的**即付保函统一规则**的规定。

签字人:_____ 签字人:_____
      (签字)   (签字)

   _____ _____
      (姓名)   (姓名)

日期:_____

PERFORMANCE SECURITY – SURETY BOND

NOTE: This form is suitable during the Design-Build Period. If a security is required during the Operation Service Period (either in the form envisaged in the Contract, or in another form), this must be carefully prepared with professional and legal help.

Name of Contract/Contract No.: ....

Name and address of Beneficiary ("the Employer"): ....

We have been informed that : ....
(*name of Contractor*)
(hereinafter called the "Principal") is your contractor for the above-named Contract which requires him to obtain a performance security.

By this Bond, ...,
....
(*name and address of Contractor*)

who is the Contractor under the above named Contract, as Principal and
....
(*name and address of Guarantor*)

as Guarantor, are irrevocably held and firmly bound to the Beneficiary in the total amount of ....
....(amount in words: ....) (the "Bond Amount") for the due performance of all the Principal's obligations and liabilities under the above named Contract.

The Bond shall become effective on the Commencement Date defined in the Contract.

Upon default by the Principal to perform any contractual obligation, or upon the occurrence of any of the events and circumstances listed in Sub-Clause 15.2 of the Conditions of Contract, the Guarantor shall satisfy and discharge the damages sustained by the Beneficiary due to such default, event or circumstance. However, the total liability of the Guarantor shall not exceed the Bond Amount.

The obligations and liabilities of the Guarantor shall not be discharged by any allowance of time or other indulgence whatsoever by the Beneficiary to the Principal, or by any variation or suspension of the Works to be executed under the Contract, or by any amendments to the Contract or to the constitution of the Principal or the Beneficiary, or by any other matters, whether with or without the knowledge or consent of the Guarantor.

Any claim under this Bond must be received by the Guarantor on or before ....
(*the date six months after the expected date of issue of the Commissioning Certificate*), (the "expiry date"), when this Bond shall expire and be returned to the Guarantor.

The benefits of this Bond may be assigned, subject to the provisions for assignment of the Contract, and subject to receipt by the Guarantor of evidence of full compliance with such provisions.

This Bond shall be governed by the laws of ....being the same country (or other jurisdiction) as that which governs the Contract. The Bond incorporates and be subject to the Uniform Rules for Contract Bonds, published as number 524 by the International Chamber of Commerce, and words used in this Bond shall bear the meanings set out in such Rules.

Whereas this Bond has been issued by the Principal and the Guarantor on this ....
day of ...., 20 ....

履约担保——担保保证书

注：本表格适用于设计 - 施工期间。如果在运营服务期间需要担保（无论是以合同规定的格式，还是其他格式），必须在专业人员和法律人员的帮助下精心准备。

合同名称 / 合同编号：＿＿＿＿＿＿＿＿＿＿＿＿＿＿＿＿＿＿＿＿

受益人（"雇主"）名称和地址：＿＿＿＿＿＿＿＿＿＿＿＿＿＿＿

我方已获知：＿＿＿＿＿＿＿＿＿＿＿＿＿＿＿＿＿＿＿＿＿＿＿

＿＿＿＿＿＿＿＿＿＿＿＿＿＿＿＿＿＿＿＿＿＿（*承包商名称*）

（以下称"**委托人**"）是上述合同的承包商，合同要求其取得一份**履约担保**。

根据本**保证书**，＿＿＿＿＿＿＿＿＿＿＿＿＿＿＿＿＿＿＿＿＿

＿＿＿＿＿＿＿＿＿＿＿＿＿＿＿＿＿＿＿＿＿＿＿＿＿＿＿＿＿

＿＿＿＿＿＿＿＿＿＿＿＿＿＿＿＿＿（*承包商名称和地址*），

根据上述合同规定的**承包商**，作为**委托人**与

＿＿＿＿＿＿＿＿＿＿＿＿＿＿＿＿＿＿＿＿＿＿＿＿＿＿＿＿＿

＿＿＿＿＿＿＿＿＿＿＿＿＿＿＿＿＿＿（*担保人名称和地址*）

作为**担保人**，对该**委托人**根据上述**合同**应履行的全部义务和责任，以总金额＿＿＿＿＿＿＿＿＿＿＿＿＿＿（*金额的文字：＿＿＿＿＿＿*）（"**保证金额**"），向**受益人**不可撤销地保持和坚定地担保。

本**保证书**自合同中规定的**开工日期**起生效。

在**委托人**履行任何合同义务中发生违约，或出现任何**合同（通用）条件**第 15.2 款所列举的事件或情况时，**担保人**应满足并偿清**受益人**因该项违约、事件或情况遭受的损害赔偿费。但**担保人**的全部责任不应超过**保证金额**。

担保人的义务和责任不因**受益人**对**委托人**做出的任何时限允许或其他宽让，或对根据合同应实施**工程**的任何变更或暂停，或对**合同**或对**委托人**或**受益人**的组成的任何修改，或任何其他事项而解除，不论是否经**担保人**知晓或同意。

根据本**保证书**提出的任何索赔必须由**担保人**在＿＿＿＿＿＿＿＿＿＿＿＿＿＿（*预定签发调试证书之日后 6 个月的日期*）（"**期满日期**"）或其以前收到，届时本**保证书**应期满，应退还**担保人**。

本**保证书**的权益可以依照**合同**转让的条款，以及**担保人**收到完全符合该项条款的证据，进行转让。

本**保证书**应由管辖**合同**的同一国家（或其他司法管辖区）的＿＿＿＿＿＿＿＿＿＿＿＿＿＿法律管辖。本**保证书**体现并应遵守**国际商会**以 524 号文公布的合同保证书统一规则的规定，以及本**保证书**使用的词语应具有该**规则**规定的含义。

本**保证书**于 20＿＿＿年＿＿＿月＿＿＿日由**委托人**和**担保人**签署。

Signatures for and on behalf of the Principal:

_____   _____
(*signature*)   (*signature*)

_____   _____
(*name*)   (*name*)

Signatures for and on behalf of the Guarantor:

_____   _____
(*signature*)   (*signature*)

_____   _____
(*name*)   (*name*)

委托人代表签字:

_____（签字）　　　_____（签字）

_____（姓名）　　　_____（姓名）

担保人代表签字:

_____（签字）　　　_____（签字）

_____（姓名）　　　_____（姓名）

ADVANCE PAYMENT GUARANTEE

Name of Contract/Contract No.: ....

Name and address of Beneficiary ("the Employer"): ....

We have been informed that : ....

(name of Contractor)

(hereinafter called the "Principal") is your contractor for the above-named Contract and wishes to receive an advance payment, for which the Contract requires him to obtain a guarantee.

At the request of the Principal, we: ....

(name of bank)

hereby irrevocably undertake to pay you, the Beneficiary/Employer, any sum or sums not exceeding in total the amount of .... (amount in words: ....) (the "guaranteed amount") upon receipt by us of your demand in writing with your written statement stating:

(a) that the Principal has failed to repay the advance payment in accordance with the conditions of Contract, and

(b) the amount which the Principal has failed to repay.

This guarantee shall become effective upon receipt of the advance payment, or, where applicable, the first instalment thereof, by the Principal. Such guaranteed amount shall be reduced by the amounts of the advance payment repaid to you from time to time as evidenced by the Interim Payment Certificates issued under Sub-Clause 14.7 of the Conditions of Contract. Following receipt by us from the Principal of each Interim Payment Certificate, we shall promptly notify you of the revised guaranteed amount.

Any demand for payment must contain your signature (s) which must be authenticated by your bankers or by a notary public. The authenticated demand and statement must be received by us at this office on or before (*the date 70 days after the expected date of completion of the Design-Build*)....................(the "expiry date"), when this guarantee shall expire and be returned to us.

If the advance payment has not been fully repaid 28 days prior to the expiry date, we undertake, upon receipt of your written demand and statement that the advance payment has not been repaid, to pay you the guaranteed amount within 28 days of your demand.

This guarantee shall be governed by the laws of ....,and shall be subject to the Uniform Rules for Demand Guarantees, published as number 458 by the International Chamber of Commerce, except as stated above.

Signed by: ....   Signed by: ....
(signature)   *(signature)*

....
(name)   *(name)*

Date: ....

预付款保函

合同名称 / 合同编号：_____

受益人（"**雇主**"）**名称和地址**：_____

我方已获知：_____

（**承包商**名称）

（以下称为"**委托人**"）是你方上述**合同**规定的承包商，希望得到一笔预付款，为此，合同要求其取得一份保函。

应**委托人**请求，我方：_____（银行名称）在此不可撤销地承诺，在我方收到你方书面要求和关于以下情况的书面说明后，向你方，**受益人 / 雇主**，支付全部总额不超过_____（金额的文字：_____）（"保证金额"）的任何一笔或几笔款额：

（a） **委托人**未能按照**合同条件**付还预付款，（以及）

（b） **委托人**未能付还的款额。

本保函在**委托人**收到预付款或，或如适用，首次分期付款时开始生效。该保证金额应按你方根据**合同（通用）条件第 14.7 款**规定签发的**期中付款证书**中证明已向你方不时地付还预付款的款额，逐步减少。我方每次从**委托人**处收到**期中付款证书**后，将立即通知你方修改的保证金额。

任何关于付款的要求都必须有经你方银行或公证人确认的你方签字。经确证的要求和说明必须在_____（*预定设计 - 施工竣工日期后 70 天的日期*）（"期满日期"）或其以前，由我方在本办公地点收到，届时本保函将期满，应退还我方。

如果预付款在到期日期前 28 天仍未全部付还，我方承诺，在收到你方书面要求和关于预付款还没有付还的说明后你方要求的 28 天内，向你方支付该保证金额。

本保函除上述规定外，应受_____法律管辖，并应遵守**国际商会**以第 458 号文公布的**即付保函统一规则**的规定。

签字人：_____   签字人：_____
　　　　　　（签字）　　　　　　　　　　　　　　（签字）

　　　　　_____   　　　　　_____
　　　　　　（姓名）　　　　　　　　　　　　　　（姓名）

日期：　　_____

MAINTENANCE RETENTION GUARANTEE

Name of Contract and/or Contract No.: ....

Name and address of Beneficiary ("the Employer"): ....

We have been informed that : ....
(*name of Contractor*)

(hereinafter called the "Principal") is your contractor for the above-named Contract and has chosen to provide a Maintenance Retention Guarantee.

At the request of the Principal, we ....
(*name of bank*)

hereby irrevocably undertake to pay you, the Beneficiary/Employer, any sum or sums not exceeding 5% of the total amount of all interim payments indicated on interim payment certificates that have been presented to us (the "guaranteed amount"), subject to the maximum guaranteed amount of .... (*insert maximum amount stated in the Contract Data, in words and indicate currency*).

Any demand presented under this guarantee shall be in writing and shall be supported by a written statement (whether in the demand itself or in a separate document accompanying and referring to the demand) stating:

(a) that the Principal has failed to carry out his maintenance obligation (s) under the Contract after having received due Notice (as defined in the Contract) to do so, and

(b) the nature of such failure (s).

Any demand for payment, and the written statement if in a separate document, must contain your signature (s) which must be authenticated by your bankers or by a notary public. The authenticated demand and statement must be received by us at this office on or before..
....(*the date 70 days after the expected date of completion of the Operation Service Period*) (the "expiry date"), when this guarantee shall expire and shall be returned to us.

We have been informed that the Beneficiary/Employer may require the Principal to extend this guarantee if the Contract Completion Certificate under the Contract has not been issued by the date 28 days prior to such expiry date. We undertake to pay you such guaranteed amount upon receipt by us, within such period of 28 days, of your demand in writing and your written statement that the Contract Completion Certificate has not been issued, for reasons attributable to the Principal, and this guarantee has not been extended.

This guarantee shall be governed by the laws of........................and shall be subject to the Uniform Rules for Demand Guarantees, published as number 458 by the International Chamber of Commerce, except as stated above.

Signed by: ....   Signed by: ....
                (*signature*)   (*signature*)

....
                (*name*)   (*name*)

Date: ....

维护保留金保函

合同名称和/或合同编号：_____

受益人（"雇主"）名称和地址：_____

我方已获知：_____
（*承包商名称*）

（以下称为**"委托人"**）是你方上述**合同**规定的承包商，并选择提供一份**维护保留金保函**。

应**委托人**请求，我方_____（*银行名称*）在此不可撤销地承诺，在我方收到你方提交的期中付款证书后，向你方，**受益人/雇主**，支付所有期中付款全部总额不超过 5%_____（"保证金额"）的任何一笔或几笔款额，以最高保证金额为准_____（插入**合同数据**中规定的最高金额，用文字表示和注明货币）。

根据本保函提出的任何要求应以书面形式，并应附有书面说明（无论是要求本身，或在随附并提及要求的单独文件中）说明：

(a) **委托人**在收到**通知**（如**合同**中所定义）后，未能履行根据合同规定其的维护义务，（以及）

(b) 此类违约的性质。

任何关于付款的要求和书面说明，如果在单独的文件中，都必须有经你方银行或公证人确证的你方签字。经确证的要求和说明必须在_____（*预定运营服务期完成日期后 70 天的日期*）（"期满日期"）或其以前，由我方在本办公地点收到，届时本保函将期满，应退还我方。

我方已获知，如果到该期满日期 28 天前还没有签发合同规定的**合同完成证书**，**受益人/雇主**可以要求**委托人**延长本保函。我方承诺，根据我方在该 28 天期限内收到你方的书面要求和关于**合同完成证书**因**委托人**应负责的原因尚未签发，以及本保函尚未延长的书面说明，向你方支付该保证金额。

本保函除上述要求外，应受_____法律管辖，并应遵守**国际商会**以第 458 号文公布的**即付保函统一规则**的规定。

签字人：_____   签字人：_____
　　　　　（签字）　　　　　　　　　　　　　（签字）

　　　　_____　　　　_____
　　　　　（姓名）　　　　　　　　　　　　　（姓名）

日期：_____

ERRATUM to the First Edition, 2008

The following erratum has been corrected in this 2012 reprint of the First Edition of the Conditions of Contract for Design, Build and Operate Projects.

SAMPLE FORMS

Page 286, the Maintenance Retention Guarantee form

The entire form has been replaced by the amended version.

GENERAL PROVISIONS

Page 168　　　　Sub-Clause 20.1: penultimate paragraph, last sentence, delete "Engineer's Representative" and substitute "Employer's Representative".

　　　　　　　　Sub-Clause 20.2: penultimate paragraph, last sentence, delete "Engineer's Representative" and substitute "Employer's Representative".

2008 年第 1 版勘误表[一]

以下勘误表内容已在 2012 年再版的第 1 版《设计、施工和运营合同条件》中进行了改正。

样本格式

第 286 页，维护保留金保函格式

整个格式被修订版替换了。

一般规定

第 168 页　　第 20.1 款：在倒数第二段最后一句，删除"Engineer's Representative"并替换为"Employer's Representative"。

第 20.2 款：在倒数第二段最后一句，删除"Engineer's Representative"并替换为"Employer's Representative"。

[一] 中文翻译文本已改正。本勘误表只是应 FIDIC 的要求而翻译，仅供参考。——译者注